Sites of Power

Sites of Power

A Concise History of Ontario

Peter A. Baskerville

OXFORD

UNIVERSITY PRESS

1904 ❦ 2004

100 YEARS OF
CANADIAN PUBLISHING

OXFORD
UNIVERSITY PRESS

8 Sampson Mews, Suite 204, Don Mills, Ontario M3C 0H5
www.oupcanada.com

Oxford University Press is a department of the University of Oxford.
It furthers the University's objective of excellence in research, scholarship,
and education by publishing worldwide in

Oxford   New York
Auckland   Cape Town   Dar es Salaam   Hong Kong   Karachi   Kuala Lumpur
Madrid   Melbourne   Mexico City   Nairobi   New Delhi   Shanghai   Taipei   Toronto

With offices in
Argentina   Austria   Brazil   Chile   Czech Republic   France   Greece   Guatemala
Hungary   Italy   Japan   Poland   Portugal   Singapore   South Korea   Switzerland
Thailand   Turkey   Ukraine   Vietnam

Oxford is a trade mark of Oxford University Press
in the UK and in certain other countries

Published in Canada
by Oxford University Press

Library and Archives Canada Cataloguing in Publication

Baskerville, Peter A. (Peter Allan), 1943-
Sites of power : a concise history of Ontario / Peter A. Baskerville.

Includes bibliographical references and index.

ISBN 0-19-541892-1

1. Power (Social sciences)—Ontario—History. 2. Ontario—History.
I. Title.
FC3061.B373 2005   971.3   C2004-906721-4

Cover design: Brett J. Miller

Frontispiece: One of the city's poor, [ca. 1915] (Archives of Ontario, F 1075-15-0-0-111)

2 3 4 5 - 14 13 12 11

This book is printed on permanent (acid-free) paper ∞.

Contents

Preface

Sites of Power is a significantly updated edition of *Ontario: Image, Identity, and Power*, published by Oxford in 2002 as part of its Illustrated History of Canada series. There is some thirty per cent more text and fewer images. The coverage of the post confederation period is, as a result, much more extensive. More maps have been included and a series of sidebars, focussing on matters of controversy and general interest, have been added. The footnotes are deliberately fulsome to make it easy for readers to follow their interests through further reading and research.

Acknowledgements

This book attempts to reflect the quality and richness of writing on Ontario's histories. As such, the book has been written on the backs of others. My first thanks are to those scholars and my hope is that I have used their research in an appropriate manner. Thanks, too, to archivists throughout Ontario who never tired responding to my long and short distance requests for assistance. Michael Piva's input has been appreciated. As of this writing the illustrated history book has received two published reviews. One concentrated on listing alleged errors; I thank that reviewer for his diligence and I have tried to correct where appropriate. The second review was of a different, more enjoyable and substantive kind. While I have not changed my overall interpretation to reflect that of the reviewer, I have tried to strengthen and broaden in areas mentioned by him. Oxford sent this book manuscript to two scholarly reviewers. While both were complimentary, both supplied useful comments which I have taken seriously and I thank them for their time and effort. Stephanie Fysh excelled as a sensitive editor. Mark Piel and Rachael Cayley helped expedite the publishing process at Oxford. Laura Macleod spearheaded the idea. As always my ultimate thanks is to Fran.

Whose Ontario?

What follows is a historical survey of a moving target, a place now called Ontario. It is, in a sense, like its subject a work in progress, a contribution toward an understanding of the many Ontarios that have a history, a present, and a future. For Ontario has never been, is not now, and never will be knowable in the singular. But to know Ontario well it is necessary to employ a historical approach. Any sufficient understanding of regions, communities, places, and provinces must be rooted in the context of particular times, places, and sets of social, economic, and political interactions that have been conditioned by their respective pasts. As Gerald Friesen and Richard White have perceptively noted, categories of thought such as regions, communities, and places have their own histories.[1] While this book does not directly confront the histories of those categories, it does attempt to complicate their meanings by privileging Ontario's pluralist past.

Regions are made and unmade by people interacting socially with one another and with their never-static natural and animal surroundings. Certainly there is reciprocity here. A region made can, at various levels, influence the character of social intercourse for those living within it. But in several ways, interaction between people and region is a variable and contingent process: not all people at any one time, place, or event see region the same way, are affected by region equally, or affect regional change similarly.

A concrete example is useful here. Since the retreat of the last ice age, what we now call Ontario has exhibited radically different environmental landscapes. One obvious distinction exists between northern and southern Ontario. Without detailing the different and changing environments and the functional definitions of 'north' and 'south', it is enough to note that those in the north have rarely been accorded parity with those in the south. This is the case whether one thinks of interaction between the southern Wendat (Huron) and the northern Anishinaabe (Algonquian) before the arrival of Europeans or of the use of the north by those living in the south at the time of Premier Oliver Mowat in the late nineteenth century. But such a demarcation is only part of the story. People within the north were affected differentially by such environmental and functional (and always self-interested) definitions. A person's gender, employment status, age, and colour, among other social characteristics, always filtered the impact of regional place. It mattered whether you worked as a miner at Silver Islet on Lake Superior in the late nineteenth century, or managed the miners, or owned the mine, or were a

Native person dispossessed, or a woman without property. Individuals' understanding of and impact on the north (or the south) varied according to their social placement and relationships with other social groups.

Power is one of the most important determinants of how people and place interact. The notion of power requires thinking relationally and appreciating how such relations constrict, define, and enable behaviour from within the tiniest of 'regions'—the family, for example—to the largest of places, in this case Ontario and its relations with Canada and the world. From the perspective of power, region has a nicely utilitarian function: political and economic leaders have often used appeals to regional identity and location as a means of padding, protecting, augmenting, and obfuscating their own more particular and never explicitly—or better, publicly—defined agendas. As we shall see, many of Ontario's political and economic leaders have been masters of that art. In presenting such identities and images, those leaders certainly represented more than themselves, but they never represented all Ontarians equally or even positively, despite the implicit and explicit claims of many of their biographers. Nor did they always succeed in inscribing their vision of Ontario on all Ontarians. Power begets resistance. This history, therefore, is as much about the visions of Ontario held by those who resisted as it is about the more 'official' visions held by those in power.

In fact, although the term 'Ontarian' is occasionally used in this study, it is not meant to imply the existence of a homogeneous group. It may be that there is something uniquely 'Ontarian' about all the people who have lived in the province, but to determine that would require an explicitly comparative analysis with people elsewhere. This historical survey has a more modest aim: it focuses on the disparate groups of people who have inhabited a space now called Ontario for the past 11,000 or so years. Indeed, the modern boundary was not itself settled until 1912. That settlement encompassed just over 1 million square kilometres in area, extending 1,690 kilometres from east to west and 1,730 kilometres from north to south. Depending on variable definitions, from two-thirds to four-fifths of that area is normally accorded 'northern' status (an area lived in by 8 per cent of the province's population in the 1990s)—a part of the Canadian or Precambrian Shield, a huge mass of bare rock, rivers, lakes, trees, and cold. The south, roughly below the tip of Georgian Bay, contains some of Canada's richest agricultural land and a more temperate, 'continental' climate. This book is about the people who lived in Ontario and about the social processes that have given Ontario's space meaning.

Chapter One

Weblike Relations: Early Ontario, 9000 BC–AD 1500

The Paleo Period, 9000–7500 BC

Some 11,500 years ago, Paleo-Indian people from northeastern Asia trekked into North America across an ice-free corridor now covered by the Bering Sea. Animal and human occupation of the southern Great Lakes—probably the first eastern Canadian region to support plants, animals, and people—began some 500 years later. Scholars have generalized broadly about Paleo life, assuming climate and vegetation resembled that of Canada's modern Subarctic: a mixed-forest tundra environment supporting few plant foods. Recent studies, however, conclude that this period experienced the greatest weather turbulence of the past ten millennia. Average temperatures approximated those of the modern Subarctic, but greater variation existed and microenvironments—near, for example, lakes—proliferated.[1]

Sensitivity to regional variation underlies recent research on Paleo-Indians. Some suggest that Paleo peoples were 'free wanderers'—hunters following big game across the tundra. In the context of patchy microenvironments, however, this interpretation loses force. Given unpredictable climatic change, Paleo peoples could not afford to specialize on one major food source to survive; rather, they moved within defined ranges, exploiting a variety of seasonal opportunities, including fish and land mammals. Base camps became focal points for activities. Paleo groups were sedentary in that they did not move long distances as a daily routine, although they travelled up to 350 kilometres on a yearly basis, suggesting a harsh natural environment.[2]

The notion of Paleo peoples as semi-sedentary has implications for the timing of the peopling of North America. Since free wanderers have low birth rates (a result of the carrying costs of transporting infants), some suggest that for North America to have been populated as quickly as it appears to have been, a population must have lived there before the Paleo peoples. But a more sedentary lifestyle in fact facilitated *greater* fertility. Paleo-Indians, then, could well have been North America's first peoples to have successfully expanded over the non-glaciated portion of the continent in a matter of a few centuries.[3]

Close attention to specific contexts has fostered other (re)interpretations of Paleo life. Some see Paleo peoples as being at the bottom end of a continuum, at the top of which perches modern 'civilization'. But Paleo-Indians possessed skills suitable for living within their demanding environment. To travel the distances they did required sleds, toboggans, and some means for water travel. They chose the best local stone (including chert, quartz, and basalt) to manufacture fluted spear points and a wide range of other implements, such as children's toys and needles for sewing hides (and, perhaps, for tattooing). Their manufacturing must have been of high quality: modern attempts to replicate it have generally failed.[4]

Did early Ontario peoples live in isolated 'paleolithic poverty'? Clearly, survival was a challenge. Yet the care taken with the crafting of implements suggests usage of a cultural rather than a strictly practical sort. On an isolated plain west of London, Ontario, a late Paleo-Indian band deliberately fractured a large cache of well-manufactured tools. Why destroy useful implements made of material brought from 175 kilometres away? Paleo peoples may have seen tools as a form of wealth—material worthy of sacrifice in the context of cultural or spiritual rituals. They prized snow white or blood red chert chipped from specific rocky outcrops. The outcrops themselves probably had cultural and spiritual significance. Tools, to use the language of archaeologists, were markers of local group identity. Reliance on specific outcrops also lends support to the argument that bands moved within defined territories. This association of tools with regions makes it possible to trace the movement of goods over space: trade occurred with bands as far away as what are now Ohio and southern Michigan. Band intermarriage ensured a wider selection of eligible partners and established a type of 'paleo insurance'—groups to whom one could turn for help when the uncertain environment proved especially inhospitable.[5]

The Archaic Period, 8000–1000 BC

During the Archaic era, Native peoples adjusted to significant warming trends. By about 6500 BC, plant growth closely resembled that of the present time. By 500 BC, forest cover already extended to only 2 degrees north of today's position. In the early Archaic era, however, water levels were 100 metres below today's, making archaeological knowledge of this era extremely difficult: by 5000 BC, water had reached or exceeded current levels. Along with hunting and fishing, subsistence activities increasingly included gathering berries and wild rice located in many marshy zones created by fluctuating water levels. Around Lake Superior, fishing probably played only a minor role; some fishbones dated to the early Archaic period have been found in Native encampments in the upper Great Lakes region. Around lakes Erie and Ontario, fishing—using nets and dugout canoes—provided a major supplement to deer in the Native diet. Population gradually increased, and single families lived in oval dwellings up to 15 by 10 metres in size, covered in spruce bough (cut, for the first time, by grooved axes) or skin. In the south, band territories emerged in specific river valleys.[6]

So too did trading routes of a surprisingly modern sort. Archaeologists speculate that the Humber River (which empties into Lake Ontario at Toronto) was a boundary point between different bands. Eastern Ontario bands exchanged goods along the Saint Lawrence, and southwestern bands traded with groups in the

Illinois, Michigan, Ohio, and Wisconsin regions. Employing a technology first developed south of the Great Lakes, Lake Superior Archaic bands picked, pounded, ground, and polished local copper into a variety of tools. This method contrasts with the use of flaking to manufacture stone tools in the Paleo era and marks the beginning of a manufacturing and trading pattern that continued up to European contact. Trade from the upper Great Lakes extended down the Trent, Severn, Rideau, and Ottawa rivers, a route in extensive use at the time of European contact and beyond. Indeed, some of these copper tools reached east to Labrador and west to Saskatchewan.[7]

The association of trade and spiritual beliefs underlines 'the web-like social relations' of the late Archaic period. Small bands lived in discrete territories but were not bounded and isolated. They traded for social and material reasons. Around 1500 BC, the graves of Native people in what is now Picton, Ontario, included white shell pendants and beads from the Gulf of Mexico along with Lake Superior copper items. Native people near Lake Nipigon and along Lake Erie's north shore placed deposits of red ochre and green clay with assorted non-local items in their graves. Some individuals were buried with more goods—occasionally, women were buried with more than men—but the general pattern suggests an egalitarian society.[8]

What were the cultural values that underlay these grave goods? At the time of European contact, many Native cultures equated red with social well-being, white with physical goodness, and copper with spiritual power. Those who see the genesis of Iroquoian- and Algonquian-speaking peoples—the two major language families in northeastern North America at the time of contact—as dating from the late Archaic period think that these beliefs extended to the time of contact. Most specialists, however, put the origin of Iroquoian ancestry at circa 500 BC and Algonquian ancestry at circa AD 700. The issues are compelling: beyond tracing roots, there are land claims. But little consensus exists, and archaeologists warn against reading post-contact values and ethnicities into the material remains of the pre-contact era.[9]

A common view that Archaic life was nasty, brutish, and short requires rethinking. The skeletal remains of the Hind Site people who lived in southwestern Ontario 3,000 years ago provide a snapshot of life at that time. Indeed, a rugged lifestyle left many adults with osteoarthritis; they coped with severe dental deterioration as a result of chewing hard substances and using teeth as tools; the average age of death was the mid-thirties. But the skeletal remains of a twelve-year-old boy who lived in chronic poor health suggest that, despite its hardships, life was not nasty and brutish. His parents ground his food into gruel. His weak bone development required that he be carried from campsite to campsite. He was never abandoned and was buried with band members, suggesting a culture that respected and protected those unable to fend for themselves.[10]

The Woodland Era, 1000 BC–AD 1500

That hunting and gathering remained the focus of subsistence activities in Ontario up to AD 500 is often taken to mean that no significant change occurred. Yet in the early Woodland period (1000 BC–AD 500), hunter-gatherers developed pottery, engaged in extensive and often long-distance trade, and, in some regions, developed complex social structures.[11]

Hunter-gatherer bands were probably patrilineal societies (tracing descent through the male line). Fairly standard pottery styles throughout southern Ontario suggest that women, the primary pottery makers, moved from band to band. As hunters, men built up a specialized knowledge of their local ecosystem and therefore stayed put. Each spring and fall, several bands met for fishing; during that time, marriages, communal burials, and general ceremonies took place, all of them affirming and reinforcing a general allegiance. The burial remains of most of these bands resemble those of the Archaic period and indicate a single-family egalitarian society.[12]

More complex socio-economic structures did evolve. Caches of specially crafted, often heat-treated Woodland-period artifacts have been found across the Great Lakes. These goods were used for trading purposes (interregional trade reached its pre-contact peak in this era) and were manufactured by part-time or possibly full-time craft workers, suggesting a specialization of function within these societies.[13]

Archaic grave goods were primarily practical items, such as polished tools and weapons, though they probably also possessed some spiritual value. By contrast, in the Early to Middle Woodland era, pipes, cut jaws, drilled teeth, and shaped skulls existed *only* for spiritual purposes and dominated burial deposits. Some scholars suggest that an idealistic rather than a materialistic notion underlay the world view of Ontario Native peoples from the Early Woodland era to European contact. A non-material notion of wealth is also indicated by the Native practice of gift-giving during trade, burial, and other ceremonies. The display of social rank through conspicuous giving rather than through conspicuous consumption began before contact.[14]

Even within early hunter-gatherer societies, cultural and social behaviours differed. At Rice Lake in southeastern Ontario, an even more complex social and economic system emerged. Seven concentrations of large burial mounds—one measuring 53 metres long by 7.5 metres wide by 2 metres high—dot the landscape. Each mound overlooked water and demarcated a local ecosystem used by fifty to a hundred people. Successive burials in each mound indicate that bands possessed these territories for generations. Burial patterns and grave-good distribution point to clear distinctions in social status. Privileged individuals were buried in discrete subfloor pits, accompanied by prized goods. They were genetically related, indicating that status was hereditary; the bodies of the less important became part of the fill used to construct the mounds. When a local leader died, those who had died since the death of the previous leader were disinterred, disarticulated, and reburied, adding to the size and status of the local mound.

Why did this complex system emerge at Rice Lake? Rich natural resources facilitated long-term residence, yet elite status also resulted from trade and craft specialization. In two gravesites, single individuals were buried with silver items, suggesting that these people had special access to the trade and reworking of silver. Silver from Cobalt, 350 kilometres north, was reworked and distributed through an elite-controlled trade system linked to southern Ohio. Rice Lake was the northern node in what is called the Hopewellian exchange system. That the Ohio and Rice Lake cultures both declined following AD 250 supports the argument for interconnection.[15]

'Unprecedented change' occurred between AD 500 and 1200. The adoption of the bow and arrow from western Canadian Native peoples—or possibly its independent invention—facilitated more efficient exploitation of game. The gradual introduction of corn and other cultivated crops led to even more dramatic lifestyle changes. Corn cultivation in Ontario commenced about AD 500 with the development of a new eight-row corn variety well suited to short growing seasons. This technology gradually spread north, perhaps via the Ohio-based trade systems that had linked late Archaic peoples. By 1100, southern Ontario Native peoples also cultivated beans, squash, sunflowers, and tobacco.[16]

Initially, villages varied little from the average size of pre-agricultural societies, at 200 to 400 people. By 1300, there is evidence of a more dramatic cultural transformation: villages began to coalesce into larger, more fortified, and more permanent sites, covering 1.2 hectares and containing over a thousand people. By the mid-fifteenth century, southern Ontario's population reached its contact level of 60,000 to 65,000; villages of 8 to 9 hectares contained 2,000 to 3,000 people. Longhouses—the first monster homes of Ontario—reached 100 metres in length and housed more than twenty families, or more than one hundred people.

Corn cultivation contributed to village consolidation, but subsistence-level societies rarely swiftly abandoned a diversified food-gathering strategy. Early Iroquoian villagers relied on a mixed economy. At seasonal hunting and gathering camps they herded deer into killing pens. The deer were then skinned, cured, and transported—by women—back to the central village. Women also collected berries, nuts, and wild rice. Corn was added to traditional ecological behaviour but did not supplant it. The full nutritional value of corn is released only when it is mixed with foods such as beans, which spread widely in the fifteenth century, a time of significant population growth. Moreover, cultivated plants replaced wild plants not meat in the Native diet. In contrast to the United States—a region of longer growing seasons where more crops were eaten—the corn, bean, and animal protein diet of the Iroquois led to fewer winter famines, a lower death rate (of some 40 per 1,000), and a higher annual growth rate (of about 1.2 per cent).[17]

From 1400 to European contact, southern Ontario Native peoples engaged in large-scale war involving territorial acquisition, cannibalism, and conquest. Warfare prompted tribal consolidations. Villages were enclosed with multiple rows of palisades, catwalks, and turrets. The emergence of larger allied groups—the Neutral and Erie in southwestern Ontario and the Petun and Wendat (Huron) in the southeast—dates to the later fifteenth century. Wendat engaged in extensive warfare with the St Lawrence Iroquois, and the Neutral vied with the Algonquian Fire Nation in the southwest. Population growth levelled off, a result of increased warfare and the spread of tuberculosis, a disease characteristic of relatively densely populated areas.[18]

Why did violence and tribal movement increase? A traditional interpretation

Iroquoian women preparing corn. Women cultivated the crops (corn, beans, squash, sunflower seeds), carrying their young children as they worked. From François Du Creux, *Historiae Canadensis*, (Paris, 1664). NA.

argues that the fur trade undermined the peaceful and sharing lifestyle practised by pre-contact peoples. But war and population migrations predate the arrival of Europeans. A commercial fur trade did not commence until the 1580s; Europeans exacerbated these developments, but they did not initiate them.

Perhaps the notion that sharing was central to pre-contact peoples has been romanticized? Despite variable-sized longhouses—the chief's dwelling, used for ceremonial and political meetings, was the largest—archaeological evidence has failed to demonstrate significant differences in wealth among the Iroquois. Conspicuous giving militated against sharp differences in lifestyles. Semi-sedentary populations (sanitation concerns and resource exhaustion caused the Iroquois to move about every twenty years) exhibited less concern for property protection than did sedentary peoples. A simple desire for territorial and material aggrandizement, then, is not enough to account for increased warlike activity.

A more intriguing perspective focuses on the impact agriculture had on traditional gender roles. Physical anthropologists have documented the continuance of a fairly constant gene mix across southern Ontario, but biological homogeneity is not accompanied (as was the case in the hunter-gatherer era) by standard pottery styles. Before corn, women—the pottery makers—married outside their bands; after corn, women, while continuing as pottery makers, tilled and cultivated crops and adopted a more sedentary lifestyle. After clearing fields, men regularly left villages to hunt, fish, gather food, and make war. Men, not women, became the primary agents of village interaction. Women, not men, became the focus of a more sedentary family life. Women oversaw the use of longhouse space, an important task given rising population levels. They also played significant roles in the (s)election of men to village councils, which oversaw the merging and commingling of different clans within specific villages.[19]

The spread of corn and of matrilocality was a gradual and reciprocal process. Initially, corn was grown close to homes. Over time a gendered ownership of this resource emerged. Mothers taught daughters to cultivate corn. If a daughter resided in her mother's home after marriage, the skills to successfully cultivate corn remained in the region. The coincidence of successful corn production and matrilocality probably encouraged other families to adopt similar matrilocal households. As corn became a more important dietary component, it made sense for men to reside in the place where the resource's owner lived. Thus, though corn cultivation had occurred in southwestern Ontario in the sixth century, the large longhouses associated with matrilocal residences did not become common until about 1300, when maize cultivation was widespread.[20]

Farming did not completely transform Native women's lives. While foraging gradually diminished, transporting game remained unchanged. The persistence of traditional labour by Native women resulted in a birth rate similar to that of the hunter-gatherer era: one child every fourth or fifth year. In order to perform her tasks, a mother could carry only one child at a time; after age five, children could keep up with their mothers. Evidence from the contact period provides further support for a low birth rate. Wendat and Five Nations women abstained from intercourse while nursing their children for two to three years. Rituals also often required sexual abstinence. Men did not marry until their mid-twenties: their families wanted them to participate economically in the maternal household as long as possible. Wendat women regarded marriage, it would seem, with ambivalence; they regularly engaged in premarital sex and may only have married when they became pregnant.[21]

In hunting-gathering economies, men achieved status and prestige by successfully guiding their families through the rigours of winter life. As women produced more of the staple food, hunting became devalued. Moreover men moved to their wife's residence after marriage and had to adapt to new challenges and expectations. Semi-subterranean sweat lodges attached to the ends of longhouses emerged in this era as an exclusive place for men to meet, smoke pipes, and become integrated into the household and provided a private place for male bonding. Still, men also needed to demonstrate individual prowess and thereby maintain status in the larger community. Courage and daring in war provided one way to do this. A pattern of conflict based on individual daring, revenge, and the pursuit of prestige—all of which could be satisfied by swift raids, the taking of captives, and ceremonial torture—emerged in the period following 1300 and extended into contact times.[22] Changing gender roles undermined traditional measures of status, but it is nonetheless hard to see how that process alone could have led to the escalating troubles of the late fifteenth and sixteenth centuries. The extent of population dislocation and the scale of conflict seem motivated by more than the need for men to bolster damaged egos.

A more holistic perspective points to underlying changes at least equal in significance to status upheaval. Even as modified gender roles challenged male egos, changing environmental conditions undermined the very conditions that had initially led to those role changes. Farming took place within a fragile ecological zone at the northern edge of productive agriculture. The locational characteristics of over three hundred Iroquoian villages settled between AD 900 and 1550 suggest that Iroquoian peoples preferred sandy, well-drained soils on moderately sloping terrain in regions with over ninety frost-free days. These characteristics suited pre-contact agricultural techniques: sandy soils could be easily worked with digging sticks made of wood, bone, or stone; moderate or undulating slopes provided adequate natural drainage.[23]

Ontario did not boast many suitable microenvironments for farming of this type. Nor was the climate predictable in this period. From 1450 to 1850, much of the world experienced the Little Ice Age. In southern Ontario, temperatures averaged 1 to 2 degrees Celsius lower than today. These low temperatures could have adversely affected corn and beans, cold-sensitive plants already being grown at their northern limits. It is difficult to be exact concerning annual temperature ranges, but the Little Ice Age increased temperature variability and to that extent made farming an increasingly risky endeavour, contributing to social destabilization.[24]

Northern Ontario Peoples

Pre-contact northern Ontario hunter-gatherers are often described as living a simple, egalitarian, and harsh life. The temptation to draw a sharp distinction between Algonquian and Iroquois is prompted in part by their different linguistic stocks: most northern Native bands spoke an Algonquian dialect; those further south were of the Iroquoian linguistic grouping. Yet it is far from clear that language determined social and economic practice. The argument for a sharp distinction also rests on the notion of contrasting ecosystems, but this perspective suffers from environmental determinism and overlooks the reality of the gradual change from an environment that supported farming to one that did not. Some Algonquian peoples did farm, and northern bands interacted both among themselves and with more southerly sedentary bands. This interaction facilitated diversity, cultural complexity, and change over time.[25]

Native peoples in Ontario's northwest practised a more diffuse subsistence strategy and resided in smaller groups than did Native peoples around the northern Great Lakes. The boreal forest cover and harsher winters made for limited food

Box 1.1　Understanding Change in the Pre-Contact Era

It is difficult to infer motivation, agency, and intent from material remains. Yet such remains—charred wood, postholes, broken pots, animal parts, and midden piles—are the sources from which those interested in understanding social, economic, and ecological change in the millennia before European contact must draw their interpretations. In order to make sense of these material remains and what changes might have occurred in their nature over time, careful classification and detailed typologies of pottery types, faunal remains, size and spacing of postholes, thickness and thinness of pots, and so on have to be systematically carried out. Comparisons of these material remains can then be made across space and time. Consistencies and changes are noted and attempts are made to explain the patterns unearthed. The following example, which touches on a major debate, suggests the rich inventiveness of scholars who work on this period of Ontario's history. Some archaeologists have argued that around AD 1300, as a result of a major conquest of southern Ontario peoples by an invading group, cultural change emerged. Others wonder if 'a sudden militaristic "hiccup"' is an adequate explanation. How, for example, might one explain changes in ceramic style that seem to emerge at this time period? Were they the result of conquest? The close study of ceramic stylistic change at one archaeological site covering the thirteenth and fourteenth centuries suggests another possibility.[1]

Today young people often introduce stylistic change. Diffusion happens 'almost entirely on an interpersonal level'. This diffusion model has relevance to the pre-contact period. We know that personal interaction was common, and ceramic change did occur; who might have initiated the process? Comparing pottery made by daughters—'juveniles'—with that made by their mothers at the Calvert site east of London, Ontario, archaeologist Peter Timmins suggests that the junior potters were the innovators in ceramic design and that these innovations could have spread over an extensive region by the mid-fourteenth century. The work of these daughters privileged horizontal ceramic motifs, while that of their mothers emphasized vertical lines. Peer interaction, in this case among young women, is thus seen as a major conduit for the diffusion of significant ceramic stylistic change in the pre-contact era. Why did young women experiment with new designs at this time? Timmins suggests that the twelfth century was an unsettled time and that responses took the form of new habitation patterns and new ceramic designs, symbols that could promote a strong feeling of group identity. Issues of gender, generation, and agency underlay the diffusion of ceramic stylistic change in the twelfth and thirteenth centuries. The argument that war was the prime cause of cultural change in 1300 seems less probable.[2]

---

1. Quotation: Neal Ferris, 'Telling Tales: Interpretative Trends in Southern Ontario Late Woodland Archaeology', *Ontario Archaeology* 68 (1999): 1. For the first argument, see J.V.

Wright, 'The Conquest Theory of the Ontario Iroquois Tradition: A Reassessment', *Ontario Archaeology* 54 (1992): 3–15.

2. Peter Timmins, 'Born Glen Meyer, Growing Up Uren: The Juvenile Ceramics from the Calvert Site', *KEWA* 97 (1997): 2–14; Kathryn A. Kamp, 'Where Have All the Children Gone? The Archaeology of Childhood', *Journal of Archaeological Method and Theory* 8 (2001): 1–34.

resources and encouraged small, seasonal group concentrations at rivers and in rich hunting territories. Some archaeologists assert that the migratory practice necessitated by the sparse ecosystem precluded strong band organization and status distinctions and fostered instead an overall economic homogeneity and social equality throughout the region—a culture that remained relatively unaltered from the late Archaic period to the eve of contact. Perhaps so, but grave goods dating to the Woodland era have been found in the northwest, suggesting cultural links to the south, a sense of band solidarity, and a degree of social stratification.[26]

Further south, between Lake Abitibi and the northeast shore of Lake Superior, a group of Algonquians whom Europeans called Ojibwa and who are now known as Anishinaabe developed a subsistence economy based on fishing. In

Princess Point Vessel, c. AD 600–900. On this typical pot, the lines near the neck were made by using a coiled string to press twigs into the clay. From Chris Ellis and Neal Ferris, eds, *The Archaeology of Southern Ontario to A.D. 1650* (London, ON: Ontario Archaeological Society, 1990), 177. Metropolitan Toronto Reference Library.

the late Archaic, Native peoples fished in the spring, using spearing and angling techniques. Largely an individual activity, the fishery supported only a few, so Native peoples did not linger at the site. According to Native creation mythology, a god named Michabous, after observing a spider 'working at her web in order to catch flies', invented fishing nets. Because Native people used the productive but labour-intensive seine net (nets had to be made, mended, and attended to by many people), larger groups stayed longer at spring fishery sites, perhaps necessitating a chieftain system for social control and food distribution. By the fifteenth century, Native people also worked a fall fishery, using gill nets, and froze much of the catch for future use and trade with Iroquois. Preserving food for winter promoted greater stability and eased the pressure to disperse into smaller groups for extended winter hunting. Artifacts found near Lake Nipissing suggest that certain nineteenth-century Anishinaabe rituals, especially the Midewiwin, date from the sixteenth century. This process of group identification—suggested also by common pottery styles—paralleled the emergence of clans among the agricultural Iroquois to the south. Indeed, it used to be thought that pottery was brought to the Anishinaabe via trade and intermarriage with the Iroquois; archaeologists now believe that the Anishinaabe manufactured their own pottery.[27]

At European contact, trade between northeastern Anishinaabe bands and Iroquois occurred within a structured set of relationships. The Wendat (called by the French 'the Huron'), who traded corn and other foodstuffs for beaver and deer pelts, believed themselves superior to northern Native peoples. Huron was the language of trade. Wendat men married Anishinaabe women, who had to relocate to Wendat territory; but Wendat women never married Anishinaabe men. Nor did the Wendat eat Anishinaabe food. The northeastern bands, who also traded with bands further to the northwest, were nevertheless nicely situated to control the flow of southern goods into the north and of northern goods into the south. As in Huronia, certain Anishinaabe families controlled these trading paths and bequeathed that right to their descendants.[28]

Even before contact, then, some northern Ontario hunter-gatherer societies were increasingly non-egalitarian and far from isolated. Cultural change occurred at variable rates as Native groups responded to and assimilated into their lifestyles various combinations of environmental pressures, indigenous traditions, cultural infusions, and trade exchanges. Recognition of the strength, durability, and protean nature of these various cultures is essential in order to understand the nature of the contact and post-contact eras of Ontario's past, periods to which we now turn.

Chapter Two

The Transformation of Ontario's Cultural Landscape, 1580–1653

European contact had catastrophic effects on Native peoples. European disease, greed, arms, culture, and trade resulted in the near—and sometimes complete—destruction of many North American Aboriginal peoples. Yet that fate did not determine the activities and perceptions of Native people or Europeans in the early contact period. Native peoples had confronted disease and war before, and they were active participants in the tumultuous events that forever altered the Native geography of southern Ontario. That said, this is not to offer an apologia for European exploitation. It is, rather, to suggest that unless we approach the contact era from that perspective, we must be at a loss to understand the re-emergence and revitalization, albeit slow and painful, of Ontario's Native peoples in the late nineteenth and the twentieth centuries.[1]

Early Contact

In the early sixteenth century, Giovanni da Verrazano (1524), Jacques Cartier (1534–6, 1541–3), and others traded in the Americas. A few European goods had reached Ontario earlier, around 1520, with Portuguese, Basque, and French cod fishermen who frequented the Grand Banks from at least the beginning of the sixteenth century. In these early exchanges, Europeans had many questions about Native societies. For example, did Native peoples have gold? Did they have knowledge of a short northern route to the riches of the East? When, by the mid-1500s, the answers seemed to be no, European exploration declined, although the fisheries expanded. After 1580, however, European demand for fur hats increased as fur supplies from Russia dwindled because of war with Sweden. Consumer pressure for fur hats provided the spur for a renewed push into the North America interior.[2]

By 1600, four separate—often competing and warring—nodes of Iroquoians lived in and around southern Ontario. The Neutral peoples had settled at the head of Lake Ontario. To the north and in close contact with the Neutral lived the Petun. The Five Nations Iroquois—the Mohawk, Oneida, Onondaga, Cayuga, and Seneca—settled in what is now northern New York State. To minimize internal conflict and facilitate the conquering of other Iroquois peoples, they formed a confederacy in 1536. Wendat (Huron) and Anishinaabe warfare with St Lawrence Iroquoian groups escalated. The latter fled their homes in the late sixteenth cen-

A beaver—'26 inches from head to tail'—as depicted in *Voyages du Baron de Lahontan dans L'Amérique Septentrionale* (La Haye, 1706). Demand for felt hats made of beaver fur spurred the development of the fur trade, but Europeans also prized beaver meat for its medicinal properties and as a source of food. The tail was especially sought after: according to Lahontan, its 'flavour and appearance resemble those of the choicest bacon'. National Library of Canada C-099255.

tury, probably to join the Five Nations Iroquois to the south, whom they then encouraged to attack the Wendat. In an attempt to put space between themselves and the Five Nations Iroquois, southern Wendat moved north, joining others already resident in the Lake Huron region. In the midst of this turbulence, Samuel de Champlain slipped into the recently vacated territory and, in 1608, set up at Quebec the first permanent French settlement in North America.[3]

In 1615, Champlain reached Huronia, where he encountered a society in the making. Occupying an area of some 1,125 square kilometres in the southeastern corner of Georgian Bay, 20,000 to 30,000 Wendat lived in eighteen to twenty-five villages that ranged from 1.5 to 6 hectares in size. Ongoing coalescence between traditional residents and new arrivals from the Trent River Valley intensified a system of decentralized political and economic control. Though there were chiefs, their power tended to be narrowly focused in either military or civil and trade functions, and even in those sectors they ruled by consensus. Thus, in 1615, Champlain affirmed a trading and general accord with each chief in the Confederacy.[4]

Native peoples made sense of Europeans by situating them within the boundaries of traditional Native world views. They perceived Europeans as otherworldly people arriving from under the water or beyond the horizon, where such beings traditionally lived. The material wealth these returning-culture heroes brought—metal goods, combs, mirrors, and glass beads—fit perfectly into a society that accorded spiritual value to red copper and to crystal or shell artifacts. The baubles

The Battle of Lake Champlain, July 1609, from Champlain's *Voyages* (1613). Like many European representations of life in the 'New World', this famous illustration of Iroquois warriors' first recorded encounter with firearms is quite inaccurate. The hammocks in the enclosed compound (not to mention the palm trees beyond) belong in Latin America—and Iroquois did not fight in the nude. Nor did they use what appear to be French river boats. CMC J10225.

were analogues to—and were, therefore, interpreted as—traditional spiritual items. The increase in the number of these spiritual items sparked the re-emergence of long-dormant cultural behaviours. Following the Hopewellian period (circa AD 300), for example, the practice of depositing spiritual goods in graves had declined; this behaviour re-emerged with the arrival of European trade goods.[5]

Europeans worked within established trading and diplomatic customs even if they did not always comprehend the significance of these interactions. For example, to trade with a Native nation also meant becoming a military ally. Similarly, when Champlain's interpreter, Étienne Brûlé, began to live on a semi-permanent basis with the Wendat in 1615, he and the French were following a long-established custom. Nipissing and Ottawa traders also resided in Huronia on a seasonal basis and while there, like Brûlé, spoke the Wendat language and adopted Wendat customs, thus acknowledging Wendat superiority.

The Wendat's traditional role in the northern trading relationship—supplier of agricultural goods in return for copper, fur, and fish—was elaborated as the result of increasing European trade. Before the 1630s, the Wendat traded directly with the French at Quebec, paying tolls to various Algonquian tribes, especially the Kichespirini, who were situated on the Ottawa River. After 1630, trade with northwest Native peoples intensified as a result of declining fur resources within Huronia. Similar declines occurred within Nipissing and Ottawa hunting territories, facilitated in part by the Anishinaabe belief that dead animals, if treated prop-

About every fifteen years, a Wendat village would celebrate the Feast of the Dead. The bones of those who had died since the last feast were disinterred and, following a night of ceremonies and gift-giving, were deposited in a common pit, probably symbolizing community solidarity. At the same time, the feast served to reinforce trading relationships with other groups (Anishinaabe and Europeans were often invited as guests) and to demonstrate, via gift-giving, status within Huronia. NA C147966.

erly, would return to earth and thus reincarnation would prevent extinction—yet another example of cultural belief mediating European inputs and pressures. The Nipissing and Ottawa became, like the Wendat, intermediaries, drawing into the developing trade network the more northerly Cree as the initial suppliers of fur.[6]

Other Iroquoian groups benefited from the control of a strategic point along an axis of European-oriented trade. Some 30,000 Neutrals occupied 5,500 square kilometres and resided in forty settlements of 0.5 to 6 hectares near Lake Ontario's west end. They may have had a more centralized political system than other Iroquoian groups, with civil and military affairs more concentrated in the hands of one chief. Neutral gravesites resemble those of the Rice Lake area in the Hopewellian period. Some grave goods had arrived from the south rather than by the St Lawrence route, suggesting the continuance of trade patterns that had been evident as early as the Archaic era.[7]

The Neutrals also took advantage of eastern trade. As the Wendat-French alliance solidified (the French and the Wendat fought the Five Nations many times between 1609 and 1634), the Five Nations found it difficult to acquire French goods, while the Wendat could not acquire goods from the south. In this context, the Neutrals functioned as a port of trade, allowing the Wendat and the Five Nations to exchange goods in a 'neutral' zone. The Neutrals charged a toll for linking these two otherwise unconnected trading systems. And just as the Wendat linked the northern Nipissing—and, through them, subarctic hunter-gatherers—to European trading zones, so the Neutrals developed a similar system via the Petun, the more northwesterly Ottawa tribes, and other northwest subarctic hunter-gatherers.[8]

South of Lake Ontario, the Five Nations Iroquois also changed in the early contact period. While attempting to control French trade, the Mohawks—the easternmost Five Nations tribe—began to deal with Dutch traders, who arrived in the upper Hudson River Valley in 1614. While the Dutch presence initially eased Mohawk pressure on French-Wendat trading routes, it exacerbated rivalries within the Five Nations Confederacy. The Onondaga attempted to establish direct trade links with the French, thus bypassing both the Mohawks and the Dutch. Trade with the Dutch did increase Mohawk power; it did not lead to the emergence of a centralized political system comparable to that of the Neutrals.[9]

Europeans were hemmed in and could trade only with the permission of certain Native peoples. Yet European posts became 'a set of fixed points to which the native trading system could be anchored.' By the 1630s, many Native people had begun to appreciate European goods for utilitarian more than spiritual reasons: no longer deities, Europeans were seen as fallible and 'ugly' beings who could nevertheless provide many practical items. Among the Wendat and the Five Nations, for example, the incidence of traditional stone tools at archaeological sites shows a dramatic decline. Desire for European metal goods prompted the intensification of intertribal relations, increased pressure on local ecosystems, sparked the evolution of more sharply graded social structures, and, in some cases, promoted the gradual emergence of more centralized political systems.[10]

Europeans did not control the winds of change sweeping over Ontario in these years. Too few in number (in 1629 there were only 117 Europeans in New France, and only 356 by 1641), Europeans, in fact, depended on Native know-how, labour, and trading links to live. For their part, Aboriginal people desired certain goods but could have survived without them. Native peoples were confronting 'a change in the processes of change, not the beginning of change'.[11] The early contact era is best characterized as one of non-directed change: host societies dealt with European inputs free from European hegemony. Change resulted from the complex interplay of Native cultural traditions, intertribal rivalries, and the specific and varied relations each Native group had with particular European powers.

Disruption

The 'scythe of infectious disease' that ravaged Native peoples (see Box 2.1) cannot by itself account for the transformation that took place in southern Ontario. Plagues knew no favourites: Native peoples along the major trading corridors were affected relatively equally. Yet by 1653, the Neutrals, Petun, and Wendat no longer existed as major confederacies and south-central Ontario had become the hunting preserve not of the immune disease carriers—the French and the Dutch—but rather of the Five Nations of northern New York. What each

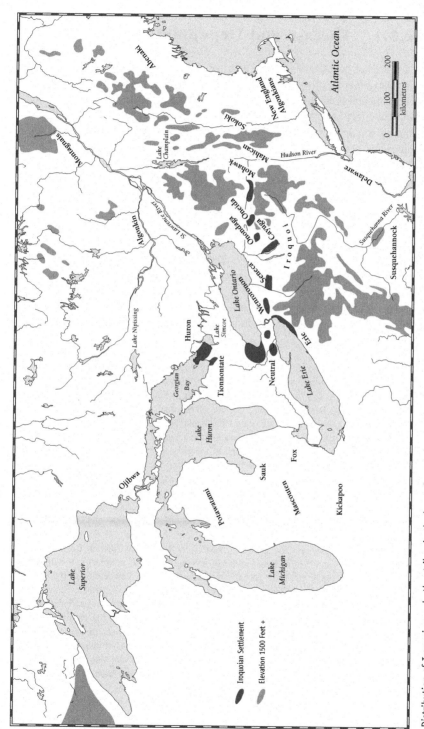

Distribution of Iroquoian and other tribes in the lower Great Lakes area, c. 1630. From Bruce Trigger, *The Children of Aataensic: A History of the Huron People in 1660* (Montreal: McGill-Queen's University Press, 1976), 92.

Box 2.1   Disease and Depopulation

It is a matter of considerable debate as to when European-introduced disease first ravaged Native peoples living in northern New York and Ontario. Archaeological and paleodemographic evidence dates the first Ontario epidemics to the mid-1630s, yet trading and direct contact with Native peoples had occurred well before that date. Why did disease arrive so late? Indeed, some scholars strongly hypothesize that several epidemics occurred earlier.[1]

Archaeologist Gary Warrick has offered a plausible explanation for the late-arrival thesis. Both smallpox and measles were more apt to be fatal to adults than to children. Before the 1630s, few children came to either New France or New England. On a ship without many children to serve as carriers, diseases could run their course during the Atlantic crossing. In June 1634, one of the first vessels with a large number of children arrived in Quebec City. The Montagnais people contracted measles and transmitted it to Wendat traders in the vicinity. The disease swept through Huronia, followed several years later by a series of virulent smallpox epidemics.[2] The effect was devastating. The population of most of the affected peoples declined by over 60 per cent in a period of about five to eight years, a death rate possibly double that experienced by Europeans during the infamous Black Death of the fourteenth century.

---

1. For the strongest statement of pandemics in the sixteenth century in northeastern North America (and elsewhere), see Henry F. Dobyns, *'Their Number Become Thinned': Native American Population Dynamics in Eastern North America* (Knoxville: University of Tennessee Press, 1983), and Georges E. Sioui, *For an Amerindian Autohistory: An Essay on the Foundations of a Social Ethic*, translated by Sheila Fischman (Montreal: McGill-Queen's University Press, 1992). Dean R. Snow and K.M. Lamphear, 'European Contact and Indian Depopulation in the Northeast: The Timing of the First Epidemics', *Ethnohistory* 35, no. 1 (1988): 15–33, and Dean R. Snow and William A. Starna, 'Sixteenth Century Depopulation: A View from the Mohawk Valley', *American Anthropologist* 91, no. 1 (1989): 142–9, present the strongest countercase: that epidemics were an early seventeenth-century occurrence, not a sixteenth-century phenomenon. Recent discussions focusing on methodology can be found in D. Ann Herring, 'Toward a Reconsideration of Disease and Contact in the Americas', *Prairie Forum* 17 (1992): 153–65; Henry F. Dobyns, 'More Methodological Perspectives on Historical Demography', *Ethnohistory* 36 (1989): 285–99; Dean R. Snow and K.L. Lanphear, '"More Methodological Perspectives": A Rejoinder to Dobyns', *Ethnohistory* 36 (1989): 299–304; David Henige, 'On the Current Devaluation of the Notion of Evidence: A Rejoinder to Dobyns', *Ethnohistory* 36 (1989): 304–7. William Engelbrecht focuses on factors other than disease to account for population in the pre- and proto-contact periods, in 'Factors Maintaining Low Population Density among the Prehistoric New York Iroquois', *American Antiquity* 52 (1987): 13–27. Bruce Trigger presents a balanced discussion of the literature, leaving open the possibility of sixteenth-century epidemics while noting that evidence for such has yet to be uncovered, in *Natives and Newcomers: Canada's Heroic Age Reconsidered* (Kingston, ON: McGill-Queen's University Press, 1985), 231–42. Susan Johnston is critical of some of Trigger's figures; see 'Epidemics: The Forgotten Factor in Seventeenth Century Native Warfare in the St Lawrence Region', in *Native Peoples, Native*

Lands: Canadian Indians, Inuits and Métis, edited by Bruce A. Cox (Don Mills, ON: Oxford University Press, 1987), 14–31. See also John A. Dickinson, 'The Pre-Contact Huron Population: A Reappraisal', *Ontario History* 72 (1980), 173–9, for a specific discussion of the Wendat, and Ubelaker, 'North American Indian Population Size', for statistics on North American population decline and growth from 1500 to 1985, derived from *Smithsonian's Handbook of North American Indians.*

2. Gary Warrick, 'The Precontact Iroquoian Occupation of Southern Ontario', *Journal of World Prehistory* 14 (2000): 457; Warrick, 'European Infectious Disease'.

European trading power brought, in addition to disease, helps to account for this radical change in intertribal affairs. The French brought missionaries; the Dutch, spurred on by the English, brought muskets.[12]

Récollet missionaries reached Huronia in 1615, followed by the Jesuits in 1626. The Récollets were the more dogmatic and the less successful. They did not learn Native languages and generally lived apart from those they sought to prose-lytize. Weakened by civil and religious intrigues in France, the Récollets left the field to the better-financed and better-organized Jesuit order.[13]

Jesuits learned Native languages and lived among those they sought to convert. In 1634, led by Jean de Brébeuf, they set up a permanent presence in Huronia; thirteen Jesuits lived there in 1639, and about twenty in 1648. In 1639, under a new Jesuit leader, Jerôme Lalemant, the construction of a large mission centre, Ste-Marie-among-the-Hurons, commenced. Lalemant also introduced *donnes*—men who, while not taking the vows of the church, gave their lives to its service. These assistants soon outnumbered the missionaries (there were at least twenty-four of them in 1648) and were essential to the missionary effort. Smaller missions of shorter duration were established among the Petun, the Nipissing, and the Ojibwa, and in 1640 a brief visit was made to the Neutrals. The Wendat accepted Jesuits as a reaffirmation of the French–Wendat trading relationship. By 1646, the Jesuits counted some 400 to 500 Wendat converts, and in 1648, with Huronia under increased seige from the Five Nations, the Jesuits baptized some 2,700 Wendat.[14]

Missionary and Wendat world views were incompatible. To accept Christianity meant, as one Wendat chief affirmed, 'overthrowing the country'.[15] The new religion challenged not only traditional Wendat spiritual beliefs, but their whole social and political order. Although more sympathetic than the Récollets to Wendat tradition, the Jesuits failed to appreciate the extent to which Wendat society was integrated with its traditional religion and hence how the process of mass conversion to a European cultural framework undermined traditional Wendat existence.

The Wendat lived in balance with nature. Good and evil spirits were constants: neither would ever triumph over the other; both required close attendance and propitiation, and each could be found inherent in all matter. The Wendat universe was in this sense a closed circle. One did not expect to move toward a state of increased perfection; good would not win out in the end; balance was the goal. This cosmological imperative underlay Native regard for the spiritual well-being of animals, rocks, and trees. A complex system of taboos governed Native conduct vis-à-vis the natural world. At bottom, these taboos were designed to maintain balance, to propitiate the good and evil spirits that were inherent in all matter.

This cosmology also underlay Wendat social relationships. Children were not physically punished, scolded, or disciplined. They were indulged and, from the Jesuits' perspective, spoiled. 'The Savages', one Jesuit reported, 'love their children above all things. They are like the Monkeys—they choke them by embracing them too closely.' In fact, Wendat children were given freedom to experiment. This educational technique fostered 'self-reliance rather than obedience, the self-directed warrior rather than the other-directed soldier'. Children came to appreciate how generosity and sharing benefited individuals and society as a whole. Balance and harmony could be attained through gift-giving and could be disrupted by personal acquisitiveness. The primacy of community over self also informed the Wendat judicial system. Reparations for wrongdoing became the responsibility not simply of the individual but also of his or her kin and clan. The generalized consequences of wrongdoing acted as a control against its repetition.[16]

Balance was not part of Jesuit cosmology. As one Jesuit wrote, 'all nations must believe in the same way.' Nothing was satisfactory save complete submission to God and the consequent eradication of the devil or evil. Vigilant control was necessary to win this war. Education had to be formally structured and policed. Justice had to be strict and punishment severe. Children had to learn to obey. Families should become microcosms of a hierarchical society. Christianity and capitalism each stressed obedience, regimentation, and the acceptance of other-direction. And just as people could manipulate or control other people, so too could people manipulate or control and transform the natural world.[17]

Christianity accorded women a subordinate role in society. The social independence that Wendat women enjoyed astonished and dismayed Jesuit missionaries. 'The women have great power here,' one missionary noted. 'A man may promise you something, and, if he does not keep his promise, he thinks that he is sufficiently excused when he tells you his wife did not wish to do it. I told him then that he was the master, and that in France women do not rule their husbands.' The missionaries especially disapproved of the freedom displayed by Wendat women in sexual relations, marriage, and divorce. At times, as even Champlain discovered, women did not wait for male suitors but had the temerity to take the initiative in propositioning men. Jesuits worked hard to end premarital sex and easy access to divorce and remarriage. But they failed to subordinate women to men in such matters. Even during the 1640s, when the conversion rate increased, women resisted and made life as miserable as they could for the men who did convert. As one Jesuit reported of a male convert, women 'drove him away from their cabins, and refused to give him anything to eat. . . . He was left without the means of support, and [did] the work of women. He was mocked at, and spurned from every company: . . . quarrels were picked with him. If . . . he was invited to a feast, some insolent persons . . . would call out that he should not have been invited, because he was a Christian, and because he brought misfortune where ever he went . . . he might certainly make up his mind to die sooner than he expected; and that he would be clubbed to death as a Sorcerer.'[18]

While the Jesuits failed to subordinate Native women, they did (as the previous passage illustrates) sow dissension and create disunity within Huronia along very broad social and political lines. Because Native religion permeated all aspects of Native society, Christian converts could not engage in governmental affairs, fight in traditional ways, hunt according to accepted practice, or take part in important religious ceremonies such as the Feast of the Dead. All these and many other functions entailed the recognition and observance of religious ceremony and practice deemed invalid and savage by Christian teaching. As converts increased in the 1640s (the French encouraged conversion by granting Christians preferential trading rights and withholding muskets from all non-Christians), there emerged a significant minority whose beliefs were at odds with those of the Wendat community at large.[19]

The epidemics that crippled Huronia between 1634 and 1640 were selective, cutting heavily into the very young (the warriors of tomorrow) and the very old (traditional leaders). By stripping Huronia of its leadership, the epidemics further contributed to the erosion of religious, social, and political beliefs. Disease reinforced a widening split in Huronia between those who saw missionaries as agents of death (why, many Wendat wondered, did so many die so soon after being baptized?) and those who saw in the missionaries and their links to the French their best hope to continue trade and to protect their homeland from the escalating attacks in the 1640s by the Five Nations Iroquois.[20]

The Dutch adopted a different policy. They viewed New World activity as a business—more a commercial than a religious venture. By the late 1630s, challenged by independent Dutch and English traders who offered muskets to the Mohawks, the Dutch West India Company began to sell guns. By 1644, the Mohawk had 400 guns, and they received a further 400 in 1648. The Seneca also acquired several hundred Dutch guns in the early 1640s. By contrast, the French sold guns only reluctantly, for fear of endangering resident Jesuit missionaries. By 1648, the Wendat had only 120 French guns, which were shorter than, lighter than, and inferior to those provided by the Dutch.[21]

Guns did not cause the wars the Iroquois won: depopulation did. The Five Nations Iroquois went to war more in pursuit of people than of pelts. Traditional Iroquoian warfare has been aptly called the 'mourning-war': in order to avenge a death, enemy captives were sought for ritual torture, whether or not the enemy had been responsible (the word used to designate a captive was the same as that used for a domesticated animal). Other captives were adopted to fill the deceased's role within the Iroquois family, clan, and tribe. The spiritual power of the deceased was thus replaced and the nation maintained its collective strength while weakening the collective spiritual and physical strength of its enemies. The demographic crisis caused by the epidemics resulted in an escalation of warfare to (at least for post-contact time) unprecedented levels. The Neutrals engaged in massive war after epidemics; one encounter with the Fire Nation of northern Michigan

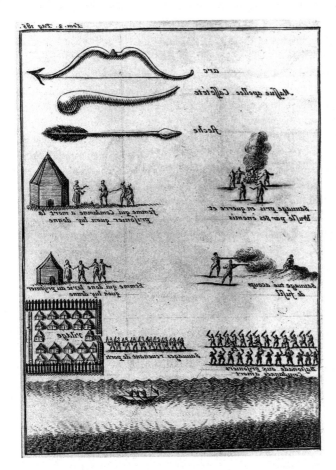

Aspects of Iroquois warfare, early eighteenth century. At the top, the weapon between the bow and arrow is a club called a cassetête. On the left are scenes from the battlefield, with warriors being burned and shot. On the right, women determine the fate of the prisoners given to them: the first is condemned to death, the second is spared (perhaps to be adopted). At the bottom, three condemned prisoners run the gauntlet, and members of a war party return to their village (note the regularity of the village depicted here, reflecting European notions of order). NA C99243.

resulted in the capturing of about a thousand women and warriors, most of whom the Neutrals adopted. Beginning in the late 1630s, the Five Nations Confederacy became the aggressor. The first large raids by the Seneca against the Wendat occurred immediately after an epidemic had hit the former. The pursuit of people to replenish their disease-depleted confederacy overshadowed the desire for pelts and for the material spoils of battle; in only five of thirty-six raids on Anishinaabe and Wendat in the ten years following 1639 did the Five Nations take fur and goods back to their homeland. But they always took captives.[22]

Stressed to the breaking point by poor harvests, disease, and social breakdown, the Wendat collapsed to a series of well-prepared and well-executed external attacks. Between 1630 and 1663, the Iroquois attacked the Wendat seventy-three times, killing or capturing some two thousand people, or between one-fifth and one-quarter of the total Wendat population. Four massive assaults in the 1640s culminated in the spring of 1649: armed with muskets and iron hatchets, 1,200 Iroquois overwhelmed two central Wendat villages, killing or capturing some 380 people. In the summer of 1649, French traders—not French reinforcements—swooped into Huronia, returning to the St Lawrence with some 2,250 kilograms of beaver fur. In the winter, many Wendat died for lack of clothing, though they even disinterred the dead and stripped them of the robes in which they had been buried. A year later, French missionaries reached Montreal with three hundred 'sad relics of a nation once so numerous'. Some Wendat joined the Petun and other refugee groups to the north and west. The Petun and the Nipissing in north-central Ontario and the once-powerful Neutrals at the head of the lake suffered similar fates. By 1653, south-central Ontario had become the preserve of the Five Nations Confederacy.[23]

Chapter Three

Contested Terrain: Cultural Mixing in Early Ontario, 1653–1763

'Contact', historian Richard White notes, 'was not a battle of primal forces in which only one could survive. Something new could appear.'[1] This chapter focuses on the emergence of the Ojibwa to prominence in Ontario; analyzes their relations with the French, British, Cree, and Iroquois; and charts the changing and increasingly powerful presence of Europeans in the *pays d'en haut*.

Cultural Mixing

By 1653, the Five Nations Iroquois seemed unassailable. Small bands of Wendat-Petun struggled to survive amid harsh winters and poor hunting conditions, driven, according to explorer Pierre-Esprit Radisson, to eat their children's beaver-skin diapers, which had been 'beshit [in] above a hundred times'. Continued raids created clusters of desperate refugees and an intermingling of hitherto separate Native peoples throughout the western interior. Different traditions and competing territorial claims impeded sustained united action, but some Native peoples created durable political alliances. Pushed from their traditional homelands (bounded by the north shore of Lake Huron and the east end of Lake Superior), some twenty bands of Mississauga, Saulteaux, and Chippewa regrouped in what is now northern Michigan to become the people known in Canada as the Ojibwa, in the United States as the Chippewa, and among themselves as the Anishinaabe. Numbering about five thousand, these Algonquian-speaking peoples were relatively sedentary, relying on hunting, fishing, gathering, and trading for subsistence. Compared to the northern Cree, they enjoyed a hospitable physical environment. The fact that these individual bands had gathered together each summer since pre-contact times in large multi-clan settlements of over a thousand people to fish, trade, and socialize facilitated the forging of substantial bonds.[2]

Cultural mixing also occurred within the Five Nations Confederacy. In order to bypass Mohawk control of trade at Albany, the Onondaga invited missionaries to reside with them and encouraged the French to set up a trading fort 'in the heart of the country'. In 1656, a short-lived mission commenced, French trade with the Onondaga increased, and internal jealousies flared. Following an Iroquois–French peace agreement in 1666, new, longer-lasting missions led to destabilization similar to that in Huronia. By the 1680s, perhaps 20 per cent of the Five Nations' population were 'sincere Christians'. Though the missions lasted only until 1687, factions developed that cut across traditional Iroquoian political structures, undermining the efficacy of traditional beliefs and rendering consensus on foreign-policy issues difficult.[3]

The extent of Iroquois victories created cultural divisions in another way. After 1650, the Iroquois adopted whole villages of conquered Wendat, Erie, and Neutral people. Unlike individual adoptees, many group captives lived apart: the Seneca, for example, granted five hundred Wendat their own village on Seneca land. These groups generally maintained their social and political distinctiveness, although they had to assist in war and other external affairs. In 1657, casualties in war combined with success in collection led one Jesuit to remark that 'more Foreigners than natives of the country' resided within the Five Nations Confederacy. Indeed, prisoners constituted two-thirds of the Confederacy in the 1660s. Many adoptees were also Christians, who, encouraged by the Jesuits, were the first to trek north to missions along the St Lawrence in the late 1670s.[4]

As the seams binding traditional Iroquois culture stretched to the breaking point, external setbacks added further tension. Ottawa, Ojibwa, Nipissing, and Wendat-Petun vied with the Iroquois for the middleman role vacated by the Wendat. In 1654, 120 traders reached Montreal with fur; two years later, double that number eluded the Iroquois along the Ottawa River. Despite Iroquois harassment, Nipissing continued to collect fur from the Cree travelling to Trois Rivières by the northern route and to Montreal by the Ottawa River. They undertook these arduous and dangerous journeys for two reasons: to acquire European goods and to affirm an alliance with the French against the Iroquois. Too often historians have overemphasized the first at the expense of the second. Yet in the case of the emerging refugee nations, diplomacy rather than material need underlay relations with the French. At Montreal, trade fairs began with the traditional Anishinaabe ceremony celebrating alliances and reciprocity, symbolized by the exchange of goods. Thus, direct contact between the Anishinaabe and New France represented both an economic and a military threat to the Five Nations.[5]

The Emergence of the Anishinaabe

At mid-century, the Iroquois had conquered several Native peoples living in southern Ontario; the central and northern terrain remained contested. In fact, by the late 1650s, the Five Nations began to suffer military defeats in central Ontario at the hands of an allied group of Nipissing, Ottawa, and Ojibwa. Losses to traditional foes to the south and increased aggression by the Mohicans and New England Algonquians to the east compounded Iroquois difficulties. The Five Nations no longer enjoyed armament superiority over their southern and eastern foes and, thanks to French trade, were steadily losing that advantage in Ontario as well. In 1662, for example, Ojibwa armed with muskets wiped out a war party of 100 Iroquois near Lake Huron. Moreover France's new king, Louis XIV, dispatched 1,200 soldiers to subdue the Iroquois. After an initial failure, the French razed five Mohawk villages and destroyed food supplies in 1666. This defeat, plus a series of debilitating epidemics, led the Five Nations to conclude a truce that lasted for sixteen years.[6]

The Treaty of 1666–7 provided the French a needed breathing space to recoup losses. Yet the Five Nations also benefited. Secure to the north, the Confederacy concentrated resources against the Susquehanna and the Mohicans. The settlement also brought greater unity to the Five Nations, and it encouraged them to look for assistance from the English, who had ousted the Dutch from Albany in 1664. Most important, the French recognized Iroquois sovereignty in south and central Ontario. The Iroquois moved quickly into 'the place where we do our hunting since the beginning of the world': by 1763, seven Iroquois villages—virtual extensions of their southern homelands, each containing some 500 to 800 people—dotted Lake Ontario's north shore from the Bay of Quinte to the lake's western tip. The Iroquois had come to stay. They constructed traditional longhouses and storehouses for food, supplies, and furs. 'All this Beaver', Jean Talon, New France's intendant, lamented in 1670, 'is trapped by the Iroquois in countries subject to the King [of France]'.[7]

Events in the north bring into sharp focus two emerging themes in this period of Ontario's history. First, while still fuelled by the economic drive to capture fur, French expansion was increasingly driven by the need to forestall the British, a people who, in the words of one acute French observer, 'did grasp at all America'.[8] Second, expansion along the fur-trade frontier began—slowly but inexorably—to restrict Native participation in that trade.

The Hudson's Bay Company (HBC), which received an imperial charter from England in 1670 operated three forts at the bottom of James Bay by the end of the decade. France now faced European competition from the north and the south. By 1685, the French had constructed a series of forts to prevent, as one map noted, 'les sauvages de descendre à la Baye de Hudson'.[9] Over the next decade, the French and English fought for control of the James Bay forts.

To forestall Iroquois movement, the French initiated a more aggressive policy, constructing a new fort at Niagara and rebuilding Fort Frontenac at what is now Kingston. In the 1680s and 1690s, governors Joseph-Antoine Lefebvre de La Barre J.-R. de Brisay, marquis de Denonville, and Louis de Buade, comte de Frontenac, attacked the Five Nations. The results were mixed. In the early 1680s, for example, La Barre, heading a flu-ridden contingent of 1,100, accepted a dictated and humiliating peace treaty with the Iroquois at Fort Frontenac. His successors, Denonville and Frontenac, mounted better-organized expeditions in 1687, 1693, and 1696. But the Iroquois fought back. Emboldened by the renewal of European hostilities between France and England in 1689, the Iroquois forced the French to abandon Fort Frontenac and other western posts and even attacked Lachine, near the heart of the colony's main settlement. The French, with the exception of the 1693 attack against the Mohawks, fought few Iroquois. Instead they burned cornfields and destroyed villages. Denonville, however, had little faith in a scorched-earth policy. He knew the Iroquois would resettle the vacated area. He therefore encouraged the Ojibwa—four hundred of whom had accompanied him in his 1687 campaign and had ridiculed the notion of 'warring on cornfields rather than Iroquois'—to stay in the southern region and maintain military pressure on the Five Nations.[10]

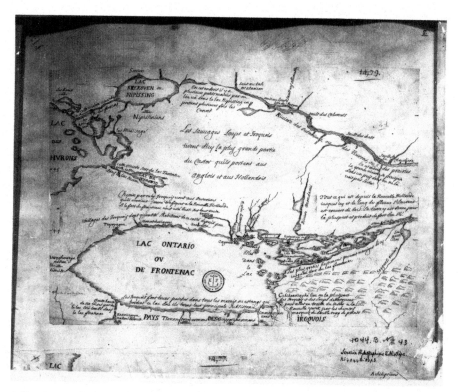

A French map of Iroquois villages north of Lake Ontario, c. 1680. As the Iroquois moved into the region, they established villages at the base of major routes into the northwest fur region: on the portage between the Grand River and Lake Ontario's western end; near the mouths of the Humber, Rouge, Ganaraska, Trent, and Napanee rivers; and on Rice Lake. NA National Map Collection 6409.

To understand the Ojibwa position, it is necessary to situate them within the evolving context of French–Native relations in the interior. By 1685, some eight hundred French traders, called 'coureurs de bois', had replaced the Ojibwa and Ottawa as middlemen in the fur trade. Some historians have argued that these changes represented a major setback to their economic and social existence. Not all French traders, however, traded with other interior peoples: many provided the Ojibwa and their allies with a form of home delivery, thus rendering unnecessary the time-consuming and often dangerous trip to Montreal.[11] Even when coureurs de bois dealt directly with the Cree, the Ottawa and Ojibwa profited by charging tolls to traders who passed through their territory.

In fact, neither the Ojibwa nor the Ottawa were dependent on the French. They fought against tribes such as the Miami and Sioux, with whom the French wished closer relations. At various times they entered into diplomatic negotiations with the Iroquois. Whenever possible they traded with the British. They arranged tithes, intermarriages, gift exchanges, and war alliances without consulting the French. They attempted to block other nations from direct contact with the

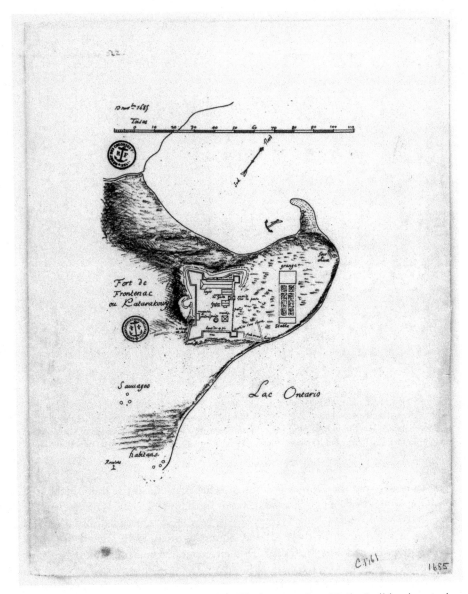

Fort Frontenac, 1685. French traders had great difficulty competing with the English, whose trade goods were of higher quality. Only a few people from the Iroquois Confederacy settled and traded at Fort Frontenac; most stayed closer to the other end of Lake Ontario, maintaining links with the British at Albany. NA National Map Collection 4755.

French at Michilimackinac, where they alone supplied the French with canoes, food, and furs. 'They make', the French complained, 'a profit on everything'.[12]

Complain as they might, the French needed to continue trade in order to maintain an alliance with the Ojibwa. By the late 1680s, however, declining demand had created a glut on the French fur market; in 1696, the government abandoned the fur trade and closed the interior posts, although some coureurs de bois remained and trade continued at Fort Frontenac. If, one angry Native leader warned, 'the French come to visit us no more—you shall never see us again'. Indeed, in the winter of 1695 the Ottawa hunted with the Iroquois, and in 1696 they refused to assist Frontenac against the Five Nations. Pursuing another option, the Ojibwa moved south to fight the Iroquois.[13]

Motivated by the desire for revenge and conquest, those who accepted French guns had a further reason for action. The British-controlled fur trade operating out of Albany through the Five Nations offered richer returns than did the troubled French trade out of Montreal. To tap the British trade required the conquest of the Iroquois. In effect the Ojibwa and Ottawa accepted French musketry in order to enter into a trading and diplomatic alliance with France's enemy. According to Ojibwa oral history, the Three Fires peoples (Ottawa, Ojibwa, and Potawatomi) and some Wendat massed in the Georgian Bay area and moved south in the late 1680s and 1690s. Bloody and brutal battles ensued (one aptly called the Battle of Skull Mound) involving at times one thousand warriors. By the late 1690s, the Ojibwa and the French had pushed the Iroquois out of Ontario and were attacking them in their villages south of the lake. Vanquished—'we are become a small people and much lessened by war', a Mohawk chief told the British in 1696—the Iroquois sought peace.[14]

In 1697, the Treaty of Ryswick ended hostilities in Europe between France and England. In 1701, at Montreal, a colonial peace was concluded between the

Box 3.1   The Ojibwa and the Defeat of the Iroquois

Not all historians agree that the Ojibwa played a primary role in defeating the Iroquois. French correspondence, Iroquois oral history, and archaeological investigation have provided no corroboration for specific Ojibwa claims. How credible, then, are Ojibwa accounts? Most historians of New France have concentrated on the French and placed their Native allies in a subordinate, if supportive, role: they are given recognition as hunters and fur providers, but in military matters the French waged the significant battles. Despite its ethnocentric bias, many historians of the Five Nations people have accepted this perspective.[1] The common stereotype is one of Iroquois strength relative to most other Native peoples. In the end, only Europeans could subdue them.

Those interested in Native history north of the Great Lakes have tended to focus mainly on the Wendat and Five Nations. While this reflects available source material, it also follows from the assumption that Native peoples north of Huronia were politically and culturally less developed. In fact, the presumed lack of cultural and

'Expedition contre les Iroquois en 1695'. NA C30926.

political organization is often used to explain why Ojibwa peoples could successfully resist the Iroquois. The nomadic Ojibwa, after all, were accustomed to moving in search of food and fur and thus could fade away before their allegedly better-organized and more powerful foe. But this perspective overlooks Ojibwa attachment to territory, as indicated by their quick repossession of traditional homelands by the late 1660s. It also ignores the fact that their local environment did not necessitate a radically nomadic way of life in order to survive. Most historians, however, have assumed that the requisite degree of planning and control was not possible within the presumed atomistic and egalitarian Ojibwa socio-cultural structure. Thus, on *a priori* grounds, whatever contributions Ojibwa warriors made to the Iroquois defeat had to have been the result of French planning and initiative. Yet this argument takes no account of the tradition of annual meetings of proto-Ojibwa peoples, dating to the pre-contact era. Interaction within the refugee settlements forged still greater unity. Even in the case of egalitarian societies, crisis situations could generate centralized response.[2]

It is possible that Ojibwa oral accounts exaggerated their contributions. Yet the French and the Iroquois knew their worth. 'They are very useful', a Jesuit wrote in 1692, 'in war against our enemies, whom they alone can reach in the woods'. 'All the nations of the Pays d'en Haut', Frontenac informed Paris the same year, 'had more than eight hundred armed men in different small parties that every day were at the doors . . . of the Iroquois or harassed them on their hunts which harmed them greatly'. In 1699, the Iroquois pleaded with the French to 'make your allies stop coming into our territories every day and breaking our heads.' In the same year, they asked the English for assistance 'for wee can endure it noe longer'. At a general level, Ojibwa oral accounts are more plausible then many historians have recognized.[3]

1. Schmalz, *Ojibwa of Southern Ontario*, chapter 2, and Havard, *The Great Peace*, accord the Ojibway much agency. Brandão and Starna, 'Treaties of 1701', 237m59, are quite skeptical concerning the alleged role played by the Ojibwa. Richter, 'War and Culture'; Richard Aquila, *The Iroquois Restoration: Iroquois Diplomacy on the Colonial Frontier, 1701–1754* (Detroit, MI: Wayne State University Press, 1983), 61; Neal Salisbury, 'The Indian's Old World: Native Americans and the Coming of Europeans', *William and Mary Quarterly* 53 (1996): 455 downplay or ignore the Ojibway's role. Brandão and Starna, 'Treaties of 1701', 230–2, 237n58, 237n59, are quite sensitive in according the Iroquois with a status and policy separate from that of the English, but they do not grant a similar independence from the French to the 'French allies'.

2. On the tendency of historians to use the term 'nomadic' in too loose a manner, see Toby Morantz, 'Old Texts, Old Questions: Another Look at the Issues of Continuity and the Early Fur Trade Period', *Canadian Historical Review* 73 (1992), especially 187–8. The notion of the passive Indian is common in exploration literature, which privileges the 'active' European discoverer. Ojibwa oral tradition turns the table: *they* discover and nurture Europeans; see D. Peter MacLeod, 'The Amerindian Discovery of Europe: Accounts of First Contact in Anishinabeg Oral Tradition', *Arch. Notes* (July–August 1992): 11–15; Leroy V. Eid, '"National" War among Indians of Northeastern North America', *Canadian Review of American Studies* 16 (1985): 125–54.

3. Quotations: Havard, *The Great Peace*, 32, 64, 88–90.

French, two hundred representatives of the Five Nations, and more than seven hundred representatives of the Three Fires and other western tribes. This meeting was the largest held until that time in New France for the purposes of achieving peace in the upper country. It would never have taken place without the support of Kondiaronk, a widely respected Wendat-Petun leader. He convinced many upper-country nations to travel to Montreal despite the outbreak of an epidemic that soon took his own life. In death as in life, the French found him to be essential. As Kondiaronk lay dying at Montreal, the negotiations were in disarray. Overlooking the fact that Kondiaronk himself was on the verge of leaving in disgust, the French gave him the equivalent of a state funeral: a regal procession that included the governor general, Ottawa and Wendat-Petun chiefs, French soldiers, clergy, and Wendat warriors, all of which seemed to symbolize French respect for Kondiaronk and the essential unity of interests that the French hoped to forge with the peoples of the upper country. The negotiations continued.[15]

The Ojibwa left the table with a full stomach. Before the Montreal meeting, the Ojibwa and Iroquois had agreed to cease fighting, in return for which the Ojibwa received an open path to trade at Albany and acquired control of hunting territory north of Lake Ontario. The Iroquois certainly painted the agreement as a victory for themselves, and, indeed, they managed to maintain formal independence from both the British and the French, in the process gaining trading rights with the latter. But even as members of the Five Nations negotiated at Montreal,

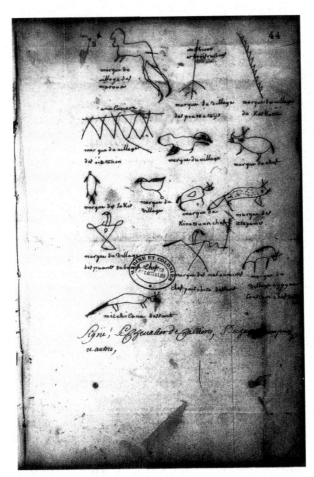

The Treaty of 1701. These are the totemic marks of some of the many chiefs—from the Five Nations, the Ottawa and Ojibwa, and other western nations—who signed the peace treaty with the French, ending the Iroquois wars. NA C137798

other Iroquois conferred with the British at Albany, where, in return for British protection, they ceded land north and west of Lake Ontario to the British—land they did not and could not possess. The arrangement enabled the British to maintain the legal fiction that the Iroquois controlled the northern hunting region and that the British, too, enjoyed some sort of proprietary right. The French were unaware of these separate agreements. They wanted the Iroquois weak, not impotent. It was not a draconian peace that the French wanted: they wanted Iroquois–Three Fires enmity to continue, and by elevating themselves to the role of guarantor of peace—a sort of mediator of last resort—they hoped to be in a position to kindle the fire while preventing a conflagration. French fortunes rested less on imperial military might than on the ability to conciliate, to act in a manner appropriate to the Native name for the governor of New France: *Onontio*, 'father'. French conciliatory skills would be closely tested in the era following the negotiations of 1701.[16]

As the War of the Spanish Succession (1702–13) broke out in Europe, French presence in the Great Lakes region seemed in dramatic decline. France, of course, had never controlled that region. Its small trading posts had been erected on Native land only in return for the giving of presents, a form of rent payable annually. Voyageurs going into the interior resembled 'a military expedition [entering] enemy country'. The closure of the fur trade, the withdrawal from many interior posts, the cessation of the brandy trade (in 1702), and the end of gift-giving stripped from the French the tools required to conciliate and mediate in the interior. The French establishment of a post at Detroit in 1701 succeeded only in bringing more Ottawa and Ojibwa within close reach of British trade. Plots against the French between British and Iroquois and between Iroquois and Ottawa became commonplace. From the French perspective, this period represented the nadir of the interior alliance system.[17]

The Treaty of Utrecht, which ended the European war, made matters worse: it seemed to cede Hudson Bay to the English. Especially devastating, it recognized British suzerainty over the Five Nations and forbade French colonists from 'Hindrance or Molestation' of those Native peoples and their allies. Moreover, the treaty permitted freedom of trade for all Native peoples. For the Ojibwa–Ottawa, such a sanction was, of course, irrelevant: they were doing this anyway. The treaty did, however, open the interior to English expansion. And expand the British did.

The Iroquois were the first casualties of the new European rapprochement. In 1714 and 1715, British traders trekked through Five Nations territory and made direct contact with western tribes. New France responded swiftly. With the French market for fur on the rise and Louis XIV's colonial policy on the verge of collapse, French administrators reopened interior posts and constructed subsidiary posts at Toronto (a well-travelled route into the interior) and, to the east, at Quinte. The Iroquois, increasingly disunited, could only watch as the British responded by building a trading fort at Oswego (in 1726) on Lake Ontario's south shore opposite Kingston.[18]

As the Iroquois increasingly became bystanders, the Ojibwa entered a golden age. France was at peace in Europe until 1744. Tense, but relatively peaceful, relations among the Europeans in the New World gave to the Ojibwa much scope for independent action. In 1725, they sold English traders two hundred 10-metre canoes, each capable of carrying three tonnes of trade goods, enabling them to travel to Lake Ontario's north shore and trade with Ojibwa virtually within sight of French posts. Faced with severe competition from Oswego, the French closed their Toronto post, even as more Ojibwa moved south. By 1736, the Ojibwa had established five permanent settlements on Lake Ontario's north shore, containing some 1,500 people. By 1768, 5,000 Ojibwa lived in twenty-five villages spanning southern and central Ontario west of Gananoque.[19]

European–Native Interaction in the North

Desperate, the French reinstituted the brandy trade, abolished open bidding for monopolies at the forts (a system that had encouraged high prices and sharp trading practices), and, to undercut British competition, traded at a loss. The effect was immediate. Licensed Montreal merchants sent some five hundred *engagés* (hired boatmen) into the interior in 1730s, double the number of the previous decade.[20] These changes had a catalytic effect on social and economic processes already in train throughout Ontario: increased population movement, enhanced cultural interaction, more intense fur-trade competition, and greater Native dependency on European goods.

In response to British competition, some Ottawa and Ojibwa moved north and west. The northward movement of the Ojibwa led to the displacement of some Cree. Encouraged by British traders, coastal Cree began altering traditional seasonal movements in search of food, camping instead for extended periods near British posts. Called the 'homeguard', they became general provisioners for the British traders. Other Cree and possibly Ojibwa, called 'uplanders' by the British, maintained a more traditional lifestyle and played off not only French against British but even British traders against one another. They both hunted furs and became middlemen traders between British and Native peoples in the western and southwestern interior. HBC men distrusted the uplanders and denied them entry to their forts, forcing them to trade through specially constructed narrow openings in the palisade. Nonetheless, they realized that a profitable trade depended on uplander assistance: in the gift exchanges that preceded trading, the British provided virtually undiluted brandy and, at times, goods at a loss in order to keep the uplanders within the British trading circuit.[21]

Cross-cultural trade between the uplanders and the British was a complex blend of market and non-market behaviour.[22] Seemingly fixed prices and a fixed protocol characterized the conduct of trade. Gift-giving, peace-pipe smoking, and speech-making—practices embedded in Native tradition—connoted more than trade and extended to military alliances. Yet almost from the first presence of the British at the Bay, it was a case of new wine in old bottles. Unlike traditional practice, speeches focused more on trade matters than on military and political affairs. Accordingly, gift-giving became less a testimony of friendship and more a means to achieve a profit. Native peoples offered low-quality fur and local produce, not traditional symbolic items, and in turn were given gifts that would entice them to return the next year with more followers. As southern trade became increasingly important for diplomatic reasons, northern trade occurred for more purely commercial ends.

British traders had limited room for manoeuvre. Goods and furs were assigned a value in terms of the made beaver (MB), one prime beaver pelt. Gift-giving, brandy sales, quality assessment, the measurement and weighing of items, and the conversion of worth in terms of MB left scope for bargaining and profit-taking. Yet several non-market factors set fairly inflexible upper limits to prices. Native peoples rarely varied from a set of fixed needs. They abhorred hoarding, and their canoes had limited carrying capacity. Thus, lowering trade-good prices did not attract more Native people bringing more fur. Rather, Native people brought less, because their needs and their carrying capacity could be more easily met. Gifts that could be consumed on the spot—alcohol and tobacco—rather than price reductions were the most effective means of attracting Native traders. Moreover, if British traders adjusted prices or altered quality to meet market pressures back home or to increase profits, Native people quickly left to trade with the ever-hovering French coureurs de bois. The uplanders remained in close contact with the French at Timiskaming, Abitibi, Michipocoton, Nipigon, and farther west, at Fort St Charles and a series of smaller tributary posts. The French more than held their own in the fierce competition for fur in the northern and northwestern hinterland.[23] So too did the Native people with whom they traded.

British and French trading posts provided yet another site for cultural merging in early Ontario. Relations between the homeguard and traders were as much social as economic. Official regulations discouraging sexual and illicit trade between HBC employees and Native people were widely ignored. Since European women were not allowed at the Bay after the 1680s, the chief trader often took a Native woman into the post to live as his 'bedfellow'. Lesser traders could entertain Native women in their quarters during the day but not overnight. Officially, company servants were denied any such contact, but the incidence of venereal disease suggests that the ban was ineffectual.[24]

Mixed-blood offspring of these many sexual liaisons soon became quite noticeable among the people who lived near the forts. These mixed-blood people were the most visible side of an intermingling and merging of cultures that took place across many areas of activity. Fur traders began to use snowshoes and moccasins. They practised other Native traditions and, in their turn, homeguard Native people (such as Sakie at Moose Factory) wore a captain's coat, 'laced hat, . . . stockings [and] a white shirt'. As early as 1721, Miscamote, a homeguard leader at Fort Albany, expressed his wish to 'be buried nigh the British', and in 1745, when Sakie died at Moose Factory, he was buried 'after the English fashion', as was his wife two years later. This forsaking of traditional burial practices is evocative testimony to the depth of cultural interaction at the Bay. And the term *is* 'interaction', not 'assimilation'. While some Cree adopted British burial practices, Hudson's Bay traders, who lived with 'country wives', conformed to Cree marriage formalities, including sanction by the bride's relatives and payment of presents to the bride's family. Upon retirement, some traders even retired with their Native wives to England, and many included their country wives in their wills. Personal as well as economic needs conditioned interaction.[25]

The merging of European and Native cultures also occurred at French posts. At Michilimackinac, as we have seen, the French depended on the Ojibwa and Ottawa for crops and fish. French fur-trade employees commonly married or lived with Native women, prompting missionaries to exclaim that they 'found . . . [Native women's] bodies might serve in lieu of merchandise and would be . . . better received than beaver skins'. But Native women were more than sexual objects to French fur traders, and fur traders were not simply sexual partners to Native women. In fact, Native women exerted an active influence on the flow of trade goods. Between 1715 and 1760, hunting items, rifles, flints, and so on represented only 11 per cent of the value of French goods traded at Michilimackinac. Clothing, which had the greatest impact on the lives of Native women, represented 60 per cent. The dominance of these trade items underlines the activity of Native women, such as the Oneida woman Sarah Ainse, who became an active trader in the mid-1760s. By the 1780s, Ainse had accounts with Detroit merchants in excess of £5,000 and owned two houses, flour, cattle, horses, and four slaves in Detroit.[26]

Ojibwa and Ottawa women and their Métis offspring, like the Cree in the north, provided merchants with potentially lucrative links to Indian traders and helped them acculturate to life in the interior. For the Native peoples, these liaisons facilitated access to powerful European traders, to prized European goods, and to higher status within Native society. Not surprisingly, then, between 1698 and 1765 almost one-half of the recorded marriages at Michilimackinac were between English or French employees and Native or Métis women. Forty per cent of all recorded births were Métis offspring of those marriages. Indeed, the increased numbers of Métis required the Michilimackinac garrison to expand its walls three times before 1763.[27]

Europe at War in North America

The complex set of social and economic relationships engendered by the competitive fur trade made it increasingly difficult for the Three Fires Confederacy to act in concert. For these Native peoples, the war that erupted between France and England in 1744—part of a general European confrontation over the Austrian succession—seemed but a more violent extension of existing trade battles. When the British began to cut off French supplies from Europe after 1745, many Ojibwa supported British providers. As early as 1738, Joseph La France, a Métis trader, pointed to the 'avarice and injustice' of the French, attitudes that 'disgusted the Natives'. Even when the war ended in 1748, many Ojibwa and Ottawa continued to be indifferent to French overtures. Some Mississauga reaffirmed an Iroquois alliance in 1751, demonstrating their independence from both European powers. Neither were the Ojibwa very receptive to French missionary overtures. Less dependent on the French fur trade than the Wendat had been, they did not have to suffer similar missionary presence. On the eve of the fateful Seven Years' War, the French in a sense formally recognized Ojibwa independence by marking southern Ontario on their maps as the 'Country of the Missesagues'.[28]

Canada was only one stage in the struggle between France and England for colonial supremacy in India, the West Indies, and America, a struggle that commenced in 1756 and ended seven years later. Throughout the late 1740s and early 1750s, British colonists pushed westward, threatening to snap the thin band connecting French Louisiana to French Quebec. English colonists for the first time began to receive significant support from the mother country. Unprecedented amounts of British money, men, and supplies reached the New World. Despite a weak position in the Atlantic, France responded as well as it could. Europe had come to fight in America: the War of the Conquest had begun.

Both British and French courted the Ojibwa on the eve of the Seven Years' War. The French ordered traders at Niagara, Frontenac, Detroit, and the newly reopened Toronto to sell at British prices, no matter how heavy the loss. Brandy flowed, for as one Ottawa chief acknowledged, the warriors 'love[d] their drink': in 1757 a missionary described Fort Rouille, at present-day Toronto, as little more than 'un cabaret d'eau-de-vie'. Through the Iroquois, the British sent wampum belts to the Ojibwa at Niagara and Toronto, inviting them to war against the French. But for many Native people, an impressive French victory at Fort Duquesne in July 1755 tipped the scales in New France's favour. Plunder obtained by the Ojibwa exceeded any they had previously known: one thousand rifles, four to five hundred horses (the first ever acquired by the Ojibwa), gold, silver, and cloth. In anticipation of even more, most Ojibwa sided with the French.[29]

From the French perspective, however, it was always an uneasy alliance. 'One is a slave to Indians in this country', Louis Antoine de Bougainville, a French officer, admitted. 'In this sort of warfare it is necessary to adjust to their ways.' Presents, plunder, food, and drink constantly had to be provided. Before successful attacks on Oswego in August 1756 and at Fort William Henry in August 1757, Louis-Joseph de Montcalm, New France's governor, sent word 'throughout all the Indian nations that there would be plunder for those who would come and fight with us'. At the conclusion of both battles, Montcalm could not back up his guarantees of safety to British survivors. His Native allies scalped as many as they could, starting with the wounded left unprotected in the infirmaries.[30]

In 1757, smallpox spread throughout the Ojibwa peoples. In 1759, the loss at Fort Frontenac of a huge cache of supplies destined for Native allies broke the back of the French–Three Fires accord. When the British attacked Fort Niagara later that year, Ojibwa and Iroquois stood aside, letting the Europeans decide the issue. Neither believed they could get what they wanted from either European power. In 1760, unable to supply New France with reinforcements as a result of British superiority at sea, France lost the war. The Ojibwa, although weakened by disease, continued to believe in their independence. Minweweh, an Ojibwa chief, put it succinctly: 'Englishmen, although you have conquered the French, you have not yet conquered us! We are not your slaves.' Claiming they had been 'wheedled and led on', they sought a working relationship with the British.[31]

But the notion of rapprochement was far from the mind of General Jeffrey Amherst, the British commander-in-chief. He totally misunderstood Native intent. French success in retaining Native allies depended on generous gift-giving, supplying arms, and conducting a liberal fur trade. It is important to emphasize that Ontario's Native peoples did not view gifts as things that the giver could withhold for whatever reason. Rather, gifts were received as payment for the right to cross, camp in, and construct forts on Native territory. They were testimonials to peaceful relations, signifying respect among allies. Gifts were also recompense for past mistakes and wrongdoing. An alliance without gifts could not be. But Amherst would have none of it. Against the advice of Sir William Johnson, the superintendent of northern Native peoples, he ended the rum trade, restricted general trade to garrisoned posts, banned gift-giving, and withheld ammunition. These were fateful decisions. Minweweh's declaration had fallen on deaf ears. Growing 'tired of this bad meat which is upon our lands', Pontiac, an Ottawa chief from the Detroit area, massed support from four tribes and, commencing in the spring of 1863, captured eight British forts, caused one to be evacuated and besieged two others.[32]

The British responded brutally. Anticipating his command, Amherst's men broke the seige of Fort Pitt in 1763 by giving Native people, as gifts, two blankets infected with smallpox. As one eyewitness recorded in his diary, 'we gave [the Natives] two Blankets and a Handkerchief out of the Small Pox Hospital. I hope it will have the desired effect.' It did. Smallpox ravaged the district around Fort Pitt throughout the spring and summer of that year. Nor was this an isolated instance of biological warfare in North America. 'Customary codes of international and military conduct', one historian has concluded, sanctioned the use of germ war- fare against perpetrators of unjust rebellions and against 'wild' and 'savage' peoples. Amherst clearly espoused that view. 'Could it not be contrived', he wrote his sec- ond-in-command in July 1763, 'to Send the *Small Pox* among those Disaffected Tribes of Indians?' 'Indeed', he wrote a month later, 'their Total Extirpation is scarce sufficient Atonement for the Bloody and Inhuman deeds they have Committed.'[33]

For some Native peoples, this campaign may have been an attempt to protect their lands and liberty from an aggressive foe. For the Ottawa and Ojibwa of the north and northwest, quest for plunder and presents remained more important: wars as French allies in the mid-eighteenth century are given little space in Ojibwa oral histories, suggesting that the later battles were peripheral to their central con- cerns. Moreover, some southern Ojibwa, led by the Mississauga Wabbicommicot, self-styled 'Chief Man North and West upon Lake Ontario and so far upon Lake Erie as ye big [Grand] River', refused to take up arms. Wabbicommicot desired freer trade but counselled peace, and it was he who ultimately convinced Pontiac to lay down his weapons in 1764.[34]

Desirous of—and, in some cases, dependent on—European goods, the Ojibway sought rapprochement, not revenge. When, at Niagara in 1764, before some two thousand chiefs from twenty-four nations, the British promised to rein- stitute trade and distributed £38,000 worth of gifts, the Ojibwa thought they had succeeded. A middle ground could be re-established. In this sense, the Ojibwa, although weakened by disease and war, could continue to view themselves if not as victors, then at least as a proud and unconquered people.[35]

In fact, however, Pontiac's uprising and its aftermath represented the begin- ning of the end to rapprochement. The conflict sent immediate shockwaves to dis- tant London, England, the seat of imperial policy-making. No longer could the British take the western and northern Native peoples lightly. Now it was impera- tive that the British deal more systematically with the inhabitants of the *pays d'en haut*. To maintain control of the conquered habitants of New France and of a rest- less Native population, the British devised a policy that laid the foundations for the settlement by Europeans of the region north of the Great Lakes. While Wabbicommicot envisioned a country within which Native peoples and Europeans could coexist, the British envisaged a colony increasingly fixed by finite borders and exclusivist notions of belonging.[36]

Chapter Four

The 'Men with Hats': Defining Upper Canada, 1763–91

In February 1763, the Treaty of Paris ended the Seven Years' War and Britain added New France to its existing North American holdings: Nova Scotia, Newfoundland, the vast expanse of Hudson's Bay Company land in the northern interior, and the thirteen American colonies to the south. By 1791, this British American Empire was altered once again. The thirteen southern colonies had successfully fought for independence during the American Revolution, begun in 1776. While Britain maintained control of her northern colonies, the form of that control had undergone significant change. By the 1790s, five northern colonies—Upper Canada, Lower Canada, Nova Scotia, New Brunswick, and Prince Edward Island—had been granted locally elected assemblies overseen by appointed councils. Two others—Cape Breton and Newfoundland—continued to be ruled without representative government, and the Hudson's Bay Company continued to oversee a vast west. From the perspective of the evolution of British imperial policy as well as from the vantage point of those who lived in North America, the closing years of the eighteenth century represented a time of tumultuous change. This was especially true of the territory north of the Great Lakes, land one disgruntled colonist termed 'this American Siberia'.[1]

From the Proclamation Act to the American Revolution

One of Britain's first acts with respect to its new territory was to issue the Royal Proclamation of 1763. To forestall the formation of any alliance between the French in Quebec and the First Peoples to the west and south, Britain hived off Quebec by prohibiting any European settlement in the newly delimited 'Indian Territory' and stipulating that Aboriginal land could be sold only to the British government. This gave the Crown firm control over future land and settlement policy while appearing to guarantee the region's Native peoples independence and traditional land rights (to this day, the Royal Proclamation remains one of the most important bases of Aboriginal title in Canadian law). In addition, imperial administrators hoped the Indian Territory would block the westward movement of American colonists, funnelling them instead north to Quebec, whose 75,000 French-speaking residents they would surely outnumber before long.

Except for twenty-five to thirty farms along the Detroit River established under the French regime in 1749, the upper country was virtually without European inhabitants. Those who traversed it—usually fur traders—did so with care; to cross Seneca land near Niagara in 1764, the British had to swear that no farming or permanent settlement would take place. South of the Great Lakes, however, where agricultural land was richer and more accessible, settlers ignored the Proclamation Line. Tensions mounted, but the British refused to dedicate the resources necessary to prevent westward movement. Rather, they allowed their security in the Great Lakes area to depend on the goodwill of the local First Peoples.

The passage of the Quebec Act in 1774 exacerbated these tensions. Territorially, New France was restored; the new Quebec incorporated the former French lands to the east and the Indian Territory as defined in 1763. This change meant little to the First Peoples of the *pays d'en haut*, who continued under the 'protection' of the British superintendent of northern Indians. But the southern colonists recognized the Quebec Act as a stratagem for keeping the west out of their control, and they considered it 'intolerable'. A year later, rebellion erupted in Massachusetts. Because Quebec administered the western lands, the rebels invaded the upper country, only to be repulsed late in 1775. In July 1776, the thirteen colonies declared independence.

North of the Great Lakes, the American Revolution represented the first major test of British Native policy since the Pontiac uprising. Retaining control of the military posts in First Nations territory at Carleton Island (off Cataraqui), Niagara, Detroit, and Michilimackinac was crucial. From these posts, garrisons to the west and south could be provisioned, and offensives into New York, Pennsylvania, and the Ohio and Illinois territories could be launched; to these posts, First Nations allies and British supporters from both the northern and southern regions could be attracted.

Aware that success depended largely on the attitudes of the local peoples, British commander-in-chief Guy Carleton and his successor in 1778, Frederick Haldimand, redoubled efforts to provision and offer presents to potential Native allies. Similarly, the Northern Indian Department, administered up to his death in 1774 by Sir John Johnson (whose wife, Molly Brant, was an influential Mohawk), made every attempt to guarantee the neutrality of and, ultimately, to win the active support of the Six Nations Iroquois in northern New York (the Tuscarora tribe had joined the Confederacy in 1722). Although Mississauga at Niagara aided the British in battles to the south, most Mississauga remained aloof, on occasion even flaunting their independence; in 1780, the 'insolent' Mississauga at Cataraqui forced the military to huddle in their blockaded fort at night.[2]

After General Burgoyne's defeat at Saratoga, New York, in October 1777, the British shifted their strategy. Henceforth they relied on guerrilla activity by Loyalists (around one out of six Americans supported the British—or at least did not support the Rebels) and, whenever possible, Native allies. A corps of Loyalists and Seneca of the Six Nations, raised and commanded by John Butler, staged a series of devastating guerrilla raids out of Niagara. These successes attracted more support for the Loyalists' cause—as did the retaliation they provoked. After an American force of 5,000 swept through the Six Nations territory late in 1779, an equal number of Iroquois retreated to Niagara, swelling the ranks of the 'loyal'.

The successful offensives waged from the northern posts did not alter the war's overall course. When the French entered on the Americans' side in 1778, battle lines were greatly extended and British resources were correspondingly stretched. Gains made could not be held. To the chagrin of the northern Loyalists, who had won their battles, the British called a halt in April 1782. Fearing retribution from the victors, many Americans who had supported the British trekked north in search of a safe haven.

Loyalists and Native Peoples in the *Pays d'en haut*

By the conflict's end, some 100,000 Loyalists had left. Most travelled on to Britain, but 7,500—of diverse classes, cultures, ethnic backgrounds, and motivations—settled in Mississauga country, mainly in the Bay of Quinte area. Seen in the context of the region's early history, this forced mingling of people from widely varied backgrounds represented simply one more in a long line of refugee movements in the *pays d'en haut*. 'Strange is the collection of people here', one visitor observed in 1784. There were farmers from northern New York State, often of German, Irish, or Scots backgrounds; African American slaves of elite Loyalists; and Iroquois and other Native people who had supported the British. Most Loyalists possessed little wealth or education. Many had arrived in America no more than a decade before. As immigrants, these Loyalists had already been uprooted: they desired stability and continuity, not rebellion and change.[3]

Under the smokescreen of war the foundations of a colonial society were being laid. Contracts for provisioning and supplying the army and its Native allies offered considerable opportunities for merchants aspiring to better their economic and social positions. To succeed, however, merchants had to be of a special sort. Strong military contacts helped but were not in themselves sufficient for success. John Butler, for example, had attracted significant Iroquois support and engineered devastating guerrilla raids. Haldimand considered appointing him superintendent of the Northern Indian Department. In the end, though, he decided that Butler was 'deficient in Education and liberal sentiments'. Several years later, John Graves Simcoe, Upper Canada's first lieutenant-governor, would make much the same point, declaring that his administrators should not be of the type 'who kept but one table, that is who dined in Common with their Servants'. The rules were clear for those who knew how to read them. Breeding, respectability, and the proper social bearing were fundamental requirements to join the ranks of the elite, whether as a merchant or as a bureaucrat. Just as the mechanism for the divestiture of Native lands had been put into operation during the Revolutionary War, so too had the ground rules for the investiture of Upper Canada's future elite been laid.[4]

Such requirements excluded most Loyalists and all Native people. In the negotiations leading to the peace settlement of April 1783, Britain's First Nations allies had been completely ignored; in fact, the British had allowed the Americans to take possession of Six Nations lands that the British had never owned. Joseph Brant, the Mohawk spokesman for thousands of Native people stranded near

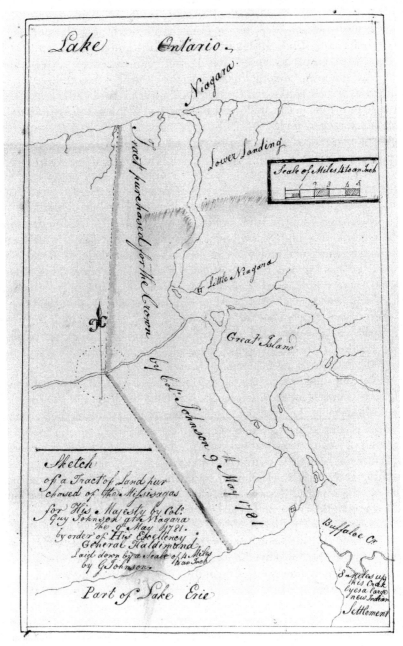

The first Mississauga land surrender, 9 May 1781. The British were hard pressed to provision the thousands of Loyalists who had fled north after the American Revolution. Accordingly, Commander-in-Chief Frederick Haldimand ordered the Lake Ontario garrisons to begin growing their own food. Advised that the best agricultural land lay on the west side of the Niagara River, under Mississauga control, in May 1781 the British appropriated 1,200,000 hectares of Mississauga land, in exchange for just three hundred suits of clothing. AO RG 1-A-1-1, vol. 1, 67.

Niagara, was outraged. To show that the British would continue to protect First Nations land (in return for the support of the First Nations in war and trade), Haldimand, now commander-in-chief and governor of Quebec, quickly took control of several western posts in American territory, initiating a dispute with the United States that would continue to simmer until 1794, when Jay's Treaty finally settled it.

Realizing that these forts could not be retained for long, Haldimand offered to find land for all First Nations allies dispossessed of their traditional territories during the Revolutionary War—even though his government had no such land to give. And when many of the Loyalists clustering at makeshift refugee centres in Quebec asked to stay in the upper country rather than move to Cape Breton or Nova Scotia, Haldimand acquiesced.

It remained to find the land. Between 1783 and 1790, Haldimand engineered nine agreements with the Mississauga, Iroquois, and other nations, acquiring for the British state territory spanning from the Upper St Lawrence to Detroit. The Detroit situation was particularly complicated since a considerable number of high-ranking military personnel and prominent local merchants had acquired land from local Native groups, in violation of the Proclamation of 1763. Such acts, were, in the mind of one British appointee, 'in apparent defiance to all authority, and repeated orders to the prevention of such Traffic'. Native people thought that these 'private' agreements allowed reciprocal access to the deeded territory. '[T]he Men with Hats who have come to reside,' one Chief complained, 'always asked for leave to build a House and for a little piece of ground for a garden—But Father, after they had got up their house, they took and fenced in large tracts of Land, contrary to our wishes and intentions.'[5]

In 1790, the British Crown and the Ojibwa, Ottawa, Potawatomi, and Wyandot peoples signed a treaty at Detroit that ceded to the British a huge tract of land along the north shore of Lake Erie. The Proclamation of 1763 had been couched in the language of protection from 'great frauds and abuses . . . committed in the purchasing of lands of the Indians', so the Native chiefs may have seen the 1790 treaty as a way of protecting their land from squatting settlers. From the British Crown's perspective, however, that treaty extinguished all Native rights to the land. The Crown could sell or grant land to whomever it wished, free of Native input. On all subsequent deeds, stamps of British approval superceded the totemic symbols of Native chiefs.[6]

The treaties made with First Nations peoples at this time share several features. The land involved was often defined only in the vaguest of terms. Northern boundaries were determined to be either as far as a man could walk in a day or as far north as one could hear the sound of a gun fired from the lakeshore. In one case a blank deed was all that 'testified' to the nature of the transaction. In another there was no formal documentary evidence at all, and in still others the evidence was contradictory. When Lieutenant-Governor John Graves Simcoe reported this sloppy documentation, in particular the blank deed, his superior (the governor general at Quebec) cautioned him 'not to press that matter or shew any anxiety about it' since it 'throws us entirely on the good faith of the Indians for just so

Box 4.1   Sarah Ainse, Oneida Trader: Land and Power

Military officers, Native agents, and white merchants were not the only speculators in Native lands. Native people also purchased from other Native people. Sarah Ainse, a successful Oneida trader, acquired a large tract of very desirable land on the north shore of Lake Erie in 1780 that included the location of the modern town of Chatham. She had moved there in 1787 with several black slaves. When she claimed that the Crown's 1790 purchase did not include her land, many local chiefs testified on her behalf. In March 1794, Ainse wrote to a highly placed British official, possibly the lieutenant-governor, John Graves Simcoe:

> Though I am an Indian Woman, (& guilty of a great indecorum in presuming to write to you in this manner,) I see no reason why I should be openly plundered on my property; of what cost me dear; which I could prove in the sight of God; but as it is allowed, for some gentlemans word to be taken & to overthrow the Oaths of Eighteen to twenty Indian Chiefs— I have poor chance to go to law; but I confide in the judicious Character of His Excellency Lord Dorchester, [the Governor General at Quebec] whom I expect to visit this Summer & I doubt not, but to be recompensed for my land and trouble.

In June, Simcoe ordered that a grant of 677 hectares—a mere 1.7 per cent of her claim—be ceded to her. But in 1798, Upper Canada's Executive Council, influenced by non-Native speculators, denied her claim. She was stripped of all land and received no compensation. 'It grieves us to observe,' Joseph Brant, one of her Native supporters, wrote, 'that it seems natural to Whites to look on lands in the possession of Indians with an aching heart, and never to rest until they have planned them out of them.' Although Ainse persisted as a trader, her fortunes took a downturn thereafter. Local merchants occasionally forgave her accounts, and the Moravian Mission at Fairfield offered her charity in 1798; in 1803, the Mission's diary noted that 'Sally . . . was here this week trading wares for corn. She is very old.' Nevertheless, Ainse continued to petition for her rights for another twenty years, until her death in 1823. All her efforts were in vain. Merchants, missionaries, and settlers would grant Native people charity but rarely justice, and never equality.[1]

---

1. Quotations: Clarke, *Land, Power, and Economics*, 139–41; Linda Sabathy-Judd, ed. and trans., *Moravians in Upper Canada: The Diary of the Indian Mission of Fairfield on the Thames, 1792–1813* (Toronto: Champlain Society, 1999), 159, 297. See also Fred Hamil, *The Valley of the Lower Thames, 1640–1850* (Toronto: University of Toronto Press, 1951).

much land as they are willing to allow'. A corollary to a subsequent agreement in 1805 attempted to paper over the blank-deed problem, but two centuries later that attempt is under dispute between the Mississauga of New Credit and the federal government and involves much of the current city of Toronto and its suburbs.[7]

Mary Ann Burges, *Lt General Simcoe*. John Graves Simcoe was Upper Canada's first lieutenant-governor, from 1791 to 1799, although he spent only four years (1792–6) in the colony. MTRL JRR T34632.

In effect, the Mississauga and eastern Iroquois, rather than the British, paid the costs of rewarding the Loyalists. But why did the Mississauga, who less than a century before had shed blood to acquire this territory (and whose oral tradition exalted those battles), suddenly give it away for so little? A number of explanations have been suggested: the slow and unthreatening rate of European settlement, a lack of unity among the Mississauga compared to ninety years earlier, increasing dependence on and desire for European trade goods, and the fact that negotiations were conducted by Indian Department military agents, who were experienced in dealing with Native people and often trusted by them.

None of these factors can be completely discounted. Yet perhaps the best explanation is that the Mississauga and Iroquois did not think that they were giving away their land rights forever. The surviving documents are vague or contradictory even in English; the translations were likely far worse. In the case of the appalling Niagara Peninsula treaty (the interpreters apparently did 'an atrocious job') Mississauga (oral) history relating to the Gun Shot Treaty of 1792 is evocative in this regard: 'I am astonished. Disappointed. When I remember the promise

Elizabeth Simcoe, *Mohawk Village*, 1793. This sketch by Mrs Simcoe gives pride of place to two outposts of civilization: the church (on the right) and the agent's house (on the left). AO F47-11-1-0-109.

made by the Govmt. His [Governor Simcoe's] words were very sweet. At that time he did not give me any writing to hold in my hands but I know all. [Hunting, fishing, and trapping rights were guaranteed to us by treaty], and I never realized anything for it.'[8]

British and Native concepts of ownership were fundamentally at odds. The Mississauga 'owned' land in a communal sense; no particular individual or group could lay exclusive claim to any of it. Although they had had contact with individual European settlers and were aware of the fences around particular properties, any notion of private freehold tenure was entirely foreign to them. In return for gifts, the Mississauga were willing to allow the British a share in the use of the land; by the time they realized what 'ownership' meant to Europeans (which was not until the 1790s), a great deal of their prime land had already been taken from them—at least as far as the British were concerned.

The British divided even as they conquered. Haldimand had planned for the Six Nations Iroquois to settle near the Bay of Quinte, but the local Mississauga worried about the influx of so many Iroquois, and Joseph Brant, the Iroquois liaison with the Indian Department, wanted to be closer to the Seneca and other western members of the Six Nations. Accordingly, Haldimand granted the Iroquois about 400,000 hectares along the Grand River. Unlike their counterparts at Quinte, the Grand River Mississauga had fought alongside the Iroquois in the Revolutionary War, and—perhaps for that reason—they welcomed the new arrivals. Brant drew his influence from the power of his sister Molly and from his ability to deal with the British Indian Department, though not all Iroquois acknowledged him as the sachem (supreme chief) of the Mohawk tribe. At least in part because they resented Brant's leadership pretensions, a smaller group of Mohawks under John Deseronto decided to stay at the Bay of Quinte.

It became clear almost immediately that British and Iroquois understandings of the Six Nations land grant diverged widely. As far as the British were concerned, under the provisions of the Royal Proclamation they, not the Six Nations, still controlled all sales, rentals, and other land transactions. Brant disagreed, and within several years he had sold or leased much land to non-Native settlers. At issue was whether the Six Nations, by accepting the grant, had become subjects of the Crown or whether they retained their sovereign independence as allies and were thus free to dispose of the land as they wished. This dispute would not be finally decided in law until 1959, when the Six Nations peoples were declared 'loyal subjects'.

It is often assumed that the Loyalists who moved north were a fairly quiescent, apolitical lot. Such was not the view of Governor Haldimand, who was beseiged with petitions for land, construction materials, food, clothing, horses, cows, sheep, arms, and ammunition, on top of the hoes, axes, ploughs, seeds, and clothes provided free of charge. In addition, the British government set up a claims commission through which Loyalists could seek compensation for goods confiscated by the Rebels. Although only 13 per cent of Loyalists settled in Quebec and the future Ontario, 52 per cent of the claims heard originated there. Payments of claims plus half-pay pensions for all officers of Loyalist regiments or their widows plus the cost of provisions totalled £1 million for the upper country alone.

In addition, of course, the Loyalists received free grants of land. In the spring of 1784, Haldimand opened thirteen townships—eight on the St Lawrence River and five west of Kingston—laid out on the strip, or seigneurial, landholding model. Settlers drew lots for the land within each township, with the size of each grant determined by military rank and social position. Unmarried civilians received 50 acres; married enlisted men received 100 acres plus 50 for each family member; field officers received 1,000 acres plus 50 for each family member. Some, like Sir John Johnson, refused to choose by lot and instead appropriated the choicest acreages for themselves and their friends. Generally, however, the lottery principle was honoured—if only because most Loyalists would not have tolerated too blatant a subversion of it.

Distinct religious and ethnic groups—Roman Catholic Highlanders, Scottish Presbyterians, German Calvinists, German Lutherans, British Anglicans—settled in their own townships. Not all, however, stayed on the land they were allotted; in some townships, as many as two-thirds of the landholders either failed to take up their land or moved within a year. Townships with higher proportions of American-born residents had higher rates of transiency, suggesting that some Loyalists may have moved back to the United States. Nor did all Loyalists conform to Captain Thomas Gummersal Anderson's nostalgic image: 'honest, attend[ing] to their own business . . . , kind'. In 1787 Hugh Gallagher, married with a young son, lost his allotment in the Niagara District because he was 'disapproved of' as a 'man of infamous character; frequently suspected of robbing Indians of their silver works and a common disturber of the peace, . . . known to fire at his neighbours' Cattle in the night time, and worry them with Dogs, through much Malice'.[9]

By 1790, the 'Loyalist' population in what had been Mississauga territory had swollen to between 14,000 and 20,000. Simply by swearing an oath of allegiance, the so-called late Loyalists (arriving after about 1783, probably motivated less by loyalty than by free land) became eligible for a grant of 200 acres—more than some of the first-comers had received. In response to vigorous protests, the Upper Canadian government ensured that all original Loyalists would receive at least 300 acres and that their children—including daughters—would each receive 200 acres when they came of age.

As the population grew, demands increased for freehold land tenure and for an elected assembly located in the upper country itself. Like their counterparts in Nova Scotia and New Brunswick, upper-country Loyalists couched their demands in the 'country party' rhetoric that in England contrasted the virtuous farmer/yeoman with the actions of an allegedly corrupt overly centralized administration in London. The colonial parallel was of course the virtuous upcountry Loyalist pitted against an appointed governor and his councils in faraway Quebec.

During the Revolution, many Loyalist women had shown exceptional courage. Left behind with their families while their husbands went to fight, some acted as British spies. Others sheltered and provisioned Loyalist raiding parties. Almost all had to fill the traditionally male roles of providing for the family and making decisions on its behalf. Those who resolved to leave the sphere of conflict often had to negotiate with the rebels for permission to go. Then, accompanied in many cases by young children, they travelled through enemy territory to find asylum either in New York refugee camps or in the British-held territory to the north.

When the dust settled, however, the new society these women helped to establish was no less patriarchal than the one they had left. Men were the decision-makers, women and children the followers. A married woman became a 'femme covert', a person with no legal identity separate from her husband. As historian Janice Potter-MacKinnon points out, when a Loyalist widow petitioned for compensation, no matter how heroic her accomplishments had been, in her plea for support she would invariably cite her status as 'a poor helpless woman', 'a Feeble Woman', a woman without a man to protect her. Even so, the all-male adjudicators of Loyalist claims awarded proportionally much more to men than to women.[10]

The subordination of women was not the only inequality built into the structure of life in the *pays d'en haut*. Far from encouraging the assimilation of French-speaking Quebecers, the Loyalist migration in many ways accentuated the reality of social diversity in Britain's northern colonies. The Quebec Act had been a sign of Britain's recognition that this cultural divide could not be eradicated, and the American Revolution had underlined the importance of acknowledging colonial needs and sensibilities. With a possible war with the United States brewing over the western forts still held by Britain, imperial administrators realized that they would have to tolerate a certain amount of diversity but keep it constrained within strict bounds. Thus, land grants and compensation payments were designed to pre-

Box 4.2   The Loyalists and the State in the Up Country

Far from wishing to overturn authority, the Loyalists sought a place of respect and power within the hierarchical structure of their new society. This is not a trivial point and reflects more than simple self-interest on their parts. As historian Elizabeth Mancke has argued, the acceptance of a strong central state is a primary characteristic that set the Loyalists apart from those who rebelled against British rule in the American colonies. Loyalists found that strong state in British *North* America: the state owned the land and resources and governed, often through appointed governors and unelected councils; where assemblies existed, the governor-in-council retained significant fiscal powers. In other words, a strong state presence and tradition existed in British North America before 1783.

The existence of that strong state and the Loyalists' willingness to work within it are important for at least two reasons. In the first place, the political debates that emerged in what became Ontario always included space for a centralized bureaucratic state. That was not the case in those colonies that rebelled. In the United States, political debate would focus on the degree to which a nation could exist without a strong state. Secondly, as Mancke says, 'If the development of the bureaucratic state is one of the hallmarks of the modern era, then Canada [Ontario] has always been modern, while the United States has resisted the institutions of modernity.' The roots of a strong state tradition extended deeper than the Loyalist migration; the institutional structures supporting a strong British state were part and parcel of the early modern British Empire (pre-1783). British and other settlers who arrived after that date 'negotiated the function, control and growth of those institutions, more than contested their legitimacy'.[1]

1. Elizabeth Mancke, 'Early Modern Imperial Governance and the Origins of Canadian Political Culture', *Canadian Journal of Political Science* 32 (1999): 3–20, quotes 18–19.

serve and enhance social differentiation: compensation to Loyalists for losses incurred during the Revolution reflected each individual's social and economic standing prior to the conflict; the highest-ranking British officers received the most land, and efforts were made to settle enlisted men in the same townships as their commanding officers (though this did not always succeed).

The Constitutional Act, 1791

A similar concern with containment influenced the design of new political structures in this period. Administration of the upper country was now costing Britain more than £100,000 per year, and the passage of the Self-Denying Ordinance of 1778 had made it illegal for Britain to tax its colonies unless they had representatives in the British parliament—an unthinkable prospect. When the Loyalists demanded an elected assembly, the imperial authorities willingly acceded. Together, the Constitutional Act of 1791 and further legislation the following year created Upper and Lower Canada. Each of the new colonies would have a locally elected assembly with the right to impose taxation and the responsibility to meet the colony's fiscal needs.

The Constitutional Act laid the legislative foundations for the first fifty years of Upper Canada's political and social development. Reflecting the vision shared by a ruling elite composed primarily of British landed aristocrats, it gave Upper Canada a lieutenant-governor who, as the Crown's representative, could grant or withhold or reserve royal assent to any legislation. The lieutenant-governor was also to appoint both an Executive Council, whose appointees sat at his pleasure to offer him advice and serve as the final legal court of appeal in the colony, and a Legislative Council, the 'upper' section of the bicameral legislature. The lieutenant-governor's power was further enhanced through his control of some funds relatively free of assembly oversight. Underlining the colony's subservient status vis-à-vis the mother country, Upper Canada's judges were appointed by London and served at the Crown's pleasure.

Legislative members were to number at least seven and, like members of the British House of Lords, to hold their seats for life. The Assembly—the 'lower' section of the legislature—was to consist of no more than sixteen representatives elected for terms of no longer than four years. To become law, proposed legislation had first to pass both the elected Assembly and the appointed Legislative Council, then receive the lieutenant-governor's assent, to be followed by the Crown's confirmation within two years. Finally, matters of local and regional concern were to be handled by district councils appointed by the central government; by the 1820s there were eleven such bodies. This complex structure left considerable control in the hands of imperial administrators, and the powers of the two councils—especially their control of patronage—generated much dissatisfaction in both the Canadas.

The Constitutional Act sowed the seeds of more than political discontent. Taking advantage of their control of Upper Canada's land, British administrators reserved one-seventh of each township for the maintenance 'of a Protestant clergy' and, by a slightly later edict, a similar amount for the Crown's exclusive use. While many then, and later, assumed that 'Protestant clergy' meant the established Church of England (the Anglican Church), the act was unclear on this point. Given that Anglicans were a small minority in Upper Canada in 1791, the possibility rankled many Loyalists.

The Constitutional Act also had significant implications for Upper Canada's economic and financial future. Lacking direct access to the sea, Upper Canada had to depend on Lower Canada to handle trade to and from Great Britain. In this situation, Upper Canadian merchants were generally the junior partners. Because the Upper Canadian commercial class had no say in the development of ports, canals, or general commercial infrastructures in Lower Canada, its ability to promote local commercial growth was limited. Moreover, at a time when customs

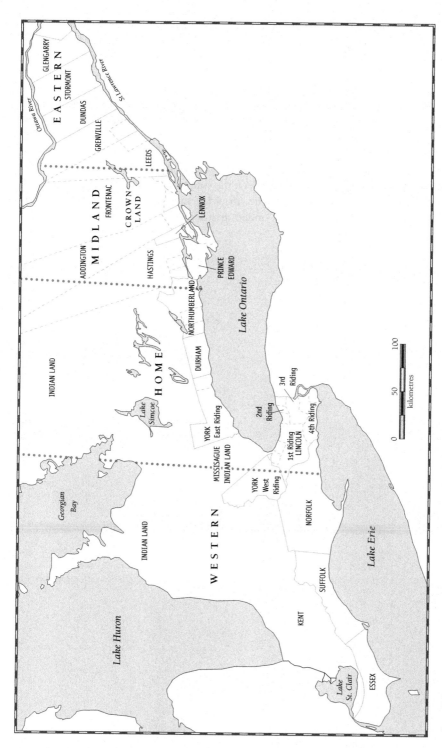

From W.G. Dean and Geoffrey J. Matthews, *Economic Atlas of Ontario* (Toronto: University of Toronto Press, 1969), plate 98.

duties were the major source of revenue for almost all British colonies, the Constitutional Act made Upper Canada reliant on Lower Canada for its share of the duties collected. This fiscal dependence would become increasingly intolerable for Upper Canada.

On a broader level, Britain retained control of the colony's commerce by means of the Navigation Laws. Restricting foreign participation in colonial trade and requiring colonies to ship raw material to the mother country in return for manufactured goods, these laws spawned a particular type of business elite. Within the British Empire's protected trade zone, colonial merchants shipped whatever they could and imported as much as possible. Up to now, strong military contacts plus an upper-crust background had been the sine qua non for social advancement in the *pays d'en haut*. Now, merchants would begin to challenge commissioned officers and the colony's nascent landed aristocracy for positions of power and prominence in Upper Canada.

Native Peoples, Nature, and Newcomers: The Making of Rural Upper Canada, 1791–1871

It used to be fashionable to comment that not much had been written on Upper Canada. After all, the argument went, it was much more exciting to study post-Confederation Ontario than the tiny Upper Canadian colonial backwater controlled by an inward-looking, socially and politically (if not economically) unprogressive colonial elite, a place peopled by emigrants who could not make it in the mother country, and economically driven by the unimaginative shipment of staples such as lumber and wheat to England, where the really significant manufacturing and processing of such raw products took place. Recent writing by such historians as Douglas McCalla and Keith Johnson has warned against reliance on simple typologies to explain the colony's development, arguing instead that the making of Ontario is best understood as the result of efforts of individual people. 'I argue,' McCalla writes, 'that we need to stress human agency, not natural resources, in the making of the Ontario economy.' For Johnson, 'There were no typical Upper Canadians. . . . There were simply individuals, or families, native-born or newcomers, well-off or struggling, educated or illiterate, who in the end, with, or despite, the leadership of the provincial economic and political establishment, contributed to, sometimes complicated, the creation of a new province.'[1]

There is much of value in this focus on agency and on deconstructing labels such as 'staples' and social categories such as religion and class. Yet, as McCalla and Johnson both acknowledge, many rural Upper Canadians endured very harsh conditions. The focus on human agency and the assertion that Upper Canadians were simply individuals can, it is argued here, carry one's understanding of success, failure, and aggregate development only so far. To a large extent, birthplace, ethnicity, gender, colour, wealth, and class determined individual expectations, behaviours, and rewards. First Nations peoples, for example, found little room in the colony that European settlers began to build in the 'Country of the Missesagues'.

Native Peoples and European Expansion

On 20 August 1796, a group of Mississauga led by Chief Wabakinine travelled from their village at the mouth of the Credit River to Upper Canada's newly designated capital at York. The fishing had been good that day, and they had caught

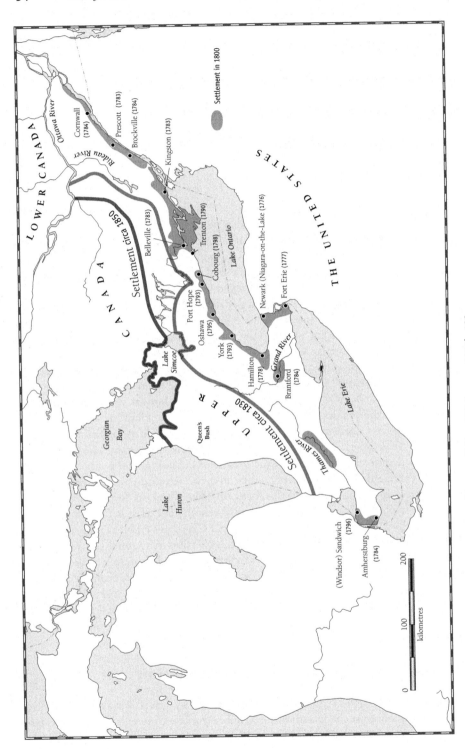

From David Bercuson et al., *Colonies: Canada to 1867* (Toronto: McGraw-Hill Ryerson, 1992), 198.

enough fresh salmon to offer some for sale. Mississauga at Upper Canada's other emerging urban centres, Kingston and Niagara, were starting up similar commercial ventures. But competition from white fishermen was increasing so swiftly that the very next year the colonial government would take measures to protect Native fisheries—though these laws were never enforced. In 1790, the Mississauga had warned that none but the First Nations would be permitted to fish the Credit. Yet by 1804, whites were catching so many salmon and the pollution caused 'by washing with soap and other dirt' was discouraging so many fish from even entering the river that the Mississauga complained, 'our families [are] in great distress for want of food'.[2]

Wabakinine did not live to see that distress. In the 1770s, he had organized the Ojibwa to fight with the British, and in the 1780s, he had helped to negotiate three treaties giving the British immense tracts of land north of Lake Ontario. Like many other Mississauga, he had thought his people were merely renting out the land and that, in return, they would 'always be taken care of' and would be permitted to 'encamp and fish where we pleased'.[3]

By the 1790s, however, First Nations people realized how misplaced their trust had been. In 1784, there were only 6,000 non-Native people in Upper Canada; by 1791, there were about 14,000, reaching some 70,000 by 1812. By then, most of Upper Canada's non-Native population were American immigrants searching for cheap land, and many brought with them strong antipathies toward Native people. These feelings were often reciprocated: when approached by 'a Yankee stranger' who wished to purchase land, one Mississauga chief refused to sell: '[the Yankee's] mouth is all sugar and his words very sweet, but I do not know what is in his heart'. In 1792, a Mississauga chief named Snake was murdered by British soldiers in Kingston and no one was punished for the crime. This was not unusual. As early as 1773, the superintendent of northern Indians counted eighteen such cases and concluded that colonists could kill Native people with virtual 'impunity'. Scarcely a week after Snake's murder, Elizabeth Simcoe, the wife of Upper Canada's first lieutenant-governor, visited Kingston and in a diary entry remarked on the 'unwarlike, idle, drunken, dirty tribe' of Mississauga who 'saunter up and down the Town all day'.[4] Such views were commonplace among Upper Canada's elite.

Numbering about a thousand in the early 1780s, the Credit River band had dropped to 330 by 1798. The survivors still faced the threat of disease, which continued to spread as white settlers moved north. As early as 1793, a Mississauga family named Different complained that 'when white people sees anything that they like they never quit us untill they have it. . . . The taking or stealing from us is nothing for we are only Massessagoes.' Some Mississauga adopted a belligerent stance, accosting surveyors, threatening settlers, burning mills, and hunting cattle. But the several bands in the lower Great Lakes region seldom acted in concert. In May 1796, in a rare attempt at united action, Wabakinine, believing that the British were about to form an alliance with the Six Nations people at the Grand River against the Mississauga and Ojibwa, sent warnings to his fellow chiefs. The British were compelled to assure six Ojibwa chiefs that no such plan existed.[5]

A month later, at the southern end of Burlington Bay, John Graves Simcoe was preparing to return to Britain after five years as lieutenant-governor. A gathering was held 'to compliment the Gov.' on the eve of his departure, Mrs Simcoe recorded in her diary, during which 'Wabekanine and a number of his tribe . . . gave us the largest Land Tortoise I ever saw.' The next evening, the Simcoe entourage enjoyed a fine dish of 'Tortoise ready dressed'.[6]

The tortoise played a crucial role among the numerous manitou (deities) that, for the Mississauga, represented 'the ultimate sources of existence'. Some of these spirits, such as the Great Lynx and the Large Snake, were evil; others, such as the Thunderbird, were powerful guardians. None, however, spoke the same language, and only Mikinak, the Great Turtle, possessed the power to translate, both between individual manitou and between manitou and humans. Who better to present to the chief of a troublesome alien culture? Surely Mikinak could translate more effectively than any human. Perhaps he would also report back to Wabakinine on the intentions of the interlopers; he had performed a similar service in 1764, when, after visiting the British at Niagara and Montreal, he advised the Ojibwa at Sault Ste Marie to seek peace because the British had superior arms.[7]

The Turtle was also a powerful protector in war. That Wabakinine looked to Mikinak for assistance suggests that he did not accept at face value the assurances of the British. With good reason: Upper Canada's administrators were indeed looking to isolate the Mississauga from potential allies. They also had their eyes on the vast stretch of Mississauga land between Burlington Bay and Etobicoke Creek, land that could constitute the final link between Niagara and York, if only it could be obtained cheaply. However, the Mississauga had seen Joseph Brant get a good price from the British for land the Mississauga had relinquished to other bands following the American Revolution. As one government official put it, the Mississauga 'are perfectly apprised of the value of money, and of its use'.[8]

We cannot know how these matters weighed with Wabakinine as he made camp on the waterfront opposite Berry's tavern in York on the night of 20 August 1796. At midnight, three white men dragged Wabakinine's sister away from the camp. (They would later claim that they had paid her money to sleep with them.) Frightened, Wabakinine's wife shook him awake and—half asleep and half drunk—he staggered after his sister's abductors. The men made short work of the chief, repeatedly kicking him and striking him with a rock as he lay on the ground. They also severely wounded his wife. Wabakinine died at his village on the Credit River the following day, the second Mississauga chief to be murdered by whites in four years, and his wife died several days later. Their murderers went unpunished.

As the government sent to Quebec for some 4,000 guns to protect the colony in the event of an uprising, the Mississauga looked to Brant for help. Promised by the government that all his land sales, although illegal under the Proclamation Act of 1763 (because they were made directly to settlers and white speculators), would be sanctioned if he counselled moderation, Brant urged the Mississauga to lay down their arms.[9] Nor could the Mississauga find allies south of the border, where several recent battles with the American army had left the local people in no position to provide assistance. Alone, the Mississauga were too weak to resist.

The government's divide-and-conquer policy culminated in a land agreement in 1805. The Mississauga, weakened by disease, alcohol, and the loss of traditional leadership, ceded 32,400 hectares—a tract of land 10 kilometres deep between Burlington and Etobicoke Creek—for a tiny fraction of its market value. The remaining local Mississauga clustered at the mouth of the Credit, the site of Wabakinine's old village, but the proliferation of mills and dams weakened the fishery. Finally, in 1847, when offered land on the Grand River by the Six Nations Iroquois (who remembered a similar offer by the Mississauga following the American Revolution), the Mississauga abandoned the Credit and moved to the southwestern corner of the Grand River Reserve. Meanwhile, to the east, Mississauga in the Kingston area ceded 1,200,000 hectares of land to the Upper Canadian government in the early 1820s.[10] In a brief twenty-five years, the

Box 5.1   Ontario's First Native Land Claim?
The Map as a Tool of Anti-Conquest

In March 1784, Sir John Johnson, Sir William's son, arrived at Johnstown (now Cornwall) seeking land on which to settle his Loyalist officers and their men. Consistent with a broader imperial mindset, Johnson viewed this land as an 'empty' space open for discovery and exploitation. Native people from the village of St Regis in Lower Canada, however, claimed the land as their own. Angered, Johnson reluctantly agreed to bargain. Joseph Brant cautioned Johnson 'to use those Indians in an easy manner . . . for many reasons, in the first place it gives the dam rebels large mouths for many things against us'. Governor General Haldimand agreed. Although he could find no record testifying to Native ownership, he counselled Johnson not to 'do anything in the Matter that might be interpreted as injurious to the Indians' and suggested that the lands could be granted them 'as an indulgence, during the King's pleasure'. Patrick McNiffe, a merchant and land speculator from New York State, quickly mapped and surveyed the territory. Land the Mohawk chiefs claimed as their own was granted to Loyalists, many of whom—including Sir John Johnson— quickly sold to others, who settled unaware of potential ownership problems.[1]

For several centuries, Europeans had routinely used surveys and maps to claim and rename land in the new world. Maps legitimated appropriation. They were instruments of power. In 1809, the Iroquois turned the tables and adopted some of the techniques of European imperialism to their own ends. Ten 'Indian Chiefs of the tribe of St Regis' 'employed Jeremiah McCarthy, Deputy Provincial Surveyor, . . . to make a correct survey of our lands'. His report, carried out 'in the presence of the . . . Chiefs and with their consent and approbation', documented deficiencies and requested 'compensation' for the Native people.[2]

Thomas Ridout, Upper Canada's surveyor general, did not accept all of McCarthy's survey but did acknowledge that the Native people were entitled to 30,690 acres of land 'on the northerly side of the River St. Lawrence'. By 1847, the Iroquois had 'let and leased out in different lots and parcels to divers persons for the benefit of the said Iroquois Indians . . . the whole or very near the whole of the said tract of land'. In that year, the 'Chiefs or Principal Men of the Iroquois Indians' relinquished their roles as rentier landlords and granted 'the whole of the said tract of land . . . to Her Majesty for the purpose of being sold, and the monies arising therefrom applied to and for the use and benefit of the said Iroquois Indians and their posterity.'[3] Thus ended what might very well have been the first 'successful' Native land claim in Ontario's history.

---

1. Quotations: Elinor Senior, *From Royal Township to Industrial City: Cornwall, 1784–1984* (Belleville, ON: Mika, 1983), 20; R.J. Surtees, *Indian Land Surrenders in Ontario, 1763–1867* (Ottawa: Indian and Northern Affairs Canada, 1984), 29. See also Ron Edwards, 'Patrick McNiffe,' *Dictionary of Canadian Biography*, vol. 5 (Toronto: University of Toronto Press, 1983), 553–4.
2. Quotations: Jeremiah McCarthy Surveyor's Report, 1809, Charlottenburg Plan and Survey, c279-0-0-0-68-3, Ontario Archives. See also Graham Huggan, 'Decolonizing the Map: Post-colonialism, Post-structuralism and the Cartographic Connection', *Ariel* 4 (1989): 115–31.
3. Thomas Ridout Reports, 14 September 1811 and 30 January 1817, Charlottenburg Plan and Survey, c279-0-0-0-63.3–68.6, Ontario Archives; *Indian Treaties and Surrenders, from 1680 to 1890* (Ottawa, 1891), Early Canadiana Online, CIHM 91942, no. 57, 136–8.

Mississauga had moved from being the state's landlords to being its clients.

The same process would be repeated as colonial settlement edged north. Close to 140,000 emigrants arrived from the British Isles between 1815 and 1835; by 1842, Upper Canada's non-Native population numbered about 450,000. By contrast, between 1770 and 1835 the Native population dropped from 14,000 to 9,300. After the War of 1812, the British military believed that it no longer needed First Nations assistance in war; thereafter, the practice of giving gifts to Native people declined, causing the need for assistance to increase. Responsibility for Native issues in Upper Canada then shifted from the military to the civil sector. In 1830, the state attempted to move a large number of Native people to a model agricultural settlement at Coldwater, between Lake Simcoe and Georgian Bay. Methodist, Catholic, and Anglican churches assisted the state in what would become an ongoing attempt to 'civilize' Native people.

But not everyone saw assimilation as the appropriate goal. In 1836, Sir Francis Bond Head, lieutenant-governor of Upper Canada, concluded that Native people would never be able to adapt to white culture; the only realistic solution was to let them die out in peace. Accordingly, he negotiated a treaty with the Ojibwa of the Saugeen region, acquiring 600,000 hectares of land for the state and relocating the band to Manitoulin Island in Georgian Bay, where, he assured them, whites would never bother them. Protests from various missionary societies led the Colonial Office to overrule Bond Head's decision, but segregation rather than assimilation remained the approach of choice for most Upper Canadians, regardless of the policies and programs espoused by the state and religious groups.

Some 1,200 Native people did settle on Manitoulin Island, where the Roman Catholic and Anglican churches vied for their souls. Farther south, the Methodists converted many of the Credit River Mississauga, including a chief named Kahkewaquonaby, who would become known to newcomers as Peter Jones. Influenced in part by Jones, the Mississauga of the Kingston area settled on Grape Island in the Bay of Quinte. Here they were beset by Methodist missionaries, who believed that to be 'civilized', a society must be based on agriculture and the raising of livestock. But Grape Island was too small to provide adequate forage; the animals had to be kept on another island, and the women had to row for two hours a day in order to care for them.

Still, for some of the Mississauga, even Grape Island offered a better life than the one they had known in the 1820s; as one recalled, 'they were all happy drunkards ... dying very fast. ... Some of them were stabbed, some were drowned, some were burned, and some were frozen to death. And thus we were going to destruction at a great rate.' Others quit the island for the back country north of Kingston. Petitioning for land, they were granted a 1,085-hectare reserve, but—to the consternation of the white authorities—instead of using the land for farming, the Mississauga resumed their traditional hunting and foraging culture. Eventually the remaining Grape Island Mississauga were moved to another reserve. Yet throughout the nineteenth century, the Mississauga never abandoned their tradition of communal ownership for the European model of individualized private property, nor did many other Native bands. Similarly, attempts by Peter Jones to enforce British criminal law among the Port Credit Mississauga were resisted; instead, they followed 'a code of several Rules and regulations among themselves'.[11]

Nevertheless, Native leaders often welcomed, and even petitioned, for residential schools, or 'teaching wigwams', to help them learn European ways. In the 1820s and early 1830s, Ojibwa in southern Ontario asked for books and eagerly sent their children to Methodist-run bilingual day schools. These schools taught a curriculum superior to that received by most European settlers in the colony. Peter Jones became an extremely effective proselytizer for residential schooling as a vehicle for teaching the Methodist faith. Shingwaukonse, a chief of the Garden River Ojibwa near the Sault, took a more pragmatic approach, looking to missionary schools not for spiritual instruction but for the education his people needed to adapt to broad economic and social change. Both, however, believed that the schools should at the earliest possible time be run not just for Native people but by them.[12]

For all societies, 'culture' is a protean term. This is equally true of Native societies. Different bands and different groups within bands took firm positions on different issues, each attempting to protect those parts of their culture that they considered most essential. Indeed, many of the most prominent Native leaders believed that participation in the new economic and social reality offered the only hope for preservation of their traditional culture. What from a distance may look like a uniform retreat in the face of an overwhelming foe was actually a complex

Newly built Mississauga homes at the Credit River, 1827. Each of these two-room log cabins housed two families. Homes were inspected by Methodist missionaries and assessed for cleanliness and organization. Kahkewaquonaby, the Mississauga chief and Methodist minister also known as Peter Jones, took part in such inspections and reported his findings in his journal: 'Bro Hurlbert's—All neat, like a white squaw's house, except the tea kettle which was out of place.' 'Jacob Snowstorm's—Floor and cupboard poor—bed tolerably good . . . one woman making baskets—one sewing—one idle.' 'Passed by one Indian Camp, a specimen of old times.' 'John Pigeon's—floor good but dirty—good tables but dusty . . . a Bible and Hymn Book etc on the shelf—everything looks like industry, and improvement in the house' (in B. Osborne and M. Ripmeester, 'The Mississauga between Two Worlds', *Canadian Journal of Native Studies* 17 [1997]: 259–91). Many Native leaders believed that preservation of their traditional culture depended on their co-operation in such activities. By 1847, the Mississauga had ceded to the state the land on which these houses stood. Image from Egerton Ryerson, *The Story of My Life* (Toronto, 1883), 59. Thomas Fisher Rare Book Library, University of Toronto.

process of accommodation, compromise, and calculated response aimed at protecting what each group deemed most central to its cultural identity. In this sense, Native peoples continued to exercise an agency, however limited, that white society never succeeded in appropriating.

Ultimately, however, efforts to promote assimilation in Upper Canada were not about providing the wherewithal to participate constructively in white society; Native people remained decidedly second-class. The successful Methodist day schools deteriorated after the Canadian Methodists merged with their more conservative British brethren in 1834. Bureaucrats allowed Native people to play no significant role in the residential schools set up in the 1840s. This was not Peter Jones's vision, and not one of his own children went to a residential school. For those children who did, such schooling did not lead to acceptance in the dominant white community. At Fort William, residential-school enrolment had been high, yet in 1871, Native and Métis men were significantly overrepresented in the lowest-paid occupational groups.[13] In short, European immigrants were not prepared to suffer the competition that a more constructive approach would produce. The real purposes behind 'Indian policy' were displacement and containment.

Nor did the white population wish the Native people to enjoy the benefits of development. Local municipal councils wanted unfettered access to Native lands for road-building. Officers in the Indian Department did act as arbitrators, providing some protection. In 1851, the Western Superintendent berated Lambton County councillors for their refusal to allow 'the poor Indians the enjoyment of a small remnant of their once rich domain' and accused them of wishing 'to see these unoffending people driven beyond the Rocky Mountains'. But in 1853 and again in 1860 (when the colony took over formal control of Indian affairs from the imperial government), the legislature of Upper Canada merged the departments of Indian Affairs and Crown Lands, making conflicts of interest inevitable. From that time forward, the state evinced little sympathy for Native peoples' right to control road development on their reserves—and this is still a contentious issue in Ontario.[14]

In fishing and mining—key 'frontiers' of contact in nineteenth-century northern Ontario—white immigrants denied Native people the right to participate as equals. Throughout the nineteenth century, Ojibwa chiefs fought valiantly to preserve their traditional fisheries from the incursions of non-Native commercial fishermen.[15] From the 1830s to the mid-1850s, Ojibwa in the Lake Huron–Georgian Bay region entered into numerous agreements with commercial companies designed to regulate, control, and rent fishery rights. As well, they signed treaties with the government that, while ceding land, retained Native ownership of aquatic and animal resources.

But commercial companies often ignored the agreements, and the state did nothing to enforce Native rights. On a number of occasions, the state even refused Saugeen Ojibwa access to money from the state-controlled trust fund (set up from the sale of Native lands), money the Ojibwa required for the purchase of fishery equipment. The first comprehensive legislation concerning fishing on inland waters, passed in 1857, facilitated the leasing of Native fishing grounds to non-Native companies. The fishery overseer, William Gibbard, believed that 'the Indians would be far better off if they attended to their farms instead of dabbling in fisheries'. Accordingly, of the ninety-seven licences he issued in 1859, eighty-five went to white applicants and only twelve to Native groups.[16]

In effect, Aboriginal people were now required to compete for the opportunity to exercise their never-ceded right to fish, and to do so within a system heavily biased against them. They fought back, destroying the nets and other equipment of the white fishermen. But by the 1860s, the Great Lakes fisheries were increasingly dominated by non-Native commercial companies, the largest of which were American-owned. Even Gibbard admitted that the Americans operated 'in a manner incredibly reckless, and altogether regardless of the most ruinous consequences', leaving 'old nets upon the ground to rot . . . with putrefying masses of fish entangled amongst them'. Meanwhile, Native people were regularly fined and

The troubles on Manitoulin Island, *Canadian Illustrated News*, 8 August 1863. Despite treaty guarantees of their rights, Native people were regularly fined and jailed for 'illegal' fishing. In 1863, fishery overseer William Gibbard led a party of armed deputies in an unsuccessful raid on Manitoulin Island. He died not long after, in mysterious circumstances. NA 134371.

jailed for 'illegally' fishing in waters to which treaties guaranteed them free access. 'It is quite natural', William Plummer, a retired Manitoulin Island Indian agent, wrote in 1878, 'that they should think that they were arbitrarily deprived by government of rights they have never surrendered.' Plainly, as an Indian agent in Grey County acknowledged in 1896, Native fishing would not be tolerated if it involved competition with whites.[17]

By the mid-1840s, the mineral resources of the north were attracting southern interests. In 1845, the colony extended its jurisdiction to Sault Ste Marie, surveyed Ojibwa land, and granted mining companies leases, despite impassioned protests from chiefs such as Shingwaukonse, who, in 1849, wrote to the governor general, 'you have hunted us from every place as with a wand, you have swept away all our pleasant land, and like some giant foe you tell us "willing or unwilling, you must now go from amid these rocks and wastes, I want them now! I want them to make rich my white children, whilst you may shrink away to holes and caves like starving dogs to die."'[18] Shingwaukonse refused to shrink away. That same year, with some twenty-five Native comrades and several sympathetic whites, he seized a copper mine at Mica Bay from the Quebec and Montreal Mining Association, occupying it until the spring of 1850.

The Ojibwa believed that copper had great spiritual power, but the mining clash was less about preservation of a spiritual resource than about access to a saleable commodity. As Peau de Chat, an Ojibwa chief from Fort William, put it, 'A great deal of our mineral has been taken away and I must have something for

Shingwaukonse, c. 1849. 'Drive us not to the madness of despair', the Ojibwa chief urged Governor General Elgin in 1849. 'We are told that you have laws which guard and protect the property of your white children, but you have made none to protect the rights of your red children. Perhaps you expected that the red skin could protect himself from the rapacity of his pale faced bad brother?' In nineteenth-century Ontario, the rapacity of white settlers, speculators, and government administrators prevailed, but Shingwaukonse's Garden River descendants kept pressing for equal rights in economic and educational development. Today, on a local level, they have achieved some success. Shingwauk Project, Algoma University College.

it.' Shingwaukonse agreed: 'We want pay for every pound of mineral that has been taken off our lands, as well as for that which may hereafter be carried away.'[19] These chiefs did not oppose resource development in itself (although many whites explained the conflict in those terms): what they wanted was a fair chance to participate in it. For Shingwaukonse, it was just one aspect of a multi-faceted approach to development, one that would include Native-managed schooling and allow for reciprocity and cultural exchange. For the state, however, resource development was a one-way street. Finance minister Francis Hincks, who had profited from northern mining speculation, consistently ignored or denied the petitions of Native leaders to set up lumber mills and mining operations.

The Robinson Treaties of 1850, which acquired for the Crown almost 140,000 square kilometres of land in the Georgian Bay–Lake Superior region, signalled the future direction of the state's Native policy. Whereas earlier treaties had left it to individual bands to decide how they would distribute the annual payments they received, the Robinson Treaties stipulated that a portion of each payment was to be given to individuals within each band, effectively undermining the collective property ownership so central to traditional Native cultures.

These initiatives were extended in 1857 by the passage of what has been called 'one of the most important bills in the history of Canadian Indian policy'. Without consulting any Native chief and with only one dissension—'Why should we wish to civilize them?' William Lyon Mackenzie wondered, 'What sort of civilization have we here?'—the government passed the Gradual Civilization Act, which granted voting rights to any Native man literate in either English or French who could answer a skill-testing question (naming the world's continents) and who was willing to renounce the principle of collective ownership in favour of individual property rights. Those who accepted enfranchisement, however, would lose their legal status as Indians. Intended, as one chief put it, 'to break them to pieces', the Gradual Civilization Act created two categories of subjects in Upper Canada: Indians and citizens. Most Native people remained the former; by 1880, fewer than fifty had become enfranchised. 'At this rate', remarked one MP, 'it would take 36,000 years to enfranchise the Indian population of Canada.'[20] True enough, but it took over a century for the state's patience to wear thin and for the Act to be repealed.

The name 'Gradual Civilization Act' reflected white society's common view of the new land and its peoples: both were wild and forbidding. Preparing for the Prince of Wales's tour of British North America in 1860, the Indian Department encouraged Upper Canadian Native people to dress in traditional costumes, complete with 'any war clubs and tomahawks they may possess, and what they do not possess perhaps they may borrow from those who have.' Press reports of Aboriginal presentations during the tour emphasized Native nudity, war paint, and savagery, ignoring those Native people who chose to dress in European style and overlooking the petitions to the prince from Native leaders decrying colonial injustices. While such depictions rested uneasily with the official policy of assimilation, they emerged naturally from the foundations of the colonizer's mindset: racial hierarchies—the boundaries between colonizer and colonized—had to be preserved whether in terms of the 'Noble Savage' or of the degenerate wild man.[21]

Nature and European Expansion

The natural world was never a simple constant. Climate, vegetation, and wildlife changed, often in ways and in response to forces that we have yet to comprehend. Compared to European settlers, Native peoples desired to live on a level of respect and equality with their environment. Europeans often experienced a kind of disorientation when confronted with the 'almost impenetrable and exceedingly dreary' bush. '[T]he landscape', one recent arrival complained in 1831, 'is unvaried and exceedingly confined—nothing but trees, trees, trees continualy'. One gentlewoman from England described the forest as a 'rural prison house'. As if to protect himself and his family from the uncharted wilderness, Jasper Grant planted a garden around his Amherstburg house: 'I have sown flowers . . . all around.'[22]

Not all settlers were afflicted with what has been called a 'garrison mentality'. Most Upper Canadian writers looked on the forest with awe and affection. Adam Hood Burwell, a clergyman and poet, believed that

> Productive nature smiles over this land
> And shows her bounties with a lavish hand
> In wild profusion—soft meandering rills,
> Deep woods, rich dales, smooth plains and sunny hills,
> Sylvan recesses, dark o'erhanging groves,

Where vocal songsters tune their throats to love.

Wonder and interest rather than fear dominated Charles Durand's 1832 short story about being lost in the woods. There are a hundred more stories of a similar sort. While most Upper Canadian writers did not view the bush as a 'rural prison house', their perspectives, as Burwell's poem indicates, were constricted by obeisance to the British Romantic tradition, a formulaic depiction of the sylvan sublime that dominated writing of the period. Concrete detail—the realistic description of the Upper Canadian frontier—awaited a later generation.[23]

Those willing to learn from the local Native people discovered that the forest was neither pathless nor unbroken. A network of trails facilitated movement north of the lakes, and for centuries Aboriginal farmers had been maintaining cleared land (often by means of fire) for planting their crops. Cleared plains abutting dense forest provided environments attractive to many of the species they hunted. Some astute settlers looked to Native examples for guidance in selecting choice farmland and appropriate crops. Others looked to the trees themselves. Government land surveyors routinely linked tree species with soil types, and many astute land speculators read those reports carefully before selecting land to purchase. 'The nature of the soil may be invariably discovered by the description of the timber it bears', notes a guidebook published in 1831, for example 'on what is called hard timbered land, where the maple, beach, black birch, ash, cherry, lime, oak, black walnut, butternut, hickory, plane and tuliptree etc. are found, the soil consists of deep black loam.'[24]

Early settlers also benefited from Native knowledge of the medicinal value of forest plants. The use of curative herbs and wild plants was a familiar practice to many settlers. Old World traditions often privileged such folk remedies. Doctors were few and, even when available, were rarely trusted in early Upper Canada. Far from a last resort, self-care was the first choice for many Upper Canadians. From this perspective the forest became an ally, not a place of danger and distress. In this context, Native people became helpmates. Lady Simcoe noted that when her husband became ill, she performed wonders using a Native remedy recommended by Molly Brant. A Moravian missionary followed a Native recipe for treating a severe burn by 'boil[ing] Sassafras root, soak[ing] the leaves and put[ting] them on the burns'.[25] Upper Canadian attitudes to the environment were thus not all of a piece. While many shielded themselves from the unknown, seemingly pathless, wilderness, others saw their environment in a more positive light: used carefully, the forest nurtured and supported life.

Few nineteenth-century Ontarians gave much thought to the reverse proposition: that in order for the forest to survive, the forest and the life it contained also required nurturing. For most settlers, clearing the land of Native people was far easier than clearing the land of forest. The axe was the 'essential weapon' in the settlers' war against nature. With it, early Upper Canadians effected 'an ecological revolution'. As Anna Jameson, visiting from Britain, reported in the 1830s, a 'Canadian settler hates a tree, regards it as his natural enemy, as something to be destroyed, eradicated, annihilated by all and any means'. Thirty years later, the president of the

Henry Francis Ainslie (1803–79), *Canada, Settler's house in the forest, on the Thames, nr London CW, April 1842*. Axes, even more than railways, transformed the Upper Canadian landscape. For settlers, trees were the enemy. Most farmers managed to clear half a hectare or less per year, and clearing and planting went on simultaneously. Crops grew up amid the stumps, which were easier to pull out once they had rotted. NA C 000544.

Agricultural Association of Upper Canada was still urging his members to apply themselves to 'the subjugation of the forest'. In 1816, Charles Fothergill observed that the Trent River Valley was surrounded by 'a thick forest of very fine Fir, Pine, Timber trees—some of the Pines were indeed magnificent from 100 to 180 and occasionally, perhaps to 200 feet in height.' A scant sixteen years later a British traveller lamented the 'nakedness' of some areas of southern Upper Canada. By 1875, lumber companies were in a continual and increasingly difficult search for rich pine stands: in southern Ontario, farmers and lumberers had stripped many areas of 80 per cent of the original forest cover. In 1871, the government passed legislation to encourage farmers to plant trees on their property near roadways. Most ignored the legislature. By the third quarter of the nineteenth century, some Ottawa Valley lumberers began to argue for the implementation of limited conservation measures, but they were a minority and achieved little success. Lumberers stripped Ontario of its pine stands and polluted its rivers with sawdust, beached logs, and eroding soil. Farmers imported useful crop seeds, but they also imported weeds, such as thistles, wild mustard, burdock, and a new and fast-spreading plant species, *Ambrosia*, commonly known as 'ragweed'.[26]

The variety and abundance of animal life astonished Europeans. In their eyes one of the first tasks was to classify and 'map' wildlife. In practice, this entailed imposing a European framework, in effect extracting animals and plants from both their natural ecological habitats and from Native peoples' understandings. Charles Fothergill, who arrived from Yorkshire in 1816, collected (often with Native help) and described 186 bird species, 105 mammals, 27 fishes, and 15 reptiles. A devoted naturalist who tried to establish a natural history museum, Fothergill believed that humankind 'has no right to injure or wantonly destroy any animal'. But such sentiments were rare. Even a man like Elkanah Billings, the founder of Upper Canada's first natural history journal, *The Canadian Naturalist and Geologist*, in recording his admiration for the pileated woodpecker, complacently noted that he 'shot several of them on the Bonnechere River in the County of Renfrew'. For most Upper Canadians, wild animals were either pests or they were game, to be hunted and killed either way. By 1892, a Royal Commission on Fish and Game would report a 'sickening tale of merciless, ruthless, and remorseless slaughter'. Its conclusion was only too predictable: 'Where but a few years ago game was plentiful, it is hardly now to be found.'[27]

Making It in Rural Upper Canada

Conservation was not much on the minds of settlers struggling to make a better life for themselves and their families. The story of Wilson Benson is representative of his time and class. Born in Belfast in 1821, Benson had worked as a linen weaver, agricultural labourer, and peddler before embarking for Upper Canada with his fourteen-year-old wife, Jemima, in 1841. Over the next eight years, he worked at twenty different occupations and moved more than a dozen times; Jemima worked as a domestic and dressmaker and bore at least two sons. Following the loss of their home and store to a fire in 1849, Jemima's brother suggested that they take up farming close to his own operation near Orillia. After sending Jemima there 'to ascertain from her how she liked the place', Benson moved his family north and became a farmer at age twenty-eight. He would move only twice more: first to a bigger farm in Artemesia Township in Grey County, and finally, after suffering a crippling accident on the farm in the early 1870s, to the village of Markdale, a few kilometres away. There, with the help of his second wife, he became a respected merchant and lived until his death in 1911.[28]

With many occupational and geographic moves in the early years followed by relative stability and moderate success in farming and storekeeping, Benson was typical of thousands of immigrants in the early nineteenth century. Upper Canada was known as a 'poor man's country', a country to which a struggling family in the Old Country could emigrate with reasonable hopes for bettering its position. Historians suggest that an agricultural ladder was in place for most of the nineteenth century in Upper Canada/Ontario. Families arrived with a little cash, worked for a period to save a down payment, purchased farmland (often on a time plan), and, after some years of intensive labour, owned and operated their own rural enterprise. Like Wilson Benson, who emigrated with the intent of scaling 'the ladder of fortune', most settlers, it is argued, aspired to and achieved a modest competency, the ability to support their family and to bequeath to their children a small stake for future development.[29]

Following the end of the Napoleonic Wars, the prospects offered by a poor man's country attracted much attention in the British Isles, where land enclosures, sluggish industrial growth in many regions, and redundancy caused by mechanization in others made finding employment very difficult. Between 1815 and 1865—a period known as the era of 'Proletarian Mass Migration'—well over one million emigrants entered British North America from the British Isles. Thomas Bunn, a wealthy British philanthropist, noted in 1834, 'It is a frequent expression among the poor people, if there were a bridge to Canada, many would pass over it.'[30] As it had for almost every decade since 1791, Upper Canada's population doubled in the 1840s, to 952,000 in 1850. Population growth and net immigration slowed thereafter, and by 1870 Ontario had 1,926,922 people.

Not all the new arrivals came from the British Isles: some 12,000 Germans settled in Upper Canada after 1850—often met at Quebec City and accompanied to their Upper Canadian destination by a German-speaking emigration agent— and by 1860 a sizeable number of African Americans were also living in the colony. Although kin groups often settled in the same general area, rural society in Upper Canada typically consisted of what, in March 1846, a Scottish farmer in Huron County called a 'mixty moxty Quire hotch potch of high and low country scotch, English, welch, irish, dutch, french, Yankees of the states, new brunswick, and novacosea with native born canadians'.[31]

This dispersal of peoples of different backgrounds was paralleled by the settlement pattern of Upper Canada's black population, itself of varied backgrounds. In 1860, only one out of five of the 23,000 Upper Canadians of African American descent was an escaped slave; two out of five had been born in Upper Canada. While some lived in separate enclaves, the 1860 census found the black population was dispersed across 312 county and city wards and that mixed marriages were fairly common. Black people suffered significant discrimination in Upper Canada at this time. The writer Susanna Moodie, whose legendary journals recount her journey from England to Upper Canada in 1832 and her settlement in the backwoods, reports a black man, who was married to a white woman, killed by a white mob. More representative was the experience of a black community in the southwest of the province. In 1829, the Cincinnati Colonization Society had arranged with Lieutenant-Governor Colborne to send a sizeable group of African Americans from Cincinnati to settle in Upper Canada. Around two hundred men, women, and children made the move to Wilberforce, but most left again within a few years. The Canada Company, which owned much of the land in the area, had refused to sell to the new arrivals on the grounds that their concentration 'alarm[ed] the present inhabitants, who appear to have a repugnance to [black people] forming communities near them'. Samuel Ringgold Ward, a black activist from the United States, noted that jobs were restricted to work as a railroad navvy, waiter, cook, or barber, or some other menial service. 'The truth of the matter', as one observer reported in 1863, was that 'as long as the coloured people form a very small proportion of the population, and are dependent, they receive protection and favours; but when they increase and compete with the labour-

Box 5.2 Upper Canadian Irish in the Mid-Nineteenth Century

The Irish potato famine of the mid-1840s contributed the greatest single influx of migrants in this period: between 1846 and 1851, 200,000 British subjects—two-thirds of them from Ireland—migrated to Upper Canada, perhaps 40,000 of these British immigrants moving on to the United States. Unlike those who came before and after, these migrants often arrived in broken health (17 per cent of those who left Liverpool died on board or in quarantine at Quebec), and most were virtually penniless. In 1847, officials recorded 20,365 deaths out of some 98,000 emigrants to Canada, and this was undoubtedly an underestimate.

An older historiography argues that the Irish were predominantly unskilled industrial labourers who populated urban slums. This interpretation, based largely on evidence from the United States, has been thoroughly discredited with reference to Upper Canada. By the end of the 1850s, about three-quarters of all Upper Canadian Irish lived and worked in rural regions, a ratio similar to that for other major ethnic groups. How can one explain the fact that often destitute and at times disease-weakened migrants were able to settle in rural areas at a time of rising land costs and diminishing arable land? First, many were already experienced small tenant farmers. They possessed technological knowledge, if not always material wealth. As well, many had artisanal skills that facilitated the accumulation of capital for farm expenses. Moreover, many received help from relatives and friends who had preceded them to Upper Canada. Migration and settlement was a stepwise process often involving many links and stops before a final destination was reached, and not just for the Irish. Finally, recent work examining the practices of Irish farmers in Eastern Ontario in the 1860s has pointed out that not all Irish farmed the same way. Some were 'go-getters', while others rested content with meeting their 'consumptive obligations'. It is dangerous to ascribe a homogenous behaviour to any 'ethnic' group.[1]

---

1. Gordon Darroch and Michael Ornstein, 'Ethnicity and Occupational Structure in Canada in 1871: *The Vertical Mosaic* in Historical Perspective', *Canadian Historical Review* 61 (1980): 305–33; Don Akenson, *The Irish in Ontario: A Study in Rural History* (Kingston, ON: McGill-Queen's University Press, 1984); Edward J. Hedican, 'Irish Farming Households in Eastern Canada: Domestic Production and Family Size', *Ethnology* 42 (2003): 15–37.

ing class for a living, and especially when they begin to aspire to social equality, they cease to be "interesting negroes", and become "niggers".'[32]

While it has often been suggested that Upper Canada's settler economy can be best understood as one dependent on the export of a central staple, such as wheat or wood, the reality is more complex. It is true that Great Britain provided a protected market for Upper Canadian grain and forest products for much of the first half of the century. In this sense, British policy-makers instituted a type of mercantile system whereby natural products from the colonies would be shipped to the mother country and manufactured goods from Great Britain would be sent to the colonies. Yet this protection was of a shifting sort, and in the 1840s the system was very nearly totally dismantled, with the ending of timber preferences and the repeal of the Corn Laws and the Navigation Acts. These changes excited violent protest on the part of some local merchants and led to a desire on the part of some to annex with the United States.

Most farms, however, produced many things besides wheat—barley, tobacco, rye, pork, ashes, lumber. One farm produced thirty-nine different crops in a single four-year period. In 1803, only half the land under tillage produced wheat, and only 20 per cent of that wheat was exported. Even at the height of wheat production in the 1850s, when the export market was buoyant, wheat took up less than a quarter of the average farmer's cultivated land, and at least half of Upper Canadian wheat exports went not to Britain itself but to its other North American colonies. A reciprocity treaty with the United States (1854–66) facilitated the existing trade flow for a wide range of natural products. Agricultural diversification intensified after 1850: by 1871, wheat, although still central to Upper Canada's rural domain, took up less than one-quarter of tilled land, and mixed farming, dairy, and livestock production had assumed increased importance.[33]

In 1814, speculator Thomas Smith probably looked to the export market to sell his copse of 34,603 oak trees; between 1815 and 1870, exports of timber and wood products brought in almost as much as exports of flour and wheat. In the mid-1830s, some 3,500 men worked—wielding saw, axe, cant hook, pike pole, and oar—in commercial logging ventures. Many came from Lower Canada to the Ottawa Valley as seasonal workers, and clashes between French Canadian and Irish Catholic loggers sometimes occurred. Commercial logging was soon also underway in the Georgian Bay region. By the 1870s, the value of sawn lumber exports to the US surpassed the traditional trade in square timber to England. By the turn of the century, logging would employ 20,000 men.

A good portion of the output of the colony's sawmills—425 of them as early as 1826—was destined for local building construction (farmers could have their own logs milled in exchange for half the lumber), and distilleries (150 in 1842) and steamboats (30 in 1840) also used large quantities of local wood. Probably as much wood went to heat settlers' homes as went to external markets. In the 1830s, John Dunbar Moodie estimated that 'a house with only two or three fires' would burn about one acre of timber in a year. Just to heat their homes, Upper Canadians in the 1840s consumed 400,000 hectares of woodland.[34]

Cash existed in only limited quantities in the colony, as in most frontier communities. It would be wrong, however, to see the exchange system as based simply on the exchange of goods for goods. Merchants would calculate the amount owed in cash and then collect the equivalent in goods. Nobody owed a literal bushel of wheat; rather, one owed a sum of money that might be paid off in wheat. This barter system shocked many recent arrivals. 'Ministers in the Townships or Country circuits', the Reverend John McLaurin told a correspondent in Scotland, 'are paid their stipends, nearly, if not altogether in produce! . . . at the then market rates; or as may otherwise be agreed upon. This appears hard to such as never have tried it; and indeed it is so, if not reduced to some System.'[35]

Clearly the promise of a higher standard of living attracted many to Upper Canada. Between 1825 and 1851, Upper Canada was the fastest-growing community in North America. In 1826 it boasted a per capita output some three times that of Ireland. Per capita income remained the same between 1826 and 1850, as did per capita agricultural output. According to one study, only 16 per cent of farms in 1860 produced less than they consumed. Another 16 per cent provided a surplus sufficient to feed three other families. The rest produced enough to feed themselves. Farming, it is clear, could sustain a livelihood. Moreover, a study of rural landholding patterns in 1870 found that as the male household head aged, the amount of land owned increased, suggesting that if farmers started at a young age they could reasonably expect to attain a modest prosperity over the course of a lifetime—similar, perhaps, to that attained by Wilson Benson. And many fathers were able to provide for their sons. A study of 250 Irish protestant families who settled on the Upper Canadian side of the Ottawa Valley suggests that more than half the sons of families who remained in the area received farms from their fathers.[36]

In this general economic environment, many settlers eked out a modest living. With the help of neighbours, a rough log cabin could be built in two or three days for less than £10. The design and construction of such structures owed a good deal to government legislation. After 1811, all buildings in Upper Canada were taxed according to the material used and the numbers of storeys and fireplaces. The astute farmer would therefore build a one-and-a-half-storey log cabin, generally about 8 by 5.5 metres, with a full attic for sleeping. Taxed at the one-storey rate and needing only one fireplace, the one-and-a-half-storey log cabin became the most popular dwelling in rural Upper Canada, outnumbering any other type by roughly two to one in the first half of the nineteenth century. After a decade or two, a settler might then hire an itinerant craftsman to build more stately front doors and windows, often following models current in Dublin. On average, it would take thirty to forty years before a farm family could afford to build a frame or brick house.[37]

Before mid-century, advice literature for migrants tended to be a decentralized activity, often produced by speculators, land companies, and travellers. By the 1850s, the Upper Canadian state, through the Bureau of Agriculture, became a major player in the production and distribution of immigrant guides and in the promotion of the Canadas at international fairs and exhibitions. In an attempt to attract appropriate settlers, official guides appeared in English, French, German, Swedish, and Norwegian. The desired settler would be one who could emulate the 'motto of the capital of Canada . . . "Industry, Intelligence and Integrity", and her emblem . . . the Beaver. These three qualifications', William Hutton of the Department of Agriculture explained, 'are required of all who desire to make speedy and honorable progress in life and . . . to command success in Canada.' A.C. Buchanan, head of the Emigration Office in Quebec, allowed that 'cases of disappointment must occasionally occur', but, he warned, 'in nine cases out of ten, they may be traced to the individuals themselves.' Failure could be averted by reading the state-sanctioned advice found in the manuals, by registering with state immigrant agents at the various ports of entry, and by following the agents' instructions. These last admonitions were of particular importance to the state: they gave the state's agents an opportunity to observe, evaluate, and direct new immigrants.[38]

This official discourse, drawn from an international emigrant literature, certainly minimized the challenges and hardships of frontier life and promised more assistance than the state would ever give. It was a slow and arduous climb to ascend even to the middle level of the ladder. One study of start-up costs suggests that only those with at least moderate wealth could afford to set up a farm and that the acquisition of such wealth could take some ten years of work in Upper Canada—very close to William Benson's experience. Speculators were among the challenges facing potential settlers. Throughout southern Ontario, large amounts of good farmland had been appropriated by a small number of speculators well before any major influx of settlers. The government itself controlled, through the clergy and Crown reserves, two-sevenths of the land in each township. In 1825, the state sold 1 million hectares of land to a British-based corporation, the Canada Company, for £295,000. The state also regularly granted prime land to favoured applicants, a practice defended by one such recipient in 1809: 'Where there was a competition, a connection with government was surely an allowable motive of preference; nor would an unprejudiced man find anything very censurable in withholding from a casual settler, admitted on grounds of favour, an advantageous location, which might afterwards be granted to a person of superior pretensions.' The writer, Richard Cartwright, a wealthy Kingston merchant, died in 1815 owning 11,000 hectares of land scattered throughout Upper Canada.[39]

As early as 1800, up to two-thirds of the land in the Home District—the site of the colony's capital, York—was in speculator's hands. Up to one-third of all patented land in Peel County was in the hands of speculators between 1820 and 1840. By 1815, in the Western District, members of two fur-trading families, the Babys and the Askins, owned about one-third of the region's best patented agricultural land. John Askin took advantage of his marriage to a Native woman to purchase Native land at a cheap cost. This practice infuriated Joseph Brant, the local Mohawk leader, but his official protests fell on deaf ears—at least in part because the government official to whom Brant complained was Askin's confidant and troubleshooter on land issues. By the mid-1850s, good land was no longer available for purchase from the government, but, according to one contemporary, some 800,000 hectares were in private hands ready for sale.[40]

Many settlers simply squatted: one student of land development in Upper Canada claims that next to government assistance, squatting was the prime mode of settlement. Few state officials argued that squatters were ideal settlers. As A.J. Russell, a high-ranking official in the Crown Lands Department, put it in 1854, squatting was 'injurious to the future character of the settlement. The land is taken up by a poorer and inferior class of settlers.' They were, however, preferable to Native people. By 1840, about one-fifth of the Six Nations reserve along the Grand River was occupied by non-Native people, whose numbers—about 2,000 individuals, or 400 families—rivalled those of the Six Nations themselves. Squatters acquired this land in one of two ways: by simply settling there or by purchasing directly from Native people. Both modes were illegal, but the latter left the squatter vulnerable to a manoeuvre employed by a number of Six Nations and other Native chiefs. After selling the land, the chiefs would complain to the Indian Department that their property was illegally occupied, the hapless squatter would be evicted, and the process would start all over again. By such schemes some Native people profited within the shadowy world of squatting. For the most part, settlers squatted on Iroquois and other Native lands with virtual impunity, gaining a cheap entry to a farming future.[41]

Other settlers leased land. In 1848, two out of every five farms were leased and tenants were bulked in the richer agricultural areas. By 1871, tenancy had declined to one in six farms, but the pattern was the same: the richer and longer-settled agricultural districts contained the majority of tenants. Interestingly, tenants tended to be concentrated in the areas that had been most marked by the activity of speculators during the early years of settlement. As one historical geographer concludes, 'It appears that Ontario was still living under the shadow of the pork barrel land granting to government favourites that dated back to the beginning of the century.'[42]

By the 1840s, the bushland of Grey County, where William Benson and his family finally settled, was Upper Canada's last best west. It was still largely undeveloped; we know that in 1852 Benson had to transport his wheat 70 kilometres for milling. (The miller would likely have received a share of the produce for his services.) Even in Peel County, one of the richer farming areas in the colony, many of the farmers had not, by 1861, 'moved beyond the primitive amenities of a pioneer society'. The many challenges faced by Wilson Benson and his family were common for people of his class in rural Upper Canada. Untold numbers simply abandoned their plots or were evicted by creditors, 'picked', as one farmer put it, 'as bare as a bird's ass'. The challenge of 'making it' in rural Upper Canada is further suggested by the number of properties over eight years in tax arrears: between 1828 and 1830, the majority of townships had over one-fifth of their properties in arrears; the penalty for non-payment was to forfeit the land.[43]

To 'make it' often necessitated more than one move. Scattered evidence suggests that acquiring land became quite difficult as early as the 1840s. The settlement of Euphrasia Township in Grey County in the late 1840s provides an excellent example of this process. In 1851, 70 per cent of Euphrasia's ninety-seven household heads had lived elsewhere in Upper Canada. Most had spent at least three years at their previous place of residence. Moves were dictated by capital needs and, equally importantly, by the stage of family composition. No one moved to Euphrasia without at least two dependents; most families, like that of Wilson Benson, already had children of working age when they arrived. Movement was pronounced even in rich agricultural regions: close to two-thirds of all freeholders in Peel County in 1861 left the county during the next decade. Those who were most successful tended to be those who arrived first and commandeered the best land; Benson's being one of the first to settle in Artemesia Township and staying in that area is consistent with this. Later arrivals predominated among those who yet again pulled up stakes—often, in the 1860s, moving with family and other

William Eliot, *Spectacle in a Tavern at Mosa, 1845*. Drinking was commonplace in nineteenth-century Upper Canada. In the 1830s, William 'Tiger' Dunlop observed—ironically, no doubt—that Upper Canada 'may be pronounced the most healthy country under the sun, considering that whiskey can be procured for about one shilling sterling per gallon'. In 1817, the Yorkshire naturalist Charles Fothergill remarked on the 'indelicacy' that prevailed in the colony's taverns: 'decent and even pretty girls hawking and spitting about the room, occasionally scratching and rubbing themselves and lounging in attitudes in their chairs in a way that in Britain would be unpardonable.' J.J. Talman Regional Collection, University of Western Ontario.

kin as far west as Manitoba in search of a secure farming future.[44]

To make ends meet, some farmers also kept stores or taverns or worked as timber contractors, putting their earnings toward the purchase of more land in order to provide adequately for their sons. Frederick William Richardson, a shoe-maker from Ireland who arrived in the Ottawa Valley in 1819, was one such. Supplementing farming with timber contracting, he amassed enough acreage to set up six sons and two grandsons on their own farms. The sale of forestry products such as timber and potash probably tided many families over the land-clearing phase, when returns from the farm itself would have been minimal. In some cases, the connection was even more intimate. Under the agroforestry system, a lumber company such as the Hamilton Brothers of the Ottawa Valley would own farms and lease them to tenants whose produce would help to feed the company's employees. Woodworkers themselves often farmed part-time to supplement their

Eliza Harris, *Moving Day*, c. 1848. In this humorous sketch, Eliza Harris (b. 1825), a member of a well-to-do London family, pokes fun at the gendered division of work. J.J. Talman Regional Collection, D.B. Weldon Library, University of Western Ontario.

wages—a practice that the Hamilton Brothers exploited to justify reducing salaries and hiring only on a seasonal basis.

In 1836, John Dunbar Moodie, who had a few years earlier settled north of Peterborough with his wife, Susanna, warned a brother-in-law in Britain who was contemplating emigration that 'Canada has often been called the country for the poor man'; however, 'the poor man here without industry, or who from habit or weakness is unable to endure hard labour is indeed in a deplorable condition,— and meets with no compassion.' Moreover, Moodie noted, 'Farmers only profit from the labour of their own families.' Like most farms, most families were still just resources in the making. The average rural home in 1850 held 6.4 people, but half of the rural population were children—indeed, for most years following 1812, Upper Canada's population increased more from births than from immigration. Few families had sufficient labour power—that is, grown sons. As early as age eight, children were expected to assist in planting and burning. For most rural children, seasonal farm work continued to take precedence over school attendance. Rural schools developed haphazardly until legislation was passed in 1846 instituting a more formal, centralized system throughout rural Upper Canada. Of his boyhood on his brother's farm north of York in the early 1820s, Methodist preacher John Carroll recalled, it was 'frugal fare and work, work, work'. It proved to be too much for Carroll: at age twelve he ran away to York.[45]

Women were essential members of the rural workforce. Upper Canadian women were more likely to marry—and to marry early—than their European counterparts. In 1791, William Chewett, a land surveyor, announced that after 'mature and deliberate consideration . . . [I] found a girl whom I mean to make a partner for life, and without which it is impossible to exist in this settlement'. One male settler noted that 'a capital help-mate . . . can do the work of a man, as well as her own domestic duties.' A black settler recalled of his wife, '[she] worked right along with me . . . for we were raised slaves, the women accustomed to work. . . . I did not realize it then; but now I see she was a brave woman.'[46]

Even those raised for a gentler life did much more than clean house. 'I had', Susanna Moodie confessed, 'a hard struggle with my pride before I would consent to lend the least assistance on the farm, but . . . Providence had placed me in a situation where I was called upon to work.' Anne Langton, who confessed to being 'somewhat too tenderly bred for a backwoodswoman', made candles, butchered and cured meat, baked, sewed, washed, gardened, cooked, and glazed windows. More generally, farm women worked with livestock, butter, cheese, poultry, eggs, and fruit and sold these products at a local market, in all probability keeping control of the earnings such work generated. Recalling the money she brought to her family by fruit and vegetable farming, Damarais Smith concluded that it took far too long to 'bring the old-time wheat farmer to see the necessity of fruit and vegetables for a family'.[47]

In urban areas the notion of separate spheres increasingly held that a women's place was in the home; extrafamilial relations were the proper sphere of the husband. Anne Langton voiced the optimistic view when she implied that rural women had greater agency: they were not 'contented to be looked apon as belonging merely to the decorative department of the establishment'. For Sarah Hill, however, farm life in Hope Township was often unbearable: between January and November 1844, Sarah recorded in her diary eighteen instances of verbal and/or physical abuse from her husband, Edwin. 'Mr. Hill so very irritable that I am constantly in a flutter at the breast', she confided in January. In May she lamented 'going to so lonely a place, his temper at times is so awful.' By November matters were far worse: 'He became *outrageous* threw the clothes off *me & became extremely violent*. I kept up my spirits but the agitation caused me to lose a great deal of blood. I think we must part, he is so very insulting—he is the most insolent & self indulgent man I ever saw.' He died ten years later but, despite the continual abuse, Sarah, in the diary she maintained for the next twenty-seven years, never referred to him as other than her 'dear husband'.[48]

Illness and injury were omnipresent features of rural life. In his first year at Orangeville, Wilson Benson cut his foot and was unable to walk for six weeks. In the early 1860s, his wife and youngest daughter died (he remarried soon after). In the ten years between 1863 and 1873, he nearly died in an incident with a runaway horse, broke his ribs in a fall from a hay loft, and crushed his arm, leg, and head in a threshing-machine accident, after which he never regained the strength to continue farming.

Horse-related injuries were especially common—perhaps not surprising given the state of the roads. Some roads were constructed and maintained by private companies that charged tolls for their use. Yet even as late as 1893, two-thirds

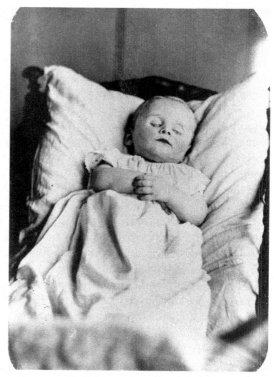

Anonymous child, c. 1870. Taken in a position of repose a few hours after death, a posthumous portrait was a common way for bereaved parents to remember their lost children, and post-mortem photography was a staple for many photographic businesses. In rural Upper Canada, children were far less likely than adults to survive illness or injury. The records of James Langstaff, a rural doctor in Richmond Hill, show that in the 1860s, one of every forty children he visited died; the rate for adults was only one in one hundred; over the four decades between 1850 and 1890, one in every six or seven babies did not live through childhood. Nor were the odds necessarily better for the children of doctors themselves: eight of the Langstaffs' own eleven children did not survive infancy. Photographic Collection, University of Waterloo Library.

of all expenditures on township roads and bridges came from statute labour (labour that residents of the district were required by law to perform) or from money paid in lieu thereof, and as a consequence the work was often badly done. Moreover, supervision was left to local residents, usually prominent farmers, and these 'pathmasters' tended to ensure the maintenance of sections near their properties at others' expense. 'In the spring, and fall of the year', complained a resident of Lanark County, 'it is scarcely possible to pass where the road has a descent. In these places the mud is from three to five feet deep. In passing horses are generally breast high, sometimes almost covered in it.' According to the Reverend Daniel Allan of London, roads were 'more properly speaking mud canals'. City-dwellers might complain, but farmers—by far the majority of the population—made do. In any case, most farm produce was sent to market during the winter months, when cartwheels were replaced by runners that slipped easily over snow-covered roads. One farmer's diary indicates that he made 75 per cent of his off-farm trips during the four winter months. No doubt, as another farmer noted in 1817, the fact that 'business is mostly contrived to be done by sleighing' contributed to 'the neglect of the roads'.[49]

For many farm households, the challenges of frontier life were eased by proximity to friends and family—relatives often lived only a few kilometres apart. Land was kept within cultural and kin groups, and families often wrote back to their home country to encourage other family members to emigrate. As James Rapson, a sawyer who had settled with two other families on the Grand River near Galt in the early 1830s, noted, 'we all assists one another, as well as we can'.[50] Many farmers also hired seasonal help, took in boarders, and invited friends and relatives to work bees, where they would help out with some large job in return for generous quantities of food and drink.

Susanna and John Moodie were typical in many respects. At times the Moodies hired occasional help (whom they could not afford to pay) and leased some of their land to tenants on a share-crop basis. Susanna's sister and brother-in-law lived, for a time, close by and helped when they could, but they too were struggling to manage a farm with a young family and insufficient cash. Susanna had just given birth at the start of the arduous year in which she managed the farm in the absence of her husband, who, like many farmers, had been forced to seek work off the farm in order to make ends meet. She already had several children under the age of eight—truly a family in the making. During this time, especially during periods of sickness, Susanna found the greatest support from 'the disinterested kindness of my female neighbours'.[51]

Many people on the rural frontier had supportive links with a broader community. Agricultural societies, designed to assist inexperienced farmers, held regular meetings where farmers could display their produce and livestock and share information (twenty-five were established before 1840 and thirty-three followed in the 1840s). The Orange Lodge, a fraternal order originally formed to support Protestantism in Ireland, proliferated throughout Upper Canada in the 1830s and 1840s and offered not only social activities, some poor assistance, and funeral support, but—as we shall see—considerable political clout.

Yet there was also a much harsher reality. When Presbyterian minister Daniel Allan set out on foot to visit his rural flock, he was subjected 'to the taunts and insolence and scorn of every vulgar waggoner and Sleigh-driver . . . merely because I couldn't afford to gratify his thirst for gold by an extravagant fee for hurling me a few miles thro the wilderness'. Wilson Benson lost a house and an acre of land to a sharp speculator, and he once had eight bushels of his wheat stolen from the local mill, very likely by a fellow Irishman. Work bees were not always occasions for the expression of brotherly love: one rural magistrate 'used to go away to the woods when [he] heard there was a fight at a bee, and keep away until the blood had cooled down'. Formal law enforcement was chancy at best. Even Susanna Moodie sheltered a man for whom 'a warrant was out' from the local sheriff.

One way of encouraging compliance with community norms was to stage a charivari—a raucous concert, typically performed on pots and pans, in which citizens would express their opinion of some dubious person or behaviour. An unusual wedding—say, between partners of widely differing ages—was a classic occasion for a charivari. In 1857 in the village of Tavistock (near Stratford), an angry crowd chased a prostitute and her client away from a hotel and continued to pursue them until they handed over an acceptable sum of cash. And in 1872, residents of Sand Point, in southeastern Ontario, disciplined a labourer caught stealing a coat by painting him with tar and parading him around the hamlet on a pump.[52]

Less dramatic but probably more effective at setting standards were the church committees that sat in judgement on members accused of transgressions in any number of areas: behaviour within the family, business practice, sexual conduct, leisure activities. Without confession and repentance, the person 'found stirring up strife' would often be expelled from the congregation. Presbyterian and Baptist Church disciplinary committees reinforced patriarchal relations within families: the husband was expected to rule 'his own house as becometh a Christian'. Allegations of wife and child abuse were rarely taken seriously by Presbyterians. Like the more secular charivari, the disciplinary activities of the local church reflected both the absence of boundaries between public and private spaces and the primacy of community values over what we now regard as individual rights. At a time when the police and judicial systems were only beginning to develop, these were important ways to enforce compliance with community norms.[53]

Community rarely meant equality. The ability to define community norms was often simply a matter of power. Especially before the mid-nineteenth century, rural magistrates and constables rarely acted against the wishes of influential citizens; in the Newcastle district, we know of fifty cases of assault on constables and magistrates between 1813 and 1840. In the Brantford area, two gangs 'often join[ed] forces to club quiet citizens left and right'. The 'swamp angels' terrorized residents in Grey County. In Durham Township, a group of self-appointed 'social regulators' called themselves the Cavan Blazers. An overtly criminal organization known as the Markham Gang operated with impunity northeast of Toronto in the 1830s and early 1840s, as did the Ribble family in Elgin county in the early 1830s.[54]

Individuals without family support were especially at risk. In 1859, in a small village near Guelph, a destitute mother and child sought assistance at the home of two bachelors; when the men refused to help, the woman collapsed and died. In 1839, a girl named Julia Higgins, working for the Cruden family near Brantford, was found 'in the most wretched condition literally naked filthy and full of bruises so much so one would hardly suppose her a human being'. It appeared that Mrs Cruden had been the worst abuser. The local magistrate judged the case to involve merely a 'petty assault', and the Crudens got off with a fine. This was not the only violent incident in which the Crudens were implicated. Almost as soon as John Thompson, a newly arrived settler, purchased a farm from them, the Crudens began vandalizing his property and physically harassing him in an effort to drive him away and enable them to reclaim the farm. Thompson received only reluctant support from the magistrate, who was loath to confront a powerful local family on behalf of a stranger. After carefully analyzing the Cruden affair, one historian has concluded that 'the gap between [the] expectation that the "myth of the poor man's country" engendered and the boredom, isolation, illness, incessant labour, and desperation which accompanied settlement created tensions peculiar to rural areas.' Such frustrations were taken out on authority figures such as magistrates and on respectable farmers such as Thompson. And, most ominously, these frustrations were exacted on those who were weakest and lowest on the social scale, vulnerable and isolated individuals like Julia Higgins.[55]

Most literature written in Upper Canada ignored this dark side of life. But John Richardson, Upper Canada's most celebrated novelist, revelled in it. In his novel *Wacousta*, he adopted the Romantic Gothic genre, but within that form he wrote in a brutally realistic manner of violence in war, in revenge, in sex, and in Native–European relations. While the Romantic form he adopted remained at odds with the realism he attempted to convey, Richardson touched the violent underpinnings of frontier society and exposed, in a way no other Upper Canadian author did, the tensions between authority and individualism. 'The colonial writer', twentieth-century Canadian poet Dennis Lee has noted, 'does not have words of his own.' While falling short, Richardson, in his unique exposé of violence, went further than any of his contemporaries in search of those words.[56]

Richardson was largely ignored by fellow colonists: 'I have seen but too much of Canadians', Richardson once reflected, 'not to be quite sensible that they would far more rejoice in a grand distiller of whiskey than a writer of books.' Yet like Richardson, aspects of popular culture reflected Upper Canada's dark underside. Drawing on a complex set of folk beliefs, rural families fashioned a range of 'decorations' designed to ward off undesirable elements of both human and natural/spiritual origin. Belief in the curative and demonic power of signs, symbols, and spirits conditioned the everyday life of rural dwellers. Many of these folk beliefs had European origins and were brought to Upper Canada by early settlers. Settlers of German origin, for example, placed hex signs on barns, furniture, and implements to ward off evil and encourage good spirits. Settlers often planted a tree on both sides of a log cabin's doorway to symbolize each spouse; on the death of a husband or wife, one tree would be cut down. The symbol of the fallen tree would often reappear on the deceased spouse's tombstone. This practice dates back to the ancient Celts in Britain. Quilt designs were particularly rich symbolically: made by wives, quilts were in a very real sense the last line of protection against the secular and spirit worlds, as well as yet another indication of the important role played by women in the defence of the home. In addition to providing warmth, quilts could encourage fertility, passionate love, long life, providence, or strength, depending on the design. These symbols were known and respected by all. They testify to a folk culture, a collective understanding that dramatically separates the rural world of early Upper Canada from our world today.[57]

Even the power of rural folk beliefs, however, proved insufficient to sustain Susanna Moodie's farming career. Near the end of her year alone, Susanna Moodie wrote to her husband, 'I Know not what to do about the farm, and I am so dispirited that I care nothing about it. I have no money to hire labour to cut the grain and the crop is but indifferent. I fear I cannot even let it on shares. . . . Jorys and Garbut [labourers they had previously hired] dun me constantly. Oh heaven keep me from being in these miserable circumstances another year. Such another winter as the last will pile the turf over my head.'[58]

In 1840, the Moodies abandoned the struggle. He became sheriff for Hastings County, while she continued to write and publish; her best-known work, the classic *Roughing It in the Bush*, appeared in 1852. But in quitting the farm, let alone in their later employment, the Moodies were exceptional. Between 1851 and 1871, the number of industrial workers in the province doubled, but as a proportion of the total workforce they increased by only one percentage point. In fact, during the 1860s, when many Ontario farm families were moving west to Manitoba, their places were quickly filled by urban labourers; in central Ontario, of the labourers listed in the 1861 census who could be traced to 1871, almost four in ten had become farmers.[59]

Was this an example of a perpetual cycle of the poor replacing the poor? 'Affairs along the lake', a Georgina Township resident lamented in November 1830, 'show very much the same, misery and poverty being the usual habitans.' As late as 1914, most Ontario farm women would still be lugging water to the house from more than 15 metres away, and only one farm in ten would have indoor plumbing. Assessment evidence dating from the 1840s points to the beginning of the regional differentiation that would characterize southern Ontario in the late twentieth century. A band of wealth stretched along the north shore of Lake Ontario from the Bay of Quinte to the head of the lake and into the Niagara Peninsula and London area. Farther east, per capita assessment returns fell by nearly half. Yet micro studies of rural migration in Upper Canada and elsewhere in North America and Europe emphasize the importance of the family as actor as much as the reality of constrictive environmental factors. Undoubtedly the majority of farmers on the move were poor, but they were far from helpless and passive. Within often rigid social and economic constraints, they strove to preserve and perpetuate their family values and household integrity, often establishing a life in the New World superior to what they had left in the old.[60]

Nevertheless, for those who, like Wilson Benson, did succeed in establishing a measure of stability in their lives, the process was fraught with pitfalls beyond their control. Rural Upper Canada did not provide equal opportunities for all. Rampant land speculation gave enormous advantages to those who arrived first. Family connections and cultural background could as easily lead to exclusion and misery as to acceptance and success. In order to find a congenial place, many had to move more than once. As on other colonial frontiers, progress was measured in acres cleared, wetlands drained, and bushels harvested. In the process, Native people were displaced and nature despoiled. In the typical parlance of the time, the white man's conquest of the wilderness was all but complete.

Place, Power, and Polity: The Emergence of Upper Canada and the Canadian Confederation, 1791–1867

Sophisticated studies of Upper Canadian political thought by historian Syd Wise point to a unique vision held for the colony by its governing elite: a fiercely maintained divine mission to create a North American polity that demonstrated the sanctity of British monarchical and status-oriented values. These values were formed in reaction to the Enlightenment-inspired French and American revolutions and developed in direct opposition to the alleged materialistic, individualistic, and democratic orientation of the American republic to the south. For Wise and other scholars, these values set the boundaries to colonial political debate.[1]

While accepting much of this depiction, more recent historians have added breadth and depth to the study of Upper Canadian politics. Jeffrey McNairn persuasively argues that political discussion was much less restrained than some have suggested, showing that Upper Canadians borrowed freely and strategically from pre-revolutionary Enlightenment discussions of democracy and political culture. Moreover, he deepens the focus from what elites said to the study of a broader discourse engaged in by a surprisingly wide range of Upper Canadian individuals, a discourse that he locates in the 'public sphere'. These political discussions, which were aired in the press and debated in a variety of public and private associations, led to the creation of a deliberative democracy or, as McNairn avers, 'to changes in the principles that legitimated authority within the colony and thus dictated changes to those structures'.[2]

Other scholars have helped us to understand the extent to which the public discourse analyzed by McNairn was itself the product of struggle. Most notably, Carol Wilton, through the study of public petitions, Paul Romney, through studies of the judiciary and reform activism, and Bruce Curtis, on the growth of the bureaucratic state, have demonstrated the extent to which political action extended beyond the lieutenant-governor, his councils, and the Assembly to encompass bureaucrats and the actions of even those without the right to vote. Building on the work of these scholars, while continuing to recognize the importance of individuals' social and economic positions and of wider institutional structures as conditioners of, in this case, degrees of political agency, this chapter considers the development of place, power, and polity in early-nineteenth-century Upper Canada/Ontario, a process that set the boundaries for political, economic, and cultural change thereafter.[3]

Rural-Urban Divide?

In the nineteenth century, differences between rural and urban life were not clear-cut: the distinctions that we see today emerged only gradually. Cities in Upper Canada developed slowly even by North American standards; on the eve of the War of 1812, Kingston was the only settlement of more than 1,000. York's population soon rivalled Kingston's, but these were small communities: there were scarcely 300 men over the age of twenty in York in the mid-1820s. By 1851, thirty-three communities boasted more than 1,000 people, yet only 15 per cent of the colony's inhabitants resided in such centres. In 1871, the province's urban dwellers constituted less than one-quarter of the province's population. Urban places remained small and dispersed: ninety-six communities exceeded 1,000 people, and the two largest, Toronto and Hamilton, together contained only one-quarter of the province's urban population; Montreal, by contrast, contained two-fifths of Quebec's urban population.

For decades to come, the great majority of the colony's people—not just farmers but also industrial workers—would live in the country. By the time of Confederation, the largest manufacturers were to be found in the cities, but many smaller firms were still craft-based and rural. In the era before railways, urban places emerged and evolved to serve the activities of farmers. Nevertheless, as those who aspired to power gravitated to them, cities became hubs of activity—political, administrative, commercial, industrial, legal, religious, educational, cultural—out of all proportion to their size. And Upper Canada's first lieutenant-governor was determined to facilitate that process.

Power, Place, and Politics, 1791–1812

'Every establishment of Church and State that upholds the distinction of ranks and lessens the undue weight of the democratic influence, ought to be introduced', declared John Graves Simcoe in 1792. In his wilderness domain, Upper Canada's first lieutenant-governor hoped to create a society mirroring the English one he had left behind—a society ruled by a landed aristocracy (through the appointed executive and legislative councils), a state church (the Church of England), and a small bureaucratic elite (at York). Indeed, Simcoe's plans for York, his newly designated capital, nicely reflected his aims: lots around the waterfront and larger, 100-acre park lots were reserved for the bureaucratic elite; smaller lots were allotted to shopkeepers and artisans. 'You will smile perhaps', Richard Cartwright confided to a friend, 'when I tell you that even at York a Town Lot is to be granted in the Front Street only on condition that you build a house of not less than 47 Feet Front, two Stories High and after a certain Order of Architecture. . . . [I]t is only in the back Streets and Allies that the Tinkers and Tailors will be allowed to consult their own Taste and Circumstance.' 'Seriously,' he concluded, 'our good Governor is a little wild in his projects.'[4]

Wild, perhaps, but serious nonetheless. Simcoe first attempted to dislodge a powerful commercial elite that predated his arrival and to establish in their place a small band of British bureaucrats centred at York. He failed. The commercial, not the bureaucratic, elite spanned Upper Canada. Merchants stood at the centre of Upper Canada's economy. Between the late 1780s and the eve of the War of 1812, several powerful and interlocking mercantile ventures at Detroit, Niagara, and Kingston exercised significant economic, administrative, and legal power. The Cartwrights of Kingston, the Hamiltons of Niagara, and the Askins of Detroit—all linked to the Todd and McGill fur-trading families of Montreal—headed the list. A system of long credit, settled in terms of goods and/or cash, underlay rural enterprise. Local merchants obtained goods on twelve months' credit from urban wholesalers. Up to roughly the 1850s, urban wholesalers practised a general business in order to protect themselves from fluctuation in any particular commodity, and imported goods (usually from Great Britain) on a similar twelve-month credit basis.[5]

While bureaucrats aped British procedures, customs, and social styles and exhibited disdain for all things American, these were not the views of most Upper Canadians. Indeed, by 1812 about 60 per cent of Upper Canadians were recently arrived American immigrants. Merchants such as the Loyalist Richard Cartwright and the Scottish-born Robert Hamilton traded, visited, and regularly communicated with Americans to the south. Throughout the 1790s and into the new century, Loyalists were renewing ties of friendship and kinship with those they had left behind in the 1780s.[6]

To rule effectively, Simcoe had to recognize the power of the commercial elite. Merchants and bureaucrats had to coexist. And so they did. Robert Hamilton owned one of the finest homes in Upper Canada; Simcoe supped there contentedly. From the outset, merchants sat on the appointed legislative and executive councils—the presumed preserve, it will be recalled, of the gentry. A form of gentlemanly capitalism characterized early Upper Canadian growth. A relatively small number of patrician-merchants promoted canal construction in the 1820s, founded banks, and even attempted to underwrite railroad development in the 1830s.

Social life in tiny York, the colony's capital, was an incestuous round of balls and suppers. Bureaucrat's wives vied to control the social calendar in the hopes of advancing their husbands' fortunes. Whom you dined, danced, and dallied with mattered. Anne Powell, wife of the chief justice, underlined the importance of a ball to honour the Queen in 1806 when she wrote, 'rank will be settled and I fear some who claim precedence, will find themselves of less importance than they expect.' Upper-class women were far from retired belles closeted in protected homes. In social affairs—affairs so central to political success—they were on the front lines. They did, of course, have help in running their households. There may have been as many as three hundred slaves at Niagara in 1791. However, legislation passed in 1793 forbade bringing slaves into Upper Canada after that date, making slaveholding an option for only a minority of the colony's elite. Already in the early nineteenth century the hiring and keeping of servants was a matter of great concern.[7]

A strong proprietary attitude surrounded the issue of office-holding: one could own offices and bequeath them to one's heirs. Sixty per cent of the major appointments made at York between 1803 and 1812 went to members of established families. Intermarriage, liberal land grants, proper education, and conspicuous consumption helped both to solidify the emerging commercial-bureaucratic elite and to separate it from the mass of Upper Canada's settlers. But the emerging commercial-bureaucratic elite did not enjoy unquestioned control.[8]

Although rural and urban merchants were generally better off than the farmers on whom they depended for business, their control was far from absolute. Debt constricted the operations even of large merchants. When Robert Hamilton—a man who profited from a monopoly over trade with the military and who had a hand in most economic and financial matters in the Niagara region—died in 1809, his mercantile affairs were in a state of bankruptcy, with £69,000 owed him by 1,200 debtors; his heirs failed to collect about a third of that sum. But large merchants had other means of subsistence: Hamilton bequeathed 130,000 acres of land, a benefice that allowed his family to maintain a privileged position in society. Few merchants could match that level of acquisitiveness. Throughout the colony's history, prices for goods were sensitive more to general market conditions than to the exercise of arbitrary local exploitation. The cost of goods in Napanee in southeastern Upper Canada in the 1830s was similar to that in Niagara, at the other end of Lake Ontario. Competition was intense: by 1846, 160 Upper Canadian villages boasted at least two stores. Itinerant hawkers and peddlers fanned out across the colony, wholesalers competed in urban centres, and farmers shopped around.[9]

Justices of the peace were often merchants, but settlers were sometimes able to use the courts to protect their own interests. In the early nineteenth century, district juries composed of small landowners occasionally overturned judicial decisions or handed down lenient sentences in matters of debt repayment, despite court displeasure. Cartwright and Hamilton complained, correctly, that the first Upper Canadian assembly (1792–6) was decidedly anti-mercantile. Elitist political leaders such as D.W. Smith, the acting deputy surveyor general, echoed that lament. Smith referred to the electors as 'peasants' and worried about the 'violent levelling principles' held by rural Assembly members. He was particularly upset by town meetings, a form of American political activity that he believed usurped the functions of the elected Assembly. Perhaps even more disturbing was the fact that such activities were independent of the lieutenant-governor's patronage, of which Smith himself was a recipient. Grievances escalated as settlers saw their taxes used to build schools located too far away for their own children to attend; imperial administrators raised land-settlement fees, padding their own pockets in the process; and the right to seize land for debts became legal in the colony even though it was illegal in the mother country.[10]

Robert Thorpe, an Anglo-Irish judge of the Court of King's Bench, became a spokesman for some of the discontented. His views reflected those of an Irish Whig group who believed that the assembly, not the Crown and its representative the lieutenant-governor, should have primary power within the British colonial system. Frustrated when he was not appointed chief justice in 1806, Thorpe criticized what he considered the oppressive actions of the Scottish clique at the centre of power. While on his judicial rounds in the central and western regions, he encouraged jurors to express their opinions on civil affairs. Their comments reflected the frustration felt by small farmers, many of them Loyalists, with respect to land-settlement fees and the perceived Scots hegemony both locally (the Hamilton family at Niagara) and at York. Despite his position on the court, Thorpe successfully ran for election to the Assembly in 1807. Then, in June 1807, Joseph Willcocks—a fellow Irishman, allied to Thorpe, who had been dismissed from his position as sheriff of the Home District for 'general and notorious bad conduct'— moved to Niagara and set up the young colony's first opposition newspaper, the *Upper Canadian Guardian and Freeman's Journal.*

Even though Thorpe stopped well short of promoting rebellion, York's bureaucrats and Niagara's 'shopkeepers' alike saw him as a troublemaker. Willcocks's new publication was the last straw. After all, both Thorpe's encouragement of independent commentary on the part of jurists (the lieutenant-governor, Francis Gore, saw that as an 'attempt to poison the minds of the lower order of the people') and Willcocks's publication of an oppositionist paper extended the arena of political debate outside of the Assembly and councils, making official control of the 'public mind' more difficult. Closing ranks against the 'desperados', the lieutenant-governor enlisted William Allan, a Scots merchant and the postmaster at York, to open Thorpe's mail, and arranged to bribe US postmasters to 'procure a sight of the letters address'd to the [opposition] parties'. When the *Guardian* printed a petition signed by 350 Thorpe supporters, mostly small landowners, the Executive Council compiled a blacklist of 64 names sorted into five categories: 'ignorant, but may be trusted' (7 names), 'ignorant and not to be trusted' (1), 'a little of the rogue' (36), 'a very great rogue' (8), and 'a dangerous fellow' (12). Finally, suspended by the imperial government, Thorpe left Upper Canada in July 1807.[11]

Petty jealousies certainly played a part, but the Thorpe affair was more than a falling-out within the bureaucratic elite. The affair can be seen as the first concerted attempt in Upper Canada to transfer power from the Crown and lieutenant-governor to the assembly while maintaining allegiance to the British connection. In this sense it can be seen as a precursor to the pressure for responsible government that emerged under the leadership of the Irish-born William Warren Baldwin and his son Robert in the 1820s and 1830s. Indeed, even in the short term, the discontent for which Thorpe served as a lightning rod did not disappear with his departure. Willcocks's *Guardian*, lamented one member of the elite, seemed to be in every household in the Western District. In 1808, Willcocks unsuccessfully attempted to gain the right to publish extracts from the Assembly's journals, which would have facilitated an unthinkable intrusion by the public into Assembly affairs.[12]

Religious matters added fuel to the rising discontent. Methodism, which had originated in England as an evangelical movement within the established church, came to Upper Canada in an American-influenced form with the Loyalists. Whereas the Anglicans stressed acceptance of the social hierarchy and deference to one's 'betters', the Methodists—the colony's largest religious group—emphasized fellowship, free choice, and individual salvation. Since most Methodists—indeed, most settlers—were of American background, their religion also represented the potential for a sense of community with the republic south of the border.

Methodist practice undermined the hierarchical values at the centre of Anglicanism. Methodist clergy generally came from the lower ranks of society and preached in a forthright, energetic, even boisterous fashion. All classes mingled on the fields where Methodist camp meetings were held. Methodism played an important social role in bringing rural people together: in 1805, some 2,500 worshippers attended a camp meeting at Hay Bay that extended over several days. Many experienced what the itinerant preacher Nathan Bangs called the 'jerks': 'a spark of Divine power' that shocked worshippers, causing them to lose control and twitch, roll, sing, and fall to the ground. This, Bangs said, was God relating directly to the individual, delivering the people 'from bondage' and bringing them 'into liberty'. Such communal religious experiences enhanced self-worth and helped create an identity separate from that of the merchant-bureaucratic elite at Kingston, York, and Niagara. How long could the social order survive if such behaviour were tolerated?[13]

Men and women, boys and girls could, as individuals, experience God's will. One woman who felt the call of God at Hay Bay left her husband and, supported by other women, continued her spiritual journey, exulting in the freedom of becoming a 'new creature in Christ'. How long could the patriarchal family order survive if such independence were permitted? A wife's place, after all, was within the home tending to children, cooking, and housekeeping. Small wonder the Anglican-dominated elite forbade Methodist ministers to conduct marriages. 'To regulate a family and keep children in proper subordination is much more difficult than is commonly supposed', John Strachan, a prominent Anglican minister and schoolteacher, lamented in 1812. He linked what he perceived to be the breakdown of the regulated family to a republican spirit loose throughout the colony.[14]

Strachan saw the links between Methodism and reformism, and recognized the danger that the Methodists' 'republican ideas of independence and individual freedom' represented. He urged the Anglican clergy to 'outpreach and outpractice our opponents'. But the Methodist clergy outnumbered their Anglican counterparts by two to one and enjoyed a virtual monopoly on the rural circuits, which they travelled on horseback while the Anglicans stayed put in their urban parishes. Additional tactics were required. Thus, Anglicans frequently questioned the moral character of Methodist preachers, and when Methodist ministers were elected to the Assembly, they were forbidden to take their seats, simply on the basis of their religion. Willcocks and his supporters, some of whom were themselves Methodist, deplored such tactics and did their best to fight back.[15]

Gradually, the composition of the Assembly changed to reflect this dissatisfaction. By 1812, under the loose leadership of Willcocks, eleven broadly reform-oriented members (out of twenty-three members in all) were generally voting together, arguing for legislative control of money bills, lower salaries for bureaucrats, lower assessment rates, and a loosening of the regulations (such as a stringent definition of 'Loyalist') that made it more difficult for settlers to obtain land grants. In 1812, however, the emerging Reform movement suffered a serious blow.

The War of 1812

Relations with Americans had stabilized after 1794, when Britain ceded its western forts to the United States, but the situation changed with the renewal of French–British conflict in the early nineteenth century. Believing that America supported France, Britain attacked an American frigate, the *Chesapeake*, in 1807, and also began to arm and supply Native groups on the western frontier. These Native peoples were never simply British allies. Between 1803 and 1805, western Native peoples had been forced to cede some 12 million hectares of land to American settlers. Already animated by a millenarian religion preached by the prophet Tenskwatawa, western Native people eagerly listened to militant messages put forward by Tenskwatawa's brother, the Shawnee chief Tecumseh. Despite British attempts to keep Native peoples on a short leash, by the fall of 1811 the Native frontier was a virtual war zone. Harassed on the seas, frustrated on the frontier, and convinced that American-born Upper Canadians awaited deliverance, the United States declared war on Britain in June 1812.

Senior Upper Canadian civil and military personnel also doubted the people's loyalty—and not without reason. When General Isaac Brock attempted to impose a form of military rule, the Assembly refused to comply. About half of the Upper Canadians summoned for militia duty between 1812 and 1814 failed to appear, and those who did rarely stayed long. Some deserted; others solicited from the Americans a 'parole of honour', promising, in return for their freedom, to refrain from fighting for the rest of the war.

From the outset, American tactics were faulty: as one top-ranking British commander admitted in 1814, while the British had done much, 'we also owe as much if not more to the perverse stupidity of the Enemy; the Impolicy of their plans [and] the dissensions of their Commanders.' Instead of severing Upper Canada from Lower Canada (the source of supplies and personnel) by attacking Kingston and Montreal, the Americans, underestimating the combined strength of Native, British regular, and militia forces, concentrated on the Detroit River and the Niagara region. Aided by Native warriors—Tecumseh at Detroit and the Mohawk Captain John Norton at Queenston Heights—the British won dramatic early victories. Although Brock lost his life at the latter battle, some 900 Americans were captured and as many as 500 were killed. The British lost only 15 regulars, with some 22 missing, plus an undetermined number of Mohawk deaths. Yet these victories only temporarily eased local dissent. Indeed, militia participation peaked before Brock's death and declined dramatically thereafter. In April 1813, 1,700 Americans sacked York. While British regulars were criticized, the reality was that Upper Canadians had virtually refused to assist in the battle. During the Americans' three-day occupation, nearly every militiaman in the Home District (the administrative district within which York was situated) negotiated a parole. Governor General Sir George Prevost responded by appointing agents to root out 'traitors'. Fearing that appointed government agencies would be strengthened at the expense of the elected assembly, many reform leaders, including Willcocks, left the colony, some to fight on the American side.[16]

Surviving warriors of the Six Nations Indians, Brantford, July 1882. These veterans of the War of 1812 are, from the left, Jacob Warner, 92; John Turtle, 91; and John Smoke Johnson, 93. Johnson said he did not scalp anyone in the war; he thought the practice was brutal. NA C85127.

In the summer and fall of 1813, Americans won several victories in the Niagara and Lake Erie regions. Information provided by the much-celebrated heroine Laura Secord, a thirty-seven-year-old Upper Canadian settler, may have aided British forces in repulsing Americans at Beaver Dams, but Iroquois assistance was far more important: the Iroquois acted as scouts, ambushers, light infantry, and flanking units in the Niagara region. On Lake Erie and in the western region, the Americans enjoyed more lasting success. Indeed, the Erie conflict shattered Tecumseh's confederation. Abandoned by the British, Tecumseh and 500 followers were decimated by 3,000 Americans at Morristown on the Thames River. Peace talks between Americans and 3,000 Native warriors commenced in July 1814, months before the war's end. For the Native peoples, the War of 1812 marked the finale to an often uneasy alliance with the British, an alliance marked by British betrayals in 1783, 1794, and again in 1813.[17]

Americans continued to probe the Niagara region instead of massing on Kingston, and after they were defeated at Lundy's Lane near Niagara Falls in July 1814, the end seemed near. In December 1814, the Treaty of Ghent brought an official end to a war that had come to a standoff. All conquests were returned. Subsequent agreements provided for naval disarmament on the Great Lakes and a boundary settlement extending to the Rocky Mountains. Yet the Upper Canadian border would remain defended. Forts, canals, and roadways would continue to be constructed with military purposes in mind, generally with British capital.

The consequences of the war varied for different segments of the population. At a broad level, non-American settlers became decidedly anti-American—so much so that following the war, the Upper Canadian government severely restricted immigration from the United States while encouraging intensive British immigration. Since settlers of American origin formed the largest segment of Upper Canada's population at the beginning of the war, this change helped to intensify identification with things British rather than American. As a mythology emerged of the heroic Upper Canadian militia—no matter how misplaced in fact—a sense of pride in being Upper Canadian, as opposed to American or British, developed. But for the first Upper Canadians, the Native peoples, the Treaty of Ghent did nothing. Indeed, when Upper Canadians filed claims for 'war losses', more than a quarter accused Native persons of theft.

The war was particularly hard on the Niagara area, severing the link to the old western fur-trading region and ending the already declining trade along the Detroit–Niagara–Montreal route. The York region, on the other hand, profited nicely from a growing trade in wheat and foodstuffs as a result of the war. As early as 1812, some farmers could afford to pay the £20 charged in lieu of militia service, and merchants like William Allan enjoyed a 100 per cent markup on goods sold to the military. The £350,000 spent by the military on supplies in York was doubtless responsible for much joy in the region. As important, the increased civil and military presence strengthened the position of York's bureaucratic-merchant elite, as men like Allan rooted out dissenters and kept alert for treasonous activity. Although the Kingston area was largely untouched by the war, merchants there also made money, from both a legal trade with Lower Canadian suppliers and an illicit trade with American merchants, largely conservative Federalists. Indeed, according to the city's historians, the war gave Kingston's development an impetus that would last a generation. Aware that the Federalists were in decline as a political force in the US, the elites in Kingston, as in York, were determined that Upper Canada's Tories should not suffer the same fate.[18]

Power, Place, and Politics, 1813–37

Coming on the heels of the American and French revolutions and the Irish Rebellion of 1798, the War of 1812 hardened conservative attitudes in Upper Canada and stiffened the elite's resolve to create a conservative fortress on the British North American frontier that would be impervious to extreme democratic influences. 'Disloyal', 'seditious', 'democratic', and 'American' became terms of opprobrium hurled by the Tories at any who dared oppose them.[19]

To further conservative ends, members of the elite often sought appointments to both the Legislative Council and the Executive Council at the same time, and many—including the Reverend Strachan—received them. Such overlapping appointments testify not only to the closed nature of the group that Reformers in the 1820s would call the Family Compact, but—more important—to the closeness of the links between the colony's political-administrative structure and its judicial system. Of course, the connections between political and judicial structures always tend to be close: politicians make laws and judges enforce them. In Upper Canada, however, they were so intimate that the same Executive Council that advised the lieutenant-governor on the colony's administration also served as the final resident court of appeal. As well, King's Bench judges sat on the executive and legislative councils; in fact, the chief justice was president of the former until 1831 and Speaker of the latter until 1840. Separation of legislative and judicial functions and personnel had already occurred in Lower Canada in 1811.

In keeping with British tradition, Upper Canada's elite viewed the law as an ally in the effort to preserve the social hierarchy within which they enjoyed privileged positions. At the same time they realized that—given the colony's vulnerable position vis-à-vis the United States along with the discontent evident within the colony before and during the war—too zealous an application of existing law could be counterproductive. Like Britain's ruling class, therefore, they opted for more subtle displays of power, such as a show trial orchestrated by Attorney General John Beverley Robinson in May 1814 at Ancaster (near Niagara). Dressed in regal robes, judges indicted seventy-one traitors and sentenced seventeen to be hanged, drawn, and quartered, before finally pardoning nine, hanging eight, and quartering none. By tempering harsh justice with mercy in a setting evocative of the Crown's majesty, the elite hoped to cultivate loyalty on the part of citizens.

A similar strategy informed jurisprudence in lower courts. In criminal cases, justices 'inclined to lenience and mercy when at all possible'. While the death penalty existed for many crimes (even after the reformation of the criminal code in 1833, fifteen separate offences required execution), it was only rarely enforced. Nevertheless, hanging was a public matter. The crowd that assembled to view the hanging of Michael Vincent in Hamilton in 1828 could buy pies and spruce beer from vendors. In this particular case, all did not go smoothly. Vincent proclaimed his innocence to the end, and that end was brutal: despite the executioner's hanging on to the strangling man's feet, Vincent writhed in the air for some fifteen minutes before dying. His parents wanted his body, but that, symbolic of the state's power, belonged to the Crown and was given to surgeons for dissection.[20]

The elite also attempted to use religious institutions to conciliate and control the population. While maintaining their belief that the Constitutional Act had established the Church of England as the state church, with all the majesty that that entailed, Anglicans recognized that they were in a weak position within a religiously diverse and pluralistic society, and they trod softly in the years before 1820. Seven denominations, all predating 1812, competed with the Church of England for Upper Canadian souls. By 1817, Scottish Roman Catholics boasted seven priests and 15,000 parishioners. Although their numbers were reduced during the war, Methodists numbered 6,875 in 1825, with thirty-five preachers. By comparison, in 1819 the Church of England had only nine resident clergy—and it was underfunded; in this period it actually received very little income from the Clergy Reserves, but Anglican parishioners believed that it was amply provided for and were reluctant to contribute themselves. The Anglican church laid low, hoping that the state's efforts to attract British immigrants would tip the religious balance in its favour.[21]

George T. Berthon, *Sir John Beverley Robinson*, c. 1846. Robinson, a student of Bishop Strachan's, personified the intimate connections between law and politics within the Family Compact. Appointed acting attorney general at the age of twenty-one—before he had even been called to the bar—in 1818 he became attorney general, and in 1820 he entered the legislative assembly, where he became the primary spokesman for the province's elite. In 1829, Robinson was appointed chief justice, a position he held until 1863. NGC 15192.

Majesty and mercy soon proved insufficient to paper over the essentially self-interested nature of the elite's program. In the 1820s, political, administrative, and legal decisions had an increasingly oppressive effect on growing numbers of Upper Canadians. By the end of the decade, some Assembly members began to coalesce as 'His Majesty's faithful opposition' (a term that had just become current in England).

Several issues prompted the re-emergence of a Reform movement. In 1817, a fiery Scots Reformer, Robert Gourlay, canvassed citizens for their grievances and encouraged them to speak out. When Strachan objected, Gourlay called him a 'monstrous little fool of a parson', sponsored a series of township meetings, and chaired a July 1818 public convention to organize the collection and dissemination of petitions. Petitioning stood at the heart of Gourlay's activities, and it had a long history in Britain as a way for common people to make their views known to authorities in an era of limited franchise (fewer than half the men in Upper Canada were qualified to vote). Upper Canadian authorities, however, saw petitions as a means to subvert constituted authority as embodied in the Assembly, councils, and lieutenant-governor and as marking an extension of political-economic debate to a public simply incapable (in the eyes of the elite) of rational thought. Indeed, they saw a parallel between the Gourlayite agitation and current unrest in England that took the form of mass meetings and demands for parliamentary reforms and economic change and that led to bans on popular meetings and the suspension of habeas corpus.[22]

Increasingly under siege, the elite abandoned any pretence of mercy. Christopher Hagerman, a Kingston lawyer, 'horsewhipped' Gourlay. Robinson had Gourlay's mail intercepted. The Assembly banned public conventions by means of a Seditious Meetings Act—drafted with the assistance of the justices of the Court of the King's Bench, thus making any subsequent appeal to that body of dubious worth. Gourlayites were dismissed from military and civil positions. Bartemous Ferguson, editor of a Niagara newspaper supportive of Gourlay, was fined £50, jailed for eighteen months, and not released until he posted the huge sum of £500 in sureties to ensure good behaviour for the next seven years. Under an 1804 law allowing the banishment of any recent arrival who disturbed the 'tranquillity' of the colony, Gourlay was arrested, put in solitary confinement for nearly eight months—during which his mental health deteriorated—and finally convicted and banished. Between 1804 and 1828, the state instituted thirty-four similar prosecutions—conceivably proportionally more than all the prosecutions undertaken in England to repress dissent during the period of the French Revolution.[23]

In 1817, Upper Canadians who had been born in the US after 1783 were stripped of the vote and the right to own land. The so-called Alien Question simmered through 1822, when—at the instigation of Robinson—one American-born representative was denied the right to sit in the Assembly. Enraged, opponents of the Tories bypassed the lieutenant-governor and petitioned directly to England for justice. Lieutenant-Governor Sir Peregrine Maitland felt this to be a 'remarkable' departure from appropriate practice—an understandable reaction since the tactic undercut the executive's control of communications with imperial authorities. Even more remarkably (from Robinson and Maitland's perspective), the Colonial Office responded by requiring that American-born Upper Canadians be granted equal civil rights.

Buoyed by increasing Anglican immigration from Britain, Strachan pushed the prerogatives of the Anglican Church in the late 1820s. Already in control of school textbook selections, he lobbied for an Anglican-controlled university. Reformers counteracted his blatantly false statistics on the numbers of Anglicans and Methodists by sending another petition (with 8,000 signatures) decrying the 'clerico-political aristocracy'.[24]

A series of violent incidents perpetrated by Tory supporters added to the rage engendered by the Alien Question, the Gourlay affair, and religious disputes. Unruly social behaviour was common at this time. John Carroll, a Methodist preacher who had lived in the colony's capital in his youth, recalled that 'York boys' were very warlike: gangs were 'pelting one another with stones and clods almost everywhere, insomuch that it was dangerous to walk the streets'; gang members were 'expected loyally to bear fealty to [their] military commanders', many of whom were 'respectably connected' boys; and even girls took part in school brawls.[25] In 1826, the printing press of the Reform newspaper editor William Lyon Mackenzie was smashed in what became known as the Types Riot; parts of the press were dumped into Lake Ontario. George Rolph, a long-time

Reformer, was stripped, tarred, and feathered by a band of sheet-covered men in blackface, including two magistrates, one of whom was also the local sheriff. In 1828, a vindictive series of libel charges initiated by Robinson against Francis Collins, another Reform editor, put Collins in prison for a year before the Crown halved the sentence.

The repression reached a climax of sorts in the case of Judge John Walpole Willis, who arrived from Britain in 1827 as a junior judge on the Court of the King's Bench. He quickly rendered himself suspect in the eyes of the elite by listening to Reform as well as Tory opinion. On several issues related to the tar-and-feather case, he disagreed with his fellow judges. Finally he questioned whether the court was empowered to sit without at least three judges present (legally it was not, but in practice it had done so countless times). That he raised these issues in public court angered the judicial elite and further undermined public confidence in the judicial system. Far from supporting the political status quo, Willis argued that loyalty was not God-given but must be earned: 'Statutes have not given to the People their Liberties; their Liberties have produced them.' The lieutenant-governor and his friends on the Executive Council ordered Willis's immediate dismissal.

The elite seemed impervious to prosecution. The tar-and-feather ringleaders evaded punishment in that case and on separate charges relating to a brutal rape. The two magistrates were even appointed to higher office by the lieutenant-governor, as were some participants in the Types Riot. A York magistrate arranged for the civil damages charged against the Types rioters to be paid by public subscription, and several of the rioters retained Robinson and his close associate, the solicitor general, as counsel. (Not only were law officers not obliged to initiate criminal proceedings against the alleged perpetrators of criminal acts, but they could even defend them in court.) On the Alien Question, Robinson demanded a strict interpretation of the law and was quite willing to ignore the tradition of permitting American-born settlers to vote; however, on the issue of allowing the court to sit with fewer than three judges, he supported traditional practice despite its illegality. As John Willson, an independent Tory and Speaker of the Assembly, noted in 1828, 'it had been difficult to awaken the people from their slumber but they had at last been roused to save their liberties; their complaints were now heard.' For many, the legal system had shown itself to be merely an extension of an arbitrary, devious, and repressive political system. Far from being above politics, the law was its handmaiden.[26]

Although Reformers won the 1828 election, they lacked unity. Political parties in the modern sense had yet to emerge. A new lieutenant-governor, Sir John Colborne helped conciliate dissenters by initiating some social and economic reforms and extending patronage beyond members of the Family Compact. Tories controlled the Assembly in 1830. Nevertheless, Colborne represented only the calm before the storm.

If violence simmered in the 1820s, it came to the boil in the 1830s. Of the fifty-one riots recorded in Upper Canada before 1840, forty-four took place in the 1830s. Indications of unrest elsewhere—the Decembrist uprising in Russia in 1825, the wave of revolution in central and western Europe in 1830, the Chartist

F.H. Consitt, *The Rival Candidates*, Perth, 1828. Early elections could be rowdy affairs: ballots were not secret, and whisky, money, and force were regularly used to influence voters. Sometimes ethnicity also played a role: note the kilts among the supporters of the Scots-born Morris. Queen's University Archives, William Morris Collection, 2139, Box 3.

movement and electoral reform in England, the rise of Jacksonian democracy in the US, increasing conflict in Lower Canada—intensified the elite's anxiety. Rising criminal activities seemed to parallel the increase in violence. Young offenders were seen as 'an omen of disorder and loss of control'. 'The vices of drunkenness and gambling, the Profanation of the Sabbath, and the frequent congregation of idle persons, apprentices and others at places of public amusement are the sources of most crimes', Chief Justice Robinson declared in 1834. '[I]t is at these wretched resorts of the idle and disorderly that young men of all conditions in Society often lay the foundation of lasting misery and disgrace.'[27] To contain disaffection (both imagined and real), the colony's elite began to look to the state and state-supported institutions.

The 1830s marked the beginnings of the rise of the modern institutional state and, in its shadow, the emergence to power of a new ruling class. Hospitals—designed, as one doctor explained, to 'repress [the] vices' of the sick—were constructed alongside state-supported 'houses of industry' charged with containing and reforming their inmates so that on release they would fit quietly within a stable society. A 'Lunatic Hospital' was authorized. Intense debate over education set the stage for institutional centralization of that sector in the 1840s. The Kingston

Penitentiary, the colony's largest public building, opened in 1835, with the first six men arriving in June and the first three women in September. It became society's showcase: its architecture embodied the moral values of the elite; its massive and imposing exterior cowed and impressed; and, until 1845, citizens could pay an admittance fee and covertly view the inmates.[28]

Reform kept the pressure on. Mackenzie adroitly used petitions as a means for the expression of popular will against the Tory elite. In 1831–2, he organized what Carol Wilton has called 'the most important outburst of popular political activity in the entire Upper Canadian period'. This took place at the same time as popular petitioning for electoral reform in the mother country reached a fever pitch. It drew on the grievances of both the politically and religiously disaffected. In short, Mackenzie brought together, for the first time, all oppositionist causes and thereby helped to create a more cohesive and colony-wide Reform culture.[29]

Reform petitions kept the Colonial Office aware of events in Upper Canada, and in the course of organizing these petitions, Reformers became adept at local political organization. Township meetings and county conventions took place throughout Upper Canada from the late 1820s onward. Careful to avoid violence, the Reformers worked to extend political debate to a sector of society the Tories had underestimated. Newspapers, which had multiplied from one in 1813 to thirty by 1833, with a total circulation of 20,000, had become especially effective vehicles for the Reform message and, as McNairn has demonstrated, for the wide-ranging exchange of public political debate. Petitions, conventions, and newspapers promoted public interest in political matters and, to an important degree, allowed some at least of those who lacked the property qualifications to vote to attend political meetings and use them, as many used petitions, to voice their needs and aspirations. Yet it should not be forgotten that these meetings and petitions were organized by propertied men with the vote and were designed primarily to attract a similar sort.[30]

Tories also worked to buttress their political position. Recourse to law was increasingly ineffective, as juries often failed to accept the Crown's evidence at face value. Tellingly, and despite their ideological preferences, Tories also began to court 'public opinion' in 1832 by initiating petitions supportive of loyalty to the British connection. Public meetings were conducted at which, as Colonel Thomas Talbot, a Tory patriarchal leader of the Talbot settlement along Lake Erie, put it, 'I gave my Children some wholesome advice.' Tories employed violence in their efforts to thwart the rising Reform movement—press attacks, strong-arm electoral tactics, disruption of political meetings, effigy-burning, and even personal assaults on, among others, Mackenzie. Moderate Reform leaders such as William Warren Baldwin and his son Robert could argue that 'every free Government [must] have two parties, a governing party and a party in check', but for the Family Compact there were only loyal Tories and disloyal Reformers.[31]

Led by the moderate Egerton Ryerson, Methodists edged closer to the Tory fold. By the 1830s, the tide of British immigration had radically altered the nature of Upper Canadian Methodism. More conservative Wesleyan Methodists from England began to outnumber American Methodists. Urban churches and educated,

Box 6.1 Women and Public Discourse in Upper Canada

A public forum for discussion emerged in Upper Canada in the pre-Rebellion years. 'Political rhetoric', one cultural historian affirms, 'may be considered the main art form and spectator sport of the period.' To become a player, however, one had to be 'manly', a term that encompassed such characteristics as independence and the ability to reason, learn, and act appropriately. Women played little public role in Upper Canadian public discourse. Women, especially married women, were 'to sooth the troubles of others' by being 'amiable' and by forgoing 'the trifling satisfaction of having your will or gaining the better of an argument.' They were the spectators. Yet their presence was palpable: images, generally negative, of weak, effeminate, promiscuous, and seductive woman were hurled by Reformers at their Tory adversaries. Women became symbolic weapons to underscore how unmanly the Tories really were. In highly gendered terms, Mackenzie undercut the elite's pretensions to rule by right of aristocrat blood. He vilified John Beverley Robinson by asserting that he and others like him were born of 'mothers who . . . were purchased by their sires for tobacco at prices according to the quality and soundness of the article. And it is from such a source that we may look for the tyranny engendered, nursed, and practised by those whose blood has been vitiated and syphilized by the accursed slavery of centuries'. Tories, too, used female imagery to denigrate their opponents. Mackenzie, according to one Tory commentator, aimed his 'editorial drivelings to the worst passions of the worst classes of the community in order to gain that fetid popularity which steams from the political brothel of a prostituted press'.[1]

There was no organized public participation by women in Upper Canadian political debates. Certainly the tenor of the debates themselves was hardly welcoming. Some women, however, were close observers: 'This Parliament amuses me', Mary Gapper O'Brien, a literate middle-class woman, wrote to her family in England. O'Brien followed political matters with interest, but she did so in private. The York Mechanics' Institute was exceptional in 'accommodating' women at public lectures. Yet some individual women did take strong public stands. Samuel Lount's widow published a letter to John Beverley Robinson in the Reform press. While acknowledging that a woman 'should not lead the way' in redressing the wrongs perpetrated by the Tories on innocent families, she, in a nice twist on the gendered rhetoric of the time, clearly felt that this time public commentary by a woman was justified. In her view, Robinson had forgone any claim to be a man. The patriotic poems of Susanna Moodie, published during the Rebellion years, provide another instance of a woman speaking frankly in public on political issues. She excoriated Mackenzie and his 'sons of anarchy'. In 1853, reflecting on her early years in the colony, Moodie noted how 'Even women entered deeply into this party hostility, and those who, from their education and mental advantages, might have been friends and agreeable companions kept aloof, rarely taking notice of each other, when accidently thrown together'.[2]

Politics affected women; images of women affected politics. Some historians see the growth of a 'public sphere' as ultimately—although not in this time period—enabling for women. Others argue that the definitions underlying that growth in a sense publicly institutionalized women's relegation to the spectator's box, from where they could whisper their comments to their heart's content.[3]

---

1. Quotations: Heather Murray, 'Frozen Pen, Fiery Print, and Fothergill's Folly: Cultural Organization in Toronto, Winter, 1836–37', *Essays on Canadian Writing* 61 (1997): 41; Jane Errington, *Wives and Mothers, Schoolmistresses and Scullery Maids: Working Women in Upper Canada, 1790–1840* (Montreal: McGill-Queen's University Press, 1991), 34–5.
2. Murray, 'Frozen Pen,' 54; Cecilia Morgan, '"When Bad Men Conspire, Good Men Must Unite!":' Gender and Political Discourses in Upper Canada, 1820s–1830s,' in *Gendered Pasts: Historical Essays in Femininity and Masculinity in Canada*, edited by Kathryn McPherson, Cecilia Morgan, and Nancy Forestell (Don Mills, ON: Oxford University Press, 1999), 12–28; Cecilia Morgan, *Public Men and Virtuous Women: The Gendered Languages of Religion and Politics in Upper Canada, 1791–1850* (Toronto: University of Toronto Press, 1996), 94–5; Carl Ballstadt, 'Secure in Conscious Worth: Susanna Moodie and the Rebellion of 1837', *Canadian Poetry* 18 (1986): 88–98.
3. Jeffrey L. McNairn, *The Capacity to Judge: Public Opinion and Deliberative Democracy in Upper Canada, 1791–1854* (Toronto: University of Toronto Press, 2000), 226–33; for women in the 'public sphere' in the 1850s, see Carmen Nielson Varty, 'The City and the Ladies: Politics, Religion and Female Benevolence in Mid-Nineteenth Century Hamilton, Canada West,' *Journal of Canadian Studies* 38 (2004): 151–71.

---

professionally trained clergymen replaced camp meetings and itinerant preachers. Public displays of emotion gave way to more rational principles. Methodists and Anglicans began to close ranks. When in 1831 the right to solemnize marriages was extended beyond the Church of England, Ryerson spoke of Methodists as moderate Tories, loyal to the Crown and averse to radical political reform.

At that moment, it has been argued, a central component of Upper Canada's political and social culture hardened, perhaps permanently. American Methodists preached a voluntary, individual route to salvation, a route compatible with the notion of a society composed of autonomous individuals. For a religion to flourish in early Upper Canadian society, its adherents had continually to sell, cajole, and persuade—in more secular terms, it had to play an active part in the marketplace. Over time, under the pressures of anti-Americanism and British immigration, that aspect of Upper Canadian Methodism withered and its place was filled, at least in part, by a form of Christian loyalism. Although Upper Canadian Methodists continued to insist on the separation of church and state, they increasingly looked to the state for sustenance, stability, and protection. While their American counterparts marketed their beliefs, major Upper Canadian religious groups lobbied their government.[32]

This shift was reflected in Egerton Ryerson's own life. Born in 1803 to a prominent Loyalist family and raised as an Anglican, at age fourteen Ryerson experienced an evangelical conversion and left home to follow his calling over his father's objections. As a young man he strongly supported the colony's British ties, and in the 1840s and '50s he became one of Upper Canada's most powerful bureaucrats, playing a central role in the creation of a state-sponsored school system and giving the Tories access, through the Methodists, to an organized religious body that proved invaluable in the management of local elections. 'Loyalty with us', one Methodist noted, 'is an integral and essential part of religion'. After the 1830s, Methodists never again challenged the primacy of the state in Upper Canada.[33]

While the anti-establishment tradition so much a part of North American Methodism was drying up, Upper Canadian Reform could nonetheless draw sustenance from another religious-ethnic stream. Scottish and Irish Presbyterian Seceders bulked large among rural Upper Canadians. Seceders opposed hierarchical church organizations and brought with them an oppositional culture grounded in over a century of dispute with the official Anglican state church. For many Seceders, Upper Canada was a place where religious diversity could flourish and a state church did not exist. For Tories, of course, the existence of a state church was a central prop of the meaning of loyalty and of allegiance to things British. Seceders, moreover, supported a religious structure predicated on communitarian ideals. Local congregations, not a central prelate or state official, selected clergy. Familiarity with and allegiance to the communitarian principle made the notion of responsible government (increasingly articulated by the Irish Presbyterians William Warren Baldwin and his son Robert), whereby members of the Executive Council should be drawn from and reflect the composition of the Assembly, quite congenial.[34]

The interplay of politics and religion/ethnicity in Upper Canada was dramatically evident in yet another way. While the Wesleyan Methodists served as a moderating influence within the Tory fold, the Irish Protestants—many of them members of the Orange Order—played a very different role. Having lived as a loyalist minority in Ireland, they were easily enlisted in the service of the Upper Canadian elite's loyalism. Organized by unscrupulous Tory placemen and aspiring Tory leaders to intimidate dissenters, they provided the physical force that increasingly substituted for the rule of law. 'If you had been in London [Ontario] at the last election', remarked a traveller named Richard Davis, 'you would have seen a set of government tools called Orange men, running up and down streets crying five pounds for a liberal; and if a man said a word contrary to their opinion he was knocked down . . . and all this in the presence of magistrates, Church of England ministers and judges, who made use of no means to prevent such outrages.'[35]

Reformers dominated the Assembly again in 1834. Hoping to promote conciliation, the Colonial Office appointed a new lieutenant-governor, Sir Francis Bond Head. Unfortunately, Bond Head did not know the meaning of collaboration. Deadlock between the Reform assembly and the Tory governor resulted in the Assembly's dissolution and a violent election in 1836. In an unprecedented move, the lieutenant-governor took an active role, speaking at public meetings and leading the Tories to an overwhelming victory, in the process exposing his office to direct public critique and thereby contributing to the growth of public debate in the colony. Moderates like Robert Baldwin were entirely shut out of office. In despair, many moderate Reformers left politics, leaving the movement's leadership open to those of a more radical bent.

Advocates of rebellion were always a small minority in Upper Canada. Most Reformers saw little to be gained through physical confrontation with an established authority capable of calling in military support; they preferred to concentrate on holding the higher moral ground. William Lyon Mackenzie thought differently. Having survived more than one attack by Tory vigilantes, Mackenzie came to believe that anything less than the complete overthrow of the system would be a waste of time. 'To die fighting for freedom is truly glorious', he wrote in November 1837. In December 1837, Mackenzie donned several overcoats (to ward off bullets) and led roughly a thousand ill-armed followers from Montgomery's Tavern down Yonge Street in an unsuccessful attempt to overthrow the government. A second uprising, near Brantford, failed as well: pursued by Loyalist militia, the rebels fled to the US. Four hundred warriors from the Six Nations assisted in putting down the western uprising, and a significant number of Chippawa and Mississauga rallied against Mackenzie and helped repulse rebel raids from the United States throughout 1838. In fact, in the hope of gaining guns and better bargaining positions on land issues, on a per capita basis more Native people defended the colony than people from other origins.[36]

Grievances had been intensified by an international financial crisis in late 1837, which was itself compounded when Bond Head refused to allow banking reform designed to ease the credit crunch. Yet the rebels cannot easily be distinguished from those who remained loyal on economic grounds. Rebels did tend to be more often American or Scottish than English in background and to be Presbyterian or Baptist rather than Anglican, suggestive once again of the significance of Scottish secessionist reform support. They also tended to be concentrated in economically healthy areas of the colony, a group of townships north of the first areas of settlement but south of those most recently settled. Historians have downplayed the role of class as a determinant of political behaviour in this era, most often on the grounds that such differences were muted in rural Upper Canada. This interpretative consensus, however, glosses over the importance of the formative years of many settlers in this immigrant society. As William Proudfoot, a Seceder missionary in London, Upper Canada, noted of his parishioners, 'The majority of people here are from the working classes of the old country, the ploughmen, or weavers or black-smiths or tailors they were in the old country before they became Canadian lairds, and they still retain the morality of the class of society they belonged to.'[37] We need to know more about the origins of the rebels, and indeed of Reform supporters as a whole, before we discount the significance of class as a factor in understanding political behaviour in Upper Canada on the eve of rebellion.

That only an ill-organized minority rebelled did not mean that dissent lacked wider support. When the government, having arrested over 800 alleged rebels, attempted to replicate the show trials of 1814, petitions for clemency signed by between 12,000 and 20,000 people (Lord Durham claimed 30,000) flooded into York.[38] In this turbulent context, the Colonial Office took steps to repair the fractured Canadian political system.

EXECUTION OF LOUNT AND MATTHEWS.

The execution of Samuel Lount and Peter Matthews. Lount (a farmer, blacksmith, and rebel organizer from north of Toronto) and Matthews (a farmer from Pickering) were the only ones executed for their part in the 1837 Rebellion. 'The general feeling', the Reverend John Ryerson wrote, 'is in total opposition to the execution of those men. Sheriff Jarvis burst into tears when he entered the room to prepare them for execution. . . . They ascended the scaffold and knelt down at the drop. The ropes were adjusted while they were on their knees. [The Rev.] Richardson engaged in prayer; and when he came to that part of the Lord's Prayer, "forgive us", the drop fell!' (Egerton Ryerson, *The Story of My Life* [1883], cited in Colin Read and Ronald Stagg, eds, *The Rebellion of 1837 in Upper Canada: A Collection of Documents* [Toronto: Champlain Society, 1985], 394–5.) NA C1242.

Setting the Stage: The Rebellion's Aftermath

John Lambton, Earl of Durham, the British emissary charged with resolving the Canada problem, disembarked at Quebec in June 1838 in full ceremonial dress astride a white horse, to the music of an orchestra. Despite this display of majesty, Durham did not side with the Family Compact. Rather, he determined to end forever the elite's hold on local political power and preferment. After six months in the colony, he returned to Britain and prepared a report in which he recommended that, to promote the assimilation of the rebellious French, Lower Canada should join with English-speaking Upper Canada in a single united province. In addition, however, Durham offered a second recommendation: that the Assembly should both initiate public policy and appoint 'the persons by whom that policy was to be administered'. Tories went into shock. Reformers rejoiced at Durham's proposal for what they called 'responsible government'. Durham, however, did not use that term. Nor—contrary to the Reformers' assumption—did he intend to strengthen the elected assembly at the expense of the appointed executive council or to turn the latter into the equivalent of a modern-day cabinet. Indeed, he left considerable power with the lieutenant-governor, who was to govern in 'harmony' with the Assembly. Political parties would not be encouraged: councillors would act as individuals, not as party representatives. In linking the Executive Council to the Assembly, Durham actually hoped to strengthen the former by giving it the credibility necessary to administer a state that was becoming increasingly complex, economically and socially.

The Colonial Office shared Durham's short-sighted view of the way the colonies should be governed. Following Durham, it sent over a succession of governors to function according to the rules Durham had sketched. Soon, however, a more comprehensive blueprint would emerge, devised by a set of moderate, business-oriented, urban-centred politicians, conservative and reform, from both parts of the new united province of Canada. Many of these men—such as John A. Macdonald, a rising corporate lawyer in Kingston, and Francis Hincks, a banker and Reform politician—had honed their skills at the level of local commercial and political activity in the 1830s. The heirs to the Rebellion of 1837, they were the ones who would help to devise the new rules and then capitalize on them.

To understand how they managed to take the reins of power requires a closer look at the economic and social context from which this new bourgeois class emerged. In the 1830s, developing urban places such as Hamilton, York (renamed Toronto in 1834), London, Cobourg, Port Hope, and Kingston vied for trade and economic power. Merchants and other urban landholders, anxious to modernize an increasingly inefficient system of civic rule by appointed magistrates, pushed for communities to incorporate, and by 1847, thirteen Upper Canadian towns had done so. A desire for increased efficiency rather than increased democracy underlay this movement. High property qualifications both restricted the municipal franchise and kept the right to hold local office out of the reach of most urban dwellers: from the 1830s to 1860, between 60 and 80 per cent of elected councillors were businessmen, many of them merchants. Paralleling a similar development in England, the municipal state offered local merchants opportunities to expand and consolidate economic power.[39]

In cities such as Hamilton and York, members of the business class developed close social ties: they purchased pews together in the most respectable churches; their children intermarried; they accepted, endorsed, and circulated each other's promissory notes. The fact that the Bank of Upper Canada—from 1821 to 1833 the colony's only chartered bank—was controlled by York's merchants gave them easier access to capital than their competitors in other cities had. In fact, this monopoly and the bank's closed-preserve mode of operations contributed as much to York's rise to dominance as did its rich hinterland and its position as capital. When Hamilton's businessmen finally chartered the Gore Bank in the early 1830s, they treated it as their private preserve.[40]

Provincial politics reflected the growth of regionally focused business elites. While most Upper Canadians farmed, their political leaders were more representative of an urban-centred, business-minded, capitalist society. Before 1830, about two-thirds of the Assembly's members had been farmers. In the 1830s, only a third farmed, and half of those also engaged in some other business pursuit.[41] These men wanted a stable political structure within which to pursue their economic ends.

Using the Union

In February 1841, the Act of Union joining Upper and Lower Canada in a single political body provided that structure. Lower Canadians, ruled by an appointed council since the rebellion, had no democratic say in the Union's creation. In Upper Canada, however, the elected assembly had continued in existence, and for the Union to become a reality the Assembly had to be conciliated. Public spending on roads and canals during the 1830s had increased Upper Canada's debt to a level that had become unsustainable. Upper Canada wanted debt relief and new development projects in the St Lawrence commercial corridor—as did Lower Canadian commercial interests. In fact, the idea of union had been broached as early as 1822 by Montreal merchants who understood how the existence of two jurisdictions hampered development along their common commercial artery. Aware of the Colonial Office's interest in promoting immigration and settlement, by 1839–40 Canadian businessmen and politicians emphasized how helpful a system of canals along the St Lawrence would be. While the construction of those canals was beyond the financial capacity of either Upper or Lower Canada alone, a union of the two might solve the problem.

The promise of a £1.5 million loan from Great Britain did the trick. Debts were merged, even though Canada West (the new name for what most people still called Upper Canada) owed thirteen times the amount that Canada East (Lower Canada) did. Consistent with Durham's plan to assimilate the French, Lower Canada received the same number of seats (forty-two) in the new assembly as its English-speaking counterpart, even though it had 200,000 more people. The official language was English, and the capital was Kingston—a stronghold of Anglo-Saxon loyalism. The deck seemed stacked in favour of Upper Canada and British Canadians.

On economic matters, most political leaders in both sections agreed: development should be supported by active state investment in transportation improvements. Views differed widely in the cultural sphere—both sides were equally committed to separate cultural development within their respective sections—but there was general agreement on responsible government. For Lower Canadian leaders such as Louis-Hippolyte LaFontaine, a lawyer and former rebel, responsible government represented a way to defeat the assimilation project. For Upper Canadian leaders such as lawyer Robert Baldwin and businessman Francis Hincks,

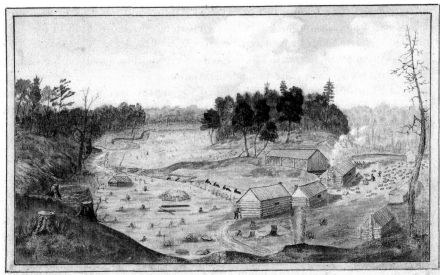

Brewer's Lower Mill;—view down the Cataraqui Creek & Clearing made for the Canal.
Sketch taken in 1829.— Excavation for the Lock just commenced.

Thomas Burrowes, *Brewer's Lower Mill; view down the Cataraqui Creek & Clearing made for the Canal. Sketch taken in 1829. Excavation for the Lock just commenced.* In 1827, the first estimate for building the Rideau Canal was £169,000; the final cost was £822,804. Between 1826 and 1832, some 9,000 men laboured on the Welland and Rideau canals each year. Human costs were high: of the 1,316 men who worked on a small section of the Rideau between Kingston and Newboro in 1830, some 500 died from disease and work-related accidents. AO C1-0-0-0-67.

it represented a way to pursue cultural and social as well as economic development in a rapidly maturing frontier society. First LaFontaine and the Baldwin–Hincks team would collaborate to achieve responsible government; then they (and their immediate successors) would set about implementing separate agendas for their respective sections.

In effect, then, the assimilationist goal was compromised from the start: a tendency toward dualism was already in place. Almost all contenders for political power agreed on the need for a strong central executive. Where Reformers and Tories disagreed was on which component of the executive branch should have primary authority: the Executive Council or the governor. Baldwin, Hincks, and LaFontaine believed that executive councillors should be the central actors. The gulf between the governor and the Reformers was no less significant over the assimilation issue. Charles Poulett Thomson (Lord Sydenham), the first Union governor, hoped that the union would serve as a container within which the French could be subdued and assimilated. Yet for the sake of their common goals as Reformers, Baldwin and Hincks were ready to stand by LaFontaine in his efforts to ensure *la survivance*: the retention and enrichment of 'our language, our laws and our religion' in Lower Canada.

Sydenham's conduct during the Union's first general election left little doubt about his position on governance. 'In present day terms', historian Irving Abella has remarked, Sydenham 'was at the same time governor general, prime minister, founder, organizer, leader and campaign chairman of his own party, chief electoral officer, commander-in-chief of the armed forces, chief crown lands agent, and head of the civil Service Commission.' He selected his own candidates, cajoled voters with promises of jobs and government largesse, and took advantage of public balloting by threatening to fire public employees who failed to vote for his candidates. He gerrymandered political boundaries, hand-picked his own electoral officers, and located polls close to his areas of strength. Since elections were staggered over roughly three weeks, he arranged for them to be held in an order calculated to generate a bandwagon effect in favour of his candidates: sure winners were elected first, sure losers last. These tactics were successful, and aspiring local politicians such as the young John A. Macdonald took careful note.[42]

In September 1841, Sydenham fell from his horse and died of tetanus. Although he had refused to recognize an alliance between Reformers, to govern effectively even he had to acknowledge that the Union's two sections possessed separate languages, religions, civil law codes, judicial systems, and forms of land tenure. Before he died, therefore, Sydenham put in place a dual administrative structure. His successors as governor general (three in the space of only four years) all contributed further to the dualistic trend. As early as 1843, each section had its own law officer, Crown lands commissioner, provincial secretary, and superintendent of education. Far from moving toward a unitary system, then, the Colonial Office's representatives were setting the administrative foundations for the emergence of a dual—or federal—structure.

The Colonial Office was not pleased. Sir Charles Metcalfe arrived as governor general in April 1843 with orders to resist further erosion. Instead, recognizing that the assimilation project made harmony impossible to attain, Metcalfe repealed restrictions on the official use of French, approved Montreal as the new seat of government, and sponsored a general amnesty for most rebels. He stood firm, however, on the issue of executive control. So too did the Reformers, who had long since tired of trusting governors. In a bitter and violent election in 1843, Upper Canadian Reformers were defeated, but their French Canadian allies, under LaFontaine, swept the lower province. Hincks and Baldwin's determination to ally with LaFontaine had paid dividends. Although shut out of power by Metcalfe, the Reformers tightened their party organization and triumphed in the 1847 election.

The LaFontaine-Baldwin government has been called the first true party government to exercise power in the Canadas. It was the first in a long line of bifurcated ministries representing the reality of linguistic duality at the highest political level. Given the Canadas' turbulent and violent political past, the transfer of power from the governor to the party in the Assembly controlling the Executive Council was suitably symbolized by the passage of the Rebellion Losses Bill in 1849, which promised to compensate French Canadians and even some rebels who had suffered property damage in the Rebellion. Coming on the heels of Britain's repeal of the

Navigation Acts and its seeming abandonment of loyal colonists, the bill aroused the fury of old Compact Tories and anglophone merchants in Montreal. Some advocated annexation to the US. When Governor General Lord Elgin signed the legislation over Tory cries, Samuel P. Jarvis, an elder Toronto Tory, prayed 'they would . . . string him up as a caution to other traitor governors'. Others did more than pray. They burned the Parliament Buildings in Montreal, pelted Elgin with ripe tomatoes and rotten eggs, and attacked the homes of Reformers like Hincks. Larratt Smith, an up-and-coming Toronto lawyer, recorded the following in his diary in March 1849: 'Mackenzie is back in town [the state had issued a pardon to all rebels] . . . This evening his effigy, with those of Robert Baldwin and William Hume Blake, was burnt by a Tory mob. . . . The howling mob, which included two city aldermen, smashed in the house of Mackenzie's friend Mackintosh and attacked and stoned the residence of George Brown, editor of the Globe newspaper; then, worn out by its exertions, the rabble sullenly withdrew.'[43]

But even Tory vigilantism could not turn the clock back. By 1850, the seeds of Canada's modern political system had been sown.

Bourgeois Politics in the 1850s

Not that Baldwin and LaFontaine reaped the rewards. Their efforts to resolve cultural and political issues were only partly successful. Like the Rebellion Losses Bill, religious and educational matters sparked strong opposition. Of particular concern to Protestants in the 1840s was the rise of Ultramontanism, a movement within the Catholic Church marked by intense devotion to the Pope and aggressive assertion of the church's primacy over the state. When LaFontaine gave in to Catholic demands for control of education, many Upper Canadians looked askance—ignoring the fact that Lower Canadian Reformers established Protestant schools as well.

In Lower Canada, elementary schools financed by the state but run by the church increased dramatically in number, as did the religious communities that were the main source of teachers. In an attempt to head off anger and anxiety in Protestant Upper Canada, Baldwin and LaFontaine passed a secular Public Schools Act and secularized the Anglican King's College, creating the University of Toronto. In 1853, their Reform successors recognized the right of religious groups to create their own religious schools. In 1855, that legislation was modified to provide funds explicitly for Catholic separate schools. The influx of Irish Catholics occasioned by the potato famines in Ireland in the late 1840s fanned fears of Catholic hegemony. As a result, the principle of voluntarism—that all religions should be supported by the voluntary contributions of their members rather than by the state—grew increasingly influential in Protestant circles.

That principle found an outspoken advocate in the Scottish-born George Brown, a successful businessman who was editor of the Toronto *Globe* and who was soon to become the voice of Reform in Upper Canada. 'It would be no exaggeration', historian Michael Gauvreau has commented, 'to state that for the Browns Presbyterianism and civil liberty were synonymous.' Indeed, Gauvreau links the religious beliefs of Brown and his father, Peter, with Scottish Seceders and the rise of an evangelical anti-Catholicism in Scotland in the 1830s. When the 1851 census revealed that Upper Canadians outnumbered Lower Canadians, Brown and the Clear Grits (Reformers who opposed religious teaching in schools and official privileges for the French language) pushed for representation by population instead of equal representation for each of the two sections. Pointing out that legislation regarding schools was often passed on the strength of Lower Canadian Catholic votes over the objections of Upper Canadian representatives, they argued that the imposition of Lower Canadian cultural institutions on the upper province vitiated the compromise at the heart of the Union—a compromise that recognized the distinctiveness of each section and in effect demanded quasi-federal political arrangements to facilitate separate social and cultural development in the two sections. Framing the issue in sectional terms garnered Brown significant electoral support in Upper Canada; however, arguing in terms of a Protestant crusade against 'papal aggression' made compromise, as even some Clear Grits realized, difficult to achieve. By the early 1860s, secular schooling and the separation of church and state had become the most divisive issues in Canadian politics and contributed to the political stalemate that characterized the Union's last years.[44]

Economic issues became another source of division for the Baldwin-LaFontaine administration. During the 1840s, British loans facilitated the completion of an impressive canal system along the St Lawrence. Initially, Baldwin and LaFontaine supported the Guarantee Act of 1849, which provided state backing for British loans to select colonial railways, but in time both men became increasingly wary of promoting unrestrained economic growth. By contrast, Hincks and other economically aggressive politicians pushed for further legislation to increase the legal rights of chartered companies and extend government guarantees to other railways. As a result, they began to part company with Baldwin and LaFontaine.

In 1851, Baldwin and LaFontaine retired, leaving their party in the hands of Hincks and Augustin-Norbert Morin, a lawyer-politician from Canada East. Economically, the new government was determined not to take a back seat to North American jurisdiction. In 1847, only three years after the telegraph had become commercially feasible, most major Upper Canadian centres were linked by it. Railway construction was equally impressive. In addition to passing financial legislation (especially the Mainline Railway Act of 1851) to facilitate borrowing abroad, the government guaranteed the loans of the St Lawrence and Atlantic Railway east of Montreal, the Great Western Railway through the Upper Canadian peninsula, and the Ontario, Simcoe, and Lake Huron Railway (later the Northern Railway) north of Toronto. By 1852, municipal governments as well as railroad corporations were allowed to borrow with the backing of the provincial government. Thanks in part to this enabling legislation, British capitalists invested some $70 million in Upper Canadian railways, and over 2,000 kilometres of track were laid in the 1850s, of which more than half belonged to the Great Western and the Grand Trunk—railroads designed, in part, to serve as links between the eastern seaboard of the US and the midwest states.

View of the accident on the G.W. Railway near Dundas, on the morning of the 19th March 1859.

Great Western Railway accident near Dundas, March 1859. In large black headlines, newspapers routinely reported on 'Frightful' or 'Fearful' railroad collisions. Between September 1853 and October 1854, seventy-nine people were killed and seventy injured in seventeen accidents on the Great Western line. A commission of inquiry cited locomotive engineers who ran over cattle for sport, gravel trains that ran on main passenger lines in disregard of published timetables, and a 'system of management unusual on the continent and ill-adapted to the circumstances and magnitude of this enterprise'. It concluded that managerial practices were haphazard and inconsistent. MTRL JRR T16587.

Railways created demand for manufactured items—from rails and spikes to engines—and facilitated the expansion of local markets. In fact, railways became effective industrial producers themselves: in 1861 the Great Western employed more than 2,000 people and the Grand Trunk more than 3,100, and in 1870 two of the three largest industrial companies in the new province of Ontario were railways. Railways were at the vanguard of managerial and corporate change. There were, however, in the Canadian context, very few imitators. Only six of the sixty largest industrial firms were incorporated in 1870. Most were partnerships or sole proprietorships, and in many, kin relations played significant roles in company management.[45]

From a political perspective, railways, like religion and culture, did little to bind the Union's two sections. The Grand Trunk, headquartered in Montreal, was originally chartered to provide the central link between the eastern and western roads, creating the backbone of a provincial system. But its managers wanted more. After absorbing the St Lawrence and Atlantic lines but failing to merge with the Great Western, the Grand Trunk used its political influence to permit it to construct a line parallel to the Great Western's, west from Toronto to Sarnia.

The Grand Trunk's ambition to channel Upper Canadian commerce through

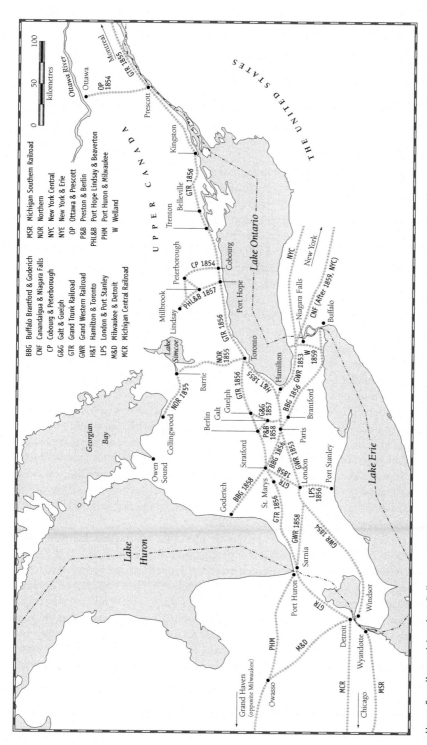

Upper Canadian and American Railways, c. 1860. From Peter Baskerville, 'Americans in Britain's Backyard: The Railway Era in Upper Canada, 1850–80', *Business History Review* 55 (1981): 331.

the St Lawrence corridor was naturally popular in Lower Canada, but it also attracted support in the Kingston area, which depended economically on the St Lawrence. Political leaders elsewhere, particularly in the southwest, regarded the Grand Trunk as a corrupt extravagance that threatened their own railway, the Great Western. George Brown, a staunch friend of the latter (the Great Western rewarded Brown by building a station on land he owned in Lambton County), became an increasingly shrill critic of the Grand Trunk in general and in particular of its political friends: John A. Macdonald of Kingston and George-Étienne Cartier of Montreal.

The push for development capital emerged from within the colony and paralleled similar initiatives from nearby American states. Local political and merchant promoters set the financial rules—and profited personally—to a surprising extent. Among them was Sir Allan Napier MacNab, the Hamilton businessman who, as premier of the Canadas in the mid-1850s, boasted that 'All my politics are railroads.' MacNab pocketed at least $400,000 (in modern values) from shady railway deals, while Hincks and Macdonald were only two of many who benefited from inside information and their political positions. Such activities did not escape the notice of Brown and the Grits. When Hincks became involved in a series of financial scandals, Reformer William McDougall suggested that the government was on the verge of being abandoned to 'Railway speculators, hungry lawyers and stock jobbers'.[46] And as social and political discontent rose, George Brown stood ready to capitalize on it.

The provincial government had agreed to guarantee the debts incurred by railways and municipalities. By 1859, acting under the Municipal Loan Fund Act, business leaders in twenty Upper Canadian centres had borrowed $7.3 million, of which $1.2 million was overdue. By the early 1860s, both Toronto and Hamilton had amassed debts of $3 million for purposes not covered by government guarantees. In all cases, the provincial government had to take steps to prevent bankruptcy. In the wake of this borrowing, municipalities curtailed spending on clean water, sanitation, social assistance, and fire protection, reducing the quality of life for the urban poor in particular. When a 'soup kitchen' opened in London, Upper Canada, in 1859, it fed seventy poor families.[47]

In the late 1850s, the state and private business alike confronted dramatic structural change. In that decade, roughly half of all businesses in Hamilton and Brantford failed. Only two of the fifteen banks chartered in Upper Canada before 1867 continued operations into the 1870s. In 1866, the Bank of Upper Canada, the colony's oldest chartered bank, closed its doors for good. 'I dont apprehend any immediate disasterous result from the Event', a prominent colonial politician confided, 'beyond loss to the shareholders.' Still, that loss exceeded $3 million and dramatically affected the lives of shareholders, such as widow Lydia Payne, who owned 215 BUC shares and 'depended on [her] stock . . . for support in [her] old Age'. Railway companies defaulted on government-backed loans. By the end of the 1850s, the colony's three largest railroads were petitioning the government for relief and half of the government's revenues went to pay interest on debt, largely connected with railways. Government and private finances were virtually indistinguishable.[48]

Social Conditions in a Bourgeois State

Workers and their families were far from passive in the midst of such change. At least fifteen strikes occurred on the Welland Canal between 1843 and 1849. In 1842, several hundred canallers, protesting low wages and layoffs, laid siege to the town of St Catharines, demanding 'Bread or Work'. At least nine strikes occurred on the Great Western Railroad between 1851 and 1856. In a phrase that captures the transitional nature of the era, one Great Western Railroad engineer recalled that railroad strikes were as common as the 'croaking of the frogs'. In 1853–4 alone, Upper Canada saw forty strikes led by skilled workers protesting the introduction of machinery and demanding higher wages. As moulders, tailors, joiners, machine workers, printers, and firemen formed unions, a new set of class distinctions began to emerge. Similar experiences—in the workplace, in living conditions, in the family—helped to create a sense of working-class consciousness. In Toronto, even skilled workers found it increasingly difficult to own a home. Different economic groups began to concentrate in specific districts of the city. As on the farm, where larger families meant greater productivity, urban families at the

John Howard, *Toronto Bay from Taylor's Wharf*, 1835. No female skaters are visible in this scene. By the 1860s, however, 'lady skaters were springing up in all parts of Canada'—a development that may have reflected the proliferation of skating rinks. 'Many a match has resulted from attentions first received there', observed Forbes Geddes of Hamilton in October 1862. In the same diary entry, Geddes notes that the city is soon to have at least one new rink: 'This will be the Aristocratic Resort. Another one for the "unwashed" is talked of to be constructed at the East end.' (In Francis Hoffman and Ryan Taylor, eds, *'Much to be Done': Private Life in Ontario from Victorian Diaries* [Toronto: Natural Heritage/Natural History, 1996].) Colborne Lodge, Toronto.

lower end of the economic scale tended to have more children than those at higher levels. Increasingly, though, the labour necessary to maintain the family was done outside the home, under the supervision of strangers. By 1871, women represented more than one-quarter of the employees in Toronto's five largest industrial groups, and children accounted for another 10 per cent. Women and children made up just under half of Ontario's tobacco workers, and in industry generally, women and children—some under ten years of age—often worked sixty hours a week for meagre wages.

In 1851, almost 45 per cent of the colony's population were under the age of sixteen. As in the 1830s, when the influx of young women and men from settled

Box 6.2   Labour, Business, and the State in Mid-Nineteenth-Century Upper Canada

Upper Canada's elite took work stoppages seriously. The very notion of a landless wage labourer ran contrary to the dominant definition of social stability: the small family farm. While essential for future growth, the wage labourer proved a present threat that had to be contained. In 1845, the legislature passed 'An Act for the better preservation of the peace and the prevention of Riots and violent Outrages at and near Public Works while in progress of construction'. A Master and Servant Act followed, in 1847, designed to help control Ottawa Valley lumber workers and, more generally, to make any labourer or servant who quit work before the terms of his or her contract expired liable for criminal prosecution. Should the 'Master' fire the worker without due cause, he was liable only for civil action, a procedure few workers would have been in a position to undertake. Labour unrest prompted St Catharines to abolish the old magistracy system of local rule in favour of town incorporation and the consequent creation of a local police board to better protect against the canallers. Twenty-five of Hamilton's uneasy entrepreneurial elite petitioned the governor general in February 1851 to call out the militia and put down striking railroad workers. Under state pressure, railroads tightened supervisory procedures and issued fat books of rules and regulations, complete with details of fines and threats of imprisonment for any transgressions. Railroad companies also began to use paternalistic as well as coercive measures to conciliate their workers: parades, picnics, reading rooms, and insurance schemes were introduced in an attempt to maintain a stable and peaceful workforce.[1]

---

1. Ruth Bleasedale, 'Class Conflict on the Canals of Upper Canada in the 1840s', *Labour/Le travail* 7 (1981): 9–39; Peter Way, *Common Labour: Workers and the Digging of North American Canals, 1780–1860* (Cambridge: Cambridge University Press, 1993); Peter Baskerville, 'Transportation, Social Change and State Formation; Upper Canada, 1841–64', in *Colonial Leviathan*.

rural areas into urban centres had contributed to the rise of the institutional state, increasing efforts were made to control unruly elements. In the 1840s, municipalities had begun to pass bylaws designed to enforce new social norms. Temperance movements flourished, police became more efficient, and 'vagrants and vagabonds' were summarily dealt with (in Hamilton, the latter made up half of all those jailed between 1843 and 1851). The Methodist *Christian Guardian* was not alone in railing against saloons, theatres, and dancing-rooms as breeding places for youthful criminals. By the close of the 1850s—despite both the professionalization of urban police forces and court systems and the proliferation of asylums, poor houses, penitentiaries, and schools—'vagrants', criminals, the insane, the poor, and even 'youth' seemed difficult, if not impossible, to contain.[49]

Church membership expanded greatly in this era. In 1842, more than one in six Upper Canadians had no church affiliation; by 1872, that figure would fall to only one in every one hundred. Before 1840, John Strachan had forcefully proclaimed the importance of the church's aiding the state, but in 1856, he sharply

HANDKERCHIEF	FLIRTATION.
1. Laying it on Right Check	1. I love you.
2. Laying it on Left Check	2. I hate you.
3. Drawing it out of Pocket	3. Do you love me?
4. Putting it over Right Shoulder	4. Follow me.
5. Putting it over Left Shoulder	5. Not just now.
6. Waving it with Right Hand	6. Will you go out to-night?
7. Waving it with Left Hand	7. I'll call for you.
8. Covering your Face	8. I don't want your company.
9. Holding it at your Right Side	9. Do you want an Introduction?
10. Holding it at your Left Side	10. Never mind an Introduction.
11. Placing it around your Neck	11. May I see you Home?
12. Crumpled up in the Right Hand ..	12. Yes.
13. Crumpled up in the Left Hand....	13. No.
14. Dropping it	14. Come now or never.
15. Folding it once	15. Call me by my right name.
16. Kissing it	16. The same to you.
17. Tieing it in a Knot	17. Remember you are engaged.
18. Holding it open in front of you....	18. If you speak I will.
19. Throwing it up...............	19. Will you see me Home.
20. Putting it in pocket...........	20. Good-by.

Courtship practices in nineteenth-century Ontario were more liberal than is often assumed. Many diarists, male and female, recorded late-night parties, and some courting couples spent quite a lot of unchaperoned time alone together. After staying out 'past dusk' with her male friend, one woman remarked that they were 'raising quite a commotion in this illustrious village'. Handkerchief flirtation was one way of circumventing the gossips. (In Francis Hoffman and Ryan Taylor, eds, *'Much to be Done': Private Life in Ontario from Victorian Diaries* [Toronto: Natural Heritage/Natural History, 1996].) MTRL Broadside Coll. 1873.

demarcated the two: the 'church and the world [are] two societies as distinct from each other as if each of the parties comparing them were of different natures'. The Gothic revival in church architecture symbolized this otherworldly message. For many, it seems, the social and economic dislocations that accompanied the advance of industrial capitalism brought a profound sense of unease. To temper the excesses of this secular life, otherworldly assistance was required.[50]

Nevertheless, it was the secular world for which schools were expected to play a central role in preparing Upper Canada's children to participate appropriately. In the 1840s, the state doubled its grant-in-aid to public schools, introduced a property tax to replace the traditional voluntary means of school finance, and created a stronger central authority with enhanced powers to regulate and supervise the selection of texts, the qualification of teachers, and the general conduct of schools. Ryerson, who became superintendent of the Department of Education in 1844, argued for a system of public taxation for the benefit of poorer classes, who 'need the assistance of the government: the rich with grammar schools and more can take care of themselves'. For Ryerson, education was an antidote for social unrest and in that sense promoted 'the rich man's security'. The object, as *The Journal of Education for Upper Canada* put it in 1854, was to facilitate the 'mental improvement' of the lower classes 'in order . . . to elevate their character rather than their station'. The practice of public opinion—of, in McNairn's terms, deliberative democracy—would then proceed on a rational, informed level and not be subject to ignorance and undue emotion. The model citizen, Ryerson believed, was the 'common sense practical' man or, more generally, 'the middle classes of society' with whose 'happiness and well being', he explained to the lieutenant-governor in 1840, he was always 'involved'.[51]

But the state's attempt to inculcate 'useful knowledge' through schooling had limited success. In the 1850s, schools were generally crowded and ill equipped; James Kyle, a teacher in Prescott in 1854, taught '40 or 50 scholars of all ages from 5 up to 15' in a space of 320 square feet. Local school boards were slow to adopt the state's slate of texts. At some schools, students set up underground libraries whose books were more widely circulated and read then those from the official libraries. In rural areas especially, it was often the religious and ethnic background of the teachers that determined whether a family would send its children to school at all. Moreover, not only were rising educational costs making it increasingly difficult for children from lower-income families to attend school past the primary grades, but middle-class parents began to pressure for state support for grammar, or upper-level, schools. State-aided grammar schools increased and, more significantly, they were enriched by the hiring of better teachers, the teaching of more advanced subjects, and the construction of new schoolhouses. In order to emphasize the distinction between grammar and common schools, school boards introduced dress regulations and the compulsory purchase of texts, making it even more difficult for lower-class children to advance upward in the public school system. As one observer ruefully remarked in 1861, state-supported schools had become 'a monster system of education for the middle and upper classes'. Schooling seemed unable to create a citizenry capable of being appropriately

THE OLD DISSECTING ROOM ON RICHMOND ST.

This is a picture taken about 1855 or 1856 in the upper room of the Toronto School of Medicine on Richmond street. The men at the table are: (1) Dr. John King, (2) Dr. Geo. De Grassi, (3) Tom Hays, a lecturer at the Toronto school, (4) Old Ned, the janitor at the dissecting room, (5) W. W. (Billy) Francis, a Toronto Med., who afterwards practised at Manitowaning, in Manitoulin Island.

Bernard R. Gloster, *Toronto School of Medicine, dissecting room, c. 1856*, c. 1904. Not all members of society had an equal chance of ending up on a dissecting table. Doctors demanded cadavers for the education of their students. How to obtain them? Grave-robbing was one way. But, following British precedent, a more efficient system was implemented by the passage of the Anatomy Act in 1843. All unclaimed bodies of inmates in public institutions (prisons, insane asylums, old age homes, Houses of Industry) were to be given to the province's medical schools. Most people in these institutions were from the working class. The act was amended several times throughout the century, but its thrust remained the same: in the name of scientific progress, the lonely destitute was dismembered simply because he or she was friendless and impoverished. MTL 1994, ACC: B 10-19a Repro t 13047.

informed and thus able to contribute effectively to the project of a deliberative democracy, which at a minimum required a populace able to debate 'rationally', a vigorous and independent press, and an elected assembly whose every action could be reviewed by an enlightened and informed public.[52]

Perhaps such a project was central to the minds of some Reformers in the 1830s and perhaps it remained so in the mind of such fringe players as William Lyon Mackenzie in the 1850s. But in the 1840s, the consensus among most politicians was that a strong central executive was required to operate an effective state. In the 1850s, the role of the Assembly and its connection to an 'informed' public opinion was further vitiated. In the two decades following the Act of Union, access to papers and to the information generated by growing state agencies became more difficult for both Assembly members and the wider public. Pleading excessive costs, party leaders such as Hincks, Baldwin, and Macdonald argued at various times against the notion of 'printing all'. '[A] mistaken idea prevailed', Baldwin lamented, 'that a member had nothing to do but to get up and ask for some information and the government must grant it.' 'The true principle', he continued, 'was to grant no information, unless a case were made out. . . .

[S]ome tangible evidence [was necessary] showing that the public would be benefited.' The question, of course, then became who was to make such a determination. '[W]hat is considered by one party as information of no moment, is precisely what by another party may be deemed of primary importance', one committee affirmed. By the end of the 1850s, however, the Assembly's printing committee decided what to exclude, how much to edit it, and what to print in its entirety. In the words of historical sociologist Bruce Curtis, the result was 'official administration of public intelligence'.[53]

Dissolution or Expansion?

In part because of the general social and economic turbulence, fissures widened within the Reform alliance. As Brown took over Reform leadership in Upper Canada, moderate Reformers from Lower Canada, led by Morin and George-Étienne Cartier (a former *patriote* who had become a lawyer for the Grand Trunk railway), broke away and joined forces with a group of Upper Canadians made up of some old Tories like MacNab and, more important, some younger moderate conservatives like the lawyer and businessman John A. Macdonald. Representing the triumph of common economic goals over religious and ethnic differences, this new alliance won the 1854 election and established a pattern that would remain the norm in central Canadian politics for the next four decades.

Even as new political coalitions emerged, railways and the state alike slowly began to professionalize and systematize their operations. British investors sent skilled British managers to upgrade the railways' managerial control and operating systems, and the Canadian state passed legislation aimed at encouraging stricter, more centralized control of labour and general operations. At the same time, the state reorganized its own internal operations to better meet the demands of the emerging industrial sphere and an increasingly complex international financial world. In addition to setting up an internal audit system, government signalled the beginnings of an independent commercial policy by adopting a tariff structure that did not simply favour British imports. A more modern bourgeois state was emerging, one that a decade later would provide the context for Confederation.

Yet in the short term, many feared for the Union's collapse. Although the new bourgeois party had won the election, the majority of Upper Canadians were not prepared to respect French Canadians' cultural differences and rejected a party that gave priority to business over the preservation of Protestant 'rights'. Many rallied around the incendiary leadership of George Brown: 'We are', Brown wrote, 'obliged to hold them [French Canadians] accountable for many of the anomalies and much of the wrong which now disgrace the system. They have evinced no forbearance, no generosity, no justice.' The election of 1858 ended in deadlock when Brown's Reformers carried a large majority in Upper Canada and Cartier's Bleus carried an equally large majority in Lower Canada. Brown and his Lower Canadian allies formed a government that lasted only a few hours. As a bitter Brown retreated, Macdonald and Cartier constructed a new Conservative administration.[54]

The key new player proved to be Finance Minister Alexander T. Galt, a liberal with close connections to the predominantly Bleu business community of Montreal. As a promoter of the St Lawrence and Atlantic Railway, he held (with Luther Holton and Casimir Gzowski) the construction contracts for the Grand Trunk line west of Toronto. But like his new political opponent, Brown, he was especially interested in western expansion. Galt's economic concerns won out over his Reformist orientation, and in 1858 he joined the Conservative government in order to expand the colonial union to include the Prairie west. Before that, however, he had to contain the financial crisis signalled by the near-bankruptcy of the Union's three major railways.

At a time when 80 to 85 per cent of all the government's revenue came from customs duties, tariffs on US goods were a crucial concern. Since 1855, the Reciprocity Treaty had allowed free trade in natural products but not in manufactured goods. Now, in order to increase revenue, foster local industrialization, and protect the commerce of the St Lawrence, Galt proposed to change the way tariffs were assessed, replacing specific duties with a comprehensive system of *ad valorem* rates. In late 1858, he canvassed boards of trade for their comments. Most Lower Canadian boards supported the plan, thinking that it would increase commerce over the St Lawrence River. Fearing a diminution of American trade, the Toronto board objected, arguing that the current system kept open the 'option of two markets'.[55]

Upper Canadian merchants believed they needed access not only to the US but also to Europe, by way of both the St Lawrence and the Erie Canal, in the US. When the Reciprocity Treaty took effect in 1855, exports of goods covered by it had doubled (from $8.5 million to $16.5 million) and imports of goods covered by it had quadrupled (to $7.7 million). But Montreal merchants felt that Upper Canadians benefited the most. Indeed, after the depression of 1857, Montreal merchants actively protested that the treaty was diverting trade away from the St Lawrence; Lower Canada was being 'sacrificed . . . to Upper Canada Agricultural interests'. Not surprisingly, these men saw Galt's plan as a 'national policy for the national advantage'.[56] Like so many policies before it, Galt's commercial policy further intensified sectional conflict.

By 1859, the intensity of that conflict threatened to split the Reform party. Militant Reformers, mainly from the southwest, demanded simple dissolution of the Union; their counterparts east of Toronto—more directly affected by commercial activity along the St Lawrence—wanted to resolve the sectional division. Matters climaxed at a Reform party convention in 1859. Whatever his personal antipathy for separate schools, the Grand Trunk, or Galt's new tariff, Brown insisted on the economic unity of the St Lawrence–Great Lakes system and continued to advocate representation by population as the solution to sectional conflicts. Taking the lead, he steered the convention toward a new proposal for a federal union. Debate focused on one key resolution: 'That . . . the best practicable remedy for the evils now encountered in the government of Canada is to be found in the formation of two or more local governments to which shall be committed the control of all matters of a local or sectional character and a general government charged with such matters as are necessarily common to both sections of the

Province.'[57] To appease the advocates of sectional autonomy, the term 'general government' was replaced with 'some joint authority'. Even though the Colonial Office had rebuffed an earlier demand by Galt for a broader union, the confederation option was left on the table. Yet further action required consent from both sections—and for that, sectional rivalries remained too intense.

The American Civil War broke the logjam. Wartime demand in the US led to an economic boom in Canada, but it also brought political risks. Although many Canadians, such as Brown, supported the abolition of slavery in the US, most followed Britain's lead in favouring the South. Relations with the US deteriorated as a result of incidents such as the St Albans raid, in which Confederate agents operating out of Lower Canada attacked St Albans, Vermont. With the ten-year term of the Reciprocity Treaty due to expire on 31 December 1863, the US Congress considered the question of renewal. In early 1864, fearing the impact of non-renewal on Upper Canada's economy, Brown approached C.J. Brydges, general manager of the Grand Trunk.

Brydges was Macdonald's political go-between with Maritime politicians regarding a proposed Intercolonial Railway, a project dear to the Grand Trunk. Now, in talks with Brown, Brydges tried to link his own interest in the Intercolonial with Brown's interest in western expansion. He offered Brown the chair of the Canada Board of the Hudson's Bay Company and—as he later reported to Macdonald—did his best to convince the Reform leader that 'nothing could be done about the Northwest without the Intercolonial.' Assuring Brydges that he was less opposed to the Intercolonial than others imagined, Brown also commented that 'the action of the Yankees on reciprocity . . . put an entirely new face on the question, and that it ought to be taken seriously into consideration'.[58] The key to Confederation had been found. Within four months, Brown, Macdonald, Cartier, and Galt had formed a new coalition government committed to a broader union of the British North American colonies.

Upper Canada and Confederation

The coalition of 1864 brought together two hitherto separate groups of the Anglo-Canadian business elite. Galt and Thomas D'Arcy McGee represented that sector associated with the Grand Trunk and Montreal. John A. Macdonald and his law partner in Kingston, Alexander Campbell, were closely involved with many of the Upper Canadian financial institutions active in railroad financing, and Macdonald was fast friends with C.J. Brydges of the Grand Trunk. Centred on the Grand Trunk, these men favoured eastward expansion via the Intercolonial. At the same time, the Grand Trunk was open to westward expansion; indeed, its president, Edward Watkin, had been actively working with the Colonial Secretary in an effort to arrange the purchase from the Hudson's Bay Company of a right of way to the Pacific coast. George Brown supported the Grand Trunk's rival, the Great Western, represented the industrial and financial interests of Montreal's rival, Toronto, as well as the more prosperous interests in rural Upper Canada, who, as good land became increasingly scarce, were pressing for expansion to the prairies.

Complementary and at times overlapping business interests formed one thread that helped to bind the coalition together. A second thread was shared attitudes toward democracy. Both Macdonald and Brown were elitists—opposed to the notion of political equality, without faith in the ability of the masses, and in favour of privilege for the propertied. This elitism was reflected in Macdonald's insistence on a strong central government. As he told one of the conferences leading to Confederation, local or provincial governments must be kept weak in order to secure 'a strong and lasting government under which we can work out constitutional liberty as opposed to democracy'.[59]

For many of the Fathers of Confederation, the rights of one minority in particular took precedence over majority rule. Which minority should be protected? Certainly not the Native people. As Macdonald wrote to the electoral returning officer of the district of Algoma in Ontario in October 1867, 'I drew the clauses relating to Algoma in the Union Act, but I really forgot all about the Indians. Had they occurred to my mind I should certainly have excluded them [from voting].' Federal legislation passed in 1868 and 1869 designed to further assimilate Native peoples prompted the Anishinaabe of eastern Ontario to form the Grand General Indian Council of Ontario, reminiscent of past Anishinaabe alliances, in order to combat federal policy. But federal politicians rarely listened to the council's recommendations. Having made his view of democracy clear during the Confederation debates ('Classes and property should be represented as well as numbers'), Macdonald specified his preferred minority in connection with the establishment of the appointed Upper House, or Senate (the North American version of the British House of Lords): 'the rights of the minority ought to be protected and the rich are always fewer in number than the poor.'[60]

George Brown was equally opposed to democracy. In the US, Brown pointed out, 'the balance of power is held by the unreasoning ignorant mass, to swing them is the grand aim of the contest and as truth, character, statesmanship, honest policy and fair argument would be thrown away upon them, both parties by consent—nay of necessity—resort to other expedients'. The pro-Confederation forces in the Canadas were united by geography (centred on the St Lawrence–Lake Ontario transportation corridor); by shared social, political, and economic views; and by common economic and political problems. Those elites, linked as they were to powerful financial interests in England, became the moving force behind Confederation.[61]

The coalition, formed in June 1864, acted with dispatch: in September they arrived—uninvited—at Charlottetown, where they commandeered a conference that had been organized to discuss Maritime union. Here they presented their broader vision: a British North American federation. Writing to his wife, the exuberant Brown described his arrival at Charlottetown in imperialistic terms:

About noon . . . we came suddenly on the Capital City of the Island. Our steamer dropped anchor magnificently in the stream and its man-of-war cut evidently inspired the natives with huge respect for their big brothers from Canada. I flatter myself we did that well. . . . Having dressed ourselves in the correct style, our two boats were lowered man-of-war fashion—and being each duly manned with four oarsmen and a boatswain, dressed in blue uniform, hats, belts, etc., in regular style, we pulled away for shore and landed like Mr Christopher Columbus who had the precedence of us in taking possession of portions of the American continent.[62]

The broad picture that the Canadians sketched—a strong central government, weak local governments, an appointed Upper House, a debt-equalization scheme, and a subsidy program—was accepted in principle by a majority of those at Charlottetown. The details would be hammered out at Quebec. Canadians controlled the conference. They prepared the draft resolutions for each day's agenda; the secretary was Macdonald's brother-in-law; the chair was Étienne Taché, from Lower Canada; Canadians made all the major introductory speeches; and Oliver Mowat, an Upper Canadian lawyer and politician, put the 'decisions into constitutional and legal shape'.[63] Canadians were reluctant to compromise on any of their proposals. Should peripheral areas such as Prince Edward Island and Newfoundland fail to agree, so be it; they could be brought in later. The seventy-two Quebec resolutions became the backbone of the constitution that, after minor modification at Westminster in 1866–7, was enacted into law by the imperial parliament as the British North America Act on 1 July 1867.

On one issue, however, the Canadians bowed to their eastern counterparts—New Brunswick's Samuel Tilley and Nova Scotia's Charles Tupper. As Tilley put it, 'We won't have the Union unless you give us the Railway'. In addition to a promise that the new government would complete the Intercolonial, Tilley secured the right both to increase the colony's debt before Confederation and to borrow money at a reduced rate of interest, pending the new government's assumption of debts. Since Canada's debt far overshadowed that of the Maritimes, even George Brown could hardly object. These concessions allowed Tilley and Tupper to raise money immediately for local railroad construction and thus to go some way toward pacifying the anti-confederates.[64]

Nevertheless, the Canadians left little room for doubt as to the roles they expected the various partners to play in the new nation: the Maritimes would supply minerals, coal, fish, and an opening to the sea; the west would supply wheat; and the Canadas would manufacture goods. Or, as George Brown put it, 'our farmers and manufacturers and mechanics shall carry their wares unquestioned into every village of the Maritime Provinces and they shall with equal freedom bring their fish and their coal and their West India produce to our 3 millions of inhabitants.' Economic affairs—including banking, currency, bankruptcy, shipping, railways, trade and commerce, and immigration policy—would be concentrated in the hands of the central government, while jurisdiction over social and cultural matters would remain local.

Brown staked his reputation on 'rep by pop'; acceptance of this principle was the sine qua non of his participation in a coalition government. Yet the virulence of his anti-Catholic, anti-French attacks on separate schools made it impossible for the francophone delegates to agree to it: no French Canadian could advocate placing French Canadian culture in the hands of an unchecked anglophone majority from Upper Canada reinforced by the English-speaking majorities of the Atlantic provinces. The solution to the impasse was a strong provincial government with jurisdiction over 'our language, our laws, and our religion'. During the Union, a quasi-federal system had grown and solidified within a legislative union. Confederation would now create two new governments to give expression to this basic political reality. The de facto pursuit of separate cultural and social agendas in Upper and Lower Canada became the de jure constitutional reality in Ontario and Quebec.

Both sections, however, contained minorities: English Protestant in Lower Canada, and Catholic—both English and French—in Upper Canada. Accordingly, the Fathers of Confederation provided protection for the linguistic rights of French and English speakers at the federal level and in Quebec (eventually Section 133 of the British North America Act), the rights of the Protestant minority to their own schools in Quebec, and the rights of Catholics to their own schools in Ontario. Where appropriate, the same rights would be extended to the minorities in the Maritimes, particularly New Brunswick.

These compromises eased the widespread fear that Confederation would weaken minority rights. Yet, as with much else in the British North America Act, other interpretations were possible. George Brown, for one, was jubilant at the conclusion of the Quebec Conference: 'All right!!!' he wrote to his wife, 'Constitution adopted—a most creditable document—a complete reform of all the abuses and injustice we have complained of!! Is it not wonderful? French Canadianism entirely extinguished!'[65]

One other general question that prompted much debate at Quebec and thereafter was the appropriate balance of power between the federal and provincial governments. John A. Macdonald pointed to the US Civil War to underline the dangers of a decentralized federalism based on 'states' rights'. Although Macdonald understood that a highly centralized union was out of the question, he pushed to expand central government powers to their maximum limits. 'I am satisfied', he wrote in December 1864, that 'we have hit upon the only practicable plan—I do not mean to say the best plan. . . . [W]e have avoided exciting local interests, and . . . have raised a strong Central Government. . . . If the Confederation goes on you . . . will see both the Local Parliaments and Governments absorbed in the General Power. This is as plain to me as if I saw it accomplished now. . . . [O]f course it does not do to adopt that point of view in discussing the subject in Lower Canada.'[66]

Macdonald believed he had achieved a strong central government and weak provincial governments in part because GENERAL residual powers had been assigned to the central government, because the federal government could appoint lieutenant-governors, and because it had the power both to disallow provincial legislation and to pass remedial legislation. His was a sanguine view: overriding provincial legislation was a political minefield. Moreover many believed that the lieutenant governors were representatives of the Crown, not the federal government. Despite Macdonald, the relative balance of power between the central and provincial governments remained ambiguous. It was only a matter of time before a centralizing prime minister in Ottawa would confront a powerful Ontario jealously promoting its autonomy.

Chapter 7

Ontario in the New Dominion, 1867–1905

Ontario was, from the start, the strongest province in the new nation. Almost half of all Canadians lived there. With 82 of 181 seats in the federal legislature, with its debt burdens eased, its economic interests mollified, westward expansion imminent, and the French problem muted, the province seemed to have little to gain from tampering with the Confederation agreement. But politics dictated otherwise. The coalition government that had carried Confederation could not last. Conservatives outnumbered Reformers nine to three in the cabinet, and John A. Macdonald passed out jobs and favours lavishly to Conservatives. Reformers became restive: in December 1865, George Brown left the coalition (while continuing to support Confederation), and he and the Ontario Reformers gradually moved toward their old sectional policies. Blithely ignoring Brown's resignation, Macdonald continued to emphasize the image of the government as a coalition and carefully prepared for Ontario's first election.

The Emergence of the Ontario Liberals

Like Sydenham during the Union's first election, Macdonald left little to chance. Claiming that a non-partisan coalition was far superior to self-interested parties, Macdonald shrewdly recruited John Sandfield Macdonald to head the Ontario Conservative party. A Scottish Catholic with Reform roots and Conservative friends, Sandfield had never supported Confederation, but he accepted it as a *fait accompli*. In an era when federal and provincial elections were held within the same period (though not on the same day), the two Macdonalds made a formidable team. John A. managed the raising and distribution of election funds, timed the votes for individual constituencies to create a bandwagon effect in favour of the Conservatives, situated polling stations far from Reform strongholds, and appointed partisan returning officers. Intimidation and bribery were widespread, and George Brown declared the process 'absurd and undignified'. But it was effective. The Conservatives carried Ontario in 1867 by a wide federal margin and won a strong provincial majority.

Close ties existed between the two governments. Five members of the Ontario cabinet also sat in the federal assembly. Both Sandfield and John A. Macdonald desired harmony between the two governments. And both were determined to keep Brown and the Reformers—now beginning to call themselves

Liberals—from gaining power at either level. Sandfield Macdonald's government passed some noteworthy measures, including a Free Grant and Homestead Act, designed to attract Americans to Ontario's newly opening north; an election act that broadened voting rights and restricted voting to one day; and an education act that made primary and secondary schooling free and, for students between the ages of seven and twelve, compulsory for four months of the year. But the Liberals, now the province's official opposition, characterized Sandfield Macdonald as little more than a federal puppet. They called for an end to dual seats (whereby a person could sit in both the provincial and the federal legislature) and argued that 'subordinate' federalism must be replaced by a more equal relationship. 'No outside control by the Lower Canadian French', the rallying cry of the Upper Canadian Reformers, now became, 'No domination by the federal government.'

When, in 1869, the federal government granted a discontented Nova Scotia 'better terms', Ontario's Liberal leader, Edward Blake, complained: Ontario's taxpayers would bear the cost of constitutional change, yet they had not been consulted; it was because Upper Canada lacked control over its destiny that the Union had failed, and Confederation had been intended to remedy that situation. Now, however, 'The former evils so far from being removed by Confederation will be intensified, the just expectations of the people will be disappointed, sectional strife will be aroused, the federal principle will be violated and the Constitution will be shaken to its base.' All provinces must consent to any changes in the Confederation agreement, Blake concluded. Ontario's Liberals had found their platform.

The last straw for the Liberals came in 1870, after the Red River Métis under Louis Riel resisted Canada's efforts to annex their territory. In response, Macdonald's federal government passed the Manitoba Act, creating a new bilingual and bicultural province that resembled Quebec far more than it did Ontario. Once again the French seemed to be dominating—now in a part of the country that many Ontarians considered their special preserve. Western settlement had been a primary goal of Confederation, and Ontarians saw the prairie region as a natural extension of their own province. 'We hope to see a new Upper Canada in the North-West Territory,' Brown's *Globe* proclaimed in 1869, 'a new Upper Canada in its well regulated society and government—in its education, morality and religion.' The intellectuals of the Ontario-based Canada First movement carried this credo to extreme lengths with their vision of a 'super race' reigning supreme in the continent's north.[1]

In the 1871 election, Liberals campaigned as if their opponents were John A. Macdonald's federal Conservatives. Sandfield Macdonald's close links to the latter hurt him, and his plans for opening up the province's north seemed woefully insufficient. The election results were close—too close. Blake moved a want-of-confidence motion that passed by a single vote, making him premier and initiating a period of Liberal dominance that would endure for more than three decades. With his sights on a political career in Ottawa, though, Blake himself remained in office only long enough to persuade Oliver Mowat to succeed him as leader in 1872. Mowat was always intensely partisan in his approach to politics. He believed that the secret to governing Ontario lay, according to the rural imagery of the

Oliver Mowat. Although trained in John A. Macdonald's law office, Mowat did not share Macdonald's political views, and the two once came close to blows during a debate in the Legislative Assembly. Mowat had entered the coalition cabinet in 1865 as postmaster general, but after the Quebec Conference, Macdonald offered him a judicial position—effectively depriving the Reform party of a very able politician. But Mowat did not stay out of politics for long. In 1872 he accepted an offer of the leadership of Ontario's Liberal party from the departing Blake; he would serve as the province's premier for the next twenty-four years. NA PA28631.

time, in the careful 'husbandry' of the business of government, and once commented that the 'distinction of parties' was 'the only principle on which free government appears to be capable of being worked'. Like John A. Macdonald, he was a product of the Union period. Indeed, he had once articled in John A.'s law office but had quit because, as a Reformer, he could not support Macdonald's political program. The two men had come close to blows in an ensuing political debate. Nevertheless, they had much in common. Both men believed in a strong executive role and the need for close control of patronage; both preferred the political centre and favoured moderate compromise over confrontation. But neither would back away from a clash of wills. On one issue—the constitutional distribution of power—Macdonald and Mowat alike were single-mindedly committed to their respective positions.[2]

Defining Confederation: Boundary Battles and Constitutional Conflicts

The boundary between the pre-Confederation Province of Canada and Rupert's Land—the Hudson's Bay Company land bought by the federal government in

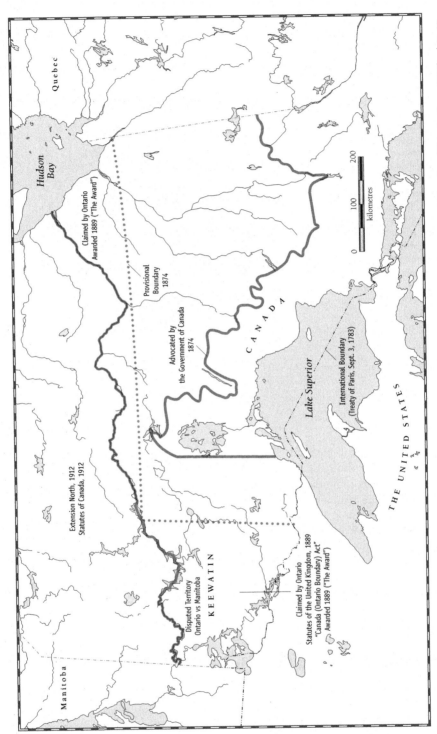

Ontario's northern boundaries, 1874–1912. From W.G. Dean and Geoffrey J. Matthews, *Economic Atlas of Ontario* (Toronto: University of Toronto Press, 1969), plate 97.

1869–70—had long been a source of dispute. If the northwest was not to be part of Ontario, precisely where was the boundary to be drawn? Even the two arbitrators charged with settling the dispute could not agree, and in 1872 they submitted separate reports. A year later the federal Conservatives fell from power. The provincial Liberals and the federal Liberals, under Alexander Mackenzie, formed a new three-man arbitration board that reported in 1878, supporting Ontario's demands. All that remained was for the two governments to ratify the agreement in their respective legislatures. Ontario stood to gain some 285,000 square kilometres of new land, and as far as Mowat was concerned, the matter was over. But before Mackenzie could ratify the agreement, the Conservatives, under the redoubtable John A., triumphed in the 1878 federal election. Not only did Macdonald refuse to implement the arbitration award, he extended the Manitoba boundary east to cover the disputed territory.

So intense was the dispute in the Lake of the Woods–Rainy River area that the federal and provincial governments each sent their own law agents, who ended up arresting each other. The region was mainly boreal forest with (everyone believed) enormous timber, mineral, and even agricultural potential. Under the British North America Act, Crown lands and natural resources fell to the provinces, and timber licences and royalties on mineral exploitation were major sources of provincial income. But the Manitoba Act reserved Crown lands and natural resources to the federal government in both Manitoba and the Northwest Territories. Whoever controlled the disputed territory would control economic development and benefit from a substantial increase in revenue. The winner would also gain control of numerous opportunities for political patronage—in the establishment of municipal government, the granting of liquor licences, the appointment of judicial and other officials—that could be used for partisan purposes. New sources of patronage in the north could give the premier a way of increasing power without antagonizing already entrenched municipal interests.[3]

Small wonder that Mowat chose to personally argue the boundary case in the courts. He prepared well: his legal department amassed five volumes of documents and maps relating to the disputed area, whereas the federal government's file consisted only of one committee report. Mowat himself set the questions that the final court of appeal, the Judicial Committee of the Privy Council in England, would consider—questions that privileged the 1878 arbitration findings in Ontario's favour. In July 1884, the Privy Council backed the province almost without qualification. Some 50,000 people cheered Premier Mowat on his return to Toronto.[4]

Macdonald had been bested, but he fought on. 'Even if all the territory Mr Mowat asks for were awarded to Ontario', he warned before the court made its decision, 'there is not one stick of timber, one acre of land, or one lump of lead, iron or gold that does not belong to the Dominion.' When the federal government signed Treaty Three with the Ojibwa in 1873, Macdonald asserted, the state acquired the rights to all the natural resources in the treaty area. In so doing he effectively acknowledged that First Nations peoples had indeed owned the land and resources before the treaty. In fact, the Royal Proclamation of 1763 had said as much, but until now no colonial or Canadian court had ever supported that position. 'We say', Mowat replied, 'that there is no Indian title at law or equity. The claim of the Indians is simply moral and no more.' Mowat argued that the Proclamation was 'provisional' and had been repealed by the Quebec Act of 1774. Even William Meredith, Ontario's Conservative leader and a strong supporter of political centralization at the federal level, wondered if it was 'worthwhile risking another litigation on the strength of the Indian title?' He wanted to put the issue to rest rather than let Mowat 'use the question as a rallying cry and in the end get a decision in his favour which would give his friends another [opportunity] to glorify him'. Besides, the increasingly angry Meredith informed Macdonald, 'in justice to the party in Ontario, it ought not to be handicapped again with another Provincial rights question in which it will be sought to fasten on the opposition here the charge of uniting with the Dominion authorities to plunder Ontario.' Macdonald ignored that good advice.[5]

The result was a legal battle called the St Catherines Milling case. The federal government had granted the St Catherines Milling and Lumber Company the right to cut timber in the disputed area. Arguing that control of that resource belonged to the province not to the federal government, Mowat sued the company. The case ended up in the Privy Council, and again Mowat won. The powers of the federal government were further weakened. In 1889, Macdonald ratified the court's decision and Ontario assumed untrammelled rights to the land and resources of the vast new territory. A further agreement between the two governments in 1912 extended the boundary to its current position.

The land dispute provides a window into more than the nature of provincial-federal relations in the evolving Canadian state. The issue turned on the definition of Aboriginal land rights. Had the federal government been able to convince the courts that Native peoples did own land before entering into Treaty Three, then Macdonald would have won. The courts, however, rejected that argument. In Chancery Court—the first of four courts to hear the case—Chancellor John Boyd concluded that the Treaty Three Native peoples had no rights to any land or resources. In the context of Upper Canadian/Ontarian jurisprudence regarding Native peoples, Boyd's language was especially racist and demeaning: 'As heathens and barbarians it was not thought that they had any proprietary title to the soil.' He felt that they 'had no fixed abode' and that these 'rude red-men' were 'a more than usually degraded Indian type'. Part of the explanation for the harshness of Boyd's attitude stems from the fact that as he wrote the decision, two of his sons were fighting against Native people and Louis Riel in the Northwest Rebellion of 1885. For their part, the federal lawyers did little to counteract Boyd's bias. They called no representative from the Ojibwa peoples, nor did they, at the Court of Chancery or later in the appeal process, ever effectively use available historical material to refute the province's claims concerning the nature of the Proclamation Act of 1763. That act had in fact been validated by many Upper Canadian leaders (including Governor General Simcoe) in the treaty process of the 1790s and later, but the federal government never exploited those instances and mounted only a half-hearted defence of Aboriginal title. As one student of the case concluded, for them 'it was merely a legal argument'.

Box 7.1　Ojibwa in the Northwest

Ojibwa in the Rainy Lake region—an area in the northwest noted for its hunting, trapping, and fishing potential—successfully pursued commercial farming. Their crop was wild rice, or *manito gitigaan*, which they had been cultivating for centuries before European contact. Hardly wild, this grain requires annual seeding, weeding, protection against predators (muskrats and blackbirds), and water control, as well as careful processing after harvesting. In the early nineteenth century, the Ojibwa sold their wild rice and other produce to both the Hudson's Bay Company and its Montreal-based rival, the North West Company. As cultivation increased, so did population: the Rainy River (Ojibwa) grew from 455 in 1822 to 1,800 in 1875.

By the 1880s, resource and railway companies provided ready markets for their produce. Farming was deemed a priority in Treaty Three, signed by the Ojibwa in 1873; yet in 1881, the federal government passed a law requiring approval by an Indian agent of all the Ojibwa's commercial transactions, lest, in the words of Prime Minister John A. Macdonald, the 'wild nomad[s] of the North-West' waste their earnings on liquor. Anyone who bought from the Ojibwa without such approval risked summary conviction. But the Indian agent could be hard to find. As a result, customers found other suppliers. The Ojibwa's troubles were compounded when, to facilitate logging, the Ontario government permitted the damming of a large river; the ensuing floods swamped Ojibwa farmland. By the 1890s, many Ojibwa had abandoned farming altogether. Then white settlers complained that many reserves were not being used in a 'productive' way: for farming—thus providing the justification that the government used to appropriate Ojibwa land a few years later.[1]

---

1. Quotation: Leo G. Waisberg and T.E. Holtzkman, '"A Tendency to Discourage Them from Cultivating": Ojibwa Agriculture and Indian Affairs Administration in Northwestern Ontario', *Ethnohistory* 40 (1993): 175–211. See also Elizabeth Arthur, 'Orientation and Disorientation in Rainy River', *Ontario History* 73 (1981): 195–218; Kathi Avery Kinew, 'Manito Gitigaan: Governance in the Great Spirit's Garden Wild Rice in Treaty #3 from Pre-Treaty to the 1990s', in *Papers of the Twenty-Sixth Algonquian Conference*, edited by David H. Pentland (Winnipeg: University of Manitoba, 1995), 183–94.

It was much more than that for the absent Ojibwa. They were well aware of the value of their land and would have made creditable witnesses. During the Treaty Three negotiations, Ma-we-do-pe-nais, an Ojibwa chief, made their position clear: 'All this is our property where you have come. . . . This is what we think, that the Great Spirit has planted us on this ground where we are, as you were where you came from. We think where we are is our property. The sound of the rustling of the gold is under my feet where I stand; we have a rich country; it is the Great Spirit who gave us this; where we stand upon is the Indian's property and belongs to them.'

In July 1888, the Judicial Committee of the Privy Council, the final court of appeal, moderated Boyd's judgement only slightly. The court did allow that before the treaty, the Native peoples had a right of occupancy, 'a personal and usufructuary right, dependent upon the good will of the Sovereign'. Other than that, the Privy Council sided with Boyd and granted full ownership to Ontario. St Catherine's Milling has become a foundational case for the settling of many twentieth-century Native title cases. But the decision that Native peoples' right to land was only 'usufructuary' meant that they were second-class peoples who could be granted only a lesser title to property (occupancy, but not ownership) than that granted white Europeans. As land claims lawyer Victor Savino noted one hundred years later, the St Catherine's case was one where 'Indians were used and fructed'.[6]

The Ontario boundary dispute helped to rally support behind those who, like Mowat, believed that Confederation had created a largely decentralized federation. As a member of the pre-Confederation cabinet, a delegate to the Quebec Conference, and an active participant in the debates over the relative powers of the central and provincial governments, Mowat had been as much a Father of Confederation as Macdonald. Now, as premier of Canada's largest province, he took the lead in the evolving process of constitutional interpretation. In addition to the boundary dispute, Mowat personally argued Ontario's case in a number of other precedent-setting appeals before the Privy Council; he won all of those cases and in the process defined the constitutional limit on the federal power to disallow provincial legislation. Together these cases confirmed the older Reform view, first articulated in the Reform Convention of 1859, of a decentralized federalism in which each province remained sovereign within its constitutional jurisdiction. Ontario's overwhelming victories dealt a severe blow to Macdonald's goal of a politically centralized Canada. The disputes were far from over, but now that Ontario's territorial ambitions had been satisfied, the province no longer had any serious quarrel with the federal system. Ever since the days of the Loyalists, when Britain had granted them land at the expense of the Native peoples, many Upper Canadians had seen themselves as occupying a position of special favour. In championing territorial expansion, Mowat and the Liberals laid claim to both the Reformist and Loyalist mantles. From now on, Ontarians would tend 'to identify the national interest as their own'.[7]

Centralizing Provincial Power

Even as Mowat chopped away at federal power, he moved to centralize political power in the province. But he did so always under the guise of government as the 'benefactor of local communities'. Numerous acts were passed in the Mowat era centralizing control of health, liquor, welfare, and education, always in the name of efficiency and always resulting in establishing direct links from the state to local communities. So entrenched did this process become that one scholar has concluded that 'even after the passage of more than a century, [it] remains recognizable in the basic contours of the Ontario government.' Debts accumulated by Upper Canadian municipalities under the aegis of the Municipal Loan Fund gave the alert Mowat his first opportunity to transfer patronage powers from local gov-

Box 7.2   The Judiciary and Politics

We have already pointed to the close relations that existed between the judicial and political spheres in Upper Canada. Those relations belie a popular notion that the Charter of Rights and Freedoms in 1982 has led to an unprecedented politicization of our courts. This current perception is further undermined by looking at the general role played by the judiciary—especially the Supreme Court of Canada and the Judicial Committee of the Privy Council (JCPC)—in resolving disputes between Ontario and the federal government in the late nineteenth century.

In the first place, both these judicial bodies had links to the political sphere. John A. Macdonald favoured the creation of a Canadian Supreme Court in order to augment federal powers: '[W]e must', he wrote, when considering a replacement to the court in 1888, 'endeavour to get a good man who will not throw Dominion rights away.' For the most part, decisions of the Supreme Court did support Macdonald's view of Canadian governance. Small wonder that advocates of Ontario's rights avoided as much as possible arguing their cases before that court. Provincial-rights advocates had greater—one might say, overwhelming—success arguing their cases before the JCPC. But that court too was strongly tied to things political. In effect, it was a quasi-judicial institution that advised the Privy Council. The Lord Chancellor, the JCPC's most powerful member, also sat in the House of Lords and generally had a seat in cabinet. While these courts were in legal theory supposed to be umpires above the fray, in reality they emerged *from* that fray and in different ways reflected contending political stances. Indeed, some constitutional historians have labelled the JCPC 'the real fathers of Canadian confederation' and assert that it was a court on 'a political mission'. Whether one agrees with this view—and it is contested—it is hard to escape the belief that the JCPC's decisions bolstered a provincial-rights interpretation of the BNA Act and to that extent actively and importantly entered into the political realm supportive of Mowat's vision of Ontario's future.[1]

1. Quotations: James Snell and Frederic Vaughan, *The Supreme Court of Canada: History of the Institution* (Toronto: Osgoode Society, 1985), 46; Frederic Vaughan, 'Critics of the Judicial Committee: The New Orthodoxy and an Alternative Explanation', in *Making the Law: The Courts and the Constitution*, edited by John Saywell and George Vegh (Toronto: Copp Clark Pitman, 1991), 181, 177.

ernments to the provincial government. Using a fat treasury provided to him by the defeated Sandfield Macdonald government, Mowat forgave some municipal debts, paid down others, and for those few municipalities not in debt he provided cash grants, in return for all of which he assumed many hitherto local functions and the appointment-making power that accompanied them. From that beginning, he instituted a centralized appointment process that rewarded deserving local party activists. Unlike the pre-Confederation Family Compact politicians,

Mowat consciously attempted to link the centre to the peripheries, through careful patronage appointments. While John A. Macdonald fell from power in 1872 as a result of his unsavoury connection to the Pacific Scandal, Mowat, through his long tenure in power, was never seriously tainted by any scandal. 'What the chiefs . . . shrink from doing', the conservative critic Goldwin Smith smirked, 'underlings do.' Put in a more favourable light, Mowat had constructed a smoothly running patronage-based political machine, one the provincial Conservatives could only dream of emulating.[8]

Religion and Language

In the 1880s, long-standing conflicts over religion and language resurfaced. Education was a particularly sensitive area in this regard. While the BNA Act had given Ontario and Quebec jurisdiction over their own school systems, it also guaranteed educational rights that 'existed in law and in practice' at the time of Confederation. In other words, Ontario's separate school system, while it need not be expanded, could not be restricted or abolished. In the aftermath of the uprising of 1870, many Ontarians mistakenly interpreted the French-speaking, Catholic Métis people's resistance to arbitrary annexation of their territory as a conflict over issues of religion, language, and schools.

In 1870, Louis Riel's provisional Red River government executed Thomas Scott, an Ontario Orangeman. To many Ontarians, Riel had become a murderer as well as a rebel. When Premier Blake issued a warrant for his arrest, Riel left the country. In 1885, however, the controversy resurfaced: Riel returned to lead an abortive Aboriginal-Métis rebellion in Saskatchewan. This time, he would be tried and hanged for treason.

In Quebec, Riel was a hero; the Québécois cheered Wilfrid Laurier, a future Canadian prime minister, when he proclaimed, 'Had I been born on the banks of the Saskatchewan I would myself have shouldered a musket.' In the heat of the Riel affair, Quebec's premier, Honoré Mercier, offered the Jesuits in his province compensation for land the British had seized from them following the Conquest of 1760. He then invited the Pope to arbitrate the settlement. Protestant extremists loudly condemned this papal intrusion into Canada's domestic politics, and several Conservative MPs from Ontario requested that the federal government disallow the Quebec legislation, known as the Jesuit Estates Act. When this request was refused, an organization calling itself the Equal Rights Association attracted widespread support from Ontario Protestants. By 1891, anti-Catholic feeling had escalated to the point that a more militant group, the Protestant Protective Association, established itself in Ontario. The PPA membership pledge required followers to 'denounce Roman Catholicism' and oppose the participation of Catholics in public life.[9]

The extremism of the PPA may in part have reflected the new visibility of Ontario's urban Irish Catholics. By the late nineteenth century, Irish Catholics were more likely than any other religious group except Presbyterians and Methodists to own houses and land. Moreover, Ontario's Catholic leaders understood that their flock had arrived—'made it'—in the urban milieu. They began to adopt a more open and accommodating attitude to the wider community within which they lived. While still protective of separate schools, they preached denominational peace and the cultivation of positive links between Catholics and Protestants. Three weeks after he had been stoned by members of Toronto's Orange Order in 1889, Catholic archbishop John Walsh promised to 'inculcate in our boys the best sentiments of patriotism and love of country, *for this is their country*, . . . despite the injustice preached against us at the present time—an injustice which will not, which cannot prevail in a free country'. Although Mowat placed some restrictions on French-language schooling in the 1880s, he generally adhered to the promises he and his Reform colleagues had made to separate schools at the time of Confederation. But Ontario's Conservative party flirted with the PPA. When Meredith resigned after losing his third election, his successor, George F. Marter, touched off an internal power struggle by announcing that he favoured the abolition of all separate schools. In 1896, James P. Whitney, the rising star of Ontario conservatism, defeated Marter and committed his party to improving relations with the province's Catholic minority. Under Whitney, the separate-schools issue ceased, for a time, to occupy centre stage in Ontario's partisan contests.[10]

Mowat and the Economy

Mowat's long rule as premier had been marked by critical developments on a number of fronts. The manner of territorial acquisition connoted a hardening of attitude toward the rights of Native peoples. Mowat's contributions to the constitutional evolution of Canada and his consistent commitment to religious tolerance were substantial and fundamental. His success on the issue of the boundary dispute provided Ontario untold potential riches. The economic policies pursued by his government to exploit those and other business possibilities were no less important.

The provincial-rights movement promoted the notion that Ontario's economic interests were not being adequately served by federal policies—a decade-long fight over control of the Canadian Pacific Railway (CPR), for example, ended in 1881 with the contract awarded to a Montreal-based company. Yet, between 1870 and 1909, the federal government spent an average of $658,571 per year on grants to northern Ontario railways. Much of that spending went to southern Ontario manufacturing companies that made rails and rolling stock. Railway-building in the rest of the province focused on feeder lines: twenty-one new lines opened for business, six of them radiating outward from Toronto and Hamilton. By 1879, 5,230 kilometres of track overlay the province. A period of consolidation occurred in the 1880s, with the Grand Trunk alone absorbing fifteen companies. Nevertheless, the major manufacturing centres of Toronto and Hamilton complained that they lacked direct rail connections to the Canadian west. Similarly, Ontario industries dependent on imported raw materials (such as coal) complained that the 1879 National Policy of high protective tariffs favoured the coal-producing Maritimes and promoted an east–west flow of trade that benefited Montreal over Hamilton and Toronto.[11]

Box 7.3   Mowat and Development

Mowat had long been what might be termed a developmental pragmatist. In 1859, he had failed to get the Upper Canadian legislature to pass a bill allowing mill owners to flood neighbouring lands on the payment of compensation. Mowat believed that existing property rights should not be permitted to impede economic growth. Accordingly, one of the first acts his government passed was the Water Privileges Act of 1873, which put into practice what he had failed to accomplish in 1859. For Mowat, resources were to there to be used, and if current occupants were not extracting the maximum benefit from them and if others offered the possibility of greater use, then the rights of the latter should have priority. When the Ontario courts denied loggers the right to float their logs downstream if such activity interfered with owners of downstream rights, Mowat passed an Act for Protecting the Public Interest in Rivers, Streams and Creeks, in 1881. Mowat claimed that the lumberers' loss of the right to float logs on some 234 streams being used for that purpose would cost the province an immense amount of revenue from timber limits and 'render lumbering over a large proportion of the public domain an unprofitable pursuit'. In 1885, Mowat passed a further piece of protective legislation that made it difficult for citizens to sue lumber mills for polluting streams with sawdust, which at times 'accumulates in great floating masses, substantial enough, occasionally for a man to walk upon'. Environmental and aesthetic values did not bulk large in Mowat's world view.[1]

1. Jamie Benidickson, 'Private Rights and Public Purposes in the Lakes, Rivers and Streams of Ontario, 1870–1930', in *Essays in the History of Canadian Law*, vol. 2, edited by David Flaherty (Toronto: Osgoode Society, 1983), 365–417.

In 1873 a major depression throughout the Atlantic economies initiated a period of general commodity price declines. Many historians view the last third of the nineteenth century as one of general economic depression for Ontario. But this interpretation requires some qualification. Dependent upon exports of agricultural and lumber products, Ontario's (and Canada's) economy was indeed tested by fundamental changes in market conditions. But the price decline was not evenly distributed; prices for wheat and barley and for some vegetable and animal products fell unevenly. Furthermore, Canada's terms of trade improved in this period as wholesale prices of imports fell and overall export prices held relatively steady.[12]

Declining prices for wheat and barley reinforced a trend toward mixed farming that had already become apparent in the 1850s. 'As far as Ontario is concerned,' the Toronto *Globe* predicted in 1878, 'the end of exporting wheat is not far off.' In fact, wheat continued to generate more profits than dairy products, but milk and butter did become major cash products for farmers. Expanding export markets were a catalyst for the development of a cheese industry, shipping to both the United States and Great Britain, and by the late 1860s, as one observer noted, farmers had 'cheese-on-the-brain'. Canadian exports of butter levelled off during the late 1870s before declining during the 1880s. Domestic consumption, however, continued to grow. In part, the decline in butter exports reflected what some thought to be poor quality. 'The dary is sometimes a gude one', a satirist wrote in the *Canada Farmer* in 1868, 'but in ten kases out of one it is a pur konstructed bildin. . . . [I]t may be a log bildin, chinkd and plasterd, with a hole five feet deep inside. On the groun floor, the mylk dishes is plasd: as ther is no vntilation here, the milk molds B-4 it sours. . . . [A] boy is dispatchd with the instruktions to get hiest markt price, as it is new.'[13]

Oliver Mowat carefully cultivated rural Ontario constituencies, where the Liberals had traditionally enjoyed strong support. Rural voters rewarded him with majorities in every election he fought. The Department of Agriculture—one of the largest provincial ministries—spent thousands annually researching the newest developments in agricultural technology and encouraging farmers to keep pace with the latest innovations. Agricultural societies, funded in part by provincial grants, dotted the province, and a new agricultural college opened at Guelph in 1874. Generally, then, the agricultural sector prospered during the late nineteenth century. But it could not provide sufficient employment for Ontario's growing population. Mechanization required capital investments beyond the reach of many marginal farmers, particularly those working the less productive land in eastern Ontario; farmers who could afford new equipment often became cash poor and unable to purchase land for their children. Increasing numbers of rural people moved to the urban areas to seek work in new manufacturing industries.

Manufacturing also experienced significant change in this period. In 1871, most of Ontario's manufacturing industries were in primary production, which encouraged the wide dispersal of production in small shops situated close to their raw materials. Even by 1871, however, several distinguishing characteristics of twentieth-century Ontario's industrial structure were in place. Ontario had 52 per cent of Canada's total industrial production; in 1929, the figure was 53 per cent. Two cities, Toronto and Hamilton, dominated industrial production in 1871, as they would throughout the twentieth century. Finally, the present-day concentration of manufacturing was in place by 1880. A manufacturing belt from Oshawa west along the north shore of Lake Ontario into the middle of the Grand River Valley marked the zone of highest concentration. Relatively little industrial activity occurred in southwestern Ontario west of London and along the Lake Ontario and St Lawrence shorelines east of Ottawa.

The 1870s economic downturn led to many business failures in agricultural implements, sawmilling, and the cotton and foundry sectors, but while the number of firms declined, the number of employees and output increased in all these areas. Consolidation and centralization of industrial capital characterized the 1870s and foreshadowed the more dramatic mergers of the late nineteenth and early twentieth centuries. The agricultural implements industry is a good example. At Confederation, such implements were produced in small 'factories' scattered throughout the province, many of them little more than upscale blacksmithing

Guelph horseshoeing forge, c. 1860. In 1861, sawmilling and blacksmithing were two of Ontario's largest employers in the industrial sectors. Even so, individual sawmills or blacksmith's shops rarely employed more than five workers. Guelph Public Library Archives.

shops producing and repairing a wide assortment of goods. By 1881, Ontario had 144 such small independent family operations, owned by men like Hart Massey and Alanson Harris. Massey succeeded through aggressive marketing, exporting even to Britain. Harris, on the other hand, was an innovator whose company created such state-of-the art equipment as the open-ended binder. In 1890, the two firms merged and moved to a new, larger factory in Toronto. Over the next two decades, the company absorbed many smaller producers (including some American firms), expanded its line of products, and became Canada's largest producer—and exporter—of agricultural implements.

Manufacturing reshaped itself during this period. Diversification and mechanization led to rapid increases in the value of production. Yet because of increased labour productivity, continued immigration, and rural depopulation, even this growth could not create enough jobs. In each year following 1873, more job-seekers left Ontario than entered it; emigration slowed population growth. Farm families adjusted to economic realities through a complex process of inheritance strategies, marriage patterns, and mobility. But movement was neither always a disruptive nor an aimless process. Rather, for some, mobility was a means to achieve stability. As well, much movement was of a regional, if cross-border (Ontario–New York) process: kin stayed in touch. Moreover, not all urban places could ape Toronto: places like Bellville and its rural hinterland offered fewer economic opportunities, but people stayed there anyway. Farmers adjusted and specialized in dairying and cheese-making, and Belleville encouraged such enterprise by offering incentives. As historical geographer Randy Willis succinctly concludes, 'local conditions modified modernization forces.'[14]

In fact, Ontario was far from homogeneous. Geographic diversity characterized the province. Not all regions contributed to or were affected by economic development in the same way. Contrasts have already been noted between rural and urban patterns, and they were even more pronounced between the north and south. In fact, the north contributed in fundamental ways to Ontario's fiscal solvency and successful southern development.

Nineteenth-century Ontarians included in their north the districts of Muskoka, Parry Sound, and Nipissing and all points north of those. One of Mowat's main challenges was how best to utilize the new northern territory's economic potential. In 1882 the *Globe* optimistically asserted that the disputed boundary territory alone contained no less than '60,000,000 acres of fertile land'. It was, of course, a preposterous estimate: by 1891, in the area northwest of Sault Ste Marie, only 57,400 hectares of land had been developed for agricultural purposes, and over three-quarters of that was unimproved pasture or woodlots.[15]

Under Mowat's leadership, systematic northern development began. The government surveyed 107 townships, settled 25,000 people on some 1.2 million hectares of land, and spent $2.75 million on building and servicing 7,350 kilometres of colonization roads. The aim was not simply to facilitate farming. Despite many attempts to promote agricultural colonization, the worth of northern Ontario, Mowat realized, lay elsewhere—politicians pandered to people, and in 1871 only 1 per cent of Ontario's population lived in the north. Exploitation of the north enabled Mowat to help finance southern Ontario's dramatic economic development without resorting to 'the bugbear of direct taxation' and thus helped to ensure his political longevity. In much of the United States resource rights went to the purchaser of the land, but in Ontario and Canada these rights remained in the state's possession. Entrepreneurs had to pay the state for the right to cut timber and mine minerals. For example, the commissioner of Crown lands would auction off the rights to a section of timberlands for a set time period, and the successful bidder would also pay ground rent and stumpage dues on the timber cut. To maximize returns, Mowat timed these auctions to correspond with favourable economic conditions in the industry. Between 1867 and 1899, payments from mines and forests represented close to a third of provincial revenues, and most of that income came from northern development.[16]

Clearly Mowat spent money in the north in order to make money; between 1872 and 1896, the Mowat government realized, after all expenses, some $17 million. This 'net fiscal benefit', made in the north and spent in the south, made possible healthy surpluses throughout Mowat's premiership at a time when most other provincial governments struggled with deficits. It also allowed Mowat to indulge an agricultural population extremely averse to direct taxation. Although some northerners complained about the unequal flow of capital, their small numbers made them easy to ignore.[17]

The decision to invest northern capital in the south probably skewed the trajectory of northern development. During the Mowat era, the north experienced extensive growth but little diversification. Mowat's policy also ushered in a long period of only loosely supervised resource exploitation. Most northern lumberers were financially vulnerable and not even remotely interested in implementing the conservation measures that some of their more wealthy southern counterparts in the Ottawa Valley were promoting. A Bureau of Forestry was not created until 1898, after Mowat had left the provincial government. Up to that time a clerk of forestry, initially resident in the Department of Agriculture and then in the Department of Crown Lands, handled forests as if they were a cash crop, properly 'part and parcel of farm management'. The clerk focused most of his energy on the effect of deforestation on southern Ontario's farm economy, encouraging Arbor Days, when communities would plant trees along roadways. Even as tourists travelled north to enjoy pristine forests, Mowat's economic policies were undercutting them.[18]

Technology and the Workplace

New technologies and the rapid expansion of the industrial factory system altered the very nature of work and with it the social conditions of wage labourers. The deskilling of labour was a feature of mines in the north no less than of factories and farms in the south. At Silver Islet, technological advances allowed mine managers to lessen their reliance on skilled Norwegian and Cornish miners, men who (in management's eyes) tended to be too independent. The company recruited cheaper, comparatively unskilled workers from mining camps in Nova Scotia and Illinois. 'If miners are plentiful', William Frue, the mine's general manager, advised, 'make up the number from mixed nationalities.' Such policies made it difficult for labour to form a unified front against management. Management exercised strict control over the labour force: the Islet had its own five-cell jail and jailer, alcohol use was carefully monitored (three drinks per day), camp watchmen were ever-present, clergymen were provided, and, of course, the company store and bunkhouses ate up roughly half of the miners' monthly pay. At Copper Cliff's nickel-copper mines, managers employed mass mining techniques, 'so the work of "mining" consisted mainly of drifting and quarrying with Ingersoll air drills'. Miners lost status; only surface labourers at the mines received lower pay. In order to control the men, Copper Cliff's management separated them from the wider community. The Company profited from housing and land leases: in 1889, the manager noted a return of 20 per cent on the rental of small houses. The workforce was ethnically diverse, but non-Anglo Saxons lived in ramshackle ghettos at the town's edge while management enjoyed separate and more substantial quarters.[19]

Technological change also affected farm work. Mechanization—the introduction of mowers, cultivators, and binders—made it possible to produce more in less time. But in the late nineteenth and early twentieth centuries, mechanization did not lead to the demise of the family farm. Rather, most implements were still horse-drawn and in that sense reinforced the family nature of farming. Yet as farms mechanized, women's work in particular was deskilled and devalued. Before the late nineteenth century, many women earned money milking cows, tending live-

Workers at Silver Islet mine, c. 1880s. Silver Islet, on Lake Superior near Thunder Bay, was the north's most successful silver mine in the nineteenth century. Between 1870 and 1884, one 24-by-20-metre outcropping located a kilometre and a half off shore yielded 3 million ounces of fine silver worth some $3.5 million. AO F1132-2-1-2 ST1237.

stock, and manufacturing cheese and butter; Lydia Chase Ranney, a craftswoman who, with her husband, manufactured cheese on their Oxford County farm, oversaw up to fourteen apprentice dairymaids in any one season. She contributed to the evolving technology of cheese manufacture and, according to the reminiscences of a male cheesemaker, deserves the credit for laying 'the cornerstone of the dairy industry in Canada'. Even in the twentieth century, cheesemakers would wield great power in rural areas; as Bertha Pope, Ontario's only solo female cheesemaker for much of that century, noted in 1967, she had the power to accept or reject the milk products supplied to her factory by the region's farmers. But she was the exception: after about 1870, when cheese production shifted to factories (farm production was halved in that decade), men generally replaced women as manufacturers, and women became factory labourers.[20]

As historian Margaret Derry has explained, change in butter manufacture was more prolonged. In the 1870s and 1880s, farmers and exporters attributed a decline in export demand for butter to poor quality, which they blamed on the central role played by women in the manufacturing process. Yet the domestic market for butter was buoyant. The low export demand may simply have reflected differences in taste: the British did not like salty butter, and Canadians apparently did.

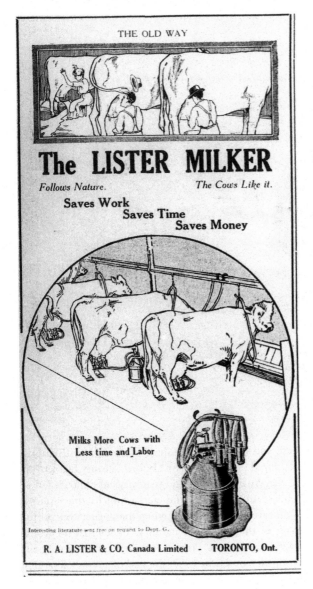

The Lister milker, *Farmer's Advocate*, 19 June 1919. According to this advertisement, 'The Old Way' meant discontented cows and spilt milk. Archival and Special Collections, University of Guelph Library.

For a while milking continued to be seen as a nurturing, female task—women's work. After 1890, however, men began to supplant women as milkers, and women were increasingly relegated to cleaning the milk pails; after all, as one writer in the *Farmer's Advocate* put it in 1885, 'for washing and keeping things clean, [men] were not equal to women'.

Yet, for a time, women also performed another function. 'If you want to know how to treat a cow you must first study how to treat a woman', one agriculturist advised 'First study the human mother, and when you have got the laws that govern her in the exercise of her maternity you have arrived at the laws that govern the bovine mother.' Woman became a sort of intermediary between man and cow. Men, of course, knew how to tame women: the same techniques could contain the female cow. With the marketing of milking machines in the 1890s, woman as intermediary became less necessary. Cows were becoming more mechanical objects than 'bovine mothers'. 'The dairy cow is not only an animal, but she is a machine', one dairyman believed. In 1895, a writer in the *Canadian Livestock Journal* went even further: 'The modern dairy cow in her best form is a highly artificial animal. The more artificial she is the better. The dairy cow has been trained and made over by the hand and brain of *man* for a perfectly natural purpose, for giving milk, yielding butter, and making money.' With the cow neutered, men no longer required women as intermediaries. It was but a small step to conceiving of the farm as a factory.

The devaluing of women's farm labour—always underappreciated at least in part because it was traditionally centred in production for local markets and in relatively non-technologically sophisticated pursuits—is nicely symbolized by the fact that by 1905, education at agricultural colleges for women concentrated on topics within the home. Men and boys, not women and girls, were offered education in traditionally women's farm work in fruit-growing and livestock production.[21]

Skilled artisans working in the small manufacturing shops that dotted southern Ontario traditionally exerted considerable control over their work. 'Let the mechanics of Ontario be true to each other', a 'Wood Worker', confident in his superior knowledge of the workplace, could write in 1872, 'and we will teach those brainless, self styled Masters [employers], that the workmen of Ontario know their power, and are determined to use it.' But specialization in manufacturing output eroded this shop-floor control. As machinists came to specialize in either brass or iron, stoves or agricultural machinery, skill sets narrowed and employee interaction lessened. Whereas previously the craftsperson had been responsible for a wide range of tasks related to the production of an item, increasingly those tasks were compartmentalized. Less skilled labourers did work that craftsworkers had done in the past.[22]

Such labour was abundant. The great numbers forced into the cities by rural depopulation were only too willing to take on such jobs, often in the face of resistance by the craftsworkers. A disgruntled Toronto tailor did not mince words: 'Between science and progress the working classes are ground as between millstones.' 'The over-production of machinery', Joseph Dickson, a carriage-maker in Chatham, believed, 'has caused a great many men to be thrown out of work. I know they have one machine in the waggon shop here that takes the place of about twenty men.' Furthermore, the long, hard Canadian winter ensured that many jobs were seasonal. 'In the trades', the federal government's *Labour Gazette* correspondent noted in the autumn of 1901, 'many are just now "between seasons" and are a little slack. . . . This by many of the men is looked forward to as an annual rest.' Much of the construction industry, which employed about a quarter of the urban workforce, shut down during the winter months. Employment in transportation picked up significantly during the late fall but declined precipitously during the long winter. Work in food-canning was concentrated into a three-month period at the end of the growing season. Even in industries such as agricultural implements, production slowed during the late summer, fall, and early winter.[23]

Workers and Unemployment

Seasonality masked a more insidious trend. Only about one-third of the urban unemployed lost jobs as a result of seasonal conditions. The remaining two-thirds were out of work because of factors more closely associated with the evolving industrial economy. In 1901, one in seven of Hamilton's wage-workers worked less than nine months of the year. Families were vital lines of defence against the impersonal workings of the labour market. In his walk through a Toronto working-class area in 1894, a *Globe* reporter came upon 'a very neat house [in which] a carpenter was found, a big, strong man eager to work, who had done nothing for months. The signs of poverty were only too apparent, and on being questioned, he admitted that his family were in want. His wife, by going out to work, earned enough to provide food, but not enough to buy fuel or pay rent. A neighbour gave him some shutters to mend, the first work he had had for sometime.' When asked where his wife was, Mr Gloynes, an unemployed Toronto labourer, provided a similar answer: 'She is out working. She makes eight or ten dollars a month scrubbing and doing chores.'[24]

The vast majority of working-class wives did not work for wages, however. A man was expected to make a 'living wage', an income sufficient to maintain his family free from poverty. A proper woman, according to the cult of domesticity, was expected to run the house and raise the family. Because of these social dicta, wives (and their husbands) may have been reluctant to admit to census-takers that they earned wages. Working-class wives raised children, tended chickens and pigs, tilled gardens, and, given adequate space, took in boarders. Younger children helped. Such non-waged contributions were often crucial to urban working-class family survival.

Children also contributed financially. Sons and daughters fourteen and older contributed on average an impressive 40 per cent of their families' income. But even with such support, many families teetered on the brink. In 1901, almost 20 per cent of Hamilton's working-class families had income close to or below the poverty line. General labourers were at the highest risk of poverty. Nearly two-thirds of labourers' families without children over the age of fourteen lived below the poverty line. In the early stages of the family life cycle, most of these families coped financially, but when children arrived, so too did poverty. Some families made ends meet by sharing the rent for a house with another family.[25]

Skilled workers reacted to the deterioration in labour conditions by organizing trade unions to pressure employers, and labour councils to lobby government. The unions of the 1860s and early 1870s were often locals of British- or American-based international unions, organizations that viewed the unskilled as potential competitors rather than collaborators. In a sense they were fighting on two fronts: against employers and against unskilled male and at times female challenges to their privileged positions. Workers pressed for a nine-hour day. In 1872, the Typographers struck in support of their demands. As the tension and rhetoric escalated, John A. Macdonald passed the Trades Union Act of 1872. Modelled on British legislation, the act exempted collective bargaining from common-law restraint-of-trade provisions. Jailed strike leaders in Toronto were freed; the union won the strike and established a nine-hour day in the printing industry.

Frequently cited as labour's Magna Carta, The Trades Union Act proved far more symbolic than real. Although it enshrined collective bargaining, the act assumed that most unions would incorporate under the civil law, which would make unions vulnerable to civil suits for damages; courts could rule that business losses as a result of strikes were recoverable through civil action. Since collective bargaining relied on economic sanctions—either strikes or lockouts—the threat of such rulings jeopardized the system. Unions therefore refused to incorporate; in turn, many employers would not negotiate labour contracts unless they could be enforced in civil courts. The Trades Union Act not only failed to address the basic issue of civil liability, it also defined as criminal offences a number of standard union practices, including picketing during a strike. Although these criminal provisions were only occasionally enforced, the act nonetheless limited the effectiveness of labour's only economic weapon, the strike, and it did little to improve the province's deteriorating industrial relations.

Under the pressure of unemployment, union membership declined in the 1870s. Not until the decade's end, when the economy showed signs of real growth,

Collecting coal by the railway tracks, Toronto, c. 1900. Despite efforts to regulate child labour, children from poor families were often working for wages before they reached the age of fourteen. Many others helped in the house, hawked newspapers on the street, or, like the very young girls shown here, scrounged for coal or scrap metal. John Kelso photo. NA PA1819261 Acc. 1975.069.

did the trade union movement begin to recover. After an initial organizing convention in 1883, Ontario's municipal labour councils firmly established the Trades and Labour Congress of Canada (TLC) in 1886. Limited initially to Ontario unions, the TLC soon included most labour organizations across Canada.

A second labour organization, originally founded in 1869, emerged in Ontario in the 1880s. The Knights of Labor represented the working class's most significant and powerful organizational effort in the nineteenth century. Through ritual and fraternity, the Knights preached the self-worth of workers and offered the promises of cultural and economic support. The movement attempted to bridge religious and ethnic, skilled and unskilled, male and female divisions and to unite all workers under a common banner, a common culture. While other unions played on the pride and 'respectability' of craft, often arguing that skills represented 'property' and thus, in a property-based economy, gave workers who possessed them the same rights as capitalists to participate in the decision-making process, the Knights questioned the capitalist system itself. Often their critique mixed notions of a pre-capitalist world of independent commodity producers with ideas anticipating the co-operative and socialist movements of the twentieth century.

According to one estimate, the Knights organized between 20 and 30 per cent of Ontario's manufacturing workers during the 1880s. Their success is further reflected in the rise in worker participation in politics, especially at the municipal level. The dramatic rise in strike activity—more in that decade than in all previous decades combined—further points to the Knights' impact. By the late 1880s, however, the movement lay in disarray. Gender, ethnic, religious, and skill-level differences could not be bridged overnight. Too often the Knights' tactics—emphasizing municipal politics and local activism—missed emerging provincial and national structures of power. In the end the Knights' rhetoric promised more than the organization could deliver. The Knights of Labor disappeared almost as suddenly as they had appeared, but they had shaken middle-class Ontario. Newspaper editorials worried about the 'class question' and the meaning of the new labour militancy. John A. Macdonald also took notice. Labour organizations had complained for years about the deteriorating social conditions that had accompanied industrialization; now a federal Royal Commission on Relations of Labour and Capital was created to investigate the social problems of the emerging industrial order.[26]

The royal commission presented an improving picture. Yet hours remained long, factories remained unsafe and unsanitary, and women and children not only continued to be employed in large numbers but were often physically abused while on the job. By the time the commission delivered its final report to the federal government in 1889, there was no longer much debate about the seriousness of the social consequences of industrialization. Since labour was a provincial matter, Mowat had to act.

The Employers' Liability Act of 1886 consolidated, but did not alter, the system by which Ontario's injured workers could recover compensation from employers. Those injured had to prove that their injuries resulted from employer negligence, but civil-law principles of risk and contributory negligence favoured employers. Nor did the 1886 Ontario Factories Act do much to ameliorate conditions. It restricted the employment of children, limited the hours of labour for both women and children, and recommended other improvements in working conditions in factories and shops. The Province even appointed a female factory inspector. Yet those industries (such as food canning) that did employ large numbers of children under fourteen received seasonal and other exemptions. Similarly, women and children under eighteen could not be required to work longer than ten hours per day or sixty hours per week, but these were already the standards in most industries, and in any event employers could request partial exemptions here as well.

Women workers were especially disadvantaged. Male craftsworkers in the printing trades, for example, successfully blocked employers' attempts to hire women at lower wages as linotype operators. Male workers were less successful controlling work in the apparel industry, Toronto's leading employer in the late nineteenth century. Three in four garment workers were women, and as in other industries, they received about half the wages of men even though they were doing comparable work. 'I don't treat the men bad', one clothing manufacturer in Toronto admitted in 1897, 'but I even up by taking advantage of the women.' The industry operated via outwork. Independent contractors engaged in cutthroat bidding for the right to manufacture clothes. Women and girls, who worked in 'low, damp basement[s]' and attics, received minimal pay on the basis of piecework. Those who worked in clothing factories rarely had the opportunity to become skilled at their trade. One employer commented, 'I have twenty or twenty-five girls working for me and not one of them could make a coat right through.' Employer strategies such as this fragmented working-class resistance.

Numerous investigations into apparel work were conducted. Typically, investigators concluded that 'the contracting system tends inevitably to the lowering of wages and degrading the conditions of labour'. In this context, the insufficiency of the Factory Act was apparent. 'Women and children work many more hours daily than would be permitted in shops and factories under the regulation of the [provincial] Acts.' Well into the twentieth century, it remained common in Toronto to see 'large numbers of women and children winding their way up and down Bay street, carrying bundles in their arms or on perambulators'. 'Some of the poor creatures', another observer affirmed, were 'hardly able to walk'. Those areas where women dominated as wage-earners tended to be those most resistant to government supervision, however nominal.[27]

More generally, the enforcement of regulations governing working conditions presented great difficulties. The act required employers to keep factories clean, ventilate workrooms, provide sanitary facilities, and install safety guards on all dangerous machinery. However, it failed to provide a standard against which conditions could be measured. 'Sanitary facilities' could mean a single outdoor privy to serve several hundred employees. No one had authority under the act to determine which machines were dangerous, what safety devices needed to be installed, the amount of space required per worker in workrooms, or the amount of air circulation needed. With depressing regularity, factory inspectors investigated and reported on inadequate conditions, but in the end the act proved unenforceable.

Nor is it clear that the province ever intended to rigorously enforce its new Factories Act. The government initially appointed only three inspectors for the whole province. By the first decade of the twentieth century, there were ten, but the Factory Inspection Branch remained understaffed and underfunded. Inspectors, meanwhile, believed that more could be gained through 'education' and public reporting than through prosecutions. Despite the ever-increasing volume of their reports, inspectors prosecuted few. When they found underage children, they charged the parents not the employers. With the Factories Act, the government established its right to regulate the conditions of labour but failed to effectively exercise that right.

The Problem of the Poor: The Bourgeois State and Its Institutions

The question of what to do with the dependent poor challenged Upper Canadians long before the Mowat era. As we have seen, institutions such as houses of industry and asylums were put in place in the 1830s, but success eluded them. Private initiatives were invariably controlled by boards made up of religious activists. Minorities such as the Catholic and Jewish communities established direct control over their own social service networks for their co-religionists. Among Protestants, denominational divisions required shared control. Ministers, wardens, deacons, and others from several denominations served together on boards of directors of a wide variety of charitable organizations. Local churches often had 'poor funds', but the amounts were small and disbursements irregular; in 1893, for example, the Baptist church in the small town of Thorold took money from the poor fund for general expenses. Religious notions often impeded the evolution of a public social welfare system. Protestants commonly believed that poverty was a punishment for sin. Social Darwinists insisted that hierarchical social structures and economic inequality were part of the natural order. Thomas Conant, a well-known Ontario publicist, asked in 1898, 'Is it wise to foster the growth of a class of persons whose filth and foul disease are the result of laziness and their own vice?' Yet Christians also fervently believed that charity was their duty. Moreover, small-town middle-class Ontarians, proud of their own good manners, industry, and sobriety, fervently believed that this 'cultivated' behaviour had to be instilled in others.[28]

The key was to distinguish between the 'deserving' and the 'undeserving' poor. The plight of the dependent elderly suggests how difficult it was to make such distinctions. Until the Mowat era, community groups such as the Ladies Aid Society had provided essential help to impoverished senior citizens in the form of 'outdoor relief'—donations of food, fuel, and clothing. Under Mowat, the government decided that the most efficient solution was to provide institutions where cheap care and, for some, rehabilitation could be offered. Mowat's Charities Aid Act of 1874 channelled money away from outdoor relief and toward private charities that supported institutional relief. Publicly assisted charity institutions increased from four in 1866 to nearly one hundred in 1900. This placed welfare

The Toronto House of Industry, 1890. Institutions like this offered unemployed men rudimentary lodging in return for work such as street cleaning. Increasingly, workers were losing control over their livelihoods. In March 1889, the Toronto *World* reported that at the local House of Industry, unskilled labourers rubbed elbows with an engineer, a stone mason, a clerk, a fuller, and a baker, among others. AO C336 #1597 5346.

measures more firmly under the central state's control, thus broadening Mowat's sphere of influence. Almost none of these institutions specialized in care of the aged; nonetheless, many soon complained of being deluged by 'the decaying and decrepit'. In fact, Ontario's institutions housed a paltry 4 per cent of the province's senior citizens. The government knew this, but in the declining economy of the 1890s it, like other North American jurisdictions, claimed that charity for the aged faced a financial crisis. The solution was to deny institutional care to all senior citizens with living relatives. This policy, the government argued, would not only save money but reinforce traditional family values. It was a con's game. The government was not close to a state of financial crisis. Most senior citizens were able to look after themselves, and families, far from abandoning their elders, were extremely active in caring for them. The tragedy of Mowat's penurious policy was that the truly poor elderly usually had families equally poor, and in the past era of municipal and community outdoor relief some assistance for these people had been available. As financing for the institutions that had supplanted that form of relief dried up, the dependent elderly and their families had few places to turn.[29]

Poverty was often equated with sloth, vice, and laziness, and for the working-class poor, it could be a short step from being denied state succour to incarceration in a state penal institution. Mowat's answer to the perceived problem of what the Toronto *Globe* termed 'a criminal class' was the establishment in 1874 of the Central Prison, designed to punish those sentenced to less than two years and thus not admissible to the federal penitentiary at Kingston. The Central Prison aspired to be 'a terror to evil-doers'. Working-class men, especially the unskilled, dominated the prison's population. Whenever possible, convicts were expected to work and to pay for their own upkeep. Whippings, frugal diets of bread and water, and extended periods of isolation typified the custodial regimen. This grim approach was a legacy of the dissatisfaction felt by mid-century Upper Canadians with costly institutions that seemed unable to effect rehabilitation and social reform. Other jurisdictions in North America and Great Britain had much more ameliorative penal systems in the late nineteenth century.[30]

In 1880, the Mowat government established a second 'special' reformatory, designed to put to hard labour another recalcitrant portion of the population. The Mercer Reformatory for Women was not only designed for female inmates, it was also run by women. Its inmates were overwhelmingly of an unskilled working-class background, often servants. Most were sentenced on moral charges, not, like Central Prison inmates, on property charges. In striking contrast with Central, punishments were few and were rarely severe. 'Our aim has been to govern with kindness', Mary Jane O'Reilly, Mercer's superintendent, affirmed, 'and we have

The Andrew Mercer Ontario Reformatory for Females, 1903. Administrators at the Mercer emphasized reform rather than punishment. Their maternal-feminist approach reflected the patriarchal attitudes of the time, but at least they treated their charges with humane consideration. AO Govt Doc PS (29th Annual Report of the Inspector of Prisons and Public Charities, Ontario sessional papers, 35 [1903], 87).

found this the most effectual way of influencing them, treating them as human beings who have a claim upon our charity as well as our justice.' One of O'Reilly's staff noted that their intent was 'to bring the girls up as if they were at home. . . . I never lock up my rooms. The front door is always open and Mrs O'Reilly's quarters are the same.'[31]

Prisons were also seen by some as fitting institutions for the socialization of Native people. In 1873 in Brantford, the home of the Six Nations, the proportion of Native people in the local jail matched the proportion in the population as a whole; by 1901, it was more than twice their proportion of the total population. Native people considered incarceration cruel and unusual punishment. Most were arrested on charges of drunkenness and jailed because they could not—or would not—pay a fine. In many localities, Native people in general were considered to constitute a criminal class.[32]

Schooling Society: A Middle-Class Project

The state also looked to education to cultivate appropriate citizens. In this context, the regulation of leisure activities assumed importance. In schools, physical education for boys emphasized physical courage, sportsmanship, and self-reliance; physical training for girls focused on health and beauty. As Lynne Marks has demonstrated, citizens of small Ontario towns strove to regulate the leisure activities of young working-class people. So too did larger municipalities like Toronto. Bull, bear, dog, and other animal fights were banned, but fox hunting continued unimpeded. Sites for sports and other games were strictly regulated, often making it impossible for working-class families to easily access the designated areas.[33]

Just as Native children were sent to special residential schools, so in many communities black children were relegated—often despite their parents' protests—to segregated schools. The uneducated in general became increasingly defined as socially unacceptable and suspect. As we have noted, John Sandfield Macdonald had passed legislation that made some school attendance for seven- to twelve-year-olds compulsory. In 1883, Mowat introduced the kindergarten, a 'garden of children' where moral values could be cultivated from the earliest age, play could be supervised, and uniform textbooks would be provided so the government could oversee their 'fitness'. Like the texts used in Upper Canada, Ontario's texts preached acceptance of a static view of life:

> Do you think the whole creation,
> Will be altered just for you?
> . . . Whatever comes, or doesn't come
> . . . do the best you can.

Poverty was self-inflicted; individuals were the architects of their own misfortunes: 'An idler is a watch that wants both hands, as useless if it goes as if it stands.'[34]

At one level, the state's project for regularizing school attendance was very successful: throughout the later nineteenth century, Ontario's children were much

Amherstburg parade, 1 August 1894. The anniversary of Emancipation Day, 1 August 1834, when Britain abolished slavery throughout its empire, was often an occasion for Ontario's black communities to assess social progress. In 1899, Reverend A.W. Hackley of Chatham asked, 'What has the negro of Kent County done that he is unable to go into the ice cream parlour? What has he done that he should be so ostracized from restaurants?' (in Colin McFarquhar, 'A Difference of Perspective: Blacks, Whites and Emancipation Day Celebrations in Ontario, 1865–1919', *Ontario History* 92 [2000], 151). AO ACC2537 S 12008.

more likely to attend school than were children in any other province. Yet patterns of schooling reflected more than the state's will. The children of working-class parents remained less likely to attend schools than children of middle-class professional and white-collar families, perhaps in part because some school boards exacted a fee of ten to twelve cents a month per child. While this charge could be waived for the poor, 'that', Hamilton's trades council noted, 'looked too much like beggary and the other children in the schools would soon know of it and point their fingers at the poor ones'. Texts were expensive, and kindergartens were very slow to take hold outside Toronto. Daily attendance continued to be lower in rural than in urban centres, although literacy levels were similar. Moreover, recent research on education in nineteenth-century Ontario suggests that parents and students in rural and urban areas used schooling for their own, rather than simply the state's, purposes. A complex interaction of gender, work rhythms, demographic trends, and family composition provides essential context for understanding schooling patterns in late-nineteenth-century Ontario.[35]

As good rural land became harder to find in Ontario, parents limited family size and young adults delayed marriage. Childhood became extended: starting as

Box 7.4   The University of Toronto: A Crossroads

The acquisition of knowledge was not a primary reason for the founding of universities in Ontario. Rather, universities emerged in order to reflect the morals and teachings of various religious denominations and, by so doing, to 'turn-out' tomorrow's leaders. Original or independent thought was not respected: duty, discipline, and adherence to strict moral codes were the values prized by university educators. But by the late nineteenth century, times were changing. Divine revelation was less and less seen as the touchstone for 'truth'. Critical inquiry unfettered by Christian dogma now challenged the very rationale for the emergence of Ontario's universities. University presidents, such as the University of Toronto's Daniel Wilson (1887–92), straddled this divide. For Wilson, scientific inquiry revealed God at work and critical inquiry had to coexist with the continued inculcation of appropriate moral teachings. It was an awkward stance.

A younger generation, often trained in Canada or the United States, began to challenge the views and power of Wilson and other British-trained academics. Many in this emerging group supported the development of a school of practical science at the University of Toronto. In an era of industrial growth and 'scientific' agricultural advancement, their arguments persuaded politicians—and politicians not only controlled the university's purse strings but also had the right to hire and fire without input from Wilson. The impotence of Toronto's university presidents would not be changed until 1906. Until then, the University of Toronto was truly an arm of the state, and the state backed a School of Practical Science at Toronto, a College of Agriculture at Guelph, and a School of Mining and Agriculture at Kingston. Humanist disciplines, which Wilson (who was among other things a poet) fought for, suffered.

Indeed, long-accepted notions of disciplines changed in this period. Wilson held a chair that covered all history and literature. Such an aspiration was not deemed arrogant; rather, it reflected, as historian Brian McKillop puts it, 'the majestic, unifying sweep of nineteenth century mental and moral philosophy'. But that was a philosophy under challenge. Disciplines became leaner and meaner. English/history split into English, political economy, and constitutional history, for example.[1]

Wilson was at the centre of yet another turning point for the University of Toronto. He believed that while women could have a university education, they should do so in institutions separate from those of men. After all, as one oft-cited expert wrote, women, being the weaker sex, could not handle the competition in a coeducational atmosphere: 'The brain cannot take more than its share without injury to other organs.' Wilson admitted that presenting lectures on Shakespeare to a mixed audience was very trying because of the sexual content of some of the writing. Nonetheless, in 1884, over Wilson's objections, women entered University College.[2]

Others feared that 'when they are educated together the men tend to become effeminate and the women masculine.' To many, such fears seemed at least in part borne out by the actions of women undergraduates in the infamous student strike of

1895. 'The class of young ladies seeking entrance [in 1895] differs very much from what we used to have ten years ago', a member of the university's senate lamented. Indeed, historians have noted that more middle-class families were sending children to university than had been the case in the past. Female undergraduates joined their male counterparts in a successful boycott of classes in protest over faculty firings. It was expected that men might engage in such activities, but 'in many instances', the *Mail and Empire* somewhat incredulously noted, the women were 'more extreme in their partisanship even then the young men'. Perhaps, many believed, a School of Household Science was required. It would enable 'a young woman to put every department of the home of which she should become mistress on a thoroughly scientific basis'. It was also, the minister of education affirmed, a field of study that would solidify the limits of 'women's sphere' and not threaten the careers of men. Accordingly, in 1902, the Lillian Massey School of Household Science was founded. The coeducational system remained intact, but the Household Science building also contained a pool (known as 'the bathtub') and gym for women only. In 1910, the construction of Hart House, a state-of-the-art recreation and cultural centre for men only, was announced. Women were not admitted until 1972.[3]

Matters of governance, gender, class, nationality, and curriculum challenged universities in late-nineteenth-century Ontario. None of these issues were firmly settled at that time. Indeed, many are still with us at the beginning of the twenty-first century.

1. Quotation: A.B. McKillop, 'The Research Ideal and the University of Toronto, 1870–1906', *Proceedings of the Royal Society of Canada* 20 (1982): 266.
2. Quotation: Sara Z. Burke, 'New Women and Old Romans: Co-education at the University of Toronto, 1884–1895', *Canadian Historical Review* 80 (1999): 219–41.
3. Quotations: Sara Z. Burke, '"Being Unlike Man": Challenges to Co-education at the University of Toronto, 1884–1909', *Ontario History* 92 (2001): 11–31. See also A.B. McKillop, *Matters of Mind: The University in Ontario, 1791–1951* (Toronto: University of Toronto Press, 1994); Keith Walden, 'Respectable Hooligans: Male Toronto College Students Celebrate Hallowe'en, 1884–1910', *Canadian Historical Review* 68 (1987): 1–34; Lynne Marks and Chad Gaffield, 'Women at Queen's University, 1895–1905: A "Little Sphere"', *Ontario History* 78 (1986): 331–49; Carl Berger, 'Sir Daniel Wilson', *Dictionary of Canadian Biography*, vol. 12 (Toronto: University of Toronto Press, 1990), 1109–14.

early as 1850, children spent longer time in their parents' home. This seems to have been most often the case in emerging middle–class urban families, but it was a trend in rural areas too. In fact, as historical sociologist Gordon Darroch has demonstrated, about half of all farm families in central Ontario in the 1860s owned middling or substantial farms. The emergence of the middle class was far from simply an urban phenomenon. For middle–class rural and urban parents, the home was a place for nurturing and inculcating respect and respectability. Parents thought schools should perform the same function. A concern for their children's material future also underlay rural and urban family education strategies. Parents increasingly provided in their wills 'cash and an education' for certain of their children. In this context, daughters benefited just as much as sons. One historian has noted that after 1870, it became 'fairly common [in wills] to insist that daughters receive an education'. Given delays in marriage, many parents realized that their daughters would be in wage work for some time prior to marriage.[36]

The teaching profession offered non-factory employment for those daughters. Female teachers received less in wages, so school districts were keen to hire them. Schools sought single, not married, women. Women were thought to be more natural nurturers than men, who were seen to be more aggressive and sexually passionate; the most nurturing teachers, then, would be unmarried women who were not distracted by raising children of their own and who, having presumably not known sexual passion, could be trusted to offer students physical nurturing (touching, hugging, and so on) in a way that men could not. In this way, social constructions of gender difference determined participation in the work of schooling just as it did in the work of farming, in some cases facilitating and in others limiting the possibilities for women and men alike.[37]

Gendered Spaces

Work was the crucible within which men proved their worth: '[I]t is in the hurry, the bustle, the turmoil of a busy active existence that we see the man', John Scrimger, a Galt liveryman, told members of the local Mechanics' Institute. 'Then we can discern whether he is an upright, virtuous, and noble character that may command our admiration and respect, or whether his be a nature that repels us, and fills us with contempt and aversion.' By contrast, women were expected to exercise their finest qualities—beauty, sincerity, warmth, purity, domesticity—in the cultivation of the home, the 'little heaven on earth'. The only acceptable public activity for married women was charitable work with churches or benevolent societies. Like housework, this was a selfless labour of love; monetary recompense could only sully such activity.[38]

But times were changing, however slowly. In the late nineteenth century, the Married Women's Property Laws gave wives the right to own and manage property and to conduct business free from their husbands' interference. At the time, relatively few women owned property, and conservative judges often refused to grant married women the potential agency inherent in the Property Laws. But soon more women began to write wills, and fathers began to write wills that put daughters on a more level footing with sons. The Property Laws created confidence that property ceded to daughters would now remain in their hands after marriage. A significant increase in landed-property ownership by women—married, single, and widowed—followed the passage of those laws.

Many women also ran their own businesses. By the turn of the century, urban women in the workforce were as likely to be self-employed or to be employers as were urban men. Some of these women may have been simply fronts for husbands who transferred their property to protect it from confiscation by creditors. Yet courts were increasingly strict about such activity, and such attempts to defraud actually provided some married women with an opportunity to take control of their lives. In 1904, when Mr Cammell of Hamilton sued his wife for recovery of property, she testified that he had deeded a hotel to her in order to avoid paying creditors but that she ignored him, paid the debts, upgraded the property, and made the business a success. The court ruled in her favour. Granted, such women were a minority. It is true, too, that women who were self-employed or employers earned far less than their male counterparts (though more than female employees) and often were self-employed simply because wage work was not available to them. Nevertheless, the Property Acts were the most important legislation affecting women's rights passed in Ontario in the late nineteenth century.[39]

Church and benevolent work provided an opportunity for women to work together in larger, more overtly political arenas. Temperance reform engaged the energies of many. Middle-class women dominated the Women's Christian Temperance Union, which looked to education and legislation to reform drinkers. Indeed, before the turn of the century the WCTU had convinced the government to insert a compulsory course on 'scientific temperance' in schools. When, in 1884, single and widowed women with property received the right to vote in municipal elections, members of the WCTU urged them to vote for local prohibition, a right ceded to municipalities by provincial legislation. The WCTU was the first organization to lobby for women's suffrage at the provincial and federal levels, arguing that women's special nurturing qualities could help reform society as a whole. In this period, few women argued that they had an inherent right to vote; rather, voting was seen as a means to realize specific reform agendas. Yet for many WCTU members, even this maternal feminist approach to reform was much too 'radical'. 'I am more than sorry', the WCTU's superintendent of franchise work lamented, 'that all our women are not in hearty sympathy with this department of our work.'[40]

If women lobbied for temperance legislation, some workers argued that women, in effect, drove them to drink. 'A love of liquor' was not what drew working men to taverns; rather, labour leaders explained to the Royal Commission on the Liquor Traffic in the early 1890s, the principal attraction was 'the love of sociable society; and the comfort that is found in the places where the sale takes place . . . often . . . not to be met with in their own homes': 'Discomfort, badly cooked food and ill-ventilated dwellings have much to answer for in connection with intemperance. Attention to these matters, *and more especially* to the training of the female portion of the population in a knowledge of domestic economy and household duties, the undersigned are satisfied would have an elevating and most beneficial effect'.[41]

In the hierarchy of the family, men enjoyed far greater rights and power than did women or children. While many families worked together to survive, and while both middle- and working-class families did protect and nurture children (indeed, advice literature in popular magazines increasingly disapproved of corporal punishment for children), there was also much abuse, exploitation, and inequality within families. The historical record from nineteenth-century Ontario provides much to challenge the notion, so often touted by contemporary family values advocates, of the patriarchal family system as a bastion of familial stability and 'a safe environment for women and children'. Penetrating the veil of family unity is not an easy task, but court records provide one imperfect but suggestive source. Various studies of Ontario court proceedings involving married women from all classes have documented a persistent pattern of wife-beating or, as the *Ottawa Citizen* reported in one case, 'reconstructing' a wife 'with a hard wood log'.[42]

A basic assumption in common law was that 'wives did not require the explicit protection of the law because they were under the guardianship of their husbands'. That assumption applied to children as well. Neighbours often aided wives who were being beaten by their husbands outside the home, and they would testify to hearing the sounds of beatings within a home, but they rarely intervened in what they—and the law—saw as private patriarchal space. Courts believed that 'moderate correction of his wife [and children] for . . . misbehaviour' was allowable. 'Proper castigation', one judge affirmed, is normal. Besides, 'it is not for magistrates or courts', he concluded, 'to step in and interfere with the rights of a husband in ruling his own household'. Wives—especially working-class wives—had little recourse before the law. It was not until 1909 that legislation was passed that recognized wife abuse as a crime separate from common assault. Some courts did fine and jail abusive and deserting husbands, but that was of little help to impoverished women and their children. Some husbands simply refused to pay fines or to post sureties as security for good behaviour, choosing jail instead. 'Why', a prison inspector lamented in 1877, 'a ruffian who is constantly beating his wife should not be *sentenced* to jail for a certain period with hard labour, instead of his electing to be *detained* there in utter idleness . . . is beyond my comprehension.' Most often, criminal courts merely gave suspended sentences and counselled mediation. Deserting husbands were rarely required to continue support payments; this changed with the passage of the Deserted Wives' Maintenance Act of 1888, but enforcement was very spotty. For women who could work, orders of protection were more effective, shielding as they did any money earned by the wife and her children from the husband's possession. Divorce was almost impossible for poor women, as it required an act of the federal parliament to effect, and the grounds for such an application were extremely limited. Violence was one ground, but, as one judge pronounced in 1873, 'the law . . . lays upon the wife the necessity of bearing some indignities, and even some personal violence, before it will sanction her leaving her husband's roof'.[43]

Public Health and the Environment

In the interests of the 'general social good', the state did on occasion intervene in family matters, but from the perspective of the poor, the result proved ambiguous. Public health reformers campaigned to restrict the keeping of domestic animals. The first to be banned were pigs (the mainstay of working-class families), long before cows (the choice of the middle class). In 1893, Sudbury's city council attempted to ban all animals from running free in the 'improved section of town', but local ratepayers forced them to repeal the prohibition on cows and, the

Sudbury Journal reported, 'these animals are again free commoners'. In Hamilton, in June 1881, a local resident reported that 'ten head of cattle were grazing along Main Street and no person in charge'. Wealthy families like the Harrises of London kept both pigs and cows and cultivated large gardens on their spacious urban estates; not until 1937 did London prohibit the raising of cows within city limits. Banning domestic animals represented a serious economic loss for many poor families: such reforms ensured better public health standards but at the cost of eliminating a key option for supplementing meagre industrial wages.[44]

Many environmental problems beset late-nineteenth-century urban Ontario. In 1878, a Select Committee of the Provincial Assembly reported that the water supplies of three-quarters of eighty responding municipalities were contaminated by human waste from privies, that disease was widespread, and that little or nothing was being done about it. Existing provincial legislation allowed for the collection of information and inspection but provided little in the way of enforcement. Municipalities were reluctant to assume costly responsibilities: dead animals in the street did not require a garbage collector; rather, Kingston's local paper advised, unhappy ratepayers should await the arrival of 'a few carrion consuming crows'.[45]

In 1882, the Toronto *Globe* lamented that the city's water system provided at best 'drinkable sewage'. In the 1890s, Sudbury's sewage was dumped raw into two creeks that ran through the centre of town. A report prepared for the town of Belleville in 1878 described the sewage system as 'overcharged cesspools, neglected privies, and filth laden sewers'; wells and springs were drying up because of 'the indiscriminate destruction of trees that formerly covered the ground' and 'the general adoption and extension of land-drainage'; and the nearby River Moira 'was completely unfit for domestic use owing to the peat colour of the water'. Lake Ontario's Bay of Quinte also fell short: in the warm months, 'large tracts of its surface resemble[d] a lawn rather than a lake'. Mowat's government tightened its supervision by establishing a Provincial Board of Health, but the board often found itself powerless in the face of local municipal councils that refused to raise local rates to establish adequate sewage systems and water supplies. In 1884, Toronto granted only $500 to its health board to oversee sanitary conditions for the city's nearly 100,000 people. In the absence of effective provincial enforcement, private concerns took some municipalities to court. In 1893 the Town of Walkerville, in the words of the Grand Jury, 'wilfully and injuriously did construct, make, build and maintain certain sewers and drains' that conveyed waste to the Detroit River, with the result that the waters were 'corrupted, fouled, offensive and unhealthy to the great damage and common nuisance' of users and residents. Walkerville and Windsor paid to clean up the mess and revamp their local sewage systems.[46]

A movement to reform city government gathered force. Historians have debated the motives that lay behind the actions and rhetoric of city reformers. Did they have the interests of the community as a whole at heart, or did they represent the needs of a more narrowly focused elite? In the case of municipal water issues, it seems clear that changes typically occurred only after one or two unwelcome events transpired. Following a big fire, municipal councils would be quick to upgrade water transmission facilities; after an epidemic, sewage systems and water quality would be upgraded. In both cases, the first step was often the purchase from private interests of local water systems: by 1891, 76 per cent of Ontario's waterworks were municipally owned; twenty years later the figure had risen to 87 per cent. The money for such initiatives usually came from increased municipal property taxes. But not all ratepayers benefited equally: water mains and pipes reached industries and wealthy residents first and the poor much later. Moreover, even as fire insurance companies pressured local councils to reform water transmission services, they routinely increased costs to residents who lived in areas with substandard systems. Thus, in many municipalities, industrialists and well-off residents also benefited from lower fire insurance rates, while those least well off—not connected to the new system—suffered from higher premiums. The benefits of municipal reform eventually trickled down, but it was a slow process and many died waiting.[47]

Nor did death by infectious diseases such as tuberculosis and scarlet fever strike the rich and the poor equally. In Hamilton, the lowest mortality rates 'were found among that segment of the population least exposed to overcrowding and environmental blight and living in the areas with the highest per capita property values'. In Ottawa, infant mortality—a sensitive indicator of overall mortality rates—was highest in Lowertown, an area of low-quality, overcrowded housing and relatively high poverty rates. In the 1870s, life expectancy for Belleville's lower-class residents (most of whom were Catholic) was about thirty-seven—some ten years less than for the better-off Protestants. Catholic infants did actually have a lower death rate than Protestant infants (Catholic mothers protected their babies from poor water by breastfeeding for a longer time), but this cultural difference could not protect against overcrowding, poor nutrition, and unsafe sewage facilities.[48]

The new century would bring even more fundamental change as economic growth dramatically quickened the pace of industrialization and urbanization. At the turn of the century, cities grew at an ever-accelerating rate, placing even greater strains on housing stock, water and sewage systems, and other urban services. As social conditions further deteriorated, old notions of laissez-faire could not contain demands for reform. The social consequences of industrialization demanded a more sustained and systematic reform response.

Chapter 8

'A New Order of Things', 1905–23

'[A] new order of things [has] come', wrote William Meredith, the retired leader of Ontario's Conservative party, to newly victorious Conservative premier James Whitney in 1905. For the first time since 1872, a Conservative government led Canada's most powerful province. Although Meredith may not have meant it, the notion of a 'new order' resonated outside of simple political change. The election results reflected profound social and economic transformation within Ontario. Liberal strength lay in rural areas, but probably by 1905 and certainly by 1911, more Ontarians lived in urban than in rural communities and more worked in manufacturing than in farming and primary industries. Both these trends, of course, had late-nineteenth-century roots. Nevertheless, their trajectories accelerated in the first decade of the new century. In 1901, 42 per cent of occupations were in the primary sector and only 31 per cent in the secondary manufacturing sector; by 1911, those figures were reversed: 31 and 41 per cent respectively. Manufacturing output in Ontario's major cities increased by 172 per cent, the greatest increase for any decade prior to the Second World War. Urban population increased by 42 per cent, still the highest growth rate for any decade in Ontario's history. At the same time, the absolute number of rural people decreased by 4 per cent and experienced only a modest growth of 2.4 per cent during the next decade.[1]

New approaches to reform accompanied these social and economic changes: the state, generally reluctantly and unevenly, became more interventionist. Reformers themselves, while still strongly religious in orientation, entered into an evolving alliance with people of a scientific (often medical) background in their attempts to preserve and cultivate an appropriately productive and moral citizenry. The state, too, increasingly relied on specialized scientific advice in the running of its affairs. The era of the talented generalist continued to give way to the expertise of the trained specialist. Machines became the symbols, efficiency the watchword of success and progress. While none of this was entirely new, the total package separated the Ontario of the twentieth century from the colony and province of the preceding century.

Amid this fast-paced change, however, continuities were evident. Four out of every five Ontarians had been born in Canada, and most, including Whitney himself, had grown up in small-town or rural Ontario. For many, farming remained a prosperous venture. Although a significant number of sons and daughters of farm families did leave for urban areas (some 700,000 people left southern Ontario's rural areas between 1881 and 1921), rural Ontario was never depopulated. As late as 1921, two-fifths of Ontarians still lived in the countryside, and many who lived in cities had moved there from rural areas. Important social, cultural, and economic links bound urban and rural Ontario. At the turn of the century, Toronto's new city hall prominently displayed murals of rural life in pioneer times. Some of the province's largest industries—agricultural implements, cheese and butter, tanning—were rural-based. As the rural population ebbed, support for traditional rural ways swelled. 'It is from our ranks', one rural activist maintained, 'that the effulgence of freedom has ever sprung.' Rural life had 'many disadvantages', one back-to-the-land advocate admitted, but, of one fact he was confident: 'there was no unemployment'. Politicians ignored rural voters and values at their peril. Meredith continued as premier until his death in 1914. His Conservative successor, William Hearst, lasted five years before being overturned by the United Farmers of Ontario (UFO), the last Ontario government elected specifically to uphold the verities of rural life.[2]

Economic Growth

Although the last decades of the nineteenth century provided a strong base on which to build, accelerated growth in Ontario depended on favourable changes in the Atlantic economy. The new century brought an end to economic stagnation and ushered in a period of rapid capital accumulation. Technological changes provided incentives for the investment of that capital in Canada. As the traditional forestry, primary manufacturing, and agricultural sectors expanded (the number of hectares sown peaked only in 1926), new industries emerged, particularly in mining and secondary manufacturing. The provincial economy became not just bigger, but also—in southern Ontario, at least—significantly more diverse.[3]

The burgeoning mining sector in 'New' Ontario proved particularly important. In 1902, the Grand Trunk Railway considered renewing efforts to build through northern Ontario en route to the west coast, and the Liberal government began work on a north–south line, the Timiskaming and Northern Ontario Railway. This led to the discovery of silver at Cobalt, a venture that yielded $206 million over the next eighteen years. Gold discoveries at Porcupine in 1909 and Kirkland Lake two years later put Ontario ahead of the Yukon as Canada's foremost gold-producing region. Around 1911, hard rock mining was further facilitated by the introduction of light hammer drills, popularly known as 'widow-makers' because of their propensity to coat the air with small dust particles that led to fatal lung diseases among the miners. By 1915, northern Ontario's railway network was basically in place. And as the north developed, in the colourful words of the historian J.M.S. Careless, 'successive opulent suburbs of Toronto [marked] a veritable progression of mining booms'.[4]

Not only did exports boom, substantial growth also occurred in primary manufacturing of non-ferrous metals. Governments imposed a 'manufacturing condition' on resource producers to ensure that primary processing occurred within the province. In addition to protecting jobs, such policies added value to

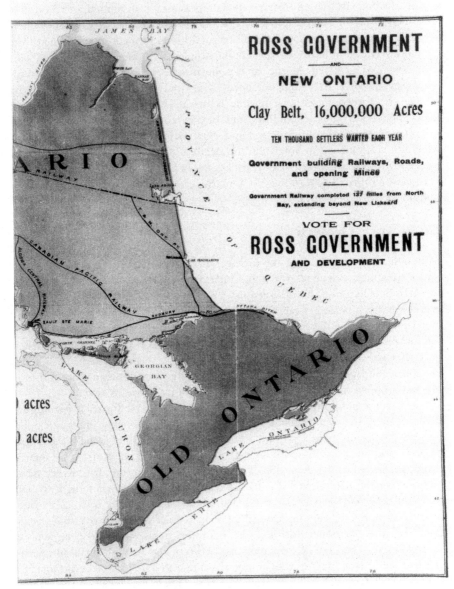

Map of Ontario, 1904. At the turn of the century, the rural life continued to be seen as a panacea for the problems of an urbanizing, industrializing society. Governments hoped that the recently surveyed clay belts of the 'New Ontario' would attract many farmers, both immigrants and Ontario-born. AO C233-1-1-2230, 5296.

Gold miners, South Porcupine region, c. 1910. Mining was dirty, dangerous work, and many gold miners contracted an incurable disease known as silicosis, caused by prolonged exposure to silica dust particles. AO ACC9160 S13751.

Canadian exports. Similarly, the development of the sulphite process for paper-making breathed new life into Ontario's forest industries. Although the emergence of newsprint and other paper-products industries was more significant in Quebec than in Ontario, the Abitibi Pulp and Paper Company's operations at Iroquois Falls became one of the world's largest by the end of the 1920s. Finally, communities such as the Lakehead, situated at a confluence of port and railway facilities, per-formed gateway functions between the west and the east in much the same way as the Algonquian peoples had between the Wendat (Huron) and more northern Native peoples in the period before European settlement. The cleaning, sorting, and shipment of wheat became an economic mainstay of the Lakehead region. Between 1900 and 1914, the storage capacity of grain elevators increased from 7.5 million to 47.6 million bushels. By the end of the 1920s, the Lakehead had become the world's largest grain port.[5]

Neither mining nor papermaking, however, proved as significant as the devel-opment of the hydroelectric industry. Ontario at the turn of the century depended on costly imported coal from the United States. If the province was to emerge as a major manufacturing centre, a cheap source of domestic energy would have to be found. The development of the hydraulic turbine, the dynamo, the alternator, and high tension wires, which allowed hydroelectricity to be produced and trans-ported cheaply and efficiently from generating stations to industrial cities, pro-vided that energy. Increasingly, manufacturers harnessed hydro's power.

This widespread growth attracted people as well as capital. Between 1896 and 1914, immigration increased sharply both to Ontario (between 1906 and 1911, about 20 per cent of newcomers to Canada settled in Ontario) and to the Prairie provinces. As settlement advanced in Manitoba, Saskatchewan, and Alberta, Ontario's manufacturing companies responded to these enlarged markets for capital and consumer goods. The hitherto dominant clothing industry grew, but it lost ground to secondary iron and steel industries, which by 1911 employed more urban workers than any other sector. Increased mechanization and the adoption of labour-saving machinery, meanwhile, led to a stabilization of the workforce despite continued growth in the volume and value of production. A major depression in 1913 briefly interrupted the extraordinary pace of economic growth, but World War I ended the slump. Between 1916 and 1918, the Imperial Munitions Board awarded over $1 billion in contracts for war material in Canada, 60 per cent of which went to communities in southern Ontario. These investments revitalized the industrial base in many small Ontario towns—Orillia, Renfrew, Peterborough, St Catharines, and Sault Ste Marie each received more orders than the entire Prairies.[6]

Industrial production continued to be concentrated primarily in Toronto and the surrounding region. Industrial jobs drew migrants both from abroad and from the surrounding countryside into the largest cities. But it is important to note that these jobs continued to rely in an important sense on the needs of rural as well as urban consumers. In 1915, the National Cash Register Company proclaimed that 'Business [was] Booming', and its advertisement prominently depicted a prosperous farmer in the foreground with industries in the background. South-central Ontario became Canada's largest consumer market, a magnet for yet more investment. As finance and trade grew ever more sophisticated, more lawyers, middle managers, and clerks were needed. Large retail department stores appeared.[7]

Government bureaucracies also began to expand in this period, and with the harnessing of hydroelectricity, the state gradually assumed a more interventionist stance. While formerly simple statutes and court cases had been sufficient to resolve most issues to do with the use of water, by the 1920s regulatory and administrative agencies were in place. The experts who staffed them attempted, often in direct response to pressure groups (the strongest of which were lumber and hydro companies), to sort out competing use rights to water. Citizens with environmental concerns only slowly coalesced into effective lobby groups.

Native Peoples

Native peoples were accorded few or no rights in environmental issues. Treaty Nine—signed in 1905–6 between Native peoples in the 'new' north, the federal government, and the province of Ontario (it was the first treaty negotiated at least in part by a provincial government)—was even less generous than Treaty Three. 'The glaring disparity between what was offered to the Indians and the potential wealth the whites hoped to realize from the land', one historian has concluded, 'makes it difficult to dispute that fraud of a high order was involved.' On the Mattagami and Abitibi rivers, Native rights were removed in favour of private corporate hydroelectric development. Much of the Mattagami band's traditional hunting area, burial grounds, and village were flooded; the only compensation for the loss of traditional lands was 25 cents an acre. Subsistence-based hunting rights meant little in the future envisioned by miners, foresters, and hydroelectric engineers. The province, through the Hydro Electric Power Commission, would not formally take over the supervision of such development until 1933.[8]

In the eyes of federal authorities, for Native peoples to make independent economic decisions was tantamount to Native self-determination—an unthinkable notion. Forests were often cut without the sanction of the bands that had been granted the land as reserves. The Garden River band at the Sault was even denied the right to cut timber on its own reserve: the federal Indian agent felt that the only proper economic activity for his charges was farming.

Native peoples resisted such interference into their sovereign affairs, with occasional success. The Garden River band had a rocky bluff known as 'wild man's stone', which it worked with local entrepreneurs who provided band members with jobs as well as money for the rock and gravel resource—a rare opportunity for the band to move out of farming. The Garden River people's success in protecting the bluff from government appropriation set a precedent for future diversification and became a story retold throughout the twentieth century. The Dokis people, a small band on the French River, managed to resist government pressure and to keep control of an extremely valuable timber reserve for which, in 1883, they had been offered a meagre $4 per person per year. When in 1906, after the death of a long-standing chief, the band finally agreed to sell, it netted $1.1 million—$600 per person per year—and 'became per capita the richest Indians in Canada'.[9]

Ontario's First Nations were becoming increasingly assertive in the protection of their rights. They especially resented residential schooling. From the 1870s, the federal government had been taking Native children from their families and placing them in the 'care of strangers' in the hope of 'civilizing and assimilating them into white society'. Anglican, Catholic, Methodist, and other religious bodies eagerly administered the state-funded program. In 1913, two Mohawk parents complained about whipping, hair shearing, poor food, and inadequate visitation rights at a local residential school. When the government ignored the complaint, one father, supported by the Six Nations council, took the school's principal to court. The jury awarded the father $100 ($5,000 had been asked for) in compensation for his daughter's having been kept on a water diet for three days and $300 for a whipping administered to her 'on bare back with raw hide'. The principal was replaced and punishments were made less severe—one government official felt the children were being 'disciplined to death'. It was only a partial victory, but not one that the government wished to see repeated; Ottawa refused to release funds to the Six Nations council for the payment of court costs.[10]

Assertive action by the Mohawk nation was far from unusual. In 1919, Lieutenant F.O. Loft, a Mohawk leader, had convened the first congress of the League of Indians at Sault Ste Marie, calling for 'absolute control in retaining possession or disposition of our lands'. Fittingly, given the prominence of women in Iroquoian society, it was a Mohawk woman who, in 1921, directly confronted the Ontario government on the central principle at issue: Native sovereignty. Eliza Sero, a fifty-two-year-old widow who had lost a son in the First World War, took a provincial fishery inspector to court for confiscating her seine fishing gear and prohibiting her from fishing in the Bay of Quinte without a licence. Fishing in the Great Lakes was big business in Ontario, which formed the northern shore of all but one of the five Great Lakes. The number of fishers had increased from 2,000 in 1879 to over 3,200 in 1920, and improved fishing technology meant larger catches. Since competition for fish in the Quinte area was intense, the local white community could only have been pleased with the inspector's actions.

Seine nets were less damaging to fish stocks than gill nets, and the licensing system had been instituted in the late nineteenth century partly as a conservation measure. But Sero's position, argued in court by white lawyers, was simply that she was a member of a sovereign nation and not subject to the laws of the whites. The presiding judge at the Supreme Court of Ontario, William Renwick Riddell, was on record as opposing the very concept of treaties being the product of negotiation with sovereign First Nations. 'In Ontario', he wrote several years later, 'there never has been any doubt that all the land, Indian and otherwise, is the king's, and that Indians are subjects in the same way as others. There are no troublesome subtleties in Canadian law.' In pronouncing in favour of the province, he asserted that seine fishing was not, in any case, a traditional Indian practice. That statement overlooked the fact that the Six Nations peoples were given seine nets by the British in 1789 and that, as we have seen in chapter 1, Ontario Native peoples had been using that technology from at least the early fifteenth century onward. But facts were never the crux of the issue. Renwick was at one with provincial government bureaucrats and, more important, firmly within the tradition of nineteenth-century jurisprudence concerning Native rights. In fact, he quoted an 1824 decision handed down by John Beverley Robinson: 'To talk of treaties with the Mohawk Indians, residing in the heart of one of the most populous districts of Upper Canada upon lands purchased for them and given to them by the British Government, is much the same, in my humble opinion, as to talk of making a treaty of alliance with the Jews in Duke street or with the French emigrants who have settled in England.' 'I cannot express my own opinion more clearly or convincingly', Riddell concluded. Eliza Sero died in 1937 at the age of sixty-eight. We do not know if she continued to fish. We do know that the Mohawk people continued to fight for the acknowledgement of their sovereignty.[11]

Women, Work, and Society

Women were leaders on other fronts. Many young farm women left rural Ontario for urban centres between 1890 and 1910. 'I've talked wid dozens of girls and I'll put ye woise', Mrs Murphy explained to Mrs Thompson in the *Farmer's Advocate* in 1918.

> 'Take it from me if ye want girls on the farm ye must be after makin' the farm more attractive nor it is now. Wan thing is the lack of conveniences. The danged men have everything they want . . . and the women is still carryin water and churnin and washin jist like the women as come over on the

Mayflower. Thin, again, the girl wants some company. On most farms her only chance is to flirt wid the hired man. . . . And there is wan more thing and that's the biggest trouble of all.'

'And what's that' says some wan.

'The long hours' says Kathlane.[12]

The exodus of young women to cities caused consternation to more than those who saw rural life as Ontario's backbone. It caused equal distress to a group of Protestant social activists committed to uplifting the moral tone of Canadian society. Science played a role here, too. Medical doctors, charity workers, and Protestant ministers worked for the good of the race, as they saw it. Members of the purity movement, part of a larger loose-knit reform group known as the Social Gospelers, looked askance at single women, bereft of suitable chaperones, working, living, and moving around in big cities like Toronto. Toronto the Good had a reputation to maintain: a sharp debate about the running of Sunday streetcars in the 1890s was troublesome enough, but the 'Girl Problem' transcended all that. Policewomen had to be hired. Places for public amusement (the number of nickelodeons, vaudeville theatres, saloons, and dance halls in Toronto increased from 5 in 1900 to 112 in 1915) had to be monitored. The imagined transgressions perpetrated by single working girls even challenged in the minds of some the purity of the Anglo-Saxon race. The single working girl, often exploited in the workplace, became, when outside her place of work, a woman adrift, a figure of suspicion. Such a person needed to be classified, regulated, and contained. From this perspective, the proper place for working girls was home service. But working girls charted their own course, and for many domestic service was not a high priority.[13]

In 1901, 27 per cent of Ontario's urban working women were employed as domestics. Working girls 'worship the god that has his throne high over the department store', the *Toronto Star* lamented in 1899. 'They prostrate themselves before the noisy chittering god of the typewriter. Upon the altar of the cruel sewing machine god they shed their blood. But the poor homely little god, whose symbols are the frying pan and the dust brush, goes a-begging for followers.' The *Star* failed to mention that 26 per cent of Ontario's urban working women toiled in factories, many undoubtedly as dark and gloomy as the International Malleable Iron Company depicted in the illustration here.[14]

For some single women, domestic work was all that was available. In order to enter the country, single Finnish women had to agree to work as domestics. Black women, too, were segregated in the domestic sector. As Caribbean-born Violet Blackman recalled of Toronto in 1920, 'You couldn't get any position regardless who you were and how educated you were, other than housework because even if the employer would employ you, those you had to work with would not work with you.' 'Really and truly', Marjorie Lewsey recalled, black women 'weren't allowed to go into factory work until Hitler started the war'.[15]

Ghettoized in low-wage, low-status occupations, frequently the last hired and first fired, women were also paid much less than their male co-workers, even in sectors where they did the same jobs. Hitherto a rarity, by 1921 female typists and

Women workers, International Malleable Iron Company, Guelph, c. 1920. By the 1920s, wages had improved and the workweek was shorter than it had been in 1900, but women were still paid much less than men. Guelph Public Library Archives.

stenographers accounted for nearly half of Canada's clerical workforce but earned just over half the salary of male clerks; even by 1971, the wage gap had narrowed only slightly. Besides, reformers asserted, women were made to be mothers. While overworked men retained their 'power for paternity', women factory workers, medical doctors affirmed, wearied from attending a machine day after day, endangered future offspring. Simply put, why pay the 'weaker sex' equal wages?[16]

Employers often believed that women were a more docile workforce than men. Such was not always the case. In 1907, four hundred primarily single women between the ages of seventeen and twenty-four walked off their jobs at the Toronto offices of the Bell Telephone Company in protest against low wages, harsh working conditions, and long hours. Moral-purity advocates chastized Bell for endangering the future of the 'race'. A better system was needed, one Methodist minister preached, one that would not 'strain women beyond their capacity and impair the interests of the unborn.' Twenty-six doctors testified to the dangers faced by the young women in Bell's employ, and a royal commission report on the strike warned that 'the breaking point of the operator's health is not far from the breaking point of efficient work.' While they did not win any of their major demands, the strikers did force Bell to rethink its often oppressive managerial practices, to introduce cafeterias, and to undertake consultation with the workforce.[17]

In 1913, two thousand Hamilton garment workers, many of them women, struck at the city's four largest clothing factories and, after two weeks, won a victory. A strike in 1912 against Timothy Eaton and Company fared less well. Religion and ethnicity as well as gender cut across the possibilities for class solidarity. 'Those [involved] are almost entirely Jewish', *The Ladies' Garment Worker* noted, 'and the chief slogan by which it was hoped to cut off public sympathy was the report . . . that this is "only a strike of Jews".' The 'slogan' worked. The future of the wrong race was at issue, and moral-purity advocates stayed away. A company spokesman arrogantly proclaimed that the action was 'nothing but a hold up game' and that the strikers could forget about their jobs—jobs already being done by Yorkshire-bred strikebreakers, often co-workers, both male and female.[18]

The First World War had a major impact on women's work. Initially, women participated in raising money for various war efforts and in prodding reluctant men to enlist. In late 1915 and early 1916, when enlistment drives intensified, women—often married women—began to work in munitions and other factories. They also worked at men's jobs in banks. At the Canadian National Exhibition in Toronto in 1918, women demonstrated their abilities to work lathes, drive tractors, and manage industrial machinery. 'They do not seem like the same women of a year or so ago', a Toronto newspaper reporter mused. 'They seemed inspired with a quiet, immovable resolve, as those who have a great mission to perform. . . . To many a man in the audience it was a new phase of womanly character which might never have been seen had it not been for the war.' Like men at the front, most women in industrial work stayed there only until war's end.[19]

Welfare Capitalism

Rising labour militancy and the rapid growth of trade unions in the 1890s led to the creation of provincial and federal Departments of Labour, which attempted to set a minimum budget necessary to maintain 'health and decency' for a family of five. Yet, by the end of the Great War, only skilled railway workers—locomotive engineers, conductors, firemen, and brakemen—earned more than the government's estimated minimum. Average wages for adult male wage earners represented less than 75 per cent of what was required.

Still, there were some improvements in the standard of living for Ontarians during these years. Changes in the structure of the labour force shifted many from lower-paying to higher-paying jobs. And, slowly, the hours of labour began to decline, from ten hours per day, six days per week, to nine hours per day with a 'half-holiday' on Saturday. During the war, the trend toward shorter hours accelerated dramatically. Employers, pushed by government studies, factory inspectors, and trade unionists, gradually recognized that industrial fatigue seriously impaired morale and thus productivity. Between 1917 and 1919, Massey-Harris reduced the workweek in its Toronto factory from sixty to forty-eight hours without any decline in production. It was a classic example of 'welfare capitalism': reform, employers discovered, was profitable. By 1920, the standard workweek in virtually all industries had been reduced to forty-eight hours; in some it stood at forty-four. Real wages may not have improved, but workers spent less time in the factory to earn those wages, and a little overtime at time-and-a-half increased incomes for many.

The wretched working conditions existing at the turn of the century also improved. Factory inspectors had argued for years that better safety measures, improved ventilation, and less crowded workrooms would pay dividends in the form of higher efficiency and productivity. The war brought new reform voices, including the Canadian Manufacturers Association; major employers led the way in workplace innovations such as lunchrooms, midday meals at cost, and pension plans designed to tie workers to their jobs and thus reduce the cost of labour turnover.

In addition, many companies sponsored sports teams, capitalizing on a vibrant tradition of community- and provincial-level competition in games such as baseball (the most popular), hockey, tennis, and lacrosse. In each case, companies' efforts were supported by provincial associations, which used the opportunity to establish rules and award prizes in order to regulate behaviour and foster allegiance to community and state. Responding to middle-class reformers' fears of idle women, Eaton's and several other companies organized leisure activities for their women employees. In addition to the chance to play basketball and learn 'Aesthetic and Ballet Dancing', the Eaton's Girls Club offered sewing, millinery, embroidery, and dress-designing classes to better enable the company's women workers to make the transition to middle-class sensibilities. What is interesting about the Eaton's case is that by the end of the 1920s, women workers had changed the company's leisure agenda from domestic courses to a more comprehensive regimen of sport-related activities reflecting a more general desire on the part of working-class women in this period for sports and, as historian Joan Sangster has noted, standing in the way of middle-class hopes for 'promoting a passive and delicate image of femininity'. Nonetheless, either scenario—domestic courses or company sports—allowed business to keep an eye on their workers during their increased leisure hours.[20]

Company publications touted the benefits to the company and its employees of welfare capitalism. Yet several government investigations in the mid-1920s concluded that, at best, these measures were very unevenly implemented within and across industries. Recreation often meant little more than an annual picnic. The condition of lavatories varied dramatically. Only about half of the province's industrial employees worked for companies that even stated they had pension plans, and twelve of sixty-one of companies making that claim did not in fact offer any such plan to factory employees. Initiatives of this kind multiplied at the height of labour unrest, between 1918 and 1920, in many cases designed specifically to blunt the bite of organized labour. Industrial councils, on which management and worker representatives sat, were meant to substitute for unions. In the end, welfare capitalism worked well for companies. While far from all workers supported such measures, many did, and to that extent, united worker action of other sorts was rendered more difficult. As the 1920s progressed, Ontario's industrial workers increasingly saw welfare capitalism as the best of a limited set of feasible options.[21]

Public Health and the Environment

In public health, little had changed since the last quarter of the nineteenth century. Cities had grown far more rapidly than housing stock or basic urban services. Slums expanded at an alarming rate. Between 1902 and 1911 for Ontario as a whole, one in six children under the age of fourteen died of a communicable disease. In 1909, the infant mortality rate rose in Toronto to an appalling 230 per 1,000 live births—over twice the level for Rochester, New York, a city of comparable size and economic structure just on the other side of Lake Ontario. Toronto dumped untreated sewage into the harbour and pumped untreated water back into the city's water system. Reform demanded state initiatives, and the state looked to scientific specialists for advice.[22]

At a broad level, scientific response focused on two areas: environmental and personal or familial. Medical practitioners campaigned for new programs based upon principles of preventative medicine. Reformers insisted that boards of health must intervene before crises erupted, not only after, in order to prevent the outbreak of disease. Dr Helen MacMurchy conducted a series of infant mortality reports between 1910 and 1913. A prominent reform advocate, John W.S. McCullough, became the chief medical health officer of the Provincial Board of Health in 1910. The following year, Charles J. Hastings became Toronto's medical health officer. Both men convinced governments to increase the resources available to boards of health at the provincial and local levels.

Pollution, Toronto harbour, c. 1912. COTA SC244, Item 1122A.

Three environmental issues were especially targeted: poor water quality, unpasteurized milk, and substandard housing. Toronto took the lead in addressing the issue of foul water. The city moved its water intake, began to filter and then chlorinate water, situated its sewage outfall six kilometres from the main harbour, and built sedimentation tanks to provide primary treatment. In 1912, the government gave to the Ontario Board of Health the power to require that municipalities erect sewage treatment plants and establish water purification measures and to promote the expansion and professionalization of public health activities throughout the province. By 1927, chlorinating plants treated 76 per cent of Ontario's water supply. The incidence of typhoid dropped dramatically. The focus on chlorinated drinking water, however, led provincial experts to ignore an equally insidious problem: inadequately treated waste from Toronto and virtually all of Ontario's and the American border states' municipalities continued to pollute the region's rivers and streams and the Great Lakes. 'Sadly', one historian has concluded, 'as the health of the people of Ontario steadily improved, just as steadily the health of its rivers and lakes declined.'[23]

Nor were health and environmental issues simply an urban problem. 'It is of little avail to our cities', the editors of the *Canada Lancet* wrote in 1910, 'to lay down the most perfect system of water services . . . if the milk dealer in the country is allowed to use water from a well that has been polluted with typhoid fever.' A study of 311 dairy farms by Queen's University chemists concluded that only 19 per cent had drinkable water. A particular concern for Toronto's Board of Health was the relation between sanitation, milk, and infant mortality. In May 1912, Dr Hastings ordered inspectors to test milk and dump 'into the sewer all milk which is obviously dirty'. They dumped 900 gallons in that month alone. In 1913, Toronto required that all milk sold must be pasteurized, and over the next five years the infant mortality rate fell dramatically. Yet it was not until the late 1930s that provincial legislation required that *all* milk produced in the province be pasteurized.[24]

An aggressive campaign to upgrade Toronto's housing stock also began in 1912. Dr Hastings underlined 'the social and national significance of "home" as being of one family dwellings'. In reformers' minds, single-family homes ensured stable families and, not coincidentally, a buoyant economy. Between 1911 and 1918, Toronto's board of health condemned 1,682 homes as 'unfit for habitation'. In the minds of many reformers, place and race were conflated. Hastings, for example, equated tenements with the 'foreign element'—Jews, Poles, and Italians—and their 'dirty habits'. In 1911, the Toronto Board of Health hired housekeepers to assist in instilling 'cleanliness, sanitation and Canadian methods of housekeeping' in working-class immigrant families. The Toronto Housing Company, formed to provide single-family rental dwellings for the working class, required two references, rent in advance, and a damage deposit. As the reproduced cartoon suggests, however, many working-class families could afford neither more expensive housing nor the rental schemes offered by the Housing Company. Indeed, between 1910 and 1913, rent in Toronto increased by 100 per cent and wages by only 32 per cent. But that did not bother the Company: it intended to appeal to the 'upper' working class, who could act as examples to the rest.[25]

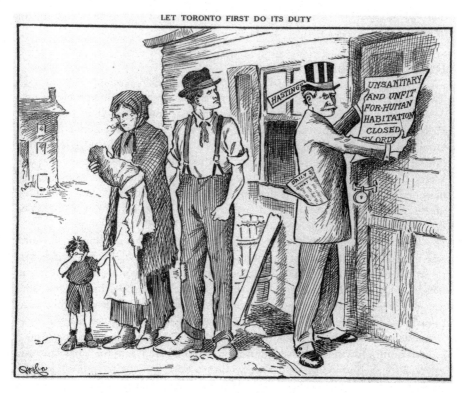

Jack Canuck, 'Let Toronto First Do Its Duty', 3 August 1912. COTA Fonds 251.

By 1920, after an extensive public works program, sewage and water facilities reached every house in Toronto, and by 1941, 90 per cent of urban households had indoor toilets—though almost 90 per cent of Ontario farms still used outdoor privies. By 1920, provincial public health standards, as measured by infant mortality, overall mortality, and morbidity rates, ranked with most in North America. In fact, in the area of public health, Ontario was Canada's leader.[26]

For scientists and other reformers, environmental issues were only one side of the problem. If the nation was to have healthy babies—the citizens of tomorrow—then mothering required close attention. Some saw infant mortality as a class or ethnic issue, and many advocated eugenicist solutions in a radical attempt to 'purify' the race. For others, if the state did not belong in the bedroom, it certainly belonged in the nursery. Led by doctors, well-baby clinics were established in Toronto in 1912 to educate 'negligent' mothers on proper child-rearing. In this conception, the environment—poverty, sewage, and poor housing—took back stage: in true nineteenth-century fashion, the culpable individual required transformation. In this case, mothers and (more generally) families were the problem; ameliorative education provided by trained medical professionals was the answer. With the death of so many of Ontario's young in the First World War, doctors and the state, as we shall see, became ever more vigilant and aggressive in the pursuit of the 'perfect' mother.[27]

Reform Movements

The tension between environment and personal character as prime problems, evident in the scientific-professional reform impulse, was reflected in the reform measures promoted by a broader group of new religious reformers commonly known as the Social Gospel movement. These reformers explicitly rejected the nineteenth-century notion that poverty was the 'wages of sin' and argued that low wages, unemployment, overcrowded housing conditions, and poor public health bred immorality and disease. At the same time, their ameliorative efforts coexisted nicely with medical professionals' desire to reform impoverished lower-class families according to the aspirations of the respectable middle class.

In this context, reformers, especially those concerned with childhood issues, often invoked the rhetoric of gardening (itself a popular middle-class preoccupation): careful planting, tending, weeding, watering, and pruning would result in lives budding and blooming in and through a controlled rearing process. This imagery nicely captured a changing emphasis within schooling from highly disciplined rote learning to encouraging the innate talents of pupils via a regimen of controlled exploration of the local environment. Excessive discipline or neglect would stunt growth; attentive cultivation would bring out the characteristics essential for the individual's and society's proper development. In addition to public schools, the Social Gospel movement's 'missions', including the Young Men's and Young Women's Christian Associations and the more secular-oriented University Settlements, provided the institutional means within which such growth could occur and in so doing began to offer the services that would in time form the basis of Ontario's social welfare system. These organizations provided community recreation for children, cheap meals, and educational programs to help the poor do more with less. Volunteers assisted men, women, and children to acquire new job skills, and their efforts touched thousands of lives.[28]

Social Gospellers quickly became the backbone of the prohibition movement. Initially, temperance advocates had demanded moderation, if not voluntary abstinence. But soon zealots demanded government intervention to prohibit the manufacture, sale, and consumption of alcohol. The Canada Temperance Act (1878) had allowed a 'local option', whereby a municipality could ban the sale of alcohol within its boundaries. Some municipalities did so, but this option satisfied few prohibitionists. Prohibition activists stepped up their campaigns, and in 1894 the province held a plebiscite asking, 'Are you in favour of the immediate prohibition by law of the importation, manufacture and sale of intoxicating liquors as a beverage?' Over half of all eligible voters cast a ballot, and the majority were in favour (65 per cent in rural areas and 58 per cent in urban areas), but the government refused to be bound by the results. Nevertheless, by the time of the Great War, prohibition dominated the reform agenda and was a central issue in provincial elections.[29]

The feminist movement too gained strength before the war, partly as a result of the growing temperance movement. Some progress was made toward improving women's access to higher education and professional training and opportunities to practise their professions, particularly in medicine. Yet little could be expected so long as women were denied the basic democratic right to express their political voice. The organizational overlap of suffrage, prohibitionist, and Social Gospel groups provided both institutional strength and ideological cross-fertilization. But women did not achieve provincial suffrage until 1917 and did not vote until October 1919. Male politicians had other priorities.

A Conservative Regime

In Ontario, as in other provinces, sitting governments have rarely been unseated, and by 1905, Ontario's Liberals had enjoyed thirty-three uninterrupted years in power. What, then, can account for the triumph of James Pliney Whitney and his Conservative party? No doubt one important factor was Oliver Mowat's resignation in 1896 to join the new Liberal cabinet in Ottawa under Prime Minister Wilfrid Laurier. Not only did Mowat's successors lack his political touch, but increasing industrialization and urbanization favoured the Conservatives, who had traditionally enjoyed the support of urban voters, particularly those of the middle class. When, despite these disadvantages, the Liberals survived a very close election in 1902, Whitney worked hard to strengthen his party's provincial organization. He dismounted from 'the Protestant horse', moderating his views on Catholic and French-language schooling, and—having lost an election early in his political career as a result of corruption within his own party—he became an advocate for electoral reform and a moral watchdog on Liberal electioneering practices.

Whitney's numerous charges of Liberal corruption led to a series of investigations in 1904, one of which revealed that the election of a Liberal in Sault Ste Marie had been effected by dint of bribes (money and whisky), 'bogus bibles' (used to swear in voters), and coercion (by a local railway company of its employees). Perhaps the last straw was the discovery that twenty Americans had been brought over from Michigan by steamboat and persuaded with liquor and money to vote for the Liberals. Editors of small-town Liberal newspapers looked askance. The 1905 provincial election turned on charges of government corruption, with Whitney asserting that he was 'honest enough to be bold!' He won an overwhelming victory, and the once-powerful provincial Liberals were reduced to little more than a corporal's guard in the legislature. Whitney was to win three more elections before his death in 1914.

Like Mowat, Whitney ran his own show. 'The Members of the Legislature must not imagine that their duty is simply that of delegates to repeat what they hear in their own localities and nothing more', Whitney believed. 'The duty of the Legislature is to help to show the people what it is right to do in the interests of the people themselves.' Whitney meant what he said. As many disgruntled back-benchers found to their chagrin, he was there to lead, not to be led.[30]

Openly pro-business and pro-development, Whitney's government proved highly innovative and at times progressive. The creation of Ontario Hydro is a revealing example of Whitney at work. Ontarians heralded hydroelectricity as the 'white coal' that promised, in the words of the *Hamilton Spectator*, 'A Smokeless City in a Coalless Province'. Hydro, proclaimed the Toronto *Globe*, represented 'the subjugation and enjoyment of nature'—Niagara Falls. No one opposed hydro development, but debate emerged over who was to control the means of production: government or private companies? And if government, municipal or provincial?[31]

By 1903, 126 Ontario municipalities owned gas, water, and electric-light facilities. Municipal control of these facilities was also common in the United States. Yet in 1906, the Whitney government chose a revolutionary option: provincial control. Whitney's biographer, Charles Humphries, argues that this action exemplifies the emergence of a 'progressive' conservative political party in Ontario. In contrast to his Liberal opponents, who favoured a monopoly in the interests of capitalists, Whitney pushed for a monopoly in the interests of consumers—among whom, of course, would be capitalists using provincially controlled hydro production to operate their enterprises.[32]

Whitney had co-opted the left. As historian Viv Nelles has pointed out, 'from the outset the crusade for public power was a businessman's movement. They initiated it, formed its devoted hard core membership and . . . provided it with brilliant leadership.' In the United States, the left was strong and business feared socialism; in Ontario, the left was relatively weak and gave middle-class business interests no reason to fear state ownership.[33]

With cheap, state-controlled power, Ontario's petite bourgeoisie could better its collective position in society, and the state could become a major player on the North American manufacturing stage. Behind the scenes, Whitney worked hard to bring the financial and business elite, who advocated private monopoly, to the bargaining table with representatives of the business middle class. Only when reconciliation seemed impossible did Whitney take the final step. In 1908, aided by the energetic leadership of Adam Beck—past mayor of London, cigar-box manufacturer, and member of Whitney's cabinet—Whitney created Ontario Hydro under Beck's control to generate and distribute electricity throughout the province.[34]

The move solidified Whitney's progressive reputation, but two other measures were, in their own ways, equally innovative. Under recent Liberal administrations, the premier had virtually managed the University of Toronto. Whitney stabilized funding in a manner that, as the commissioners appointed to report on the university's affairs put it, provided 'a home for culture and science under the same academical roof'. Whitney's 1906 University of Toronto Act also freed the university from direct government control. In the words of his biographer, that legislation 'must be ranked as one of the major achievements of the Whitney era'. Nor did he ignore the working class. While careful to heed the wishes of employers, Whitney responded to trade-union demands for protection in the face of numerous industrial accidents. Labour exerted pressure on the government the level of which had not been seen in Ontario since the Nine Hours movement of the 1870s. Whitney enacted a new Workmen's Compensation Act in 1914 that, unlike Mowat's 1886 legislation, went beyond employer's liability and provided automatic compensation to injured workers through a government fund administered by a public board. Ontario was no leader in this—only New Brunswick and Prince Edward Island had yet to pass such legislation—but Ontario's workers saw it as a major triumph. One historian believes that the campaign for worker's compensation marked the birth of the provincial labour movement in the twentieth century. For Whitney, it was a way of consolidating the urban vote, of maintaining and strengthening the coalition of interests from which he drew his support.[35]

When it came to issues of religion and language in Ontario's school system, however, Whitney stumbled. Although he had tried to improve relations with the Catholic community, he was 'typically Ontarian in his outlook and sensitivities'; as a young politician he had been an unabashed supporter of Meredith's anti-Catholic, anti-French electioneering tactics, and in 1890 he had proclaimed Ontario to be 'an English province [in] every respect'. Whitney's deep-seated bias was revealed in 1912 after the provincial Ministry of Education found a number of bilingual separate schools in the Ottawa Valley and northeastern Ontario to be substandard, particularly in teacher training and English-language instruction. The government might have responded by working with the Franco-Ontarian community to address these problems, but it did not. Instead it introduced Regulation

Box 8.1   The Orange Order and Bilingual Schools in Ontario

As we have seen in chapter 6, the Orange Order emerged as a force in Upper Canada in the 1830s. Between 1830 and the end of the century, the order expanded to most Ontario townships: by 1900, there were some 1,000 local Orange Lodges comprising some 40,000 men; perhaps twice as many more had been members at one time in their lives, out of a total male Protestant population of 600,000. Two historians of the Ontario movement assert that 'nowhere, outside of Ulster, did the Order attain such numerical strength and centrality to the mainstream of life as it did in the protestant colony of Ontario.'

The order provided welfare support to its members and their families, especially in the area of burial, sick, and work benefits similar to those provided by the Catholic Hibernian and other societies. Primarily, however, it was a male secular institution that adhered strongly to ultra-Protestant teachings and unwavering allegiance to the British monarchy. It attracted support from all classes, but working classes predominated. It also had a history of engaging in street violence, and for that reason the Upper Canadian government revoked its incorporation as a public association in the 1840s; it was not until 1890 that the order was once again incorporated, this time by a federal act.

Generally the order sided with the Conservatives at the provincial and federal levels. It also had an impact on municipal politics: twenty of Toronto's twenty-three mayors after 1845 were Orangemen. Orangemen were strong supporters of Ontario's manifest destiny: the expansion of loyal Ontarian Protestants to the Pacific. They were quick to march west in opposition to Louis Riel in 1870 and again in 1885. As well, the order watched warily the establishment of French Catholic dioceses in the west and the fate of bilingual schools in Manitoba in the 1890s.

In the context of declining Orange membership at the turn of the century, the movement of French-speaking Catholics into eastern and northern Ontario (from 5 per cent of Ontario's population under Mowat to about 10 per cent on the eve of the First World War) alarmed the order and provided the occasion for its last major public demonstrations. 'It is admirable to deal generously with the conquered race', the Orange *Sentinel* declared in April 1910. 'But is it not fatal to grant them concessions which threaten the stability of our institutions? . . . Talk as we may about the loyalty of the French to Britain, the fact is patent to every observant man that Imperialism as it is understood in the English speaking provinces finds no favour amongst the French Nationalists.' 'It is', the *Sentinel* wrote, several months later, 'this refusal to assimilate that makes the French Canadian so difficult to get along with.' Not surprisingly, the order firmly opposed the establishment of bilingual schools in the province.[1]

The bilingual schools question provoked more than Orange and French Catholic imperialist aspirations. As we have seen, Irish Catholics were increasingly prospering in Ontario. They did not want to unnecessarily incur widespread Protestant enmity. Irish Catholics believed that a wide discussion of separate schools might lead to a backlash against the schools themselves and feared that the wider public would not differentiate between bilingual schools, bilingual separate schools, and unilingual English separate schools. On a more fundamental level, Irish Catholics perceived the expansion of French Catholics as a threat to their own expansive vision of a province and country peopled by English-speaking Catholics. Competing imperialisms—or, as historian John Zucchi has suggested, competing 'diasporic imaginations'—fuelled heated debates concerning the proper fate of Ontario's bilingual schools.[2]

---

1. Quotations: Marilyn Barber, 'The Ontario Bilingual Schools Issue: Sources of Conflict', *Canadian Historical Review* 47 (1966): 227–48.
2. Cecil Houston and William J. Smith, 'The Orange Order and the Expansion of the Frontier in Ontario, 1830–1900', *Journal of Historical Geography* 4 (1978): 251–64; Hereward Senior, 'Orangeism in Ontario Politics', in *Oliver Mowat's Ontario: Papers*, edited by Donald Swainson (Toronto: Macmillan, 1972), 136–53; John Zucchi, trans. and ed., *The View from Rome: Archbishop Stagni's Reports on the Bilingual Schools Question* (Montreal: McGill-Queen's University Press, 2002).

17, restricting the use of French in Ontario's schools. The result was a marked deterioration in French–English relations.[36]

Whitney's overwhelming electoral victories no doubt reflected his identification with programs that promoted economic growth, but the disarray of the provincial Liberals—unable to find either a viable leader or a viable issue—also contributed. Between 1905 and 1914, internal party squabbling twice led to the resignation of the Liberal leader in the middle of a provincial election. In the 1914 election, the Liberals campaigned for prohibition as if it were the only issue. The demise of the once-powerful Liberal machine came in 1917 when N.W. Rowell, the provincial leader, resigned in order to join the 'coalition' Union government in Ottawa, headed by Conservative prime minister Robert Borden.

Following Whitney's death in 1914, the premiership fell to William Hearst, northern Ontario's most prominent cabinet minister. Hearst lacked his predecessor's talent for dealing with interest groups. Rowell's policies as Liberal leader had driven virtually all the so-called liquor interests into the Conservative camp, but Hearst was a devout Methodist who sympathized with the prohibitionists. In 1916, his government passed the Temperance Act (alcohol could be purchased only by the bottle and on a doctor's prescription) and delayed a referendum on the issue until war's end. When the Conservatives 'abolished the bar . . . they completely destroyed their organization in the city', one contemporary observed. 'The bar-room has been the back-bone of the Conservative organization for many years.' Hearst also furthered 'progressive' aims by passing a law giving women the vote in provincial elections. His attempts to court rural voters, however, often backfired. In 1918, at a cost of $18,000, he distributed calendars to farmers replete with such homely advice as 'Do not kick over the lanterns' and 'This is a good month to oil the harness.' Farmers found such tips insulting and wondered aloud why other classes did not receive similar literature. Nor could Hearst satisfy the mammoth egos of important party members such as Adam Beck.[37]

Ontario and the First World War

An ardent imperialist who strongly identified with British political and cultural ideals, Hearst wholeheartedly supported the war effort and deferred to Ottawa's leadership in that area. When war was declared on 4 August 1914, Ontarians expected a short, decisive encounter. Many believed that the outpouring of local recruits would never cross the ocean. Municipalities throughout the province provided life insurance for local recruits, little suspecting that a year later they would cut back their guarantees in the face of large numbers of casualties. A German assault on the Allied position at Ypres in Belgium in April 1915 shattered Ontarians' illusions. Mired in filthy rat-ridden trenches and subjected to mustard gas, Canadians and their allies repulsed the attack, but at great cost: 5,261 Canadians were killed or wounded and 776 were taken prisoner—over half the Canadians in the battle. Newspapers began to publish letters from survivors testifying to the carnage of war: 'the dead are piled in heaps and the groans of the wounded and dying will never leave me', wrote one man. The torpedoing by Germans of the allegedly unarmed *Lusitania* in May of the same year further shocked Ontarians. Aliens, especially Germans, became targets of oppression throughout the province. The Battle of the Somme in the fall of 1916 further underlined the brutality of the war: 8,000 Canadians died, and 16,000 were wounded; 2,800 meters of land had been gained. In April 1917, the Battle of Vimy

'Aliens' under armed guard sawing wood at Camp Petawawa, c. 1916. During the First World War, many Canadians of German and Ukrainian descent were treated as 'hostiles' and shipped to remote internment camps. Most German Ontarians lived in and around the town of Berlin, which changed its name to Kitchener in 1916. Toronto renamed streets such as Bismarck Avenue, which became Asquith. A.A. Chesterfield Collection, Album #2, Queen's University Archives.

Ridge marked a sort of turning point: although one-third of the 30,000 attacking Canadians suffered casualties, the joint Allied assault on this key observational post was successful and of strategic significance.[38]

By 1918, 75 per cent of Toronto's eligible recruits had volunteered. And Ontarians did more than enlist: with less than one-third of Canada's population, they contributed over half of the total money received by the Imperial War Fund over the course of the war. How should one account for the extent of this support? Although there were pockets of Italians and other non-British immigrants in Toronto, of Germans around Berlin (now Kitchener), and of French and Scandinavians in the north, fully 75 per cent of Ontario's population claimed to be of British origin, and Hearst could count on general backing for his war policies. Young imperialists were trained in many ways: Empire Day was instituted in Ontario schools to promote 'a greater love of Ontario, for Canada and for the Empire' in schoolchildren. It would have been difficult for boys born in Ontario after 1870 to have resisted the inculcation of militaristic values by children's literature, toys, clothing, schools, sports, Boy Scouts, cadets, local militias, and the teachings of an emerging 'muscular Christianity'. In Ontario and much of the English-speaking world, the male generation raised before the First World War was taught the need to be 'manly men'. In fact, the emphasis on military drills in schools diverted funds from girls' physical activities, limiting them to 'joyless, formal callisthenics'. As one prominent advocate of the manly ideal put it in 1910, 'courage is to a man what chastity is to a woman—the one indispensable virtue.' That 'manly' was the antithesis of 'womanly' could not be doubted: any boy, one

Box 8.2   Ontario and the War's Aftermath

What did the war mean for Ontario? Some historians have argued that the war was a turning point for Canadians in general. Canadians began to think of themselves less as a colonial country and more as an independent nation. Others have argued that Canadians—including Ontarians—were deluded by a carefully orchestrated state-run propaganda campaign designed to obfuscate the war's grim reality in order to keep up recruit levels and popular support for the war. This interpretation nicely fits the general mood of dismay and disillusionment among Ontarians and Canadians at the war's end. Returning veterans experienced great difficulties in adjusting to peace: they complained bitterly over poor pensions and the lack of jobs, and they accosted 'aliens' who were fully employed. Municipalities were expected to shoulder the near-impossible challenge of looking after local veterans. By then the truth could no longer be hidden: horror, grief, and outrage emerged. One historian of the war's impact on Toronto, however, has asserted that, at least in Toronto, Ontarians were always well informed of and knowledgeable about the war's harsh reality and despite—or perhaps because of—that knowledge, demonstrated overwhelming support throughout the war. Disillusionment at war's end followed more from an increasing realization that the ends for which the war had been fought were not, in the peace process, being realized.[1]

1. For Canada as independent nation, see J.L. Granatstein et al., *Nation: Canada since Confederation*, 3rd ed. (Toronto: McGraw-Hill Ryerson, 1990), 204–5; R. Douglas Francis, Richard Jones, and Donald B. Smith, *Destinies: Canadian History Since Confederation* (Toronto: Holt, Rinehart and Winston, 1988), 198. For the propaganda theory, see Jeffrey Keshen, *Propaganda and Censorship during Canada's Great War* (Edmonton: University of Alberta Press, 1996). On veterans, see Margaret E. Frenette, 'The Great War's Defeats: "Doing Your Bit" on Thunder Bay's Home Front, 1914–1919', MA thesis (Lakehead University, 1996). On disillusionment, see Miller, 'Our Glory and Grief'.

officer asserted, who 'does not like drill and military exercises . . . is not a boy and has been put into pants by a mistake'. Ontario's manly boys heeded the message: nearly half of all Canadian volunteers—205,808—came from Ontario.[39]

But more men and materials were needed. Even in Ontario enlistments dwindled by the end of 1916. Ontarians strongly supported compulsory military service in 1918. Then, as the Germans were slowly pushed back in the fall of 1918, Ontario was hit by an influenza epidemic: by war's end on 11 November 1918, some 5,000 Ontarians had died of the disease and nearly one-third of Ontario's volunteers were missing, killed, or wounded.

Ontario's support for the war did not necessarily lead to support for federal policies when they seemed to threaten the province's interests. After all, 76 per cent of the province's population had been born in Ontario. Moreover, at a time when political leaders like Mowat, Whitney, and Hearst were moving to centralize power and establish a strong bureaucracy staffed by experts, recruitment for war service was decentralized and largely dependent on local volunteers, and recruiting propaganda stressed community as much as provincial and national pride. One could, then, be pro-war and anti-Hearst. With the armistice, support for the war effort no longer even partially masked opposition to other federal policies, and this opposition quickly rebounded on the provincial Conservatives. In October 1919, the Hearst government fell to an unlikely combination of agrarian progressives and urban labour. The *Globe* believed it had witnessed a 'political revolution' on the part of voters.[40]

Political Change: Rural and Urban Discontent

Praised as 'patriots' for their essential contribution in producing food for the Allies, farmers nonetheless felt aggrieved. They had long faced economic difficulties as production costs rose far faster than income, and problems intensified under the inflationary and other pressures of the war economy. Indeed, many rural men had refused to enlist, perhaps in part because there were fewer British-born men in southern rural Ontario than in urban areas and because farmers were more likely to be married than, and tended to be older than, the male urban population. The reeve of Huron County thought the government wanted to take 'our farm hands who make money for the country' while letting 'shiftless young men continue to hang around towns and cities'. Poorer or part-time farmers often protested with their feet, but not all farmers did. Those in the middle class tended to stay put and commenced political action: in southern Ontario, the number of farms with four hectares or less declined by two-thirds between 1891 and 1911; between 1911 and 1931, the number of farms over four hectares declined by only 5 per cent. Moreover, some of the rural depopulation that was decried at the time (often for political reasons) and that was written about by later scholars involved people who engaged in non-farm work—artisans such as coopers, blacksmiths, saddlers, and shoemakers. Given expanding transportation networks, men in these occupations had increasing difficulty competing with larger industries in urban areas. Much of the actual farming population decline that did occur resulted from shrinking birth rates as well as from movement of generally young adults to cities: the average size of farm families decreased by one person between 1871 and 1931.[41]

Farm leaders opposed protective tariffs that kept costs high and farm incomes low. Issues such as these had been articulated by the Patrons of Industry in Ontario in the early 1890s, when they gained seventeen seats in the 1894 election. But that movement had a short life. In 1914 E.C. Drury, a well-educated farmer and active farm organizer, and J.J. Morrison, a capable, hard-nosed agrarian advocate, helped found the United Farmers of Ontario (UFO). Maintaining that rural depopulation had led to reduced political influence, lower land values, and higher mortgages, they argued for the expansion of co-operatives (a sister organization, the United Farmers Co-operative Company provided a centralized way to buy and sell at lower prices), a progressive income tax, and the nationalization of banking to improve the collective lot of struggling farm families.

The UFO drew on an educated farm electorate: primary and secondary school attendance had been increasing since the turn of the century; newspaper readership was high; rural libraries flourished. While farmers from all economic levels joined UFO clubs, they tended to be younger and more often Presbyterian than the general farm population. These social characteristics probably gave the movement much of its energy and idealism. Very likely the Presbyterians were sympathetic to the reformist Social Gospel ideals and the young brought to the movement an impatient desire for change. By 1918, with a membership of 25,000, the UFO moved into politics.[42]

Farm women too were attempting to better their position. Mechanization had not lessened their work; although weaving, spinning, and cheese-making were increasingly done outside the farm household, poultry raising, vegetable growing, canning, and some dairying more than filled the potential void. While their urban counterparts used their husbands' money to run their homes, farm women earned their own money. A Simcoe county farm woman reported in 1917 that she managed sixty hens and had earned $400 from the sale of dressed poultry and eggs. 'Men like to pet their wives and make children of them', another farm woman wrote in 1908. 'They seem to inherit the patriarchal air. . . . We love to be petted but we want to be treated as an equal in the partnership of life.'[43]

Rural women began to organize to deal with economic and social change. Most of the province's teachers were women, two-thirds of them employed by rural or small-town school boards. In 1918, the Federation of Women's Teachers' Associations of Ontario formed to push for equal pay for equal work. A scant year later, the association represented one-third of the province's women teachers. An older women's organization, the government-supported Women's Institute (WI), had been founded in 1897, and by 1919 boasted 900 branches and 30,000 members. The WI provided rural women with an opportunity to develop leadership skills and a heightened sense of common problems. Its leaders were largely conservative, small-town, middle-class women who believed that the answer to rural decline lay in pursuit of the domestic ideal: farm women needed to stop working for money and concentrate on home management. It seems, however, that WI leaders did not have absolute control over members. The leadership counselled against pushing for women's suffrage, but many branches went their own way: 'We have got the suffrage microbe', a member from Massey, Ontario, declared. 'Headquarters may give all the orders they like . . . [but] our Institute . . . has been the best medium we have had to spread the suffrage doctrine.'[44]

A more radical group, the United Farm Women of Ontario (UFWO), was founded in 1918, and by 1921—without support from the UFO—had reached a peak of 6,000 members. The UFWO assumed as its main task the education of rural women for political action. In rural newspapers and at rural meetings, members stressed the necessity of class consciousness as a precursor to political action. The UFWO put the primary blame for the harsh conditions of rural life on men—'with all the political power in their hands [they] have made a terrible muddle of affairs'—but they also criticized women's passivity.[45]

Male rural leaders tended to stress other problems. Farmer leaders and local

UFO members argued that both traditional political parties represented the interests of urban business. According to the UFO's Morrison, parties abetted 'the power of the vested interests that are destroying [what] our pioneer fathers wrested from the wilderness'. In 1919, with a membership of 48,000 (it reached a high point of 60,000 in 1920, about 20 per cent of the province's farmers), the UFO nominated its own candidates and, with only 22 per cent of the popular vote—less than either the Liberals or the Conservatives—won forty-five seats in the provincial legislature. Much to the surprise of Drury and Morrison, neither of whom had run in the election, the UFO had suddenly become Ontario's largest party.[46]

Farmers were not the only discontented newcomers to the provincial legislature. In the context of the Winnipeg General Strike of 1919 and of radical labour activity in the mining areas of British Columbia, Ontario's workers have been labelled as conservative. At best that is a half-truth. The province's industrial workers saw their standard of living deteriorate during the war, when costs increased faster than wages and rents escalated. Craftsworkers lost ground as deskilling accelerated. The Imperial Munitions Board, the purveyor of million-dollar contracts, had no time for workers and their unions. Its contracts often specified the production of a standard machine-tooled item; an angry Hamilton machinist proclaimed in 1916 that to run such machines 'piece workers move with automatic precision and perform a certain operation with unerring facility. Yet . . . they are not skilled. . . . [T]hey have become automatons.' Less than a month later, 2,000 Hamilton munitions workers went on strike. The Hamilton metalworkers acted on a tradition of aggressive labour activity. Ontario's urban metalworkers had been the most active in the nation in striking for lower hours, increased pay, and, most important, the maintenance of shop control.[47]

Ontario saw more strikes between 1916 and 1919 than in the previous fifteen years. Within established unions, membership numbers grew, and many new unions were formed. Women workers continued active: in one case, a strike in the metal industries included women. Nor was all this activity restricted to the industrial heartland of southern Ontario. In the north, forestry and mine workers organized and struck; gold miners in South Porcupine held out for seven months in 1912–13 against strikebreakers, detectives, and state pressure; and a 1913 street-railway strike in Port Arthur led to bloodshed between police and strikers. Yet, as in the nineteenth century, so too in the twentieth: working-class protest was not all of a piece. In one instance, Ontario iron moulders allowed management to introduce a machine in preference to maintaining work for women. Male workers resisted the employment of women by Toronto's street-railway company during the war. As we have seen in the strike against Eaton's in 1912, gender and ethnic issues cut across working-class solidarity and facilitated cross-class collaborations.[48]

The United States and Great Britain included labour leaders in their wartime planning, but Canada did not; perhaps this was one reason why the state's repressive instincts had unusually free rein. The federal government's War Measures Act denied the right of collective public protest. Police raids took place in some Ontario communities. When labour leaders mounted a general strike in Toronto in 1919, many workers did not participate.

Compared to their counterparts in western Canada, Ontario workers had been treated relatively well, especially under the Whitney government. From workers' point of view, any problems had less to do with the political and economic system itself than with the people who currently managed it. This perspective has been called 'labourism', a set of beliefs anchored by the conviction that change for the better was possible within the capitalist system. A new political movement reflecting this vision began to take shape among Ontario's non-unionized workers. Special interests were seen to be the root of the problems with the current government. A new party had to represent all people; it had to be the harbinger of a new democracy. There was no special place in this vision for unions and their collective, particular needs. A product of such thinking, the Independent Labor Party (ILP), emerged in July 1919.

The ILP courted the female electorate. In Hamilton, women formed a separate Hamilton Women's ILP. In labour newspapers, working-class women attacked the notion of separate spheres and the image of the 'sentimental and false ideal of womanhood'. Yet labouring men continued to refer to these women's groups as 'auxiliaries', and women continued to knit socks for returning veterans and to bake cakes for commemorative events. For women, the social, economic, and political space created by worker protest was not unbounded.[49]

Although the ILP ran far fewer candidates than its farmer counterparts, it did elect eleven members in 1919 (defeating Adam Beck in London) and garner substantial votes in most cities except Toronto, where factional squabbling divided the labour vote. For some, political success made strikes and militant unionism less necessary. While strike activity continued in Ontario in 1920, it seemed less spirited, less radical, more muted. In the face of renewed employer intransigence, it was certainly less successful. And, as quickly became evident, labour's political basket was not designed to hold all of labour's eggs.

Reform and the 'Progressive' Coalition

With fifty-five seats between them, the UFO and the ILP formed a 'Progressive' coalition government under E.C. Drury. Farmers supported Drury's rural credit plans, which included the establishment of a Provincial Savings Bank. Strong support also existed for the creation of the Ontario Athletic Commission in 1920—to regulate boxing and the 'aggressive masculinity' it symbolized and to provide worthwhile alternatives to moving pictures and other popular entertainments of 'dubious' moral value. But the Drury government never coalesced into an effective administration, nor did the Progressives ever articulate a clear vision. Indeed, the UFO's Morrison denied that the movement was ever a political party: '[Y]ou cannot broaden out the political association [of farmers] because there is none'. This was not Drury's view: his father had been Mowat's minister of agriculture—Drury had been weaned on party politics.[50]

Conflicts within the UFO and the ILP were matched by difficulties between them. After electing so many members to the legislature, some in the UFO immediately questioned the wisdom of a coalition with labour. Both the UFO and the trade unions condemned Drury's plans to merge the two parliamentary caucuses into a single Progressive party. ILP members in industrial centres vigorously opposed the farmer-dominated coalition's anti-tariff stance. Labour became even more disillusioned when Drury refused to concede the eight-hour day to striking workers at Ontario Hydro. Farm and labour leaders grew increasingly critical of the new government.

They were not alone. The right to vote had been granted to women in 1917 by Hearst and his Conservative administration. In 1919, rural women took immediate advantage of their new power by turning out in large numbers (in part because Hearst had scheduled the long-awaited referendum on prohibition for the same day as the provincial election) and voting against his government. 'This election was the first time that the franchise was granted to women and I knew', one UFO leader later recollected, 'that the farm women were strongly for temperance and would certainly go to the polls to vote for the Temperance Cause and when there would mark their ballot for the farmer candidate.' The prohibition side won, but those who had pinned their hopes for broad social reform on prohibition were to be sorely disappointed. Many Ontarians simply defied the new law. Enforcement was spasmodic, doctors' prescriptions were easily obtained, and pharmacies ready to fill those prescriptions proliferated. Lured by the prospect of increased tax revenue, by the end of the 1920s the province would repeal prohibition and take control of alcohol sales itself.[51]

In the 1920s, more women than ever before were participating in organized sports (especially tennis and golf) and notions of female frailty were beginning to be dispelled. Yet most hopes for improvements in general social and economic conditions for women were disappointed. Although Drury enacted a minimum-wage law for women in the workforce, no such protection was provided for men, and some observers have suggested that this move may have contributed to the institutionalization of gender discrimination in pay. The presence of single working women in cities had been accepted by the late 1920s, and concern now focused on married women. The passage of an act that provided an allowance for widows with more than one child proved to be a two-edged sword, since recipients were expected to stay home with their children and their behaviour was regularly monitored. As the government-published *Labour Gazette* explained, 'the allowance is considered a salary from the government to enable the mother to make good citizens of her children.'

Like industrial workers, mothers—'the workers in our greatest, most vital and most profoundly important productive industry'—attained value only through the products of their labour: their children. Mother's allowances, Ontario's superintendent of trades and labour noted, were 'primarily in the interests of the child; the mother being only a secondary from the standpoint of the state'. Mothers became automatons dedicated to the rearing of children (described as 'little machines' in government publications such as *The Baby*) who would grow up to be productive citizens and never represent any burden to the state. As the new act's first annual report noted, '[I]f she [the mother] does not measure up to the state's standards for such guardians [that is, be efficient, thrifty, clean, industrious, non-complaining, and, of course, loving], other arrangements must be sought in the best interests of the children.' Similar attitudes had underlain child care legislation concerning measures such as Children's Aid Societies passed by Liberal and Conservative governments before the UFO.

In that it was more an entitlement than a charity, mother's allowance went beyond previous government welfare initiatives. Mothers had crucial roles to fill, and if they performed their tasks in the state-prescribed way, they would be rewarded. But government allowances were never intended to provide enough to survive on: throughout the 1920s and especially during the depression of the 1930s, widowed mothers were expected to find additional funds on their own, whether from employment or from family members. If the state were to provide sufficient money, politicians and bureaucrats believed, it would erode the 'incentive to effort' deemed so crucial by Ontario's laissez-faire governments. As one close student of this progam has concluded, 'By failing to come close to adequacy despite recognizing entitlement and need, mother's allowances thus became an ominous indicator of contradictions that would soon bedevil other welfare programs to emerge within Ontario.'[52]

So much for the hopes of the female labour activists who had dared to oppose the notion of separate spheres. Industry and science combined to reinforce and even increase gender specialization within Ontario's households. Ironically, the ideals of the home did not transform the factory; instead, the ideals of the factory—such as the efficiency pursued through time-and-motion studies by the American engineer Frederick Winslow Taylor—invaded the home. Parental advice manuals provided rigid schedules for babies' handling, feeding, playing, cleaning, sleeping, and even crying. Nor did the introduction of new technologies speed up housework. A new understanding of the role of bacteria in the generation of disease underpinned a new domestic science that promoted spotless homes. More, not less, work was needed to keep a home really clean.

The emergence of a medical science that advocated cleanliness coexisted well with a religious reform movement that extolled moral purity. Homemakers were increasingly portrayed as fighting on the front line in the prevention of disease and the fostering of virtue. By spending more time cleaning the home, cooking nutritious foods, doing laundry, and nursing and teaching children, homemakers could cultivate a physically and morally healthy family, and in the process put Ontario in the vanguard of an international movement against disease and moral lassitude. Ontarians wanted cleanliness *and* godliness.

Women, of course, did not always follow such prescriptions. Immigrant Jewish women fought for their rights by staging consumer boycotts: as historian Ruth Frager notes, their activism focused at '"the point of consumption" rather than "the point of production"'. Many Ontario women resisted the 'mothering' call: family size, which had already shrunk dramatically in Ontario before 1890, declined by a further 36 per cent by 1930, a rate that outpaced the natioanl average. Still, the prevalence of such beliefs doubtless served to keep many married women in the home and delayed by many decades their more widespread labour participation.[53]

And what of the ideals espoused so aggressively by the UFWO's leadership? In the 1920s, single women joined the workforce in significant numbers, but, in contrast to their male counterparts employed in factory work, they entered traditionally low-paying jobs in smaller workplaces, making collective action extremely difficult to organize. UFWO membership declined dramatically; many women moved to the more conservatively led Women's Institutes. Yet, in part because of this infusion of UFWO members, the WIs began to speak more forcefully on a range of issues. They demanded upgraded technology in the home and critiqued public health measures and educational systems—hardly what one might expect from contented, well-domesticated matrons. As before, however, their emphasis was on what some have termed 'social' as opposed to 'economic' feminism: they were willing to challenge patriarchal attitudes operative within the home and farm but stopped short of demanding equity in pay. It would be close to a half a century before Ontario's rural women would again organize in an explicitly political manner within equity feminist groups.[54]

Finally, the co-operative ideal, which for many had initially promised an alternative to a capitalist profit-oriented society, seemed by the mid-1920s to reflect little other than the means to put 'a few extra dollars in one's pocket'. Yet if the UFCC increasingly resembled a capitalistic enterprise, a proliferation of locally based co-operatives continued the more idealistic agenda of local control and decentralized co-operative management.[55]

Although the social reform and feminist movements had lost much of their earlier vigour, neither entirely disappeared. Drury's coalition government suffered a different fate. Continued internal squabbling jeopardized any chance Drury might have had for re-election. It surprised no one when the Conservative party under G. Howard Ferguson swept back into power in 1923 with more than half the popular vote.

Chapter 9

'The Inequality of Our System':
Boom, Bust, and War: 1923–40s

Similar to other parts of the Western world, Ontario's social, political, and economic structures were subjected to extreme stress in the second quarter of the twentieth century. During the relative boom years of the 1920s, the state stepped back from social and economic interventionism, resting content with the laissez-faire ideals of the nineteenth century. The Depression of the 1930s tragically exposed the limits of that orientation and revealed, as one worker reflected years later, 'the inequality of our system'. The Second World War provided, amid carnage and death, opportunities for white women and especially white male workers to pressure political and business leaders to adopt more interventionist agendas—agendas designed at least in part to answer some of the social and economic needs of Ontario's 'underdog[s]'.[1]

Pragmatic Politics

'I have', G. Howard Ferguson told federal Conservative leader Arthur Meighen in December 1922, '. . . directed all efforts toward keeping the Drury government on the defensive and creating a critical attitude in the minds of its own friends. I think we have fairly well succeeded.' So he had. Ferguson's biographer argues that Ontario's new premier and the party he led reflected the province's basic character. Ferguson, who was from the eastern Ontario rural village of Kemptville, firmly believed that British culture and ideals represented the essence of Ontario's soul. He was a small-town Protestant imperialist: Mitch Hepburn, a rising star in the Liberal party, criticized him for his affected 'imperialism' in naming 'Ontario roads the "King's Highway."' More significantly, Ferguson was an at times outspoken member of the Orange Order and was closely identified with the passage of Regulation 17. 'This bilingual question is the greatest of the issues before us', he asserted in 1916. 'The government I represent upholds British traditions, British institutions and one flag and one language for the Dominion. Unless something is done to meet this French speaking invasion, this national outrage, this Dominion will be striken to its foundations as this war has not striken it.'[2]

By the late 1920s, Ferguson had the political sense to moderate his views. In 1928, about one of every six elementary-level students was registered in the provincially funded Catholic school system. Regulation 17 was modified, and inspection at the individual school level by a French and an English inspector allowed for local adjustments rather than across-the-board inflammatory measures. The resolution embodied a high degree of pragmatism. Ferguson could continue to sell it in his private correspondence as simply a more effective means to anglicize the French while he reaped the political benefits from having defused a volatile political and cultural issue. He would not be the last Ontario premier to confront and attempt to contain the tensions that bilingual issues engendered in the minds of many voting Ontarians.[3]

Pragmatism also coloured Ferguson's notions of the proper sphere for government action. He firmly believed in an 'economical' government: a government that spent and legislated little. The notion of a positive state was foreign to him. Limited government intervention, a heavy reliance on essentially unfettered private enterprise (excepting Ontario Hydro, a 'special case'), and reluctant assistance to only the most needy added up to a nineteenth-century conception of the role of government in the economy and society. In 1927, for example, Ferguson opposed Mackenzie King's plan for old-age pensions, delaying provincial implementation for as long as he could. When police magistrates urged him to implement a plan to relieve them of the 'depressing duty of committing friendless, penniless, offenceless and homeless old men to Gaol', he replied that the men's families should look after them. Ferguson presided over change; he did little to facilitate, contain, or harness it for a general good.[4]

In certain sectors, his government nevertheless reflected dominant ideologies. Efficiency became a byword of his administration. Where Mowat had talked of efficiency in terms of husbandry, Ferguson adopted the rhetoric and behaviour of industrial capitalism. By the 1920s, Taylor's 'scientific management' ideas were well publicized in Ontario. These techniques hastened the transfer of control over production from workers to managers and underlay the growth of corporate personnel/human resource departments that helped mute strike activity in the 1920s. Notions of efficiency, as we have seen, also informed conceptions of motherhood in this era. Similarly, the gospel of efficiency influenced conservation and park development. Wilderness was assessed in terms of its productive capacity. Timber, fish, wildlife, and recreation were viewed in terms of revenue production. Algonquin Park had been managed according to those principles since its founding in 1893.[5]

Given this general climate of opinion, it is not surprising that administration by experts rather than legislation by elected politicians typified Ferguson's approach to government. In the 1926 election, a central campaign booklet bore the title 'Business Methods in Public Administration'. Ferguson responded to rising unemployment and increasing poverty in 1929 and 1930 by centralizing government welfare activities under the Department of Public Welfare. Efficiency became the answer to poverty and unemployment.

The premier presided over all. With the exception of Drury's administration, which highlighted the role of the Assembly and backbencher, one would be hard-pressed to find any of Ferguson's predecessors who thought differently. Many historians have seen this tendency to focus power in the premier's office to be a core component of Ontario's political culture, one that stemmed from the power of the crown and the lieutenant-governors of the pre-Confederation era and one that evolved from the privileging of the Executive Council in the era of responsible government. Ferguson advised his successor, George Henry, to provide 'distinctive courageous leadership, and dominate the Government and Party', for 'the average fellow likes to be dictated to and controlled.' A conservative, temperate democracy, contained by executive direction and increasingly by expert bureaucrats, marked the boundary of democratic influence in the province. Ferguson never pushed that boundary: Whitney's version of a 'progressive' conservatism found little echo under Ferguson's superintendence in the 1920s.[6]

Ferguson protected provincial rights and, along with Quebec premier Alexandre Taschereau, wrestled with the federal government over several developmental issues, all of which built on the Mowat era and led to further curtailment of federal powers. After unsuccessfully promoting the sale of a light beer known as 'Fergy's Foam', Ferguson ended the prohibition era by instituting government liquor stores, a move that did not please the die-hard dries but at least held out the promise of government control and supervision. He gave relatively free rein to mining and forestry development, especially in northern Ontario, and little aid or encouragement to conservation of natural resources. Indeed, one of the province's major forestry enterprises, Abitibi Power and Paper Company, implemented a more far-sighted northern forestry renewal program than any offered by the provincial government. Between 1919 and 1929, the government distributed 3,380,224 tree seedlings in southern Ontario but ignored the heavily logged back reaches of northern areas seen by few voters. As in the Mowat era, the north existed to serve the south.[7]

Regulating Society

Leisure, too, had to be regulated. Workers were working fewer hours; adolescents entered the formal workforce at a later age and stayed in school longer than had their parents; on average, more money was available for play. It seemed to many that homes were only 'parking place[s] between shows and dances'. In 1927, Dorothy Herriman, a single woman living in Toronto, referred in her diary to 'the modern craze for excitement and stimulation'. As one historian notes, 'the dance halls, cinemas, spectator sports, automobile trips and "speakeasies" were energizing an emergent youth culture that would come to signify mass culture itself.' Just as corporations attempted to organize and control worker activity outside of working hours, so too did parents and schools, both with the assistance of trained professionals, attempt to contain the lives of adolescents outside home and school. High school attendance ballooned: enrolment quadrupled between 1918 and 1938, and the average number of years spent in school increased from eight to ten and a half between 1911 and 1941. Nor was this growth simply an urban trend: in rural areas, secondary enrolment increased by over 150 per cent between 1901 and 1931, despite an overall declining rural school-age population. In high schools, extracurricular activities for boys and girls—sports, clubs, student councils, yearbooks, and dances, all supervised by trained staff—became increasingly common. Regular assembly meetings took place in school auditoriums designed, according

Box 9.1   The Ku Klux Klan in Ontario

The Ku Klux Klan experienced only a brief public existence in Ontario in the 1920s. Some view their mercurial presence as testimony to the conciliatory nature of Ontario's political culture, a culture more directed to accommodation than to exclusion. There is merit to that view, yet a closer look at the reasons for the quick demise of the Klan as a public political threat suggests that some qualification is necessary. The

Klansmen and burnt cross, Kingston, 13 July 1927. NA PA87848.

Klan's flouting of law and order was what most disturbed provincial leaders. Racist concerns were less an issue, especially within the Orange stronghold of the Conservative party. In fact, the Orange Order already occupied the ground that the American-based Klan wished to settle. It is well to remember here the discrimination that black women like Margaret Blackman and Marjorie Lewsey experienced in the labour market in this era. The Klan had difficulty in Ontario not so much because Ontarians were less racist than people in other provinces (such as Saskatchewan, where the Klan enjoyed much success) as because Ontarians already had in place a relatively home-grown and well-entrenched, albeit more moderate, outlet for such views.

Press and community reaction to the separation of 'a negro and his intended white bride' by hooded and cloaked Klan members in Oakville in the late 1920s support such a view. The local police chief knew and spoke highly of the perpetrators. Oakville's newspaper felt that 'it was really impressive how thoroughly and how systematically the Klan went about their task'. A Milton paper affirmed that 'if the Klu Klux Klan conducted all their assemblies in as orderly a manner as in Oakville . . . there would be no complaint'. The *Globe* and the *Toronto Star* both praised and supported the Klan's motives. The final resolution of the matter occurred before Ontario's Court of Appeal in April 1930. One of the perpetrators was sentenced to a three-month jail term—not for his philosophy or his rationale for his actions, but for his tactics and strategy, which verged on mobocracy and which therefore had to be contained. The judgement did not mention the issue of race.[1]

1. Allan Bartley, 'A Public Nuisance: The Ku Klux Klan in Ontario, 1923–27', *Journal of Canadian Studies/Revue d'études canadienne* 30 (1995), 156–73; Constance Backhouse, *Colour-Coded: A Legal History of Racism in Canada, 1900–1950* (Toronto: University of Toronto Press, 1999), 173–225.

to the minister of education's 1929 annual report, to instill 'a healthy school spirit, to train the pupils in public speaking, in self control, in orderly habits, in consideration for others, and in respect for authority'.[8]

The Economy

Although less dramatically than in the pre-1914 era, in the 1920s Ontario entered another period of sustained growth. Electrical appliances and automobiles—classic examples of the 'consumer durable' industries located near south-central Ontario's primary markets—headed the list. The automobile industry dominated because of its capacity to generate jobs, not only directly in the manufacture of vehicles but also indirectly in primary steel production, parts production, and vehicle servicing. Automobile production added higher-than-average value to products, which in turn sustained relatively high wages. Yet car manufacturers hired mainly unskilled labourers for the assembly-line work pioneered by Ford, which first set up in Ontario in 1904. In the 1920s and early '30s, before the introduction of unions, layoffs were common. As one GM worker recalled, in the 1920s they 'did anything for the foreman . . . go and shovel their sidewalk, put on their storm windows and all the rest of it . . . because there was always this lay-off and this is what we dreaded'. Indeed, by 1923 Ford 'employed' as many electrically powered machines as men. It was a volatile industry: no fewer than fifty Canadian-owned car manufactories and some twenty American-owned firms began operation in Ontario before 1931. By the end of the 1920s, automobile production had emerged as Ontario's single most important industry.[9]

Ontarians took to cars like ducks to water. In the London region in 1914, about 56 per cent of summer traffic was horse-drawn; by 1922, it had dropped to 3 per cent. In the 1920s, farmers continued to employ horse power instead of gasoline tractors on farms—only 3.5 per cent owned a tractor in 1921 and only 10 per cent did so in 1931—but they took a back seat to no one in the purchase of cars. Farmers were the largest occupational group who owned Fords in 1920. Twenty years later, 70 per cent of rural households owned cars compared to 43 per cent of urban households. Decreasing car prices in the 1920s (the Model T cost $650 in 1914 and $415 in 1926) broadened ownership possibilities among members of the labouring classes. By the end of the 1920s, Ontario boasted the second highest per capita car ownership in the world, next only to the United States.

Increased auto use necessitated increased planning and regulation. Ontario established a Department of Public Highways in 1915, and road improvement and construction proceeded apace, financed in part by increased gasoline taxes. As early as 1911, Hamilton employed plainclothes police to apprehend speeders. Licensing of drivers commenced in 1927. Rural space became more accessible to urban dwellers, even as cities were forced to redesign interior roads and provide parking facilities. In 1926, Toronto's chief constable complained that the streets were 'just an open air garage'. Pedestrians and horses had to yield control of the streets to cars. Noxious exhaust fumes replaced blowing manure as a primary source of air pollution. 'Reckless walking' became punishable by fines. City playgrounds kept

Sunnyside, Toronto, 1926. By the end of the 1920s, Ontario boasted the highest per capita car ownership in the world—next to the United States. NA RD151.

children off the streets where they used to play.[10]

Car imagery became part of common rhetoric. Anyone wishing to make a case for the modernity or far-sightedness of a particular policy or program did so by analogy to auto manufacture or operation. The car was the ultimate machine, against which all else was to be measured. The renowned physician Sir William Osler warned that the human body needed care; one should not 'neglect his machine, driving it too hard, stoking the engines too much'. The premier, however, stood apart from this enthusiasm. Ferguson never owned a car, and he sympathized with those rural dwellers who complained of the noise, dust, and intrusions of urban drivers in rural areas. At one rural church picnic, he asserted that the auto was a curse on human civilization. The next day, to his surprise, the Ford Motor Company threatened him with a lawsuit.[11]

The Depression: The Economy

A buoyant period of economic growth ended abruptly in 1929. Economic setbacks spanned the North Atlantic and led to a sharp decline in Canada's exports. As exports collapsed, employment contracted and consumer spending dropped. As consumer spending—already unable to absorb production—declined, manufacturers facing growing inventories of unsold products cut production and fired workers. Layoffs resulted in even less consumer spending, more production cutbacks, and bankruptcies.

Although depressions or recessions had occurred in 1873, 1893, 1913–14, and 1921, none affected Ontario's and Canada's well-being like the Great Depression of the 1930s. Between 1929 and 1932, employment fell by 32 per cent in Ontario. Not all regions or workers suffered equally. For those who were able to keep their jobs through the Depression, falling prices made a decent living possible (the cost of living declined by 20 per cent between 1930 and 1932). The risk of unemployment was lower in the service sector and greater in construction. It was also greater for younger workers, older ones, and recent immigrants. Because women worked for lower wages than men, their risk of unemployment was lower. Unemployment was, with the exception of gold mining, particularly high in northern resource industries: in the summer of 1931, two-thirds of Sudbury's men were jobless. At some northern mines, shift bosses sold jobs to hapless miners. As one unemployed miner wrote in 1933, 'I don't know what the government intends to do with all those men who have been taken out of the mine. There is nothing else to do in the North except mining. The government may as well take these men and shoot them as let them starve.' The Depression devastated single-industry towns and cities such as Oshawa and Windsor, dependent on an automobile industry that between 1929 and 1932 could use only 15 per cent of its capacity. Native men from the Six Nations reserve who had been working in Hamilton, Buffalo, and Detroit, often as high riggers, returned with their families to the reserve to live with relatives and grow their own food. Annual meetings of the Grand General Indian Council were discontinued in 1936 because of lack of travelling funds for delegates. In 1934, a government report documented that 2,000 of Toronto's working-class families lived in destitute housing conditions. Ontario's farms, spared the droughts that already plagued the prairies in the 1920s, had prospered, but declining prices in the 1930s rendered much farm work unprofitable: by the end of 1931, the government ceased foreclosing overdue farm mortgages because there was no one to buy the properties. Farm incomes declined by over 40 per cent in the four years following 1929.[12]

By mid-decade, rates of business failure and personal bankruptcy began to slow as investment and employment gradually revived. Commodity prices stabilized and then increased marginally, and corporate profits recovered. But wages did not. Despite measurable growth, the Depression had only eased, not ended. By 1939, the standard of living (measured in real wages) was only marginally better than it had been four decades earlier.

The Depression: State and Society

Efficiency advocates found themselves without effective answers to the catastrophe of the Depression. Ferguson retired in 1930, leaving his successor, George Henry ('George the maladroit', one conservative organizer lamented on the eve of the 1934 election) to face unprecedented social and economic problems with little upon which to build.[13]

On the pressing issue of relieving poverty, Henry remained bewildered. He rejected the idea of a provincial unemployment insurance program to assist urban

Box 9.2   Park Reform

Probably the most positive initiative to emerge during Henry's tenure as premier was one with which he had little to do. With the construction of Highway 60 into Algonquin Park, several ecologically minded groups had formed to pressure the government for more enlightened park management. J.R. Dymond, a zoologist at the University of Toronto and co-founder in 1931 of the Federation of Ontario Naturalists, argued that with proper supervision, environmental and utilitarian interests could both be served. The park's superintendent, Frank MacDougall, was open to a multi-use policy that would privilege conservation over timber and tourism. The scientist and the government forester made a creative and formidable team. In the midst of the Depression, the foundations of Ontario's post-Second World War parks policy were laid.[1]

1. Gerald Killan and George Warecki, 'J.R. Dymond and Frank A. MacDougall: Science and Government Policy in Algonquin Provincial Park, 1931–54', *Scienta canadensis* 22–3 (1998–9), 131–59.

workers on relief, instituting instead a program to encourage people to become farmers, generally in the north; it accomplished little. He attempted to bring 'efficiency' to the administration of ever-increasing relief expenditures, which in practice meant cutting payments. His answer to dissent and destitution was to invoke 'law and order'. Communists became the prime target. Through the Workers Unity League, communists were actively organizing workers in Toronto, Hamilton, Windsor, London, and other Ontario centres. In close collaboration with R.B. Bennett's federal Conservatives, Henry and his attorney general engineered raids against communist leaders in Toronto, deported alleged immigrant radicals, and ordered local militias to contain protests and put down strikers in several Ontario municipalities. In October 1933, police took brutal action to break up a demonstration in Port Arthur. Ivar Nordstram, one of the demonstrators, recalled the police 'hitting people over their heads with fists and batons. The demonstrators dispersed in all directions. The police [on horseback] chased after them mercilessly. . . . While I was running I could see many men lying bleeding and unconscious. The Mounties seemed to be enjoying themselves riding after people. It was very unreal, like watching a British foxhunt, only here they were hunting people. Finally some cop noticed me and knocked me unconscious with a baton.'[14]

Responses such as these constituted overkill. Certainly the unemployed did protest and the communists, through the Workers Unity League, did agitate, but most such activity remained local and fragmented. In fact, as early as the mid-1920s organized labour seemed to be in retreat: membership had declined, most industrial unions had collapsed, and craft unions, desperately trying to defend the

Ontario Police Patrol officer, Toronto, c. 1925. During the Great Depression, 'Red Squads' intimidated and harassed suspected communists, and provincial motorcycle police were used to repress dissent. A mass meeting in Toronto's High Park in August 1933 was contained by motorcycle police, who encircled the crowd with their exhaust pipes pointed inward. Ministry of Education photo. AO RG 2-71 COT-156.

interests of a shrinking membership, had adopted a conservative stance. To resist wage cuts too vigorously was to run the risk of losing your job and earning no wage at all. 'What, strike in the 30s?!' one Hamilton worker exclaimed, remembering that time, 'You've got to be kidding!' 'I think unions were just starting to come into being then', Kerry Bass, another Hamilton worker in the 1930s, recalled sixty years later. 'You know, 'cause I don't think people who had jobs then, would protest too much. If they protested they could fire them, couldn't they?' 'I was angry!' a third worker affirmed. 'But there was nothing I could do about it.' 'We had it in mind', Ed Donaldson observed, 'that there were hundreds more out there looking for work.' 'They were all a bunch of scaredy crows', one Hamilton woman mill worker flatly concluded.[15]

Hard times reinforced the conservatism of the existing craft unions. The average number of strikes per year between 1930 and 1933 was less than half that for the century's first two decades. Although some collective violence did occur in the Depression's early years, it was the exception. More typical was the report of a police officer in Cochrane in 1931 to the effect that the local communist organization held its meetings in orderly fashion: 'The unemployed themselves have been very good during the past winter. . . . [N]o disorder of any kind (as might be expected from men who are hungry). . . . The only useful thing we as Police Officers can do at the moment is to keep these unemployed moving.'[16]

In 1933, the Liberal opposition leader, Mitchell 'just call me Mitch' Hepburn, roundly criticized Henry's decision to send troops to strike-torn Stratford: 'The provincial government has seen fit to send artillery, machine guns and tanks to Stratford because the citizens are objecting to the treatment given them by wealthy manufacturers. . . . They take all they can from the people and give as little as they can to the workers. My sympathy lies with those people who are victims of circumstances beyond their control and not with the manufacturers who are increasing prices and cutting wages at the same time.' Portraying himself as a populist, the protector of the poor and dispossessed, Hepburn claimed to 'swing well to the left, where some Grits do not tread'. He led the Liberals to a sweeping victory in 1934 and, as premier, appointed a number of pro-union Liberals to his cabinet.[17]

By 1933, relief provision for the unemployed had drained federal, provincial, and municipal resources and pushed the boundaries of state participation in the economic lives of its citizens. The three levels of government blamed one another for inadequate relief funds, but they agreed on the necessity for rigorous evaluation of relief applicants. In 1932, a provincial inspector praised the attitude of East Windsor's relief administrators, who were Ford Motor Company managers: 'These officers work on the theory that . . . most men squeal before they are actually hurt.' Municipalities where 33 to 45 per cent of the population was on relief—Windsor, Niagara Falls, Pembroke, and many Toronto suburbs, among others—often elected sympathetic councillors who, in attempting to provide adequate relief, pushed their municipalities into bankruptcy. The provincial government had no sympathy for what David Croll, the minister in charge of relief, called 'pampered, inefficient and political cry-baby municipalities'. 'Relief for Workers, Nothing for Shirkers' became the motto of the welfare department.[18]

Like the Conservatives before them, Hepburn's Liberals began to use state force to repress dissent. When in April 1935 relief recipients refused to work on public projects in Crowland Township on the Niagara peninsula, the mercurial Hepburn swung hard to the right, declaring a 'battle to the bitter end'. Falsely accusing the strikers of 'terrorization' and 'breaking heads and damaging property', he sent the provincial police to end the strike. He blamed 'professional agitators' who pressed 'for the day when Canada will be a communist state. . . . That day will never come', he promised, 'in this or any other Anglo-Saxon country with the majority of people rural dwellers'. Yet it took until 1937 for the provincial government to break the back of the unemployed's relief movement.[19]

Craft unions may have adopted a conservative stance, but one would be wrong to conclude that workers accepted their fate with resignation and relative passivity. Workers protested in many other ways. Not all could be called 'scaredy crows'. The Crowland relief strike raises a number of significant issues surrounding the nature of worker response to the pressures of the Depression years. First, such strikes were common: over the course of the Depression, almost two hundred relief strikes involving 24,000 workers occurred in the province. Relief payments in kind or by vouchers were rarely sufficient: one had to work to get relief. Protest focused on the uncharitable and demeaning processing of applicants that occurred throughout Ontario. In Gravenhurst, relief recipients could not own a car licence or hold a liquor permit and had to plant a vegetable garden on their land. The telephones of relief recipients in Fort William were disconnected. In 1932, the Timmins town council voted to publish relief recipients' names on a monthly basis. In Hamilton, 'Relief Visitors' inspected the homes of those on relief every ten days to sanction how vouchers for food, heat, and clothing had been used. Means, hygiene, and morality tests provoked rage and at times collective outcry.[20]

Second, the strike underlines the continuity of political regimes. Liberals as well as Conservatives employed state-sanctioned force to repress dissent. Third, the Crowland affair points to the fact that, under some conditions, workers of different age, sex, marital status, and nationality (relief recipients from over a dozen ethnic groups participated in the strike) could stand united against repressive authority. A similar bonding of different national groups occurred at the Lakehead where, Ivar Nordstram noted, 'every strike got support from such organizations as the Women's Labour League, the Canadian Labour Defence League, the Council of the Unemployed, the Young Communist League, the Finnish Organization, the Ukrainian Farmers' and Labourers' Temple Association, the Croatian Worker's Club, the Slovac Home Association, the Scandinavian Workers' and Farmers' Club, the International Co-op Stores and the Thunder Bay Co-operative Dairy'. Indeed, the Finns, working through a variety of political, cultural, and educational associations, had long been organizing in northern Ontario's lumbering camps.[21]

More commonly, however, ethnic, age, sex, and marital status differences cut across class and helped weaken any concerted worker response to Depression-related problems. Immigrants in many municipalities, such as Sarnia and Oshawa, were routinely excluded from relief. Anglo-Celtic workers broke up a strike by immigrant workers at the Holmes Foundry in Sarnia in 1937 under the cry of 'We'll give their jobs to white men!' Jews represented some 45,000 of Toronto's half-million residents and often lived in mixed ethnic neighbourhoods. In August 1933, following a baseball game between Jewish and Protestant church teams in a west-end park called Christie Pits, local toughs known as the Pit Gang taunted the Jews with 'Heil Hitler' chants and unfurled a huge swastika banner. The riot that erupted was quelled with difficulty by city police. '[I]t is', Miss Annie Meighn wrote Premier Henry in August 1932, 'the foreigner and the Jew who are taking our trades and work from us.' Mrs C.R. Cline assured Henry that her family were 'true, loyal Canadians from the same descent as your wife Mrs Henry. Her ancestry Laura Secord was mine also as well as Sir Allen McNab and the other faithful early settlers'. Ethnicity was used as a justification for relief, and to be white, British, and Canadian became prime requisites for citizenship and entitlement.[22]

The Crowland situation also casts light on rural–urban tensions in twentieth-century Ontario. The traditional divide between rural and urban was fast receding. In an aptly titled novel, *Day before Yesterday*, published in 1925, Fred Jacob nostalgically noted the changes from his childhood in the 1880s, when 'the older towns of Ontario were self-contained social entities, loosely connected with the world outside their walls', to town life in the 1920s, which had been 'ironed out, and standardized, and knit more closely together town to town'. The relief strikers all lived in urban Crowland near a number of manufactures, but Crowland's farming population dominated the local council and restricted relief grants to a non-subsistence level—hence the necessity for the strike. It is in this context that one might best understand Hepburn's stance. A farmer himself, he could easily identify with the attitudes of Crowland's farmers and could even assume that a majority of Ontarians lived in rural areas. The reality, of course, was quite different: in 1931, 61 per cent of Ontario's population lived in urban centres. Yet from a slightly different angle, Hepburn was quite correct: despite being outnumbered

---

Box 9.3   From Rural to Urban: Approaching Toronto by Train from Orillia, February 1933

Dorothy Choate Herriman, Diary, 21 February 1933

C.N.R. leaving [Orillia] 3.25 pm. Not cold but a blizzard of soft snow.

[6 stations later]
Maple— . . . snow less and less
    At Concord—six o'clock passed northbound train.
    The trainsmoke rolling low over the brown fields is grimly reminiscent of wartime—of poison gases and muddy trenches. And now we pass the 'Home of Moth Aeroplanes'—a somewhat forlorn and unsubstantial structure in ridiculous proximity to Shacktown. Now comes an isolated tile-factory and soon the city closes on the right of way: —houses push and crowd & rush to the fences; factories too, elbow their way and stand akimbo, taking up space and craning their tall chimneys and spindling water-tanks. Their blank windows stare like bleared eyes looking from vacant minds.
    The sky glows but here must be no twilight—no time for folding hands and idly dreaming—the lamps are lit, they shine in every street and park and avenue.
    St Clair—the homeward traffic halts for us. The bells of streetcars jangle and the horns of motors bleat.
    The ground is like a bone,—dry, frozen. There is no sign of snow. Six passengers perhaps or nine get off. I put my coat and gloves on.

Parkdale next.

Source: Kathryn Carter, ed., *The Small Details of a Life: Twenty Diaries by Women in Canada, 1830–1996* (Toronto: University of Toronto Press, 2002), 362–3.

by urban voters, rural voters continued to have a proportionately greater say in Ontario elections. Whatever else Hepburn was, he was an astute politician.[23]

Finally, the Crowland strike points to the fact that unemployment was a family affair and that familial response challenged traditional gender roles. 'Men, women and children do not parade the streets every day because they like it', the Crowland Unemployed Association averred in April 1935. Women and children stood at the front of the public protests organized by Crowland's relief strikers. Women staffed picket lines and harangued the local police. In a letter to a union newspaper titled 'Union Builder and a Wife', a northern Ontario miner's wife noted that wives 'insist[ed]' that their husbands join the union 'for their sakes anyway'. With their parents' sanction, children routinely stole coal from railway yards for heating. Many children refused to attend school because of their shabby clothes or because they had to try to find work to help support their families. With less money available for extracurricular school activities, youth gangs seemed to one writer to be 'developing into a contaminating source of infection'.[24]

Militant mothers protested publicly in many locales throughout the 1930s. They were far from passive victims: for these women, protest was a form of political resistance. As one woman who had voted for Henry warned the premier, 'if I get no help I give none'. The ideal of a male breadwinner bringing home a family wage was always difficult for working-class families to achieve, but mothers now demanded it as their right. The head of the Oshawa Mothers' Association criticized the mayor for 'telling me what to feed my family and preparing my budget. . . . We can go and ask for what we want nicely first, but if we don't get what we want we can try something else.'[25]

As the employment of men dropped, women's work both inside and outside the home became ever more important for family maintenance. Boarding, sewing, gardening, budgeting, shopping, and cooking were central to families' 'making do'. In some cases, unemployed men simply left town, too depressed and demoralized to cope, their sense of masculinity and familial authority undermined by job loss and by the demeaning reality of charity or simply its prospect. 'If I had to [ask for relief]', Russell Morris of Toronto assured Premier Henry, 'it would break my heart, all I want is some work to make my own Living.' Desertion left women to fend for themselves and their families. The state advised that they prosecute their husbands for desertion, a difficult process at best. Government only reluctantly lowered the five-year desertion rule to three years for eligibility for mother's allowance payments. Often married women worked to support the family, activity that undermined the sanctity of the male breadwinner and seemed to endanger the running of a proper home. It occasioned much critical commentary from government and even from central associations representing professional women. The Canadian Federation of Business and Professional Women's Clubs and the National Council of Women in Canada both suffered from what one historian has termed 'gender jitters'. Neither offered a strong defence of the right of married women to work outside the home. The Trades and Labour Congress urged married women who could afford it to leave their jobs.[26]

May Hoyle left Eaton's in 1938 after working there as a stenographer for eight years: 'I loved it. I really hated to leave work but in those days you just didn't work once you were married.' Some unions, as at the textile mills in Cornwall in 1939, pressured management to fire married women, despite their seniority and desirable skill levels, before firing men and single women. When the Toronto Board of Education passed a 'marriage ban' for female teachers, most of the province's school boards followed suit. In the 1930s, only 5 per cent of teachers were married women, while the proportion of male teachers soared.[27]

Skill sets, the availability of work for men, and local cultures all affected employment patterns in this period. In 1936, married women represented 40 per cent of the female workforce at Penman's in Paris, Ontario; women possessed the skills the company needed, and the local community offered only marginal employment for men. More commonly, however, as one journalist observed, 'Nowadays, any stick seems good enough to beat the business girl with.' Magazines in the 1920s had advocated that single women should work prior to marriage, but that changed during the Depression. Criticism of women's working extended beyond that of married women. 'When I went to get a job at 16', Vida Richard recalled, 'I was told by some smart-aleck man, and not just one but many—why don't you get a man and get married?' Such attitudes rendered extremely vulnerable widows with children, who had to survive on a partial mother's allowance, yet they dared not publicly complain: local supervisors were quick to retaliate by decreasing or terminating their allowances.[28]

Only Prince Edward Island granted proportionately fewer old age pensions than did Ontario in the 1930s. Moreover, those Ontarians who received such assistance rarely got the full twenty dollars a month allowed by federal legislation. Local, especially rural, boards employed rigorous means tests. The expected income of children, an arbitrary figure, was deducted. Appeal processes were not widely known, and when they were pursued they often proved futile. In the interests of cost control, Ontario centralized pension payments in 1933 and instituted even more draconian means tests.[29]

An increasing number of middle-class Ontarians pushed for a more drastic familial response to the travails of the Depression era. Arguing that much of the province's social and economic ills were the result of excessive breeding by inferior social groups, eugenics and birth-control movements gained adherents throughout the 1930s. Alvin Kaufman, president of Kaufman Rubber Company in Kitchener, founded the Parents' Information Bureau to disseminate birth-control advice and devices. But the bureau did more: in 1939, Kaufman boasted that his organization had performed more than six hundred sterilizations during the Depression years, notwithstanding that the provincial government allowed such procedures only for extreme health reasons. Kaufman and others, such as Ontario's lieutenant-governor and Mary Hawkins, the founder, with other upper-middle-class Hamilton women, of the Birth Control Society of Hamilton—argued that sterilization was necessary for the health of the wider society. While Hawkins and (to a lesser extent) Kaufman supported the argument that women should have control over their bodies, it is clear from their public statements that they saw birth control and sterilization as required primarily to stop the poor from producing children who, they believed, would become financial drones on the middle classes. Moreover, as the province's lieutenant-governor averred, if the poor were to continue to reproduce at current rates, then in seventy-five years 'half the population would be in insane asylums, while the other half laboured to support it'.

Outside of the Roman Catholic Church, few argued differently. A celebrated court case in 1936–7 involving Dorothea Palmer, a Kaufman employee who was arrested for disseminating birth-control information (which was legal only if it served the 'public's good'), sanctioned the legality of birth-control societies. The magistrate noted how the 'poorer classes' had the largest families: 'They are a burden to the taxpayer. They crowd the juvenile court. They glut the competitive labour market.' Clearly, in the court's view, birth control—and, given the strong links between organizations promoting birth control and those promoting sterilization, the eugenics movement as a whole—served the good of the wider public. The eugenics movement reached its peak in the Depression years, but as public knowledge of the link between fascism and eugenics gained ground, Ontario's eugenicists faded from view.[30]

Coincidently but revealingly, in 1934, as birth-control advocates strove to convince lower-class women to curtail births, a working-class French Canadian Catholic woman in Corbeil, a small northern Ontario village near North Bay, gave birth to the world's first known surviving identical quintuplets. Elzire Dionne was already the mother of five. Ontario's—and, indeed, North America's—reaction to the Dionne quintuplets sheds much light on the social mores of the era. Acting on advice of his parish priest, Oliva Dionne, the girls' father, travelled to Chicago to enter into contracts for a touring exhibition of the quintuplets. Such exhibitions were not out of the ordinary at this time, but English Ontarians publicly objected to the idea of American money grubbers capitalizing on the 'wondrous' birth. Within a few weeks, the Hepburn government shunted the girls' mother and father aside and took over as the children's legal guardian. The state permitted 'parental experts' to raise the quintuplets according to scientific principles of child-raising. Reflecting the advice literature of the inter-war years, everything was to be done by the clock; if the baby—even under the age of one—failed to have a bowel movement at the appropriate time, then the mother could stimulate the movement in one of two ways: by grunting 'ugh, ugh' or, should that fail, by inserting 'a glycerine suppository or soap stick into the rectum for a few days'. The quintuplets became educative tools—examples for mothers to follow, especially working-class mothers. Although the means differed, the end in view was completely in line with the ultimate goals of birth-control advocates and eugenicists: to control and educate the lower classes so that they would become productive and inexpensive members of society.

But the state desired more. As the Toronto *Globe and Mail* put it, 'We value the quintuplets for several . . . reasons . . . sentimental . . . [in their uniqueness]. And there is the very practical consideration of the quintuplets as a tourist asset.' Ontarians and their government may not have wanted Americans to profit from the birth, but they saw nothing wrong from doing so themselves. The girls were state wards of a different sort. At a site called Quintland, the girls were put on view twice daily. By 1943, some three million people had driven to the small northern Ontario town to gaze on these natural wonders, thus launching northern Ontario's tourist industry. In some years these quint-tourists rivalled the numbers who went to see another natural wonder, Niagara Falls. The province made millions from the tourists; the quints profited from a state-administered trust fund set up for them, out of which the state quietly paid for most of the expenses of their upkeep. They appeared in films and in myriad advertisements, including for Lysol, corn syrup, General Motors, and diapers. The quintuplets had become servants of science and capitalist commodities. As one psychologist wrote approvingly, 'no petty consideration of individual rights have been permitted to interfere with the carrying out of this trust.'

He wrote too soon. The trust fractured on the collective issues of language and culture. Even as advertisers such as the American Grocers Association urged that the girls learn English to improve their 'advertising value', concerned francophone associations—most notably the Fédération des femmes canadiennes-françaises—pressured the Ontario government on the issues of teaching the girls in French and their right to attend a Catholic Church. At age eight, the girls had the last word: on a show broadcast by the English-language radio station CFRB in Toronto, the Dionne quintuplets spoke only in French. Anglo-Ontarians were outraged. The Dionne quintuplets, overshadowed by the war, gradually receded from public view and, in relative solitude, struggled to realize a more normal life.[31]

The Depression years saw the growth of a number of radical movements, ranging from the moderate-socialist Co-operative Commonwealth Federation (CCF) to the agrarian-based New Canada Movement (NCM, a precursor of the more broadly based Canadian Youth Council) to more radical communists. Emphasizing the connection between masculinity and breadwinning, Mrs Charles Lickman warned Premier Hepburn that 'millions of men are driven to being red. A man can stand a good deal but when his wife and children suffer if *he is a man* he becomes desperate.' Art Haas, recalling his membership in the New Canada Movement, a primarily rural organization influenced by the Social Gospel, said, 'I know that in 1932 I had a great sense of the inequality of our system and that sense is with me 56 years later. I am sure that it was the motivation that kept me interested in improving the conditions of the underdog.' Ivar Nordstram recalled that 'in the study groups in the Scandinavian Hall [at Port Arthur] I learned to make sense of the world through a class analysis of society. . . . No, the 30s were not tragic years for those of us who became part of the Movement. They were only tragic for those that didn't.' 'The way the union talked', Mary Fox, a Depression-era worker in Hamilton, remembered, 'I had such great belief in them. . . . I am sure unity brings strength. . . . We all thought that.' Both CCFers and communists looked to the trade unions as the primary organizations to defend industrial workers. Critical of the conservatism of existing craft unions, they joined forces with advocates of industrial unionism inside the labour movement to push for major changes in organized labour in North America.[32]

In the United States, President Roosevelt's New Deal, which required all employers to bargain collectively with unions, provided a catalyst for the rebirth of the labour movement. The craft-dominated American Federation of Labor expelled its militant industrial unions, which in 1935 organized themselves into the Congress of Industrial Organizations (CIO). The CIO organized the steel, automobile, rubber, and electric industries, and by 1937 had established itself as a major force in American labour-management relations. The majority of Ontario's unions were local branches of American-based AFL unions, but the CIO's sudden success inspired many Canadian workers to organize their own CIO unions.

In 1935, Hepburn's government passed the Industrial Standards Act, which encouraged the institution of minimum wages and standard working conditions within various industrial sectors. The act promised stability within industrial areas by preventing cutthroat price-cutting and wildcat labour unrest. By 1936, thirty-five separate industrial codes had been established, but the government refused to act as an enforcer, leaving it up to the unions to police their own activities and deal with unfair employers. Strike activity increased. Between 1934 and 1940, the province averaged eighty-eight strikes a year, almost exactly the number for the turbulent 1914–21 period. Strikes grew more violent. The struggle to establish industrial unionism and collective bargaining had been joined in Ontario, Canada's most industrialized province and the centre for most of the nation's mass-production industries.[33]

The most famous battle took place at the General Motors plant in Oshawa. In the 1920s, GM had bought out the McLaughlin Carriage Works and made its Oshawa facilities the largest GM assembly plant in Ontario. In early 1937, the company simultaneously announced record profits of $200 million, an assembly-line speed-up from twenty-seven to thirty-two vehicles per hour, the fifth wage cut in five years, and new medical examinations that threatened the jobs of older workers. Workers downed their tools and a spontaneous strike swept through the factory. When the Oshawa organizers asked the United Automobile Workers in Detroit for assistance, the UAW dispatched Hugh Thompson, who, opposed to disorganized, spontaneous strike action, advised them to return to work.

Ignoring Thompson, the strikers formed UAW Local 222, signed up workers, established a negotiating committee, and presented a set of concrete demands to GM's management. GM in the United States had just fought a long and bitter strike with the UAW at its plants in Flint, Michigan, which had ended in union recognition and collective bargaining. GM Canada seemed prepared to follow suit when suddenly Mitch Hepburn, who opposed the establishment of any CIO union in his province, stepped in. With the premier on the side of management, talks broke down in April 1937 and 4,000 GM workers in Oshawa struck. Why did Hepburn intervene? The explanation seems clear. Ontario's mining magnates—close friends and financial backers of Hepburn—feared CIO organizing drives in the north. Hepburn concluded that this threat might be avoided if the CIO could be prevented from establishing a foothold in the auto industry.

When he dispatched a special force dubbed 'Hepburn's Hussars' (or, among those of a different political perspective, 'Sons of Mitch') to Oshawa, two of his cabinet ministers resigned in disgust. Hepburn demanded that the federal government send in the RCMP; King refused. GM workers achieved union recognition and improvements in wages and working conditions, but other breakthroughs in collective bargaining proved more difficult to obtain. In 1937, economic stagnation again gripped the province and organizing drives in Ontario's other mass-production industries faltered.

Ontario and the Second World War

Even after ten years of economic depression, Ontario remained Canada's economic centre: it boasted over 40 per cent of the nation's gross national product, over 50 per cent of its total manufacturing production, and just under half of all mineral production. As in 1914, the transition to wartime production accompanied by an influx of investment capital reinvigorated the sluggish economy and generated new employment opportunities. By 1943, war production hit full stride and the province came closer to the ideal of full employment than at any previous time in its history. New technologies, particularly in the chemical and metal industries, ensured an explosion in productivity. Incomes increased as swiftly as productivity.

In 1939, Ontario's population stood at 3.8 million, of whom 72 per cent claimed British ancestry, 80 per cent had been born in Canada, and 70 per cent attended Protestant churches. As in 1914–18, Ontarians overwhelmingly supported the war effort. But there was a difference: in the First World War, Ontarians had expressed their support for Britain; in the Second, they opposed Germany 'out of their informed convictions that fundamental issues were at stake'. A measured commitment substituted for the naive enthusiasm that had greeted the First World War, but enlistment was high nonetheless: 120,000 in 1941, and by 1945 some 350,000 of the province's men and women had mobilized for military duty. Among the few dissenters were many of Ontario's Native peoples (about 3 per cent of the population). Arguing that they did not enjoy the rights of citizenship, the Six Nations band 'strongly protested the imposition of 30 days military training upon the single men of this reservation', and though many did enlist, their participation rate was far lower than it had been in the earlier war. People of German and Italian origin (6 and 2 per cent of the population respectively) were deemed suspect by many Ontarians: in June 1940, the RCMP arrested 700 Italians and incarcerated them at Camp Petawawa. Many of German origin also ended up in one of the approximately fifteen interment camps scattered across the province. But, in the face of an acute shortage of farm and lumber workers, the Ontario government welcomed the resettlement of 3,742 Japanese evacuees from British Columbia, despite much outrage from the municipalities in which they settled.[34]

As in 1914, the federal government led Canada's domestic war effort. Hepburn and King had been at odds throughout the 1930s on provincial–federal power sharing, the development of hydro on the St Lawrence, and Liberal party issues in Ontario. Hepburn believed that King was too weak to lead Canada in the war. Only reluctantly did he concede leadership to the prime minister, and on one occasion he actually passed in the provincial legislature what amounted to a resolution of non-confidence in the federal leader's war policies. But following May and June 1940, when Hitler swept through France, King upped the ante. Conscription for home defence was implemented, and Hepburn agreed to it. Yet the war was going badly—it seemed that more would be required. In April 1942, King asked the nation to release him from an earlier pledge that no conscription for overseas service would be mandated. Eighty-three per cent of Ontarians supported him, while just short of three-quarters of Quebecers voted no. King walked a narrow fence.

The prime minister assembled a team of hard-nosed managers headed by industry minister C.D. Howe, whose mandate was the procurement of war materiel. Though Hepburn complained that federal usurpation of taxes on corporations, incomes, and wills unfairly stripped needed revenue from Ontario, he ultimately backed down. When inflation threatened to get out of hand in 1940–1, the federal government imposed wage and price controls. Imports ensured that some inflation was inevitable, but government regulators proved flexible and allowed prices to rise in a controlled fashion. Similarly, they allowed wages to rise either to pre-Depression levels or to industry standards. Cost-of-living bonuses made it possible to cope with inflation. Indeed, wages in Ontario and elsewhere rose faster than prices during the war, a result of government policy and a marked increase in productivity.

Many of the jobs created by the war effort went to women. In the Great War, women workers had been overwhelmingly young and single, but now married women with children also took jobs for wages. Many expressed anxiety about these new work roles and worried, as did the *Toronto Star*, that with father at war and mother at work, the prospect of delinquency 'doubled'. And indeed, many teenagers, male and female, filled jobs on farms (near the end of the war some 35,000 students worked on Ontario farms) and in other sectors of the war economy, receiving income and more unsupervised free time than would otherwise have been possible. For some women, work was liberating: in 1943, *Chatelaine's* editor noted that four years earlier 'the term "womanpower" had yet to be coined'. 'I showed', recalled Leena Turner, a bullet maker in Ajax, Ontario, 'that we were capable of doing so much more'. After working three months as a streetcar conductor in Toronto, Clara Clifford thought she could 'cope with anything in life'. For others, especially working-class women with families to raise and husbands overseas, work was a necessity and far from glamorous: a poll of female workers in Toronto in March 1943 found that 60 per cent worked because of financial need; 32 per cent would cite only 'personal reasons'. In some employment sectors, women continued to face discrimination and low wages: unions in the textile mills at Cornwall prevented employers hiring women to do traditional 'men's' work, and male workers at the Ford plant in Windsor struck against the hiring of women workers. Even when white women did obtain auto-industry jobs (black women were denied employment), they worked in only a few areas: one firm restricted women to 13 of 158 job classifications. By contrast, in teaching, married women benefited, and they maintained that advantage in the years following the war. Despite much debate about the propriety of women—especially married women—working, women's wartime work activity 'helped', as one historian has

Women at work at Stelco, Hamilton, 1940. Hamilton Public Library, Industrial Coll.

concluded, 'to kick-start a campaign for equal pay legislation and other workplace improvements' in the postwar era.[35]

Labour unions organized mass-production workers in all sectors. Between 1940 and 1945, Ontario's workers averaged about 90 strikes per year, with the peak years being between 1941 and 1943, when the average hit 113. Four thousand Kirkland Lake gold miners struck in 1941; they were defeated in their attempt to gain union recognition, but their defeat stimulated protest across a number of industrial sectors and some of Kirkland Lake's labour leaders, no longer welcomed in the north, moved south to help organize a growing wave of protest. Labour began to actively support the Co-operative Commonwealth Federation, which was becoming a threat to the two traditional Ontario parties. Under this pressure in April 1943, the Liberals passed an act recognizing the principle of compulsory collective bargaining, thus ending the need for union-recognition strikes. In late 1943, the National War Labour Board recommended that the federal government introduce compulsory collective bargaining; King, fearful of CCF gains at the federal level, obliged in February 1944.[36]

Yet at the end of the Second World War, Ontario's working class remained fragmented by gender and ethnic cleavages. Throughout the war, immigrants had been the most radical workers. Moreover, with the passage of the collective bargaining acts in the auto industry, more power was devolved to union leaders, who were skilled workers of Anglo-Celtic and Protestant background, in contrast to the majority of unskilled workers, who were often of Finnish, Slavic, and Catholic backgrounds. Indeed, union leaders had social backgrounds more akin to those of management than to their unskilled brethren. At the level of leadership, the potential for cross-class alliances remained strong into the postwar era and some scholars argue that backroom dealings stymied the emergence of a grassroots labour movement. Notwithstanding these divisions, compulsory collective bargaining led to substantial gains for Ontario's industrial workers. With a population of only 12 million in 1946, Canada could rightly claim membership in the G7 group of the world's largest economies. Ontario, the nation's most heavily industrialized province, provided the economic engine for modern Canada. By 1946, many Ontarians had embarked on a new era of affluence.[37]

Chapter 10

Modern Ontario: 1940s–2003

War left little the same. It brought rising incomes and widespread personal tragedies. A decade and a half of economic depression and war also affected long-standing attitudes concerning the proper relationship between government and society: the Depression had undermined public confidence in unfettered markets, while five years of wartime economic management had spurred interest in the possibility of public economic planning. Some analysts have employed the term 'Fordism' to characterize social, economic, and political relations in the postwar era. They argue that Henry Ford's introduction of an increasingly automized and mechanized assembly-line shop floor, which resulted in greater output at lower labour cost, was married to a political/social agenda sponsoring increased consumption. According to this theory, to achieve this union, organized labour had to be enlisted as a 'junior' partner in the project. In the Cold War years, labour was cleansed of radical (communist) influences and bought into the notion of a liberal-capitalist world order as the best system for assuring rising affluence. While this argument has been most often applied to development in the United States, it is fair to say that a particular variant of the Fordist theme took root in Ontario. As will be argued, the Ontario case differed from that of the US in two respects: first, the state was more socially active and, second, labour, although tamed for a time, was more oppositional—and successfully so—than was the case in the United States.[1]

Conservative Agendas

Hepburn's Liberals represented the old school in which government managed a public budget and, to some degree, regulated business practices but otherwise left the market to its own devices. As the new notions of Keynesian economics spread among Ottawa's economic managers, the provincial Tories rethought their traditional assumptions concerning the appropriate sphere for state activities. Over the next three decades, the 'Big Blue Machine' pursued economic management, including planning, with an openness and on a scale that few could have imagined when the war began.

The Depression, together with Hepburn's anti-labour policies during the 1930s and the substantial growth in labour organizations and collective bargaining during the war years, encouraged the emergence of a socialist alternative in

Interior, Canada Cottons Ltd, Cornwall, 1948. During the war, it often fell to factory managers to inform women workers of their husbands' deaths. A textile worker in Cornwall recalled the constant fear that authorities would be 'coming with papers that their husbands got killed. Everyday there was a note to someone who went to see the boss and he was looking at you and you knew there was something wrong there' (in Ellen Scheinberg, 'The Tale of Tessie the Textile Worker: Female Textile Workers in Cornwall during World War II', *Labour/Le travail* 33 [1994], 164). NA PA179681.

Ontario. Although Hepburn won re-election in 1937 on the basis of his anti-labour policies, by 1941 the CIO unions had formed a national federation, the Canadian Congress of Labour, which endorsed the CCF as organized labour's political voice. In the 1943 provincial election, voters now had three viable choices.

George Drew, the new Progressive Conservative leader, welcomed the challenge. Dismissed as Ontario securities commissioner by Hepburn in 1934, Drew worked hard at rebuilding a fractious Conservative party in the intervening years. In 1937, he briefly resigned in protest over what he considered to be too soft a stance on the CIO. Aggressive and outspoken, Drew worried Conservative organizers. One thought that while he 'revealed a latent ability for leadership', he 'would have to be toned down somewhat as he has the traits of a martinet, and . . . the R.B. Bennett weakness of autocracy'. In reality, of course, such a tendency had a long tradition among Ontario's Conservative leaders. So too did Drew's attitude toward the French: 'It is not unfair to remind the French', he declared in November 1936, 'that they are a defeated race, and that their rights are only rights because of the tolerance of the English element, who, with all respect to the minority, must be regarded as the dominant race.' In 1938, Drew returned as leader and promptly centralized control of constituency nominations and funding in the leader's office. Fearful of 'socialism', Drew was nonetheless a pragmatist. Noting the great success enjoyed by the CCF, the Conservatives took freely from the left in preparing their own postwar agenda.[2]

The Tories' sweeping Twenty-Two Point Programme promised a federal–provincial social security system, new infrastructure projects, agricultural marketing boards, commissions for forest resources, expanded education and health services, and tax and administrative reforms. The Tories, however, received only four seats more than the CCF. Two years later in the spring of 1945, with the war in Europe clearly won, Drew called another election. Emphasizing the 'Progressive' element in his party's name, he equated the CCF with fascist Germany's National Socialism. 'The decision', he warned, 'rests between freedom and fascism.' The scare tactics worked: in 1945, the CCF won only eight seats. Drew had his majority.[3]

He first worked to reclaim Ontario powers appropriated by the federal state during the war. The Depression had exposed a basic weakness in the Canadian federal system: while the provinces had jurisdiction in labour and social policies, the federal government had far greater financial resources. This mismatch of money and jurisdiction hampered the provinces' capacity to respond to economic crises. Unemployment insurance, for example, could be brought in only with a constitutional amendment. After 1937, a federal Royal Commission on Dominion–Provincial Relations became a forum for centralists, who advocated expansion of the federal jurisdiction at the expense of the provinces. The war provided a golden opportunity for them to implement their ideas: King used the War Measures Act to expand federal control over taxation while pressuring the provinces to share other jurisdictions.

In 1945, King's government called a Conference on Reconstruction to deal with the demobilization of Canada's wartime economy. Federal civil servants proposed that various wartime financial arrangements be retained during the postwar period. But Drew blocked the wartime drift toward a more centralized Canada. 'If', federal spokespersons lamented, 'the selfish interests of the two principal Provinces [Ontario and Quebec] are going to hamstring the Federal Government in its efforts to provide machinery which will permit it to fulfil the functions of a central government in this modern age, then Confederation is a failure and Canada cannot be a nation.' That was not Drew's view. He fought for the older federalism of Oliver Mowat.[4]

Drew began to implement his Twenty-Two Point Programme through the Department of Planning and Development (DPD), designed to parallel a similar agency set up by the federal government to oversee the nation's postwar reconstruction. It divided its work into four parts: conservation, community planning, immigration, and trade and industry. Notably absent was any department for social issues. Drew saw no role for the state in such areas as hospital insurance and old age pensions, and his Conservative successors as premier shared these notions.

Drew's vision of Ontario's future was clear: it should be 'traditionally British both by ancestry and inclination'. Through the Department of Planning and Development, Drew used Ontario House in London, England, for the encour-

Box 10.1   Conservation and the Holland Marsh: Ontario's Future?

The conservation movement served many ends. The Immigration section of the DPD commissioned a report on settlement in the Holland Marsh region just north of Toronto. This poorly drained land, the report's authors noted, attracted 'foreign' farmers, people 'used to working on farms where soil is counted in inches not in acres'. Indeed a third of the five hundred farmers were Dutch and the rest were 'East Europeans, Italians, Germans as well as a few Japanese'. What was especially troublesome was that they were all very successful. Could this be the thin edge of the wedge? Did this portend a virtual ethnic transformation of the countryside? Certainly, the authors concluded, 'the lack of Anglo-Saxon names on the Marsh is most noticeable and significant'. In this context, proper conservation measures such as flood-control and soil-reclamation projects could create a countryside congenial to British immigrants. Conservation had cultural as well as material ends in view.[1]

1. Steve Jobbitt, 'Re-civilizing the Land: Conservation and Postwar Reconstruction in Ontario, 1939–1961', MA thesis (Lakehead University, 2001), chapter 3.

agement of British trade, investment, and immigration. He encouraged British war brides to come to the province. In 1947, he even authorized 'the transport by air of selected British immigrants to Ontario'. Conservation, too, was seen as a means to this end. In 1946, Drew passed the Conservation Authorities Act, and Ontario led all provinces in implementing a comprehensive conservation program in the postwar era. By 1961, thirty-four separate conservation authorities had been established in the province—all but seven in southwest and south-central Ontario—designed to rebuild and render useful Ontario's physical infrastructure.[5]

Conservation authorities were designed for several ends, including the protection of 'natural' land and water features and the provision of recreational outlets for an increasingly urban population. As such, the conservation and community planning divisions of Drew's DPD were nicely linked. The Ontario Community Programmes Branch attempted to facilitate the local development of active recreational opportunities. Indeed, Drew wanted the program to act as an example of 'how free people live together'. But some recreational activists took Drew's challenge in a direction he never intended: they hoped to use local organization of recreational activities as a means for enabling working-class people to set up their own programs. They interpreted the Ontario government's agenda seriously and believed that local citizens should be more than consumers of a plate of activities provided by others. Rather, citizens themselves should be the originators and administrators of recreational plans. This initiative had a short life—most notably in Brantford in the 1950s. By the end of that decade, as the recreation movement's historian has concluded, participants were no longer activists in the policy process: they were consumers of programs created and directed by professionals. While for many this was but a limited expression of citizenship, it seems clear that the process fit well with how Drew and his Conservative successors envisaged 'free people' interacting.[6]

Drew's 1943 election victory began a long Conservative reign. Unlike the bombastic and flamboyant Drew, his three conservative successors—Leslie Frost (Drew's finance minister, and premier from 1949 to 1961), John P. Robarts (Frost's education minister, and premier from 1961 to 1971), and William Davis (Robarts's education minister, and premier from 1971 to 1985)—projected bland images. In other ways, however, they followed in Drew's footsteps. Their governments were 'progressive' but cautiously pragmatic. 'Government is business', Frost liked to say—'the people's business.' Robarts proclaimed himself a 'management man', a chief executive officer whose shareholders were the voters. These premiers 'managed' economic and financial policies with a view to making Ontario attractive for private investment. Although dedicated to free market capitalism, they did not hesitate to intervene with major public initiatives whenever they saw an opportunity. As Frost admitted, 'I'd listen to [the radical opposition]. Often I'd just grab off one of their ideas.' The state's bureaucracy increased dramatically, and by the 1960s the government routinely hired university-trained experts. Social reform, however, took a back seat to economic development. Conservative leaders feared that if Ontario led in social reform, the province, under the federal equalization program, 'might become paymaster in one way or another in ensuring that the other provinces could follow suit'. Instead they maintained a centrist position, co-opting policies from the right and the left to attract new followers—and renewing the party in the process. In the tradition of Mowat, all three leaders rewarded deserving party workers.[7]

Economic Development

Following the 1945 Reconstruction Conference, Ontario aggressively expanded its industrial and resource sectors. Infrastructure became the top priority. Drew initiated the rationalization of Ontario's hydro system to better conform to the North American electricity systems of which it was a part. Frost pushed for the development of the St Lawrence River, both for hydro and as a direct shipping route from the province to the Atlantic. The St Lawrence Seaway Treaty was negotiated in 1954 and construction was completed five years later. A controversial pipeline made Alberta gas available to southern Ontario by the end of the 1950s. Uranium finds soon made the use of atomic power for hydro production irresistible; the first Ontario nuclear power plant opened in 1961.

To improve northern rail service, the government upgraded roadbeds and signalling systems, promoted use of the region's lignite coal for fuel, and supported the conversion to diesel. In the immediate postwar years, the north boomed: timber production tripled between 1947 and 1949, and mineral production doubled between 1945 and 1951. Uranium finds either rivalled or topped production values for mineral exploitation in the 1950s. Yet despite rising freight rates, the viability of the Ontario Northern Railway declined. Like railways elsewhere, the

ONR became increasingly dependent on bulk freight as trucks and buses siphoned off passengers and regional freight.[8]

Ontarians' love affair with the automobile continued: between 1945 and 1975, the number of registered vehicles increased sixfold, to 3.3 million private cars and more than 600,000 commercial vehicles, necessitating massive public construction projects. One of the grandest, begun under Hepburn and completed in 1947, converted the 'Middle Road', which ran parallel to highways 2 and 5, into one of North America's first limited-access parkways, linking Toronto to Hamilton and continuing to Niagara and Buffalo. The highway facilitated the making of what soon became known as the 'Golden Horseshoe', a band of industrial and urban development stretching from Oshawa to Niagara Falls. But the highway also wreaked havoc with one of Canada's richest fruit-growing regions, below the escarpment between Hamilton and Niagara Falls. Farmers and local merchants protested to no avail, and compensation for expropriated property seemed insufficient. 'The Queen Elizabeth Way', a local politician admonished the provincial legislature in 1951, '. . . passes through the most beautiful and prolific fruit-growing section of Ontario, and yet in this modern Garden of Eden, a serpent still wanders . . . called the Department of Highways.'[9]

Aided by the federal Trans-Canada Highway program, Ontario added 25,000 miles of highways and roads between 1950 and 1975 in a system focused on the Toronto region, fast emerging as one of the continent's most densely populated metropolitan areas. Tourism benefited from this ease of access: as early as 1950, some one million tourists arrived in Ontario annually. But the government underwrote more than roads. In 1967, taking advantage of existing underused railway lines, the province introduced the Government of Ontario ('GO') trains between Pickering to the east of Toronto and Oakville to the west. These subsidized trains (in 1987 the government provided 37 per cent of the operating costs) diverted commuter traffic—some 12 million riders in 1987. Nonetheless, growth in the numbers of automobiles meant that traffic arteries remained choked at rush hour.[10]

Continuing a tradition, the north received less attention than the south. Interminable discussions of cost-sharing with the federal government delayed significant highway construction until the mid-1950s. Even then, the state-assisted transportation network promoted the movement of natural resources to the south rather than facilitating travel within the northern region. In the forest industry, however, skidder and truck were replacing horse and river drive, so forest companies built several thousand miles of roads in the north and northwest that increasingly also served tourists, campers, naturalists, and sportspeople.[11]

Promoting industrial expansion and fostering investment, public infrastructure programs contributed significantly to the extraordinary economic growth following the war. Ontario was well placed to share in the Western economic boom that initiated, in John Kenneth Galbraith's words, the 'affluent society'. The value of pulp-and-paper production tripled between 1946 and 1958. Aided by the Auto Pact agreement signed by the United States and Canada in 1965, permitting close-to-free trade in autos and auto parts, automobiles remained the leading industry, boosting production of iron, steel, and auto parts and generating well-paying jobs.

The province supplied most of Canada's cars, half of its textiles and clothes, and over half of such assorted items as rubber, chemicals, and electronic products, primarily from the Golden Horseshoe region. In 1961, Ontario confidently advertised itself as 'the Heartland of Canada.'[12]

Yet the provincial economy as a whole became less dependent on primary and secondary production: it was the service sector that experienced the fastest growth in the postwar era. Consumer spending on services more than tripled in the twenty years following 1951; by 1971, that sector accounted for 57 per cent of output and 60 per cent of employment in the province. Much of this increase came in the public sector, with the expansion of health, education, and welfare. In a boom driven by consumer spending, both retail and wholesale activity also grew rapidly. Stores relocated from downtown cores to the new suburban shopping centres, with their vast expanses of free parking.[13]

The financial sector grew substantially. Banking and finance had always been highly concentrated in Toronto and Montreal. Of the two, Toronto had historically been a regional metropolis, second to Montreal on the national stage. The latter, however, declined, while Toronto, fed by booming regional and national economies, burgeoned. As early as 1934, the value of trading on Toronto's stock exchange exceeded that of Montreal's. Finance capital became more concentrated during the 1950s and 1960s. In 1955, the Bank of Toronto and the Dominion Bank merged to form the Toronto Dominion Bank. This led in 1956 to the merger of the Imperial Bank and Barclays, which in turn merged in 1961 with the Bank of Commerce to form the Canadian Imperial Bank of Commerce. Newer near-bank financial institutions, such as trust companies, came onstream during the 1960s, while insurance companies also expanded the range of their operations. Economic power became more and more concentrated in Toronto's boardrooms at the expense of Montreal and smaller cities, and by the year 2000, almost half of Canada's millionaires lived in Toronto.[14]

The postwar era was a time of dramatic change for rural Ontario. Farm production remained extremely important to the province's economy, and cash receipts in this sector led the provinces. Indeed, in 1991 agricultural production was the province's leading primary industry, ahead of mining and forestry. In the immediate postwar period, however, many feared for rural Ontario's future. Moreover, as one expert put it in 1944, 'the reconstruction and conservation of the countryside is by no means a matter of interest to the countryside alone.' An idealized picture of the sturdy (British) farmer and his happy, united family could serve as a counterweight to changing gender roles, labour unrest, and the hectic stress of urban life.[15]

In the shadow of that image, however, young people continued to 'drift . . . to the larger centres of industry and population'. Farm life was not easy for women: a 1960 survey indicated that in addition to cooking, cleaning, and other housework, 89 per cent of Ontario's farm women gardened, 61 per cent helped with milking and feeding cattle, 53 per cent tended to poultry and eggs, 26 per cent worked in the fields, and 13 per cent did sundry other farm work, such as driving tractors. Small wonder that young girls headed the rural exodus and, interestingly,

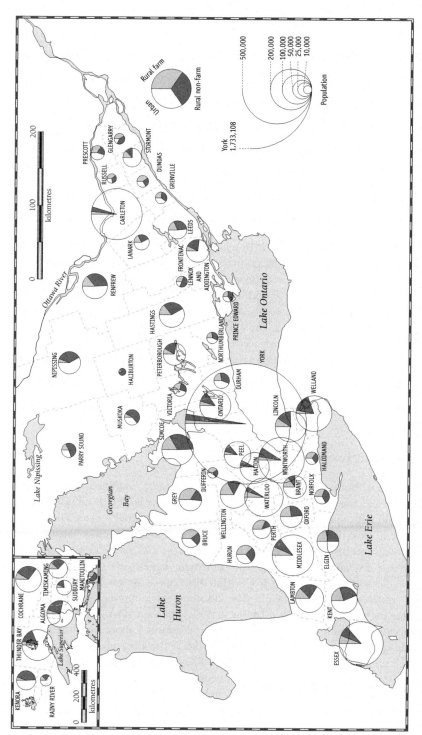

Urban, non-farm, and farm population by county, 1961. From W.G. Dean and Geoffrey J. Matthews, *Economic Atlas of Ontario* (Toronto: University of Toronto Press, 1969), plate 21.

attended school longer than boys. The non-farm rural population increased by nearly 300 per cent between 1931 and 1991; by 1991, farmers made up only 15 per cent of Ontario's rural population. '[W]here there used to be picturesque, unprofitable farms', the novelist-chronicler of southwestern rural Ontario, Alice Munro, wrote in her short story *Prue*, '[n]ow there are one-of-a-kind, architect designed, very expensive houses on half-acre lots.'[16]

In the 1950s, experts noted that there were too many small farms, which were unable to take advantage of modern advances. They need not have worried. As tractors became more reliable and less expensive in the 1950s, farmers for the first time switched in great numbers from horse to tractor power; by the end of the decade there were more tractors than horses on Ontario's farms. The mechanization of agriculture commenced in earnest, and one not-often-noted consequence was the increase of machinery-related injuries: one study of the post-1985 period concluded that Ontario lost some $17 million annually through such injuries. Farmers began to consolidate their holdings and to abandon a diverse system of mixed crop growing and livestock raising for single-enterprise operations focused on one crop or one animal breed. Between 1951 and 1996, dairy farms declined in number from 40,000 to 7,200 and hog farms from 93,000 to a mere 5,500. By 1971, farm acreage had fallen to about the level recorded in 1871. At the same time, average farm size increased. The era of factory farming—'industrial' farming, the government termed it—had arrived. The use of fertilizers and chemicals increased exponentially, leading to increased contamination of water. Woodlots and unimproved areas declined, with negative consequences for wildlife habitat. By the late 1990s, one-quarter of Ontario's farms accounted for three-quarters of total farm revenues, and a majority of farm families depended at least to some extent on off-farm income.[17]

Social Policies: 1945–70s

After the war, both Canada and Ontario opted for a modified welfare state. Depression and war had demonstrated that older private and state-subsidized programs could not cope with the problems of modern industrial society. The federal government took the lead with the development of unemployment insurance in 1940 (covering only 40 per cent of the workforce) and mother's allowances in 1945. Those federal initiatives had, one historian suggests, the 'effect of dulling whatever sense of urgency existed within Queen's Park on issues of welfare reform'. In the context of the Cold War and sustained economic growth, the CCF and (after the CCF's alliance with labour in 1961) the New Democratic Party had little success in pushing for state-sponsored social reform. Labour unions, too, were relatively quiet. Following a massive 1945 strike at the Ford plant in Windsor in 1945, the United Auto Workers accepted the Rand formula, which made management responsible for deducting union fees and made all those hired subsequent to union ratification dues-paying workers even if they were not union members. This gave a degree of legitimacy and stability to union organizations and was quickly fought for by other unions in Canada. But the Rand formula led to a further distancing between union members and union leaders. Weekly contact to collect dues was now no longer necessary; arbitration procedures were mandatory for most issues; strikes were illegal during the life of the agreement; union leaders were responsible for policing wildcat activity and purging communists. Unions became more bureaucratic and legalistic, and contracts became more detailed and difficult for the rank and file—especially recent immigrants—to understand. Consistent with the Fordist paradigm, an era of accommodative unionism commenced.[18]

Moreover, by the late 1940s, prosperity, not poverty and discontent, seemed the order of the day. Over the next three decades, Ontario's per capita personal income in constant dollars more than doubled. 'Everybody just wanted to relax', Ontario CCF leader Donald MacDonald explained. 'The normal apathy of the electorate vis a vis politics became even more pronounced with relatively good times.' In the affluence of the 1950s, a time of rising living costs and inflation, Ontario's poor were given little thought. As Louis Cécile, Ontario's minister of public welfare from 1956, admitted in 1965, 'to say that I have studied the topic [poverty] very deeply, I must confess . . . no'.[19]

Yet, for several reasons, Ontario could not entirely ignore the issue. In the first place, the province's regions did not enjoy equal per capita income. 'Eastern Ontario from North to South has a lower average income and a higher welfare rate than the remainder of the province', government officials acknowledged in 1965, 'because the area lies within the Laurentian Shield whose rocky terrain and colder climate makes it less attractive to manufacturing and less profitable to agriculture.' A Design for Development study, commissioned by the government in 1971, concluded that northern Ontario 'has a narrow and relatively slow growing economic base. . . . If . . . the dominant industry declines substantial hardships follow because few, if any, alternative forms of employment are available.'[20]

Many Ontario families lived in fairly new homes; some 43 per cent of homes in the province had been built in the twenty-five years following the war's end. Yet even at the centre of the postwar boom, finding adequate housing was extremely difficult for a sizeable minority of southern Ontario's urban working-class families. In 1959, a report issued by the Metropolitan Toronto Housing Authority documented a need for some 15,000 more state-assisted housing units in the city. 'I have not phoned too often', one increasingly anxious applicant wrote, 'cause I thought you were too busy with other people. I have had my application in [for three years] but I have not heard nothing from you people. What is the matter, I do not no . . . I just have to get out of here for my kid's sake.' 'I have been looking for a place', Marian Hartley, a single mother wrote, 'but . . . as soon as you tell anybody you have six children you might as well stay on the sidewalk than to go ask for a place.' In 1965—the same year that the minister of public welfare admitted his ignorance of the living conditions of the poor—a City of Toronto housing committee claimed that one in five of the city's families 'were unable with their own resources, to provide decent, safe and sanitary housing'.[21]

Certainly not all Ontarians were fat cats. Not all participated equally within the emerging consumer society. A federal senate report on poverty in Canada determined that in 1968, 13 per cent of Ontario's population—over one million people—lived below the poverty line; in 1991, the percentage remained the same. Those who sold consumer items, such as Eaton's store employees, were promised by union activists in the early 1950s 'access to the newest inventions' if they would join the union. Many recent immigrants could not afford to purchase the newest appliances or the food deemed appropriate for middle-class families. Moreover, many Ontarians were pragmatic about what they would give up for something new and untried and were quite willing to 'make do'. A modern electric stove would be nice, one rural householder admitted in the late 1940s, but a wood-burning stove gave better heat in winter. Although automatic washing machines held out the promise of efficient and easy wash days, many Ontario homemakers continued with their traditional wringer washers after their homes were hooked up to municipal water systems. The wringer washer gave the user greater control over the washing process and, as Mrs H.G.F. Barr of London explained in 1955, 'I have been appalled at the amount of water that seems necessary to do a normal family washing in the new spin dry type of machine. I believe one brand boasted that it rinsed clothes seven times, and all of them threw the water out after one use. There is hardly a city or town in Canada that does not have some water short-age in summer months. Large sums are being spent on reforestation, conservation and dams. It would appear that this trend toward excessive use of water should be checked now.'[22]

In the 1940s and 1950s, 80 per cent of people on general welfare assistance were women and children. Deserted and unmarried mothers headed the list. Social workers' heavy case loads virtually precluded individual counselling. Even when counselling occurred, the advice bore a depressing resemblance to the attitudes toward married women that had dominated nineteenth-century public discourse. The case of Mrs R., an abused woman with two young children, is typical. Her 1949 case report reads as follows:

> The family . . . felt there was no hope of reconciliation. Mr R. . . . possesses a violent temper, and last fall after beating his wife, he deserted her. . . . His wife was a somewhat immature girl who might have made a success of the marriage . . . but was unable to help her husband adjust to the situation. Much discussion [occurred] whether she could herself make some concessions and be the strong person in her marriage, attempting to bring her husband out of his emotional difficulties and making allowances for his immaturity. . . . Mrs R. fully cognizant of what her choice would entail, decided that she would make the effort at reconciliation.

In the caseworker's view, living with an abusive husband was better than living on public welfare. In the end, it was the wife who had to adjust. And what of those deserting husbands who could not be found? 'There must be some reason why men leave their families', a welfare administrator reasoned in 1963. 'I hate to admit it, but there may be some women who are hard to live with. We let these men drift, we don't make too great an effort to bring them back.'[23]

Since welfare lay within provincial jurisdiction, many expected the province

Box 10.2   The Costs of Consumerism: 'Yesterday and Today'

In this poem published in *Home and Country* magazine in 1956, Gertrude Lipsett expressed a common nostalgia for the pre-consumer era and a common lament that, despite modern inventions, free time in the present age was never enough.[1]

My Mother had a spinning-wheel,
And in the afternoon,
To spin a hank of stocking yarn,
Paced up and down the room.
My Mother had an old box churn,
Equipped with rod and dash,
And then for hours, she'd turn and turn,
Till butter milk would splash.
My Mother had a scrubbing brush,
To clean a rough board floor,
Down on her knees she had to rush,
From front, to the back door.
My Mother had an old wash tub,
And washing board to match,
And then the clothes she'd rub and rub,
And made the soap suds splash.
My Mother ran a leach of lye,
To make the season's soap,
She also had a pot of dye,
To give worn raiment hope.
But Mother had a lot of time,
To help a little child.
To help a neighbour who was ill,
With confidence and smile.
She taught a class in Sunday School,
She helped the Ladies Aid,
And for the children of the poor,
Some useful clothing made.
She sang the alto in the Church.
The golden rule she lived.
Her hopeful voice was ever near,

To comfort the bereaved.
Now, I have not a spinning wheel,
My yarn is factory made,
If I, by chance, choose then to knit,
The articles all fade.
I haven't got a churn at all.
The cream man at the door,
Hands out my butter,
Takes my cream,
To factory make some more.
I do not use a scrubbing brush,
Upon my hardwood floors.
My Electrolux will soon take up
The mud from out of doors.
A Leach of lye I never made-
So many new designs
Of soaps, and powders, do the work,
In all the cleaning lines.
But I have not a lot of time
To lessen others toil,
No time to help my neighbour out
With willing hands or smile.
My garments all must fit just so,
My nose must never shine,
My lips and nails must both be bright,
My whole appearance fine.
But I am missing lots of fun
My Mother must have had,
In giving all a helping hand
While looking after Dad.

---

1. In Monda Halpern, *And on That Farm He Had a Wife: Ontario Farm Women and Feminism, 1900–1970* (Montreal: McGill-Queen's University Press, 2001), 193n71.

to act. Yet there was the problem of transfer payments. As a 'have' province, Ontario resented shared-cost welfare programs that transferred money outside of the province. As John Roberts put it, Ontario was not 'a fat cat to be stripped'. At the same time, Roberts realized that transfer payments facilitated growth throughout Canada and that Ontario, as the largest producer of goods and services, would profit nicely from enhanced interprovincial trade. Thus, Roberts could assure the Ontario legislature that the problems were 'not so serious as to dictate the whole-sale abandonment of . . . the system. . . . We are Canadians first and foremost.'[24]

Private charity was gradually supplemented by a public welfare system admin-istered by municipalities and funded primarily by the province through transfer payments. In 1949, for every dollar of state assistance, private charities granted Toronto welfare families forty-one cents. But the nineteenth-century concept of poverty as a moral failure—caused by 'general subjective inadequacies', not by inadequate housing, education, or daycare—persisted. The Canadian Welfare Council argued for the need to educate 'clueless consumers'. Roberts wondered, 'How far, [should] society, through government . . . go to aid people who are not prepared to help themselves?' More ominously, he mused, 'How far does one go in making sure they do not reproduce themselves?' In the economic downturn of the late 1950s and early 1960s, many municipalities turned to the Depression-era policy of workfare: 'the threat of work stimulates people to find other support than welfare', according to the Ontario Welfare Officers' Association. But the federal government, which funded 50 per cent of unemployment benefits, refused to con-tribute if workfare policies were implemented. In 1966, Ottawa passed the Canada Assistance Plan, consolidating shared welfare costs with the provinces and formally prohibiting workfare practices.[25]

In 1961–2, Saskatchewan implemented Canada's first medicare program; in 1965, Lester B. Pearson's federal government committed itself to national medicare; and in 1966 and 1968, the federal Liberals passed legislation that pro-vided transfer funds to cover 50 per cent of the costs of provincial health insur-ance programs. Ontario responded slowly. An unenthusiastic Davis created the Ontario Health Insurance Plan in 1972: Ontarians would pay small premiums for medical insurance against virtually all hospital and doctor bills, up to a minimum standard of care.

Demographic Cha(lle)nges

The postwar years brought profound changes in the nature of Ontario's popula-tion. Between 1941 and 1971, population more than doubled, to 7,703,000 Significantly, over one-third of that expansion was accounted for by the five-to-nineteen age cohort. As a number of authors have demonstrated, the youthfulness of society affected Ontarians in a number of ways. The anti-establishment tone of youth culture was well symbolized by Elvis Presley's debute on the Ed Sullivan show in 1956; just under 80 per cent of Ontario households had at least one TV. A younger labour force emerged, one that was increasingly less willing to follow the instructions of older union leaders and very wary of international and

Rusins Kaufmanis, 'Say OO . . . Ohip', *Ottawa Citizen*, 1976. Not everyone was a fan of medicare; Ontario was one of the last provinces to implement a universal health program. Courtesy Rusins Kaufmanis. NA C147960.

American–run unions. Wildcat strikes increased: 16,000 left work at Inco in 1966; in the same year, workers stopped production at the Steel Company of Canada in Hamilton. Young 'hotheads' were pointed to as the instigators of work stoppages. The close union–management culture that had emerged during the war and in the early Cold War years was under attack. As public–sector employment increased, so too did public–sector unions, in both size and number. Justice Ivan C. Rand, an important crafter of the postwar union–management relationship, decried public-sector strikes as 'irresponsible behaviour'. Public-sector workers ignored him: in the 1970s, they threatened to (and did) strike hospitals, schools, and the post office. In Ontario, the Fordist rapprochement between unions, industry, and the state was under growing pressure.[26]

The 1943 Twenty-Two Point Programme had promised a comprehensive expansion of educational services. Between 1940 and 1975, the number of students enrolled at the primary and secondary levels jumped from 661,000 to 2 million, reflecting the postwar baby boom as well as rising school participation. The economic prosperity of the 1950s and 1960s allowed local school boards to build new schools, hire new teachers, and diversify programs. Established pedagogical practices were discarded for more 'progressive' ones. By the 1980s, the largest boards in metropolitan regions such as Toronto and Ottawa offered a wide variety of programs, including French immersion and alternative education programs for gifted children. The separate school boards also rapidly expanded their offerings, while French-language boards emerged within both the separate and the public systems. By 1990, Ottawa—one of the province's most linguistically and culturally diverse communities—had no fewer than six local school boards, each offering a variety of programs.[27]

In the 1960s, the first baby boomers neared high school graduation and brought with them a sense of entitlement surprising to those of their parent's generation. Twenty thousand students had attended Ontario universities in 1953; 50,800 enrolled in 1964–5, a figure that would increase to 216,000 by 1990. John Robarts and Bill Davis—each of whom came to the premiership after serving as minister of education—delivered on the postsecondary component of Drew's educational promises. The number of universities tripled in the 1960s. Older universities such as the University of Toronto expanded rapidly; private institutions such as the University of Ottawa became publicly funded; new institutions such as Laurentian and Lakehead universities expanded to serve northern Ontario. The government's major new initiative came in 1965 with the creation of the colleges of applied arts and technology, which provided vocational training to satisfy labour-market demands while at the same time offering a postsecondary option other than university. Within a decade, twenty CAATs operated in the province. Annual provincial expenditures on the CAATs, supplemented by federal transfer grants, increased from $2.5 million in 1966 to $63 million in 1971.[28]

Ontario and the Tories had to come to terms with increased cultural diversity. An assertive francophone community commanded attention (in 1941, francophones represented the largest ethnic group in rural northeastern Ontario, and in 1980 constituted some 6.5 per cent of all Ontarians). In Quebec, sweeping social and economic changes had found political expression in the Quiet Revolution ushered in by the Liberal Jean Lesage in 1960. Friendly with Lesage, Robarts understood Quebec's concerns about linguistic equality in the federal system. In August 1967, Robarts expanded publicly funded French-language teaching beyond the elementary level, with new funding for French-language secondary public schools for francophones where numbers warranted. Yet concerns emerged about the potential loss of separate-school supporters to the public system and about the prospect of two French-language systems, one public and one separate. Moreover, both Education Minister Bill Davis and Premier Robarts favoured promoting French immersion and French-as-a-second-language programs rather than directing funds to Franco-Ontarians for minority-language support. On becoming premier in 1971, Davis appointed a co-ordinator for bilingualism to facilitate the right of Ontarians to communicate with the government in French or English. Pushed by the Association canadienne-français de l'Ontario, the government gradually extended French-language services throughout the province, especially in health. By 1978, in the educational sector, however, almost all of the French programs were paid for with federal dollars, and because of real fears of an anglophone backlash, the Conservatives resisted acknowledging

French-language educational services as a right. This progress satisfied Conservatives, but for the francophone minority the policies were piecemeal, only grudgingly granted, and favoured programs that benefited anglophone rather than francophone children. Nevertheless, the Conservatives under Davis did make many parts of Ontario functionally, if not officially, bilingual.[29]

Ontario's First Nations fared less well. In the 1950s, Ontario had more Native people (41,803) and more acreage in reserve status than any other province. If numbers were not enough, other incentives were in place that encouraged provincial attentiveness to Native issues. In 1924, the federal and Ontario governments agreed that Ontario would transfer all its rights and interests in reserve lands and resources to the federal government, which would administer those rights on behalf of the Native bands, save that the province would receive 50 per cent of all mineral sales. Should bands become extinct or abandon the reserves, the province would gain all economic rights to the land and resources. In this context, the provincial government worked toward integrating Native peoples into white society. After all, with full integration, Native people would no longer officially exist as such and the government would control all of the province's reserve land. Ontario and the federal government agreed that the province would share costs for social services to Native peoples—such as old age assistance and allowances for blind people, to which were added a number of other services in an omnibus act in 1965—thus saving the federal government some money and allowing the provincial government to further the integration project.[30]

In 1954, a provincial Report on Civil Liberties and Rights of Indians referred to their 'now almost imaginary disadvantages' and recommended policies that would 'speed the integration of the Indian with the rest of the community.' One result was the granting to Native peoples of the right to vote in provincial elections, in 1954. Social welfare assistance also ameliorated the lives of many impoverished Native people. But as poverty-stricken Aboriginal people began to move off their reserves in search of employment, their deplorable living conditions became apparent to the wider population. Stigmatized as drunkards, vagabonds, prostitutes, and social threats, Native men and women were thrown en masse into local and provincial jails. In an attempt to instill respectable values and fit them for domestic or wage work, Native children, especially girls, were removed from their families and put into training schools. In 1958, 9 per cent of the admissions to the Ontario Training School for Girls were Native women; Native women were about 0.5 per cent of the province's population at that time. In major cities like Toronto, Native people had much lower home-ownership rates than comparable socioeconomic and demographic sectors of the city's white population.[31]

A federal white paper on Indian policy in 1969 brought policy matters to a head. It became clear to Native peoples across Canada that integration meant the denial of the Aboriginal peoples' past. The assumption of full rights as Canadian citizens could not be achieved without the renunciation of Aboriginal culture and identity—the policies underlying the Gradual Civilization Act of 1857 were alive and well over a century later. First Nations' resistance led to the shelving of the white paper. With integration no longer a strong possibility, the Ontario govern-

Mrs Echum of Moose Factory skinning snowshoe hare, 1959. A rare glimpse inside a northern kitchen. John MacFie photo. AO C330-13-0-0-141.

ment understood that its desire to acquire Native riches was less probable. Accordingly, the province began to ease out of its commitments to providing care for Native peoples, and in 1977 it ended the province's participation in delivering services on reserves.[32]

Energized by their resistance to the white paper, Native peoples in Ontario and across Canada became ever more assertive. Reserves acquired greater administrative and fiscal autonomy. In the 1970s, the province responded to Native land claims by establishing the Office of Indian Resource Policy. The Mattagami and other northeastern bands entered into accords with Ontario Hydro to protect against untrammelled hydro development in the future. The development of museums, language courses, and traditional festivals throughout the 1970s signalled Native peoples' renewed interest in their own cultures. By the decade's end, eighteen Friendship Societies existed in urban areas throughout Ontario, and political associations, bringing together bands from various Ontario regions, began to lobby for economic, social, and political reforms.[33]

Ontario has long been a destination for large numbers of immigrants. At the beginning of the twentieth century, arrivals from continental Europe and the United States increased sharply, although the United Kingdom continued to provide 40 per cent of all new immigrants. Non-British European immigrants tended to settle in northern Ontario. British immigrants gravitated to the industrial cities and towns of southern Ontario. About one-half of all arrivals between 1941 and 1971 settled in Ontario: 150,000 between 1941 and 1951, 562,000 between 1951 and 1961, and 473,000 between 1961 and 1971. They were a highly diverse group

Box 10.3   Changing Geographies: Fire, Blueberries, and Indigenous Land Management

The idea of a natural landscape is romantic. Cultural landscapes emerge via the inter-action among societies, environments, and resources. Different societies prize dif-ferent resource management systems, and so cultural landscapes continually evolve. Take, for example, the northwest corner of Ontario south of Kenora.

In the early nineteenth century, wild rice stands along the Rainy River were cre-ated in part by the Anishinaabe's routinely burning those lands. Burning also facil-itated the growth of rich blueberry fields. When white settlers entered the area, lum-bering and mining became the dominant culture's preferred economic resource and routine firing of the landscape was discouraged. Ontario passed its first fire-man-agement legislation in 1878, but control came slowly. Fires from railway trains, lightning, and sundry other causes facilitated the commercial harvesting of blue-berries by northwestern Ontario Anishinaabe until the 1940s. As Walter Redsky, a member of the Shoal Lake Anishinaabe, recalled, in that period, 'fire burnt a long way, almost to the Manitoba boundary. . . . After the fire . . . the berries came. There were berries all over. . . . They could pick all the berries here on Shoal Lake and sell them.' In the postwar era, a more extensive and well-trained fire-ranger system, using radar, radios, logging roads, and airplanes, made burning by the Anishinaabe people virtually impossible, and the blueberry landscape and the enterprise it sup-ported ended. The new ecological management system displaced the Anishinaabe from the evolving landscape they had tended for centuries. Ontario's Native peoples continue to pressure for opportunities to contribute to the creation of the province's future cultural landscapes.[1]

---

1. Iain J. Davidson-Hunt, 'Indigenous Lands Management, Cultural Landscapes and Anishinaabe People of Shoal Lake, Northwestern Ontario, Canada', *Environments* 31 (2003): 21–41.

mainly of non-British Europeans, and their arrival slowly altered Canada's and Ontario's demographic complexion. By 1971, one in four Canadians and close to one in three Ontarians were neither British nor French in origin. Unlike the early-twentieth-century wave of immigration, postwar arrivals settled mainly in southern Ontario's industrial cities, especially Toronto, which had long been dom-inated by English, Irish, and other British ethnic groups. This diverse cultural mix hugely enriched Ontario's social fabric. But social tensions also appeared.[34]

Undercurrents of racism within the province made life difficult for many. Most of Ontario's social and economic institutions, from boards of directors of major corporations to labour unions to local police forces, continued to be dom-inated by individuals of British ancestry, and discriminatory hiring and accommo-dation practices were common. Many Ontarians, often supported by courts and

Kindergarten Sunday school, Chinese Presbyterian Church, Toronto, c. 1950. From the early twentieth century on, Presbyterian, Methodist, and other churches commonly offered kindergarten classes for the children of new immigrants. The first such classes for Asian children were held in British Columbia in the late nineteenth century. Presbyterian Church of Canada Archives, G-1929-FC.

governments, argued that the right to discriminate was itself democratic. Pressured by Jewish and African Canadian organizations, George Drew's minority government passed the Racial Discrimination Act in March 1944, prohibiting public signs that promoted religious or racial discrimination. In the 1940s, Toronto passed a model bylaw that required places of amusement to allow all customers use of the premises regardless of 'race, colour or creed'. Legislation concerning fair employment and accommodation, however, found no state sponsor. In Hamilton, a typical land covenant read, 'None of the lands described herein shall be used or occupied, let or sold to Negroes, or Asiatics, Bulgarians, Austrians, Russians, Serbs, Romanians, Turks, whether British subjects or not, or foreign born Italians, Greeks or Jews.'

In the immediate postwar period, horror at the Holocaust, recognition of the United Nations' condemnation of discrimination, and pressure from African Canadians, Japanese Canadians, and most particularly Jews led to the passing of further human rights legislation. In 1950, Frost's government, somewhat reluctantly, passed precedent-setting (for Canada) legislation prohibiting discriminatory covenants in any future land transactions. Following the infamous Dresden Affair (in December 1949, the small southwestern Ontario town had voted to maintain discriminatory practices in accommodation, access to restaurants, and so on),

Frost—pressured by a coalition of human rights advocates led by Jews and including some seventy-one separate organizations from across the province, and aware of several Gallup polls that indicated strong provincial support for fair-employment legislation—introduced Canada's first Fair Employment Practices Act in 1951. It prohibited employment discrimination 'because of race, creed, colour, nationality, ancestry, or place of origin'.

In 1954, the Fair Accommodation Practices Act forbade the withholding of services on the grounds of birthplace, colour, creed, or ancestry. Frost assured his small-town Orange colleagues that doing away with restrictions would benefit business by facilitating urban growth and community development. He pointed to the fact that many US states had passed similar legislation. Finally, he noted the real possibility that Ontario's self-image of fairness would be besmirched internationally should the province not take action. Given the nature of his political support, Frost felt he had to take an incremental approach to human rights. Nor were these laws perfectly enforced. In fact, from the government's point of view, the legislation was really meant as a declaration or advertisement to the world of Ontario's innate goodness: from that perspective, not only was enforcement unnecessary, it would underline the falsity of the message itself. Small wonder that the state had to be pressured by civil rights groups to prosecute non-compliers in Dresden.

Often an intransigent bureaucracy impeded adequate implementation. Despite pressure from more liberal-minded reformers, it was not until 1962 that the province consolidated all its anti-discrimination statutes into one code and established a human rights commission to oversee its implementation, with powers to investigate and prosecute. Nevertheless, pressured by Jewish organizations in alliance with a wide group of racial and ethnic rights activists, the Conservatives under Frost did legislate on human rights, putting in place what one historian has nicely termed a 'protective shield' guarding citizens from discrimination by other citizens and in the process moving Ontario's political culture further away from its nineteenth-century laissez-faire roots. Yet in an important sense those roots remained strong: the state and the wider public had formally recognized the reality of prejudice, but for postwar Ontarians, the roots of the problem lay within individuals, not within the socio-economic system itself.[35]

In what has been called 'a species of flexible sovereignty', the federal government under Pierre Elliot Trudeau announced in 1971 that the state would recognize and promote multiculturalism, an intent passed into law in 1988. Expressions of ethnic diversity were welcomed, and indeed federal money facilitated many cultural events, in part in an attempt to exert some control over multifarious ethnic group activities. Predicated on the assumption that the various ethnic groups were equal participants in society, multiculturalism promoted lifestyle rather than life-chance opportunities. Provincial states such as Ontario bought into this 'pluralist national project' and rewarded those ethnic groups willing to nurture their culture within the Canadian/Ontarian context.[36]

Italians were quick to do so. They represented one of the largest non-British ethnic groups to arrive in Ontario in the postwar years. Before the Second World War, a small Italian community of 15,000 to 20,000 had lived in Toronto in several neighbourhoods known as 'Little Italies', and smaller groups lived in northern Ontario. With the 1947 liberalizing of restrictive 1930 federal immigration legislation, male Italians were sought to work on farms, mines, and railways. After a period of indentured labour—and often before the end of the period of indenture—many men gravitated to larger urban centres such as Toronto to work in construction, where they contributed to the building of the modern city. They encouraged families and friends to join them. Between 1947 and 1966, 160,000 mostly southern-Italian-born immigrants—about 90 per cent of whom were sponsored by Canadian family members—settled in Toronto. By 1971 they represented 6 per cent of the province's population, and by 1991, there were some 450,000 Torontonians of Italian origin (about 10 per cent of greater Toronto's population), and 700,000 in the province as a whole.[37]

Italians tended to own homes and to live in highly segregated residential areas, the latter a response to the British population's nativist reactions to the rapid influx of Italians in the 1950s and 1960s. Primarily in order to help purchase a home, some 40 per cent of Toronto's Italian women were in the workforce in the 1950s and '60s, higher than for Canadian-born women. Many became active in labour unions. 'Sure we should get more money', one Italian woman asserted. 'We work hard for it, we leave our kids, come home tired, do the dirty jobs.' Social service workers targeted southern European rural immigrants such as the Portuguese and Italians and attempted to inculcate middle-class Canadian values in terms of food and family life. Eaton's considered Italians hard to reach 'because of language difficulties and inherited indecisive shopping habits' and thus ignored them in its advertising. The implicit message was clear: become 'Canadian' or miss out.[38]

Encouraged by multicultural policies and subventions in the 1970s and beyond, Italians increasingly founded and joined community organizations that provided social, cultural, political, and welfare services, as did other ethnic groups. In various ways, these associations were a blend of Italian influences and accommodation to the newer and immediate Canadian environment. They reflected diversities within Italian Canadian communities as well as aspiring to protect and speak for Italians in Canada. Often these communities were bounded by local kin links or similar territorial origins and were based in local churches. Some of the larger associations received funding support not only from the Ontario government, but also from Italian central and regional governments. By the 1990s, there were some four hundred Italian community organizations in Toronto, three Italian newspapers, and two radio and TV stations. Expressions of Italian identity through communication systems and associational culture were paralleled by distinctive architectural styles emphasizing marble, tile, stucco, and arches, in contrast to the British Georgian red brick buildings characteristic of pre–World War II Toronto.[39]

On a wider front, Toronto's and Ontario's artists and cultural institutions—from Glenn Gould to Jack Bush and Michael Snow to the National Ballet—and its vibrant literary and publishing community were making a mark on the city, the nation, and the larger world. By the 1980s, Toronto was home to half of Canada's visual artists. Artists helped redevelop Toronto's inner city—Yorkville in the 1970s and Queen Street West in the 1980s and '90s. In 1987, Toronto artists founded the

Power Plant Gallery, which has since immodestly proclaimed itself to be Canada's leading contemporary art exhibitor. While strong regional centres for theatre emerged at Niagara-on-the-Lake and Stratford, Toronto led the way. Helped by disproportionate grants from the Canada Council, Toronto could boast that it was the third largest English-language theatre centre in the world, behind only London and New York. 'English-speaking theatre artists', one arts commentator noted, 'gravitate [to Toronto] like filings to a magnet.' Toronto was also the centre for national English-language radio and television. By the late 1980s, some 10 per cent of the city's labour force was involved directly or indirectly with the cultural industry.[40]

Women and Work

After 1945, 'experts' warned that families would suffer if wives and mothers did not stay in the home, a home often isolated in the burgeoning suburbs of the postwar era. A counsellor for Toronto's Family Court in 1953 asserted that 'where the husband and wife are both working outside the home, very often a dangerous spirit of independence exists'. Dr Benjamin Spock's widely read how-to-raise-children books and TV sitcoms such as *Father Knows Best* sent the same message. The government discouraged married women from working by dismantling many child care support programs established during the war and encouraging married women to abandon their jobs in favour of demobilized soldiers. In 1965, a government official admitted that to make do with the existing number of subsidized daycare spaces 'was like hoisting a small umbrella to shelter a stadium full of people in a downpour'. Fathers were increasingly advised to help with raising and nurturing children, but they could not be expected to do housework. Dr Alistair MacLeod, a prominent Montreal psychiatrist, warned, 'Father no longer has opportunities for pursuing aggressive competitive goals openly at work. Some of his basic masculine needs remain unmet. Mother no longer feels she has a real man for a husband and becomes openly aggressive and competitive herself.'[41]

Under this pressure, some women left their wartime paid jobs to become homemakers, but many did not. In 1941, fewer than one in five workers in the paid labour force was female. By 1961, the ratio was more than one in three, and married women had moved from 13 per cent of working women to 60 per cent. Rural women, too, increasingly worked outside the home: 'many of our rural women have returned to teaching school, working in the stores and offices in nearby towns', one commentator noted in 1958. In the short story *Queer Streak*, Alice Munro nicely catches this transition when Violet refuses to quit her wartime job with Bell Telephone despite community disapproval: 'There was some feeling that she should have stepped down when the war was over. . . . [It] would have been the gracious thing to do.'

Prior to 1940, women had been rigidly ghettoized in a small number of occupations, typically in areas that could be seen as extensions of domestic work—textiles and clothing in industry, teaching and nursing in the professions. Although women performed many traditionally 'male' tasks during the war, particularly in manufacturing, after 1945 rigid gender segregation reasserted itself in many industries. As late as 1970, a third of Ontario's working women toiled in clerical and unskilled positions. Moreover, their pay rates were dramatically lower than men's. Yet the range of occupations available to women did expand and the numbers of women in positions of some power and influence grew, albeit slowly.[42]

Women activists did push hard for equal pay for women workers and for greater representation for women within the governing structures of trade union locals and (as did CCF organizer Marjorie Wells Pinney) in riding associations within political parties. The family-centred notion of women's lives, however, changed only gradually. A large strike against Inco in 1958 witnessed workers' wives demanding an end to the strike: as one male worker reflected, the company 'got the wives to speak against the union'. Twenty years later, at a strike involving the same company, women played a different role: workers' wives founded a support group called Wives Supporting the Strike. 'I'll never be quite the same again', one woman participant recalled. 'I learned that ordinary women like me can fight a big multinational company like Inco and win.' Change occurred gradually in the rural sector, too. The rural-oriented Women's Institute slowly reassessed its traditional focus on 'good homemaking' and began to argue for equal pay for equal work. But many young farm women believed that the times had passed the WI by. In the 1970s and '80s, young farm women joined a series of non-state-funded women's groups and, like many of their urban sisters, pushed for economic equity in the workforce and within the family.[43]

Resistance was strong. Even leading human rights activists ignored women. Agnes Macphail, the lone woman in the provincial legislature, pointed out that the proposed Fair Employment Act of 1951 'gives everybody else equity, but does not give equity to women. What are women to think? . . . [A]nybody of any creed, anybody of any colour, anybody of any nationality, anybody of any ancestry or anybody of any religion, so long as they are male will get equal treatment, but, if it is a woman involved, even if her ancestry is strictly Canadian, she has been here all her life and her family for generations, she can be discriminated against.' Macphail also critiqued the government's Female Employee Fair Remuneration Act of 1951 because it referred only to 'same work' for an individual within the same occupation and workplace rather than equal pay for comparable work across genders. As such, the legislation reflected the individualistic strain of human rights discourse in postwar Ontario. 'Pious and pretty sentiment in print', Macphail concluded. 'It has no meaning in the world.'[44]

In 1963, the Roberts government established the Ontario Women's Bureau. Patterned after 1953 federal legislation, the agency was meant to perform an educative role. The bureau focused on discrimination against married women in the workforce: '[T]here are no laws which prevent you from being fired when you are married', the Ontario Human Rights Commissioner informed a North Bay woman in 1968. '[I]t is an amazing form of discrimination in this period, with so many married women in the workforce.' Following the bureau's recommendations, Ontario passed the Women's Equal Employment Opportunity Act in 1970, allowing unpaid maternity leave, prohibiting the firing of women upon marriage, and discouraging gender discrimination in job postings and seniority rights.

The first issue of *The Other Woman: A Revolutionary Feminist Newspaper*, May–June 1972. The feminist movement regained much of its lost vitality in the 1970s as activists forced new issues such as child care and abortion onto the political agenda. Feminists demanded greater recognition of women's rights and an end to discrimination in all its forms. Archives and Special Collections, University of Ottawa Library Network/CWMA Fonds.

THE OTHER WOMAN

MAY-JUNE '72   TORONTO   Vol.one No.one

25¢

A Revolutionary Feminist Newspaper

Though one General Motors woman worker thought 'we [had] died and gone to heaven', the act did not cover women in smaller workplaces. Often these women were recent immigrants or women of colour for whom employment possibilities were more restricted than for white middle-class women. These women were never part of any Fordist alliance. Similar to the rights legislation of the 1950s, the Equal Employment Opportunity Act reflected an emphasis on individuals and the optimistic view that relative equality of opportunity would soon result in equality of outcome. The state left issues surrounding systemic workplace discrimination— whether along lines of gender, colour, ethnicity, or class—untouched.[45]

Understandably impatient, black women fended for themselves. In 1951, they founded the Canadian Negro Women's Club/Association in Toronto, which sponsored public fundraising for scholarships for black students; in 1957, they inaugurated the first Negro History Week in Canada; and in 1973, they helped form the Congress of Black Women of Canada, which lobbied for fairer immigration policies and more relevant school curriculum. In 1970, Windsor women organized Black Heritage to promote knowledge about black history and to combat racial intolerance.[46]

Gay community activists, Toronto, 1978. The occasion for this protest was a speech by right-wing family-values advocate Anita Bryant. AO C193-3-0-3167, 78285-20, 5290.

Regime Change: 1970s–2003

For three decades, the Twenty-Two Point Programme introduced by George Drew in 1943 served as the blueprint for Ontario's Progressive Conservatives. During the 1970s, however, the province's economy began to sputter as it had not since the war's end. The Conservatives attempted to adjust, but in 1985 they fell from power, thus ending the longest uninterrupted reign for any provincial or federal party in twentieth-century Canada. For forty-two years the Conservatives had ruled, having won twelve straight elections with less than 50 per cent of the vote, aided as they were by having two other parties always splitting the opposition tally. Over the next eighteen years, three different parties ruled Ontario. The first, the Liberals (1985–90), would oppose free trade, a policy they had traditionally advocated. The second, the NDP (1990–5), would alienate an important section of its labour base. The third, the Conservatives (1995–2003), would forgo brokerage politics, leave the centre, and renounce the activist state, opting instead for small government.

In 1973, war in the Middle East resulted in an oil crisis. More fuel-efficient vehicles from Europe and Japan cut into North American manufacturers' market dominance. By the mid-1970s, unemployment reached 6 per cent, its highest point since the war. Inflation seemed out of control. Economic growth slowed and production dropped. The service sector became the primary creator of new jobs in the 1970s and 1980s. Yet expansion in health care, education, and welfare increased government expenditures without increasing revenues. '[F]or the first time in years', the government warned in 1975, 'the long prevailing prosperity and buoyant growth of the Province of Ontario has been challenged.' In 1977, Bill Davis repackaged Drew's Twenty-Two Point Programme as the Ontario Charter, but it was the last hurrah for an interventionist Progressive Conservative party. Davis cut welfare payments and funding for education. Following the federal government, in the early 1980s he implemented a 5 per cent limit on wage settlements and a one-year moratorium on any public-sector strike action.[48]

The Fordist alliance between labour, business, and the state weakened. While neo-conservatives railed at excessive bureaucratic/state regulation and undue interference in the marketplace, workers went their own way. Over the last third of the twentieth-century, plant closures threatened labour stability. Though closures were much more prevalent in the northern United States (the 'rust belt'), Ontario workers could not rest easy. Plants closed in the American north often reappeared in the American south; plants closed in Ontario's Golden Triangle often reappeared in more rural areas, where labour costs were lower. There were several reasons for the greater impact of closures on the American rust belt than on the Golden Triangle. Industrial plants were on average more modern in Ontario than in the northern states—more a product of postwar than of pre-war growth. A second factor relates to the difference in labour's response. Even when closures did occur in Ontario, workers received benefits superior to those granted their American counterparts. In part this success can be attributed to a combination of youthful activism and nationalist ideology. In the 1970s and '80s, workers, on their own and with the support of some unions (especially the United Electrical and the United Auto Workers), illegally occupied plants, inviting press and politicians to join them. Ontario's workers wrapped themselves in the Canadian flag and argued that multinational plants, mainly of American origin, were closing in order to protect the jobs of workers in another country. The government, one disgruntled worker declared in 1980, should 'throw all the Americans out of Canada. . . . [They] rape the country dry, make big profits here, then they pull out.'[49]

The extent to which this argument reflected reality has occasioned much debate. What is not debatable is the fact that Ontario's, and indeed Canada's, politicians listened and—to a degree, at least—acted. In this time of rising economic nationalism, premiers Robarts and Davis passed legislation requiring 'timely' notification and mandating severance pay for workers dismissed because of plant closures. While the legislation did not stop closures and had significant loopholes, it did result in higher benefits being paid to Ontarian than to American workers and may have made some employers think twice about summarily closing Ontario plants.

In 1985, on the eve of a controversial extension of separate-school funding, Davis announced his resignation. He then closed his party's member lists, effectively excluding new members and new blood. As its new leader, the party chose Frank Miller, a small-town populist from its right wing who was widely seen (particularly in Toronto) as the last vestige of 'little Ontario'. Unable to manage the minority government he inherited from Davis, Miller lasted less than half a year.[50]

The NDP under Bob Rae agreed to support a Liberal minority government led by David Peterson for two years in exchange for concessions on rent controls, environmental regulation, and public access to government. In 1987, Peterson won a large majority and, prodded by the NDP, embarked on a major social-spending agenda financed by hefty tax increases. In 1989, the Liberals substituted an employer tax for individual medical insurance premiums. They increased social assistance payments; welfare payments for a couple with two children rose by one-third between 1986 and 1993. For perhaps the first time in the twentieth century, Ontario became a leader in the implementation of social programs in Canada. And in terms of combating poverty, the Liberal–NDP policies worked: a measurement of poverty intensity put Ontario near the middle of provinces in 1984; by 1989, Ontario's level of poverty was significantly lower than that for all other provinces and was on par with such northern European countries as Sweden.[51]

Nor was the north ignored. The government listened to the findings of a Royal Commission on the Northern Environment in 1985 that, as in the Mowat era, the 'North serves and is dominated by Ontario's more populated industrial south. This reality underlines the environmental degradation and social malaise that has characterized the exploitation of Northern natural resources. . . . [T]he bulk of development benefits have flowed south. . . . The North has not shared equitably in the profits that have flowed from the exploitation of its natural resources.' The government instituted the Northern Ontario Heritage Fund to facilitate tourism and infrastructural improvements and moved the headquarters of the Ministry of Northern Development and Mines, along with the chief administrative offices of four other ministries, to various northern communities in an attempt to diversify employment opportunities and deal with a growing sense of alienation in the north.[52]

Yet the timing for these reforms was problematic. In 1984, the federal Conservatives under Brian Mulroney came to power, promising to control debts and deficits, to pursue closer economic ties with the US, and to resolve the constitutional dispute with Quebec. In 1988, the Free Trade Act was passed. Extensive social-spending cuts and privatization followed. Debts skyrocketed despite massive tax grabs such as the Goods and Service Tax. Moreover, the efforts of the Bank of Canada to achieve zero inflation kept interest rates artificially high relative to the United States. As a result, every cut in program spending was wiped out by mushrooming debt-service charges.

Though Peterson opposed Mulroney's social cuts, he fully agreed with the prime minister on constitutional issues. Mulroney aimed to bring Quebec— which had not agreed to the Constitutional Act of 1982—on board. His first attempt, the Meech Lake Accord, which Peterson firmly supported, was defeated in the Manitoba legislature by a single vote. Peterson's high-profile support for Mulroney's constitutional agenda linked him too closely to the federal Tories. High debts, high taxes, and a perception that the Peterson government was delivering services inefficiently gave credence to the NDP's electoral message that the

Liberals and Conservatives were status quo parties: real change could come only from the NDP. Surprising even the NDP, Ontario's voters agreed: in 1990, with 37 per cent of the popular vote and 74 of 130 seats, the NDP took power for the first time in Ontario. Significantly, only 17 of the new ruling party's MPPs had had previous parliamentary experience.[53]

In contrast to Peterson, who had enjoyed a buoyant economy within which to implement social reform, Rae entered power on the eve of the worst recession to strike Ontario since the 1930s, with taxes already near a record high. 'I wanted to be premier in the worst way', Rae later quipped. 'I had no idea my wish would be granted so literally.' Shortly after the signing of the North American Free Trade Agreement in 1990—opposed by Peterson and Rae for its threats to Canadian culture and out of fears that it would lead to de-industrialization—the Canadian economy went into a tailspin. Manufacturing jobs disappeared. The recession hit Ontario harder than any other region in Canada: by the spring of 1991 unemployment reached 9.6 per cent, double what it had been in 1988. Between 1989 and 1993, Ontario lost 200,000 manufacturing jobs.[54]

Even after the supposed shift from economic nationalism to economic continentalism, as signalled by the free trade acts, Ontario's workers looked to the flag. In 1989, the American-owned Inglis appliance factory in Toronto shut down. Threatened with a nationwide boycott of their parent company's products, the company granted a 'very good' closure package (the company was owned by Whirlpool). For its part, the NDP initially reacted in a Keynesian manner by increasing government expenditures. By the spring of 1994, welfare payments amounted to more than $6.2 billion annually and just under 1.4 million Ontarians were on social assistance. Provincial debt mushroomed from $42 billion to $97 billion between 1990 and 1995.[55]

The fiscal pressures of expanding social services had been building for years. The added burden of artificially high interest rates further increased budgetary deficits. OHIP, together with rapid advances in high-technology medicine, dramatically increased government health expenditures. In the midst of the recession, Mulroney froze transfer payments to Ontario. '[W]e're getting a kick in the teeth', Tony Silipo, Rae's social services minister, moaned. The NDP launched a retrenchment campaign. A 'fraud squad' was set up to catch welfare cheaters (only 0.4 per cent of over a quarter of a million cases examined were deemed illegal). The rise in health expenditures was slowed. Universities and schools had to cut spending drastically. Perhaps most dramatically, the New Democrats introduced a 'Social Contract' designed to reduce compensation paid to public-sector workers by $2 billion. A cycle of layoffs, fiscal crises, budget cuts, and more layoffs began.[56]

The Social Contract generated savings by requiring public-sector workers to take up to twelve unpaid 'holidays' annually. In an astounding assault on the basic principles of collective bargaining, employers could act unilaterally if workers did not 'voluntarily' agree to concessions by the government's deadline, even to the extent of changing contract terms in non-wage-related areas. Under pressure, the government allowed unions that agreed to unpaid holidays to protect existing non-wage clauses.

The NDP viewed the Social Contract as a defensive measure designed to avert even worse job restrictions and losses. Rae attempted to reward labour interests through Bill 40, which revised Ontario's Labour Relations Act, in part by restricting the use of scab labour and facilitating unions in the agricultural sector. The legislation led to a significant increase in union organizing and a decline in decertifications. But while Bill 40 unified business interests as a solid phalanx against the government, the Social Contract split Ontario's labour movement. Many private-sector industrial unions, such as the United Steel Workers, the Machinists, and the United Food and Commercial Workers, believed, as they put it, that 'the New Democratic Party must remain labour's central pivot point in the political arena.' But the Canadian Auto Workers—former NDP supporters—sided with the province's largest unions, those in the public sector, in condemning the government. Rae's problems were exacerbated when, in 1993, a new federal government under Jean Chrétien began to slash transfer payments for health, education, and welfare. In 1995, the Chrétien government ended the Canada Assistance Plan and with it went the prohibition on workfare, a policy change quickly seized on by a rejuvenated Ontario Conservative party.[57]

In this rapidly changing social and economic environment, women, immigrant communities, and Native groups continued to pressure politicians to combat discrimination. Women's fight for pay equity reached 'a milestone' with the passage of the Pay Equity Act in 1988. Supporters of the act referred to it 'as one of the world's most effective laws in redressing the wage gap'. Most gains occurred in the public sector. In female-dominated jobs in the private sector, the impact was 'minimal', in part because most such workplaces were small and the costs and complexities of implementation significant. As a result, poorly paid women—often immigrant women or women of colour—were bypassed by pay equity. Women continued to be underrepresented on both company and union boards, but eleven women were appointed to Rae's first cabinet and about 50 per cent of the government's deputy and assistant deputy ministers were women, visible minorities, or both.[58]

The state was slow to grant married women the right to share in property acquired during marriage. In the mid-1960s, the Ontario Law Reform Commission was formed to recommend changes to marital property law. 'More and more', the commission stated, 'marriage is being recognized as an economic partnership in which both husband and wife have equal stake.' Indeed, many married farm women became active reformers, pressing the government to recognize their contributions to the business of farming and not to allow husbands to walk away from marriage with all the assets in their pockets. The Family Law Reform Act of 1978 went some distance in that direction, but it was not until 1986 that Ontario legislated that a couple's net worth, including the worth of a home and property acquired during the marriage and money made on property brought to the marriage, was to be divided equally.[59]

Demographic and cultural change continued at a fast pace. Accelerating in the 1970s, large numbers of people arrived from developing nations in Asia—China, India, Sri Lanka, Pakistan, and Vietnam—and from the Caribbean and the

Middle East. Over the last third of the century, Toronto became truly cosmopolitan: in 1995, the United Nations proclaimed it to be the most 'culturally diverse in the world'. By 2001, visible minorities (non-white or non-Caucasian, other than Aboriginal peoples) accounted for just under 20 per cent of the province's 11.9 million people and for 43 per cent of Toronto's 2.4 million residents.[47]

'All political parties . . . now scramble to attract the support of various new ethnic groups in the province', one commentator noted. In the 1970s, British subjects living in Ontario were finally put on a par with other immigrant groups and were required to become Canadian citizens before voting in Ontario elections. New Canadians sat on school boards; in 1989, Peterson required school boards to provide heritage-language instruction if twenty-five or more students petitioned for it.[60]

Yet problems persisted. City and provincial leaders proclaimed that cultural diversity promoted greater tolerance than 'where it's just black against white'. But over the last thirty years of the century, fifteen separate reports highlighted 'differential treatment of racialized groups' in Ontario. In 1991, next to Native communities, blacks had the lowest rates of home ownership in Toronto after controlling for wealth, age, and some three dozen other variables. By the 1990s, polls found that most Ontarians favoured state-sponsored programs to counteract racism. Rae passed significant employment-equity measures favouring women, the disabled, Aboriginal people, and visible minorities. In 1992, after racial rioting erupted in Toronto, Rae appointed Stephen Lewis, a former ambassador to the United Nations and former leader of the Ontario NDP, special adviser on race relations. 'While it is obviously true that every visible minority community experiences the indignities and wounds of systemic discrimination throughout southern Ontario', Lewis concluded, 'it is the Black community that is the focus. . . . Just as the soothing balm of "multiculturalism" cannot mask racism, so racism cannot mask its primary target.' The state quickly endorsed Lewis's recommendations. But racial tensions remained, and further commissions were struck. While some social rights activists, who recognized the existence of racism and discrimination, nonetheless maintained that compared to the United States 'we always look better', a black civil rights lawyer noted in 1995 that 'in the United States you have dim-witted racism, here . . . we have a British form of racism that is much more subtle, more finessed': 'There is not less racism . . . , we just have systems to contain racism.' A report on racial profiling issued by the Ontario Human Rights Commission in 2002 agreed: '[R]acial stereotyping and discrimination . . . exists in institutions such as law enforcement agencies, the education system, the criminal justice system . . . which are microcosm(s) of broader society.'[61]

Native peoples used a variety of protest tactics to press for their rights. In the summer of 1990, Native people at Long Lake Reserve 58, northeast of Thunder Bay, blocked the CNR mainline carrying banners saying 'Let's Get Canada Back on the Right Track'. Most protests were peaceful. In 1995, however, a local band occupied Ipperwash Provincial Park in southwestern Ontario, objecting to incursions on a traditional burial ground. In a standoff between police and protestors, one Ontario Provincial Police officer came up with the following plan, recorded on tape: 'We thought if we could get five or six cases of Labatts 50, we could bait them. And we would have this big net and pit. . . . Works in the South with watermelons.' In the ensuing clash, police killed Dudley George, one of the protestors. Some have argued that the newly elected Harris government was behind the aggressive police response. Eight years later, a new Liberal government promised to set up a commission of inquiry.[62]

As they had in the past, the First Nations used the courts in their struggle for justice. The most celebrated case concerned the Teme-Augama Anishnaabe, who claimed ownership of some 6,500 square kilometres of land in the Lake Temagami region. They lost at the level of the Supreme Court in 1991. But in 1990, before the court's decision, they signed a memorandum of understanding with the province, which promised an ultimate 'treaty of coexistence'. In June 2000, Chief Doug McKenzie and Chief Raymond Katt of the Temagami First Nation and Teme-Augama Anishinaabe announced that after having 'spent the last century of the previous millennium in a struggle to obtain justice . . . there is a light of hope that we may achieve some justice through a negotiated settlement within the first few years of the new millennium'. In the same year, the provincial government reported that seventeen land claims were in active negotiation, ten others had been settled, and forty-two were in the 'pre-negotiation' stage.[63]

By 1995, the NDP had lost much labour support, yet business still preferred Conservative 'fiscal conservatives' to socialist ones. Mike Harris's Conservatives started publicly campaigning a year before an election was called by issuing their Common Sense Revolution platform, designed to attract disgruntled Liberals at odds with the spending and welfare policies of their party and the NDP. As had the NDP's campaign for change in 1990, so too the Conservative's campaign worked in 1995. With Harris's election, the drift from Drew's Progressive Conservatives, advocating state intervention, to Miller-style populists who believed Ontarians were all overgoverned and overtaxed was complete. Although it explicitly targeted the deficit, the Common Sense Revolution clearly aimed to rein in government as well. Privatization was the new mantra: even Ontario Hydro was on the auction block.[64]

Typical of populists, Harris played on popular distrust of politicians. The polls indicated that people were willing to support parties that fulfilled their promises. The Tories delivered, often in a highly interventionist and doctrinaire fashion. Harris 'sucked power into the Premier's office'. The Conservatives passed Bill 7, which repealed not only the unpopular provisions of the NDP's labour legislation but even the parts business had supported. Union organizing decreased and union decertifications increased. The Common Sense Revolution document also indicated that $400 million—3 per cent of the total budget—would be cut from primary and secondary education through administrative reform and added vaguely that the postsecondary sector would be expected to 'contribute' to deficit reduction. It did, to the tune of another $400 million, the equivalent of a 16 per cent cut.[65]

A clear signal of the government's direction came with the introduction of Bill 26, the so-called Omnibus Bill. Its central intent was to 'achieve Fiscal Savings' and 'promote Economic Prosperity through Public Sector Restructuring,

Streamlining and Efficiency'. In practice, this meant increasing cabinet power, offloading expensive responsibilities (such as regional roads) onto the municipalities, and giving the province more direct control over health, education, and welfare, whose funding was immediately cut. The same bill created a Health Services Restructuring Commission with open-ended powers that were used to close hospitals throughout the province. The province forced the amalgamation of many school boards and took direct control over funding, imposing a new formula based on operating capacity. This forced local boards to begin closing schools that used less than 100 per cent of their potential capacity. By the end of Harris's first term, school closings were the subject of bitter disputes between local school boards and parents, and public concern was rising over closed hospitals, overcrowded emergency rooms, and the amalgamation of municipal governments.[66]

Like Peterson before him, Harris reaped the benefits of a rising economy. Unlike Peterson and Rae, he slashed social assistance rates by 22 per cent in October 1995, reinstituted workfare, abolished equity legislation, and implemented welfare policies that especially disadvantaged single mothers and their families. Jobs in the north, the region that Harris represented, declined by 10,000 between 1995 and 1998. Not surprisingly, between 1994 and 1996 an index of poverty intensity charted a statistically significant increase in poverty in the province. While in a sense this put Ontario in the mainstream with many other

Rusins Kaufmanis, 'Acid Rain Damage Spreading', *Ottawa Citizen*, 1979. Not even Grant Wood's American classic was immune. NA C147961.

Box 10.4   Sulphur, Science, and the Politics of Pollution: A Case Study of Government Non-Regulation

Nickel smelters at Sudbury have polluted Ontario's environment since before the beginning of the twentieth century. In November 1902, a Toronto *Globe* reporter wrote that the area near Sudbury 'is one of the most unattractive places under the sun, for the sulphur fumes from the bed where its nickel ore is roasted have destroyed vegetation in the whole locality, leaving the rocky hills bare of trees and the streets and lawns innocent of a blade of grass'. Farmers regularly protested the damage done to their crops, with little result. In 1916, Ontario's Supreme Court granted farmers modest damages but did nothing to curtail polluting by the Canadian Copper Company (the precursor to the International Nickle Company).

Ontario's governments condoned and facilitated the production of pollution for the better part of the twentieth century. In 1918, the government passed the Industrial Mining and Compensation Act, which allowed nickel producers to purchase smoke easements, which many of the area's property holders had. These easements provided some recourse for affected property owners. In 1957, for $3,200, Erkki Hautamaki gave to Inco the right to 'at any and all times . . . emit . . . over the lands . . . all such noxious or other smoke, fumes, vapors, gases and all kinds of dust including tailings dust as . . . [Inco] deem necessary, proper or expedient in carrying on its operations . . . to have and to hold . . . absolutely forever'. In 1921, the Damage by Fumes Arbitration Act prohibited courts from hearing cases and instead set up an arbitrator to handle claims. In 1924, the act was amended, transferring the administration of pollution issues from the Department of Agriculture to the unsympathetic Department of Lands, Forests and Mines. The arbitrator, an employee of the latter, dramatically lowered claims payments to farmers.

In 1928 Inco did away with open pit roasting, and in the 1930s the company erected two 120-metre smokestacks that distributed the fumes over a wider area, resulting in fewer claims from local farmers. Concern shifted to a second environmental issue: the effect of sulphur dioxide on the surrounding forests. Regular forest monitoring began in 1945 and continued through much of the rest of the century. In an example of the state's general accomodative approach to environmental management, the government set up a Sulphur Dioxide Committee composed only of industry and government representatives. The committee met annually for some thirty years to consider scientific inputs. By the 1980s, the government had received at least nine detailed multi-year scientific studies of the impact on forest growth of sulphur fumes emitted by Sudbury's nickel producers. All the studies chronicled devastation or, in the words of one historian, 'forest ecoside'. But the government did nothing: nickel production, in the words of one bureaucrat, 'is far more important to Canada and to the world than are the agricultural crops and forests likely to be damaged'.

By the 1960s, there was a growing realization that sulphur fumes affected more than forests and farms. Published scientific studies documented the effect of acid rain on lakes and fish life. Pressured by environmentalists, cottage owners, sports fishers, and tourist operators, the Ontario government legislated controls on sulphur emissions at Sudbury in 1969 and 1970. Inco refused to comply, erecting instead a 380-metre-tall superstack in 1972. But tall pollution-emitters facilitated the transformation of sulphur oxide into acidic compounds capable of travelling over huge distances. Many polluting industries in the United States adopted similar practices. Acid rain became a recognized transboundary issue, and in that context, Canadian governments and industries had to be seen to be doing something to counteract the problem. In 1985, a federal–provincial agreement was arrived at whereby assistance was granted to the major smelters to modernize in a way that lessened sulphur outputs.

For the better part of a century, Ontario was the tail that nickel wagged.[1]

---

1. D.N. Dewees with Michael Halewood, 'The Efficiency of Common Law: Sulphur Dioxide Emissions in Sudbury', *University of Toronto Law Journal* 42 (1992): 10n43; Don Mutton, 'Fumes, Forests and Further Studies: Environmental Science and Policy Inaction in Ontario', *Journal of Canadian Studies* 37 (2002): 156. See also Don Mutton, 'Acid Rain and Transboundary Air Quality in Canadian–American Relations', *American Review of Canadian Studies* 27 (1997): 327–58, especially 355n12.

governments in the English-speaking world, it also harkened back to the punitive welfare policies in place in Ontario before 1960. Ontario's private-sector workers, benefiting from new job creation in the south (especially in the Golden Horseshoe area), and small-town fiscal conservatives, for whom small government was beautiful, re-elected Harris to a second term.[67]

During the first eighteen months of his first term and in the shadow of draconian cuts to welfare, education, and health, Harris had slashed funding for the Ministry of the Environment by 40 per cent and its staff by one-third and had devolved responsibility for many environmental issues to the municipal level without providing any new funding to facilitate the transition. At the beginning of the 1980s, Ontario had pushed for an agreement with the US on air quality and acid rain and had co-operated with Ottawa over Great Lakes water issues. Indeed, by the late 1980s, Ontario was the Canadian leader in environmental issues. Moreover, throughout the 1980s and 1990s, polls consistently indicated strong public support for these policies. In response, Rae's government had passed an Environmental Bill of Rights, consolidating and extending government initiatives in the environmental sector and broadening evaluative and consultative procedures to include non-industry and non-state sectors. But the Harris government seemed oblivious to such matters. Its curtailing of municipal recycling led to a proposal that Toronto should dump, over a period of years, 20 million tonnes of garbage down a mine shaft in northern Ontario. The accumulation of airborne pollutants—smog—in six Ontario's cities in 1981 cost, according to one economic study, 'tens of millions of dollars for each of the city centres' in work days lost by males between eighteen and sixty-five. Harris's reluctance to provide adequate funding for public transportation, charged Eva Ligeti (the province's quasi-independent environmental commissioner), 'will only add to Ontario's excessive reliance on the automobile . . . the number one source of smog-causing pollution in this province'. These measures plus the general budget cuts led some experts to claim that Harris had made it impossible for the province to honour its commitments to the Canadian and American federal governments concerning acid rain, clean air, and Great Lakes water management.[68]

Until May 2000, it seemed that Harris had dismantled environmental programs with quiet impunity. Then tragedy struck the town of Walkerton, Ontario. *E. coli* from livestock manure had infected the local water supply and caused seven deaths. Giving only eight weeks' notice, Harris had shut down government water-testing labs that had conducted some 400,000 tests a year. Ligeti herself had advised in 1997 that municipalities had neither the money nor the knowledge to test drinking water properly. Complaints about the environmentally unsound practices of industrial farming had been increasing (Ontario's 3.4 million hogs produce as much raw sewage as Ontario's 10 million people). Regulations concerning manure management were few and inadequate despite municipal requests for provincial assistance in these matters.[69]

Like the politicians he had critiqued in order to get elected, Harris stonewalled before finally admitting that he and his government bore major responsibility for the tragedy. He had ignored government reports detailing the radically insufficient monitoring of local water supplies, documents reminiscent of the reports written by medical reformers in the late nineteenth and early twentieth centuries. Harris's stringent fiscal conservatism and rigorous downsizing of government were now seen to be far from risk-free. As the Sierra Club of Canada put it, the air 'is as contaminated as Walkerton's water. Both suffer from an addiction to unregulated economic activity, cut backs and lack of commitment to protect health and the environment.'[70]

Harris resigned as premier on 16 October 2001. As he explained his reasons, the Ontario Coalition against Poverty led thousands of demonstrators in a protest to disrupt Toronto's financial district. It was one of an ongoing series of 'street theatre' tactics, influenced by the actions of the anti-globalization protestors at Seattle and Quebec City and reminiscent of nineteenth-century charivaris, where citizens attempted to impose their own ethical standards. Previously, the coalition had extended sit-ins from factories and universities to the offices of politicians and their riding associations. While the Toronto demonstration was not directly a cause of Harris's resignation, it was symbolic of the social and economic upheaval that his policies had sparked. Two years later—despite, or perhaps aided by, a leaked conservative memo calling Liberal leader Dalton McGuinty 'an evil, reptilian kitten-eater from another planet'—the Liberals swept to power with 72 of 103 seats and 46 per cent of the vote.[71]

During the latter part of the twentieth century, Ontario's trade flows were shifting significantly from an east–west to a north–south axis, prompting some analysts to argue that the province was moving away from Canada, transforming into a kind of regional state. Before Harris assumed power, Ontario's vision of itself as the lynchpin of a united Canada had already been in question. Ottawa was no longer quick to side with Ontario on fiscal and constitutional issues, and it had failed to support the welfare spending programs Ontario had adopted under its Liberal and NDP governments. With Alberta now the province with the healthiest income, it seemed that Ontario was no longer Canada's centre. Could there be an Ontario outside of Confederation?[72]

The argument for dissolution is primarily based on trade flows and other economic factors. But are attitudes formed simply by economic matters? Since 1943, voter turnout for Ontario's provincial elections has been one of the lowest for all provinces, at about 64 per cent, whereas the province's turnout for federal elections has been one of the highest, at close to 74 per cent, suggesting that Ontarians are more concerned about federal than provincial politics. Most polls designed to test the relative strength of allegiances to province and nation support that contention. In the early 1970s, half of Ontario respondents identified more closely with the federal than the provincial government; only a third identified more with the provincial government. It is true that ten years later the figures were virtually reversed, yet between 1995 and 1998 those professing a strong attachment to the province declined from 81 to 64 per cent. In the same period, a sense of strong attachment to Canada remained stable, around the 90th percentile. Moreover, recent polls have indicated that for Ontarians, allegiance to province or nation is not a zero-sum game (in Quebec such is not the case: the relationship is much closer to either/or). That many Ontarians can simultaneously exhibit strong allegiances to both levels of government probably reflects the continuation of a heartland mentality, a sense that to be Ontarian is to be Canadian, even in the face of provincial–federal disputes. Given the growing multicultural/multi-ethnic makeup of Ontario's population, it is also interesting to note that the sense of belonging to an 'ethnic group or national ancestry' did not significantly affect respondents' attachment to Canada. In fact, it might be argued that recent immigrants conceived of themselves as coming to Canada, not to a particular province, and thus new loyalties were directed to the nation not to the province.[73]

A common sense of what was Ontario was sold more easily (but never perfectly) by the province's governments in the century before the Second World War. In 1901, more than 80 per cent of Ontarians were provincial-born and around 75 per cent claimed to be of British origin. Before 1912, the province was much smaller than its current 1 million-plus square kilometres. As we have seen, social, economic, and geographic diversity intensified in the post-war years. There is more than one Ontario political and economic culture. Those in the north look for assistance beyond the Ontario state since, in the minds of many in that region, the provincial state has rarely been their ally. There, a politics of disaffection, not affection, exists.[74]

Moreover, just as the water crisis had a history, so too did the idea of a secessionist Ontario. The annexation crisis of the late 1840s—a crisis occasioned by Britain's abrogation of protective trade and fiscal policies (an early form of government downsizing)—is a case in point. One of the ways bourgeois politicians at that time deflected the crisis was by moving toward freer trade with the United States. Goldwin Smith, a nineteenth-century neo-conservative, was only one of many voluble advocates of a pan–North American union. It was only after George Drew that Ontario began walking—cautiously—with the federal government.[75] For most of its history until then, the province had stood at odds with federal policies. The notion of a regional state has a history. Ontario and the nation of which it is still a part continue to be under construction.

Population

Table A.1   Upper Canada/Canada West Population

Year	Population
1791	14,000
1812	70,000
1824	150,000
1831	237,000
1841	455,000
1851	952,004
1861	1,396,091

Table A.2   Ontario Population

Year	Population
1871	1,620,851
1881	1,926,922
1891	2,114,321
1901	2,182,947
1911	2,527,292
1921	2,933,662
1931	3,431,683
1941	3,787,655
1951	4,597,542
1961	6,236,092
1971	7,703,106
1981	8,625,107
1991	10,084,885
2001	11,410,046

Government

Table B.1 Upper Canadian Parliaments

	Term
1st Parliament	1792–1796
2nd Parliament	1796–1800
3rd Parliament	1800–1804
4th Parliament	1804–1808
5th Parliament	1808–1812
6th Parliament	1812–1816
7th Parliament	1816–1820
8th Parliament	1820–1824
9th Parliament	1824–1828
10th Parliament	1828–1830
11th Parliament	1830–1834
12th Parliament	1834–1836
13th Parliament	1836–1840

Table B.2   Province of Canada Elections and Broad Party/Groups

		Party/Groups		
	Region	**Reform**	**Conservative/Tory**	**Other**
1841	Canada West	29	10	1
	Canada East	21	17	4
1844	Canada West	28	12	1
	Canada East	28	13	1
1848	Canada West	23	18	1
	Canada East	32	6	3
1852	Canada West	20	18	1
	Canada East	36	3	3
1854	Canada West	39	25	1
	Canada East	54	9	0
1858	Canada West	39	24	1
	Canada East	15	48	0
1862	Canada West	35	29	0
	Canada East	29	35	0
1864	Canada West	43	24	0
	Canada East	25	36	1

Source: Data from Paul G. Cornell, *The Alignment of Political Groups in Canada, 1841–1867* (Toronto: University of Toronto Press, 1962), 93–111.

Table B.3   Dual Premiers: Province of Canada

Canada West	Canada East	Tenure
Samuel Harrison (Ref.)		Feb. 1841–Jan. 1842
William Draper (Cons.)		
William Draper	Charles Richard Ogden	Jan. 1842–Sept. 1842
Robert Baldwin	Louis-Hippolyte LaFontaine	Sept. 1842–Nov. 1843
	Dominick Daly (acting;	
	others resigned on	
	patronage issue)	Nov. 1843–Dec. 1843
William Draper	Denis-Benjamin Viger	Dec. 1843–June 1846
William Draper	Denis Benjamin Papineau	June 1846–May 1847
Henry Sherwood	Denis Benjamin Papineau	May 1847–Mar. 1848
Robert Baldwin	Louis-Hippolyte LaFontaine	Mar. 1848–Oct. 1851
Francis Hincks	Augustin-Norbert Morin	Oct.1851–Sept. 1854
Allan Napier MacNab	Antoine-Aimé Dorion	May 1856–Nov. 1857
John A. Macdonald	George-Étienne Cartier	Nov. 1857–Aug. 1858
George Brown	Antoine-Aimé Dorion	Aug. 1858–Aug. 1858
John A. Macdonald	George-Étienne Cartier	Aug. 1858–May 1862
John Sandfield Macdonald	Louis Sicotte	May 1862–May 1863
John Sandfield Macdonald	Antoine-Aimé Dorion	May 1863–May 1864
John A. Macdonald	Antoine-Aimé Dorion	May 1864–July 1865
John A. Macdonald	Narcisse-Fortunat Belleau	July 1865–June 1867

Table B.4   Ontario Premiers and Parties

	Term	Party
John Sandfield Macdonald	1867–1871	Coalition: Liberal-Conservative
Edward Blake	1871–1872	Liberal
Oliver Mowat	1872–1896	Liberal
Arthur S. Hardy	1896–1899	Liberal
George William Ross	1899–1905	Liberal
James Pliny Whitney	1905–1914	Conservative
William Howard Hearst	1914–1919	Conservative
Ernest Charles Drury	1919–1923	United Farmers of Ontario
George Howard Ferguson	1923–1930	Conservative
George Stewart Henry	1930–1934	Conservative
Mitchell Hepburn	1934–1942	Liberal
Gordon Daniel Conant	1942–1943	Liberal
Harry Corwin Nixon	1943	Liberal
George Alexander Drew	1943–1948	Conservative
Thomas Laird Kennedy	1948–1949	Conservative
Leslie Frost	1949–1961	Conservative
John Robarts	1961–1971	Conservative
William Grenville Davis	1971–1985	Conservative
Frank Miller	1985	Conservative
David Peterson	1985–1990	Coalition: Liberal–New Democratic Party
Bob Rae	1990–1995	New Democratic Party
Mike Harris	1995–2002	Conservative
Ernie Eves	2002–2003	Conservative
Dalton McGuinty	2003–	Liberal

Table B.5   Ontario Elections: 1867–2003

	Conservative	Liberal	CCF/NDP	Other
1867	41	41		0
1871	38	43		0
1875	3652	0		
1879	31	57		
1883	37	50		1
1886	32	57		1
1890	36	55		0
1894	23	45		17 Patrons of Industry; 9 others
1898	43	51		0
1902	48	50		0
1905	69	29		0
1908	86	19		1
1911	82	22		2
1914	84	24		3
1919	25	28		55 UFO & ILP; 4 others
1923	75	14		22
1926	72	14		26
1929	90	13		9
1934	17	65		8
1937	23	63		4
1943	38	15	34 CCF	3
1945	66	11	8 CCF	5
1948	53	13	21 CCF	3
1951	79	7	2 CCF	2
1955	83	10	3 CCF	2
1959	71	21	5 CCF	1
1963	77	23	7 NDP	1
1967	69	27	20 NDP	1
1971	78	20	19 NDP	0

Table B.5   *continued*

	Conservative	Liberal	CCF/NDP	Other
1975	51	35	38 NDP	1
1977	58	34	33 NDP	0
1981	70	34	21 NDP	0
1987	16	95	19 NDP	0
1990	20	36	74 NDP	0
1995	82	30	17 NDP	1
1999	59	35	9 NDP	0
2003	24	72	7 NDP	0

Labour and Industry

Table C.1   Upper Canadian Farm Production, 1848–1870 (bushels per capita)

	1848	1851	1860	1870
Wheat	10.4	13.3	17.6	8.7
Oats, barley, rye	11.0	13.2	17.9	19.8
Peas, corn	4.0	5.0	8.5	6.6
Potatoes	6.5	5.2	11.0	10.6
Butter	4.7	16.9	18.5	23.2

Source: Adopted from Douglas McCalla, *Planting the Province: The Economic History of Upper Canada, 1784–1870* (Toronto: Univesrity of Toronto Press, 1993), 267.

Table C.2   Occupational Distribution: Ontario (percentage of total employment)

	Primary	Secondary[a]	Tertiary
1871	51.4	34.4	14.2
1881	48.4	35.7	15.9
1891	47.6	32.5	19.9
1901	42.3	30.6	27.1
1911	31.1	40.8	28.1
1921	27.9	40.2	31.9
1931	24.9	41.0	35.1
1941	21.6	40.0	38.4
1955	13.7	38.3	48.0
1961	9.6	33.3	57.1
1971	6.1	33.5	60.4
1975	4.7	30.8	64.5
1993	3.2	27.4	69.4
2002	1.8	29.8	68.4

[a] includes transportation

Source: Data from Ian M. Drummond, *Progress without Planning: The Economic History of Ontario* (Toronto: University of Toronto Press, 1987), 364; K.J. Rea, *The Prosperous Years: The Economic History of Ontario, 1939–1975* (Toronto: University of Toronto Press, 1985), 83; Ontario, Ministry of Finance, *Economic Outlook and Fiscal Review, 2003*, table 29.

Table C.3   Ontario's Ten Leading Industrial Sectors: 1870–2002

1870[a]	1910[a]	1941[b]	1971[c]	2002[d]
1. Flour and gristmill	Log and lumber	Automobiles	Motor vehicles	Auto industry
2. Log and lumber	Flour and gristmill	Electrical apparatus and supplies	Iron and steel mills	Primary and fabricated metal
3. Foundry, machine shop	Clothing	Machinery	Motor vehicle parts	Chemical products
4. Woollen, yarn and goods	Foundry, machine shop	Pulp and paper	Misc machinery	Food
5. Clothing	Slaughtering, meat packing	Non-ferrous metal smelting	Pulp and Paper	Machinery
6. Liquors, distilled	Iron and steel	Primary iron and steel	Misc. food industries	Computer and electronic products
7. Slaughtering, meat packing	Agricultural implements	Automobile supplies	Industrial chemicals	Plastic products
8. Carriages and wagons	Butter and cheese	Rubber goods, incl. footwear	Rubber products	Paper
9. Bread, biscuits, confectionery	Printing, publishing, bookbinding	Aircraft	Metal stamping, processing	Beverage and tobacco
10. Oils	Leather, tanning	Hardware and tools	Commercial printing	Printing

[a] Ranked by gross value of output

[b] Ranked by net value of production

[c] Ranked by value added by manufacture

[d] Ranked by real gross domestic product

Source: Data from Ian M. Drummond, *Progress without Planning: The Economic History of Ontario* (Toronto: University of Toronto Press, 1987), 401; K.J. Rea, *The Prosperous Years: The Economic History of Ontario, 1939–1975* (Toronto: University of Toronto Press, 1985), 201; Ontario, Ministry of Finance, *Economic Outlook and Fiscal Review, 2003*, table 7.

Notes

Introduction: Whose Ontario?

1. An excellent introduction to the extensive literature on regions is Gerald Friesen, 'The Evolving Meanings of Regionalism in Canada', *Canadian Historical Review* 82 (2001): 529–45. For Richard White, see 'Is There a North American History,' unpublished paper, 1995, cited Friesen, 545n23.

Chapter 1: Weblike Relations: Early Ontario, 9000 BC–AD 1500

1. P.F. Karrow and B.G. Warner, 'The Geological and Biological Environment for Human Occupation in Southern Ontario', in *Archaeology of Southern Ontario to AD 1650*, edited by Chris J. Ellis and Neal Ferris (London, ON: London Chapter of the Ontario Archaeological Society, 1990), 21–3; Andrew Stewart, 'Relating Environmental Change to Cultural Behaviour in the Late Pleistocene Great Lakes Region', in *Great Lakes Archaeology and Paleoecology: Exploring Interdisciplinary Initiatives for the Nineties*, edited by Robert I. MacDonald (Waterloo, ON: Quarternary Sciences Institute, University of Waterloo, 1994), 141–54.

2. Peter Storck, 'Case Closed: The Fisher File', *Rotunda* 27, no. 4 (1994): 38–40.

3. Todd A. Surovell, 'Early Paleoindian Women, Children, Mobility and Fertility', *American Antiquity* 65 (2000): 493–508.

4. Chris J. Ellis and D. Brian Deller, 'Paleo-Indians', in *Archaeology of Southern Ontario*, 37–64; R. Cole Harris, ed., *Historical Atlas of Canada*, vol. 1 (Toronto: University of Toronto Press, 1987), plates 1–4.

5. Storck, 'Case Closed', 37; Chris J. Ellis, 'The Explanation of Northeastern Paleoindian Lithic Procurement Patterns', in *Eastern Paleoindian Lithic Resource Use*, edited by

Christopher J. Ellis and Jonathan C. Lothrop (Boulder, CO: Westview, 1989), 139–64; D. Brian Deller and Chris Ellis, 'Evidence for Late Paleoindian Ritual from the Caradoc Site (AfHj-104), Southwestern Ontario, Canada', *American Antiquity* 66 (2001): 267–84.

6. Chris J. Ellis, Ian T. Kenyon, and Michael W. Spence, 'The Archaic', in *Archaeology of Southern Ontario*, 65–124; Conrad Heidenrach and Robert W.C. Burgar, 'Native Settlement to 1847', in *Special Places: The Changing Ecosystem of the Toronto Region*, edited by Betty I. Roots, Donald A. Chant, and Conrad H. Heidenreich (Vancouver: UBC Press, 1999), 63–5; Paul A. Lennox, 'The Rentner and McKean Sites: 10,000 Years of Settlement on the Shores of Lake Huron, Simcoe County, Ontario', *Ontario Archaeology* 70 (2000), 16–65; B. Fox, 'Native Man', in *Legacy: The Natural History of Ontario*, edited by John B. Theberge (Toronto: McClelland and Stewart, 1989), 215–20; Harris, ed., *Historical Atlas of Canada*, vol. 1, plate 14; Toby Morrow, 'Continuity and Change in the Lithic Technology of the Precontact Great Lakes Region', in *Taming the Taxonomy: Toward a New Understanding of Great Lakes Archaeology*, edited by Ronald F. Williamson and Christopher Watts (Toronto: Eastend Books, 1999), 228.

7. Susan M. Jamieson, 'A Brief History of Aboriginal Social Interactions in Southern Ontario and Their Taxonomic Implications', in *Taming the Taxonomy*, 173–92.

8. Quotation: Ibid., 177. See also James V. Wright, *Ontario Prehistory: An Eleven-Thousand-Year Archaeological Outline* (Ottawa: Archaeological Survey of Canada, National Museum of Man, National Museums of

Canada, 1972), 12, 20.

9. Ellis et al., 'The Archaic', 121; Bruce Trigger, *Natives and Newcomers: Canada's 'Heroic Age' Reconsidered* (Kingston, ON: McGill-Queen's University Press, 1985), 82–3; Bruce Trigger, 'Master and Servant: A Conference Overview', in *Taming the Taxonomy*, 318; K.C.A. Dawson, 'Prehistory of the Interior Forest of Northern Ontario', in *Boreal Forest Adaptations: The Northern Algonkians*, edited by A. Theodore Steegmann, Jr (New York: Plenum, 1983), 75.

10. Tamara L. Varney and Susan Pfeiffer, 'The People of the Hind Site', *Ontario Archaeology* 59 (1995): 96–108.

11. Barbara Bender, 'The Roots of Inequality', in *Domination and Resistance*, edited by Daniel Miller, Michael Rowlands, and Christopher Tilley (London: Unwin Hyman, 1985), 83–95.

12. Michael W. Spence, 'Band Structure and Interaction in Early Southern Ontario', *Canadian Journal of Anthropology* 5 (1986): 91–3; Michael W. Spence, Robert H. Pihl, and J.E. Molto, 'Hunter-Gatherer Social Group Identification: A Case Study from Middle Woodland Southern Ontario', in *Exploring the Limits: Frontiers and Boundaries in Prehistory*, edited by Suzanne P. De Atley and Frank J. Findlow (Oxford: B.A.R., 1984), 123.

13. Morrow, 'Continuity and Change', 230–1.

14. George R. Hamell, 'Strawberries, Floating Islands, and Rabbit Captains: Mythical Realities and European Contact in the Northeast during the 16th and 17th Centuries', *Journal of Canadian Studies* 21 (1986–87): 72–94; D.W. Penney, 'The Origins of an Indigenous Ontario Arts Tradition: Ontario Art from the Late Archaic through the Woodlands Periods, 1500 BC–AD 600', *Journal of Canadian Studies* 21 (1986–7): 37–55.

15. W.A. Kenyon, *Mounds of Sacred Earth: Burial Mounds of Ontario* (Toronto: Royal Ontario Museum, 1986); Michael W. Spence, 'The Social Context of Production and Exchange', in *Contexts for Prehistoric Exchange*, edited by Jonathan E. Ericson and Timothy K. Earle (New York: Academic Press, 1982), 183–9; Ian Hodder, 'Toward a Contextual Approach to Prehistoric Exchange', in *Contexts for Prehistoric Exchange*, 199–221.

16. Quote, Michael S. Nassaney and Kendra Poyle, 'The Adoption of the Bow and Arrow in Eastern North America: A View from Central Arkansas', *American Antiquity*, 64, 1999, 258; J.H. Blitz, 'Adoption of the Bow in Prehistoric North America', *North American Archaeologist*, 9 (1988): 135. Frank A. Dieterman, 'Princess Point: The Landscape of Place', unpublished, PhD thesis (University of Toronto, 2001), 46; M. Anne Katzenberg, H.P. Schwarcz, M. Knyf and F.J. Melbye, 'Stable Isotope Evidence for Maize Horticulture and Paleodiet in Southern Ontario Canada', *American Antiquity*, 60 (1995): 341; Bruce D. Smith, 'Origins of Agriculture in Eastern North America', *Science*, 246B (1989), 1566–1571; R.F. Williamson and D.A. Robertson, 'Peer Polities Beyond the Periphery: Early and Middle Iroquoian Interaction', *Ontario Archaeology*, no. 58 (1994): 39. For a contrary opinion see Dean R. Snow, 'Migration in Prehistory: the Northern Algonkian Case', *American Antiquity*, 60 (1995): 59–79.

17. Neal Ferris, 'Telling Tales: Interpretive Trends in Southern Ontario Late Woodland Archaeology', *Ontario Archaeology* 68 (1999): 31; Conrad E. Heidenreich, 'History of the St Lawrence Area to AD 1650', in *Archaeology of Southern Ontario*, 478; G. Warrick, 'Comment on Varley and Cannon', *Ontario Archaeology* 58 (1984): 99; W.R. Fitzgerald, 'Contact, Contraction and the Little Ice Age: Neutral Iroquoian Transformation, AD 1450–1650', *KEWA* 92 (1992): 3–24; Williamson and Robertson, 'Peer Polities', 38; M. Annie Katzenberg, 'Changing Diet and Health in Pre- and Protohistoric Europe', in *Health and Lifestyle Change*, edited by Rebecca Huss-Ashmore, Joan Schall, and Mary Hediger (Philadelphia: MASCA, University Museum of Archaeology and Anthropology, University of Pennsylvania, 1992), 27; Mary Jackes, 'The Mortality of Ontario Archaeological Populations', *Canadian Journal of Anthropology* 5 (1986): 33–48; Bruce C. Trigger, 'Maintaining Economic Equality in Opposition to Complexity: An Iroquoian Case Study', in *The Evolution of Political Systems: Sociopolitics in Small-Scale Sedentary Societies*, edited by Steadham Upham (Cambridge: Cambridge University Press, 1990), 119–45.

18. Gary Warrick, 'European Infectious Disease

and Depopulation of the Wendat-Tionontate (Huron-Petun)', *World Archaeology* 35 (2003): 268.

19. *Historical Atlas of Canada*, vol. 1, plate 12; Trigger, *Natives and Newcomers*, 84–91; Mima Kapches, 'The Spatial Dynamics of Ontario Iroquoian Longhouses', *American Antiquity* 55 (1990): 49–67; David Kingsnorth Patterson, Jr, *A Diachronic Study of Dental Palaeopathology and Attritional Status of Prehistoric Ontario Pre-Iroquois and Iroquois Population* (Ottawa: National Museum of Man, National Museums of Canada, 1984), chapter 3.

20. John P. Hart, 'Maize, Matrilocality, Migration and Northern Iroquoian Evolution', *Journal of Archaeological Method and Theory* 8 (2001): 151–82; Ferris, 'Telling Tales', 26–33, 68, 199.

21. W. Engelbrecht, 'Factors Maintaining the Low Population Density among the Prehistoric New York Iroquois', *American Antiquity* 52 (1987) 13–27.

22. Mima Kapches, 'Chaos Theory and Social Movements: A Theoretical View of the Formation of the Northern Iroquoian Longhouse Cultural Pattern', in *Origins of the People of the Longhouse*, edited by André Bekerman and Gary Warrick (North York, ON: Ontario Archaeological Society, 1995), 86–96.

23. Celina Campbell and Ian D. Campbell, 'Pre-Contact Settlement Pattern in Southern Ontario: Simulation Model for Maize-Based Village Horticulture', *Ontario Archaeology* 53 (1992): 3–25. For a critique, see Dieterman, *Princess Point*, 42.

24. Ibid., 22; Ian D. Campbell and J.H. McAndrews, 'Cluster Analysis of Late Holocene Pollen Trends in Ontario', *Canadian Journal of Biology* 69 (1991): 1719–31; David Demeritt, 'Agriculture, Climate and Cultural Adaptation in the Prehistoric Northeast', *Archaeology of Eastern North America* 19 (1991): 183–202. For an alternative view, see William D. Finlayson, *Iroquoian Peoples of the Land of Rocks and Water, AD 650–1650: A Study of Settlement Archaeology* (London, ON: London Museum of Archaeology, 1998), 58–66, 94–107.

25. David A. Robertson and Ronald F. Williamson, 'The Archaeology of the Dunsmuir Site: 15th-Century Community Transformations in Southern Ontario',

Canadian Journal of Archaeology 27 (2003): 50–1; Thomas N. Headland and Lawrence A. Reid, 'Hunter-Gatherers and Their Neighbors from Prehistory to the Present', *Current Anthropology* 30 (1989): 43–66.

26. Kenneth C.A. Dawson, 'Northwestern Ontario and the Early Contact Period: The Northern Ojibwa from 1615–1715', *Canadian Journal of Archaeology* 11 (1987): 150–60; Dawson, 'Prehistory of the Interior Forest of Northern Ontario', 79; Charles A. Bishop and M. Estellie Smith, 'Early Historic Populations in Northwestern Ontario: Archaeological and Ethnohistorical Interpretations', *American Antiquity* 40 (1989): 52–65; Charles A. Bishop, 'The Emergence of the Northern Ojibwa: Social and Economic Consequences', *American Ethnologist* 3 (1976): 49–51.

27. Victor P. Lytwyn, 'Ojibwa and Ottawa Fisheries around Manitoulin Island: Historical and Geographical Perspectives on Aboriginal and Treaty Fishing Rights', *Native Studies Review* 6 (1990): 5; C.E. Cleland, 'The Inland Shore Fishery of the Great Lakes: Its Development and Importance in Prehistory', *American Antiquity* 47 (1982): 776–81; David A. Robertson, Eva M. MacDonald, and Martin S. Cooper, 'Among Marshes and Gneiss Mounds: The Archaeology of La Vase Island', *Ontario Archaeology* 64 (1997): 8–38.

28. Bruce G. Trigger, *The Children of Aataentsic: A History of the Huron People to 1660* (Kingston, ON: McGill-Queen's University Press, 1987), 62–5.

Chapter 2: The Transformation of Ontario's Cultural Landscape, 1580–1653

1. This revitalization is not limited to Ontario peoples. See Douglas H. Ubelaker, 'North American Indian Population Size, AD 1500 to 1985', *American Journal of Physical Anthropology* 77 (1988): 289–94; Nancy Shoemaker, *American Indian Population Recovery in the Twentieth Century* (Albuquerque: University of New Mexico, 1999).

2. M.A. Latta, 'Iroquoian Stemware', *American Antiquity* 52 (1987): 718, 723; Peter Ramsden, 'A Society Transformed', *Rotunda* (Spring 1988): 45–8; James W. Bradley,

Evolution of the Onondaga Iroquois: Accommo-
dating Change, 1500–1655 (Syracuse, NY:
Syracuse University Press, 1987), 94–5; John
Dickinson, 'Old Routes and New Wares: The
Advent of European Goods in the St
Lawrence Valley', in 'Le castor fait tout':
Selected Papers of the Fifth North American Fur
Trade Conference, edited by Bruce Trigger,
Toby Morantz, and Louise Dechêne
(Montreal: Lake St Louis Historical Society,
1985), 25–41; James Axtell, 'At the Water's
Edge: Trading in the Sixteenth Century', in
After Columbus: Essays in the Ethnohistory of
Colonial North America (New York: Oxford
University Press, 1988), 144–81; Conrad E.
Heidenreich, 'History of the St Law-
rence–Great Lakes Area to AD 1650', in The
Archaeology of Southern Ontario to AD 1650,
edited by Chris J. Ellis and Neal Ferris
(London, ON: Archaeological Society of
Ontario, 1990), 481n16.

3. Jose A. Brandeo, 'Iroquois Expansion in the
Seventeenth Century: A Review of Causes',
European Review of Native American Studies 15
(2001): 7. Gary Warrick argues that the Five
Nations conquered the St Lawrence Iro-
quois, in 'The Precontact Iroquoian Occu-
pation of Southern Ontario', Journal of World
Prehistory 14 (2000): 456.

4. Bruce Trigger, The Children of Aataentsic: A
History of the Huron People to 1660 (Kingston,
ON: McGill-Queen's University Press,
1987), 27–32.

5. Ibid., 218–19, 245; Bradley, Evolution of the
Onondaga Iroquois, 110–11, 223n26; Chris-
topher L. Miller and George R. Hamell, 'A
New Perspective on Indian–White Contact:
Cultural Symbols and Colonial Trade',
Journal of American History 73 (1986): 311–28;
George R. Hamell, 'Strawberries, Floating
Islands, and Rabbit Captains: Mythical
Realities and European Contact in the
Northeast during the Sixteenth and
Seventeenth Centuries', Journal of Canadian
History 21 (1986–7): 72–94.

6. Charles A. Bishop, 'Territoriality among
Northeastern Algonquians', Anthropologica 28
(1986): 47–50, 58; Charles A. Bishop,
'Northeastern Indian Concepts of Conser-
vation and the Fur Trade: A Critique of
Calvin Martin's Thesis', in Indians, Animals,
and the Fur Trade: A Critique of 'Keepers of the
Game', edited by Shepard Krech III (Athens:

University of Georgia Press, 1981), 39–58.

7. William C. Noble, 'Tsouharissen's Chief-
dom: An Early Historic 17th Century
Neutral Iroquoian Ranked Society', Cana-
dian Journal of Archaeology 9 (1985): 133–46;
William C. Noble, 'Historic Neutral Iroquois
Settlement Patterns', Canadian Journal of
Archaeology 8 (1984): 3–27; Susan Jamieson,
'Economics and Ontario Iroquoian Social
Organization', Canadian Journal of Archaeology
5 (1981): 19–30; A. Rotstein, 'The Mystery
of the Neutral Indians', in Patterns of the Past:
Interpreting Ontario's History, edited by Roger
Hall, William Westfall, and Laurel Sefton
MacDowell (Toronto: Dundurn, 1988),
11–36; William R. Fitzgerald, Lest the Beaver
Run Loose: The Early 17th Century Chris-
tianson Site and Trends in Historic Neutral
Archaeology (Ottawa: Archaeological Survey
of Canada, 1982); Bradley, Evolution of the
Onondaga Iroquois, 99–103; Axtell, 'At the
Water's Edge', 176–7.

8. Lev G. Waisberg, 'The Ottawa: Traders of the
Upper Great Lakes, 1615–1700', MA thesis
(Carleton University, 1979), 35; Charles
Garrad, 'The Plater-Fleming B of H 6-2
Site: A Review', Ontario Archaeological Society
Newsletter 89 (1989): 14–20; Jamieson,
'Economics and Ontario Iroquoian Social
Organization'; Rotstein, 'The Mystery of the
Neutral Indians'.

9. Bradley, Evolution of the Onondaga Iroquois; W.
Engelbrecht, 'New York Iroquois Political
Development', in Cultures in Contact: The
Impact of European Contact on Native American
Cultural Institutions, AD 1000–1800, edited
by William W. Fitzhugh (Washington, DC:
Smithsonian Institute Press, 1985), 163–83;
William A. Starna, 'Seventeenth Century
Dutch-Indian Trade: A Perspective from
Iroquoia', Halve Maen (Holland Society of
New York), 69, no. 3 (1984): 5–8, 21.

10. Quotation: Bradley, Evolution of the Onondaga
Iroquois, 90. See also Jesuit Relations, cited in
Catharine Randall, 'Cathedrals of Ice:
Translating the Jesuit Vocabulary of
Conversion', International Journal of Canadian
Studies / Revue internationale d'études canadi-
ennes 23 (2001): 28; Bruce G. Trigger, 'Early
Native North American Responses to
European Contact: Romantic versus Ra-
tionalistic Interpretations', Journal of American
History 77 (1991): 1207–8.

11. Population figures: Gary Warrick, 'European Infectious Disease and Depopulation of the Wendat-Tionontae (Huron-Petun)', *World Archaeology* 35 (2003): 270; Ian K. Steele, *Warpaths: Invasions of North America, 1513–1765* (New York: Oxford University Press, 1994), 72. Quotation: Thomas D. Hall, 'Historical Sociology and Native Americans: Methodological Problems', *American Indian Quarterly* 13 (1989): 224. See also C. Heidenreich, review of *Natives and New-comers* by Bruce G. Trigger, *Native Studies Review* 2 (1986): 140; Heidenreich, 'History of the St Lawrence–Great Lakes Area'; Trigger, 'Early Native North American Responses to European Contact,' 1195–1215.

12. Warrick, 'European Infectious Disease'.

13. Olive Dickason, *The Myth of the Savage and the Beginnings of French Colonialism in the Americas* (Edmonton: University of Alberta Press, 1984); Trigger, *Children of Aataentsic*, 399–401; Francis Jennings, *The Ambiguous Iroquois Empire: The Covenant Chain Confederation of Indian Tribes with English Colonies from Its Beginnings to the Lancaster Treaty of 1744* (New York: Norton, 1989), 86–7; Sean O'Neill, 'French Jesuits' Motives for Baptizing Indians on the Frontier of New France', *Mid-America* 71, no. 3 (1989): 121–36; Cornelius Jaenen, *Friend and Foe: Aspects of French-Amerindian Cultural Contact in the Sixteenth and Seventeenth Centuries* (Toronto: McClelland and Stewart, 1976).

14. John W. Grant, *Moon of Wintertime: Missionaries and the Indians of Canada in Encounter since 1534* (Toronto: University of Toronto Press, 1984), 28–9; Charles E. Heidenreich, plate 34, in *Historical Atlas of Canada*, vol. 1, edited by R. Cole Harris (Toronto: University of Toronto Press, 1987); Léon Pouliot, 'Jerome Lalemant', *Dictionary of Canadian Biography*, vol. 1 (Toronto: University of Toronto Press, 1966), 413–4; Trigger, *Natives and Newcomers*, 255, 266.

15. Grant, *Moon of Wintertime*, 40.

16. Quotations: Carol Devens, 'Separate Confrontations: Gender as a Factor in Indian Adoptation to European Colonization in New France', *American Quarterly* 38 (1986): 477n11; Olive Dickason, 'Campaigns to Capture Young Minds: A Look at Early Attempts in Colonial Mexico and New France to Remold Amerindians', *Historical Papers* (1987): 62. See also Grant, *Moon of Wintertime*, chapters 1 and 2; Trigger, *Children of Aataentsic*, 59–62; Bruce Trigger, 'Maintaining Economic Equality in Opposition to Complexity: An Iroquoian Case Study', in *The Evolution of Political Systems: Sociopolitics in Small-Scale Sedentary Societies*, edited by Steadman Upham (Cambridge: Cambridge University Press, 1990), 119–45.

17. Quotation: Randall, 'Cathedrals of Ice', 27. See also Grant, *Moon of Wintertime*, chapters 1 and 2; Dickason, *The Myth of the Savage*; Nancy Bouvillain, 'The Iroquois and the Jesuits: Strategies of Influence and Resistance', *American Indian Culture and Research Journal* 10, no. 1 (1986): 29–43.

18. Quotations: Devens, 'Separate Confrontations', 468; Karen Anderson, 'Commodity Exchange and Subordination: Montagnais-Naskapi and Huron Women, 1600–1650', *Signs: Journal of Women in Culture and Society* 11 (1985): 59. See also Karen Anderson, 'As Gentle as Little Lambs: Images of Huron and Montagnais-Naskapi Women in the Writings of the 17th Century Jesuits', *Canadian Review of Sociology and Anthropology* 25 (1988): 560–76; Karen Anderson, *Chain Her by One Foot: The Subjugation of Women in Seventeenth-Century New France* (London: Routledge, 1991); Devens, 'Separate Confrontations', 461–80.

19. Trigger, *Natives and Newcomers*, 256–9.

20. Trigger, *Children of Aataentsic*, 547, 632–3; Heidenreich, review, 146; John Steckley, 'Developing a Theory of Smallpox: Huron Perceptions of a New Disease', *Ontario Archaeological Society Newsletter* 90, no. 1 (1990): 17–20.

21. On the European gun trade, see Howard Vernon, 'The Dutch, the Indians and the Fur Trade in the Hudson Valley, 1609–1664', in *Neighbours and Intruders: An Ethnohistorical Exploration of the Indians of Hudson's River*, edited by Laurence M. Hauptman (Ottawa: Canadian Ethnology Service, 1978), 204, 298–309; Olive Dickason, 'Europeans and Amerindians: Some Comparative Aspects of Early Contact', *Historical Papers* (1979): 198–200; Jennings, *The Ambiguous Iroquois Empire*, 71; Jennings, *History and Culture*, 132; Trigger, *Natives and Newcomers*, 334; Trigger, *Children of Aataentsic*, 633; Jan Piet Puype,

'Dutch and Other Flintlocks from Seventeenth Century Iroquois Sites', in *Proceedings of the 1984 Trade Gun Conference*, edited by Charles F. Hayes III (Rochester, NY: Rochester Museum & Science Center, 1985), 9, 81–90; James Hunter, 'The Implications of Firearms Remains from Sainte-Marie Among the Hurons, AD 1639–1649,' in *Proceedings of the 1984 Trade Gun Conference*, 5–7. On the Wendat, see Trigger, *Natives and Newcomers*; Jennings, *The Ambiguous Iroquois Empire*, 80–1, 102–3; Bradley, *Evolution of the Onondaga Iroquois*, 125–6, 142–5; J. Frederick Fausz, 'Fighting "Fire" with Firearms: The Anglo-Powhatan Arms Race in Early Virginia', *American Indian Culture and Research Journal* 3 (1979): 33–50; Puype, 'Dutch and Other Flintlocks', 90–1; Barry C. Kent, 'More on Gunflints', *Historical Archaeology* 17 (1983): 28–9; Donald E. Worcester and T.F. Schilz, 'The Spread of Firearms among the Indians on the Anglo-French Frontiers', *American Indian Quarterly* 8 (1984): 104–15; Daniel Karl Richter, *The Ordeal of the Longhouse: The Peoples of the Iroquois League in the Era of European Colonization* (Chapel Hill: University of North Carolina Press, 1992), 62–4; Heidenreich, 'History of the St Lawrence–Great Lakes Area', 491; Brian J. Given, *'A Most Pernicious Thing': Gun Trading and Native Warfare in the Early Contact Period* (Ottawa: Carleton University Press, 1994); Craig Keener, 'An Ethnohistorical Analysis of Iroquois Assault Tactics Used against Fortified Settlements of the Northeast in the Seventeenth Century', *Ethnohistory* 46 (1999): 778–807.

22. Richter, *Ordeal of the Longhouse*, 32–8; Jennings, *The Ambiguous Iroquois Culture*, 94–6; James V. Wright, 'Archaeology of Southern Ontario to AD 1650', in *Archaeology of Southern Ontario*, 502; Brett Rushforth, '"A Little Flesh We Offer You": The Origins of Indian Slavery in New France', *William and Mary Quarterly* 60 (2003): 783; Susan Johnston, 'Epidemic Effects as Causes of Warfare in the Northeast after 1640', MA thesis (Carleton University, 1982), 94–131; W.R. Fitzgerald, 'Contact, Contraction and the Little Ice Age: Neutral Iroquoian Transformation, AD 1450–1650', *KEWA* 92 (1992): 12; Heidenreich, 'History of

the St Lawrence–Great Lakes Area', 488n21; Jose Brandão, *'Your Fyre Shall Burn No More': Iroquois Policy toward New France and Its Native Allies to 1701* (Lincoln: University of Nebraska Press, 1997); Brandeo, 'Iroquois Expansion', 7–18.

23. Quotation: Keith Otterbein, 'Huron vs Iroquois: A Case Study in Inter-Tribal Warfare', *Ethnohistory* 26 (1979): 141–52. See also Brandeo, 'Iroquois Expansion', 15; Keener, 'Ethnohistorical Analysis of Iroquois Assault Tactics', 790–1; Trigger, *Children of Aataentsic*, 775–6, 781–2; Hunter, 'Implications of Firearms Remains', 7; James A. Clifton, 'The Re-emergent Wyandot: A Study in Ethnogenesis on the Detroit River Borderland, 1747', in *The Western District: Papers from the Western District Conference*, edited by K. Pryke and L.L. Kulisek (Windsor, ON: Essex County Historical Society, 1983), 1–17; Bruce W. Hodgins and J. Benidickson, *The Temagami Experience: Recreation, Resources and Aboriginal Rights in the Northern Ontario Wilderness* (Toronto: University of Toronto Press, 1989), 15; Trigger, *Natives and Newcomers*, 271; Garrad, 'The Plater-Fleming B of H 6-2 Site', 18–20; Rotstein, 'The Mystery of the Neutral Indians', 16; H.H. Tanner, *Atlas of Great Lakes Indian History* (Norman: University of Oklahoma Press, 1987), 30.

Chapter 3: Contested Terrain: Cultural Mixing in Early Ontario, 1653–1763

1. Richard White, *The Middle Ground: Indians, Empires, and Republics in the Great Lakes Region, 1650–1815* (Cambridge: Cambridge University Press, 1991), ix; see also Marcel Moussette, 'An Encounter in the Baroque Age: French and Amerindians in North America', *Historical Archaeology* 37 (2003): 29–39.

2. Peter S. Schmalz, 'The Role of the Ojibwa in the Conquest of Southern Ontario, 1650–1701', *Ontario History* 76 (December 1984): 345n1; Neal Ferris, Ian Kenyon, Rosemary Prevec, and Carl Murphy, 'Bellamy: A Late Historic Ojibwa Habitation', *Ontario Archaeology* 44 (1985): 3; Charles A. Bishop, 'The Emergence of the Northern Ojibwa: Social and Economic

Consequences', *American Ethnologist* 3 (1976): 39; White, *The Middle Ground*, 16–18; Charles A. Bishop, 'The Indian Inhabitants of Northern Ontario at the Time of Contact: Socio-Territorial Considerations', in *Approaches to Algonquian Archaeology*, edited by Margaret G. Hanna and Bryan Koogman (Calgary: University of Calgary, 1982), 259; Edward S. Rogers, 'Southeastern Ojibwa', in *Handbook of North American Indians: Northeast*, edited by Bruce Trigger (Washington: Smithsonian Institution, 1978): 762; Leroy V. Eid, 'The Ojibwa–Iroquois War: The War the Five Nations Did Not Win', *Ethnohistory* 26 (1979): 300; Leo G. Waisberg, 'The Ottawa: Traders of the Upper Great Lakes, 1615–1700', MA thesis (Carleton University, 1978), 10–15.

3. Quotations: Stephen S. Webb, *1676: The End of American Independence* (New York: Knopf, 1984), 259; Daniel Richter, 'Iroquois vs Iroquois: Jesuit Missions and Christianity in Village Politics, 1642–1686', *Ethnohistory* 32 (1985): 8, 16n72.

4. Quotation: Daniel Richter, 'War and Culture: The Iroquois Experience', *William and Mary Quarterly* 40 (1983): 354. See also Gilles Havard, *The Great Peace of Montreal of 1701: French-Native Diplomacy in the Seventeenth Century*, translated by Phyllis Aronoff and Howard Scott (Montreal: McGill-Queen's University Press, 2001): 36–7, 49, 68; Ian Steele, *Warpaths: Invasions of North America, 1513–1765* (New York: Oxford University Press, 1994), 72, 118; James Lynch, 'The Iroquois Confederacy and the Adoption and Administration of Non-Iroquoian Individuals and Groups Prior to 1756', *Man in the Northeast* 30 (1985): 91.

5. Waisberg, 'The Ottawa', 70, 82–3; White, *The Middle Ground*, 25, 104–7.

6. Waisberg, 'The Ottawa', 62–8; Gordon M. Day, 'Nipissing', in *Handbook of North American Indians*, 15, 789; Schmalz, 'Role of the Ojibwa', 332–3; Francis Jennings, *The Ambiguous Iroquois Empire: The Covenant Chain Confederation of Indian Tribes with English Colonies from Its Beginnings to the Lancaster Treaty of 1744* (New York: Norton, 1984), 128–30; Jose Brandão, *'Your Fyre Shall Burn No More': Iroquois Policy toward New France and Its Native Allies to 1701* (Lincoln:

University of Nebraska Press, 1997), table D.1; Webb, *1676*, 265–9.

7. Quotations: J.A. Brandão and William A. Starna, 'The Treaties of 1701: A Triumph of Iroquois Diplomacy', *Ethnohistory* 43 (1996): 211; Victor A. Konrad, 'An Iroquois Frontier: The North Shore of Lake Ontario during the Late Seventeenth Century', *Journal of Historical Geography* 7 (1981): 138. See also W.J. Eccles, *France in America*, rev. ed. (Markham, ON: Fitzhenry & Whiteside, 1990), 66–7; W.J. Eccles, 'Rémy de Courcelle', *Dictionary of Canadian Biography*, vol. 1 (Toronto: University of Toronto Press, 1979), 571; Bruce G. Trigger, *Natives and Newcomers: Canada's 'Heroic Age' Reconsidered* (Kingston, ON: McGill-Queen's University Press, 1985), 340.

8. Eccles, *France in America*, 66.

9. Quotation: E.E. Rich, *The Fur Trade and the Northwest to 1857* (Toronto: McClelland and Stewart, 1967), 55. See also Russell M. Magnaghi, 'The Jesuits in the Lake Superior Country', *Inland Seas* 41 (1985): 202.

10. R. La Rogue de Roguebrune, 'Le Febvre de La Barre', *Dictionary of Canadian Biography*, vol. 1, 445–6; Jennings, *The Ambiguous Iroquois*, 191; *Historical Atlas of Canada*, vol. 1, plate 38; Schmalz, 'Role of the Ojibwa', 329.

11. On change as setback, see *Atlas*, vol. 1, plates 37, 38; Waisberg, 'Ottawa', 70–83; L.V.B. Johnson, 'The Early Mississauga Treaty Process in Historical Perspective, 1781–1819', PhD (University of Toronto, 1986), 47. See also Thomas Wien, 'Selling Beaver Skins in North America and Europe: The Uses of Fur Trade Imperialism', *Journal of the Canadian Historical Association* 1 (1990): 293–317.

12. Quotation: White, *The Middle Ground*, 131. See also Waisberg, 'The Ottawa', 87–100, 181–3.

13. Yves F. Zoltvany, 'New France and the West, 1701-13', *Canadian Historical Review* 46 (1965): 302; Eid, 'The Ojibwa–Iroquois War'; quotation from White, *The Middle Ground*, 130.

14. Quotation: Brandão and Starna, 'Treaties of 1701', 235. See also Peter Schmalz, *The Ojibwa of Southern Ontario* (Toronto: University of Toronto Press, 1991), chapter 2; Donald B. Smith, 'The Life of George Copeway or Kuh-ge-ga-gah-boroh 1818–

1869—and a Review of His Writings',
Journal of Canadian Studies 23 (1988): 22; D.
Peter MacLeod, 'The Anishinabeg Point of
View: The History of the Great Lakes
Region to 1800 in Nineteenth-Century
Mississauga, Odawa and Ojibwa History',
Canadian Historical Review 73 (1992):
194–210.

15. William M. Fenton, 'Kondiaronk', *Dictionary
of Canadian Biography*, vol. 2 (Toronto:
University of Toronto Press, 1982), 320–3;
John Steckley, 'Kandiaronk: A Man Called
Rat', in *Untold Tales: Four 17th Century Huron*
(Toronto: Associated Heritage, 1992), 41–52;
White, *The Middle Ground*, 143–5; Havard,
The Great Peace, 104.

16. Most often, historians have accorded that
status to the French, Iroquois, or English; see
W.J. Eccles, 'The Fur Trade and Eighteenth-
Century Imperialism', *William and Mary
Quarterly* 40 (1983): 343–4. See also R.
Hahn, 'The Problem of Iroquois Neutrality:
Suggestions for Revision', *Ethnohistory* 27
(1980): 318; Aquila, *The Iroquois Restoration*,
133–9, 266n6; Neal Salisbury, 'The Indian's
Old World: Native Americans and the
Coming of Europeans', *William and Mary
Quarterly* 53 (1996): 455; Richter, 'War and
Culture', 552–3; Zoltvany, 'New France',
304; Brandão and Starna, 'Treaties of 1701'.
Havard, *The Great Peace*, 160–78, provides
the most balanced account. On the Ojibwa–
Iroquois agreement, see Schmalz, 'Role of
the Ojibwa', 341, 351n7; Eid, 'The Ojibwa–
Iroquois War', 311; Jennings, *The Ambiguous
Iroquois Empire*, 209; Daniel K. Richter, *The
Ordeal of the Longhouse: The Peoples of the
Iroquoian League in the Era of European
Colonization* (Chapel Hill: University of
North Carolina Press, 1992), 202–3. On the
British, see Jennings, *The Ambiguous Iroquois
Empire*, 212–13; R. Hahn, 'Covenant and
Consensus: Iroquois and English, 1676–
1760', in *Beyond the Covenant Chain*, 52–3.
On the French, see Schmalz, 'Role of the
Ojibwa', 351n87; Yves F. Zoltvany, 'The
Problem of Western Policy under Philippe
de Rigaud de Vaudreuil, 1703–1725', *CHA
Historical Papers* (1964): 10–11.

17. Quotation: W.J. Eccles, 'Sovereignty
Association, 1500–1783', *Canadian Historical
Review* 65 (1984): 500. See also Cornelius J.
Jaenen, 'Characteristics of French-Amer-

indian Contact in New France', in *Essays on
the History of North American Discovery and
Exploration*, edited by Stanley H. Palmer and
Dennis Reinharz (College Station: Texas
A&M University Press, 1988), 79–101;
Zoltvany, 'New France', 307–9; Richter,
'War and Culture', 354–5; Catherine M.
Desbarats, 'The Cost of Early Canada's
Native Alliances: Reality and Scarcity's
Rhetoric', *William and Mary Quarterly* 52
(1995): 609–30.

18. Zoltvany, 'The Problem of Western Policy',
16–25; Dale Miquelon, *New France,
1701–1744: A Supplement to Europe*
(Toronto: McClelland & Stewart, 1987),
52–3, 171–2; Eccles, 'Sovereignty
Association', 491; Hahn, 'Covenant and
Consensus', 57; Hahn, 'The Problem of
Iroquois Neutrality', 325–37; Francis
Jennings, *Empire of Fortune: Crowns, Colonies
and Tribes in the Seven Years War in America*
(New York: Norton, 1988), 73–5.

19. Schmalz, *Ojibwa of Southern Ontario*, chapter
3; Schmalz, 'The Role of the Ojibwa', 67;
Zoltvany, 'The Problem of Western Policy',
23n55; Helen Hornbeck Tanner, et al., eds,
Atlas of Great Lakes Indian History, 66, map
13.

20. Zoltvany, 'The Problem of Iroquois
Neutrality', 24n62. Figures calculated from
data in *Historical Atlas of Canada*, vol. 1, plates
40 and 41. See Eccles, 'Fur Trade', 355n66,
for a cautionary statement concerning such
statistics. See also Miquelon, *New France*, 174;
Eccles, 'Fur Trade', 155.

21. Bishop, 'Indian Inhabitants', 259–61; Arthur
J. Ray and Donald Freeman, *'Give Us Good
Measure': An Economic Analysis of Relations
between the Indians and the Hudson's Bay
Company before 1763* (Toronto: University of
Toronto Press, 1978), 42–3; Carol M. Judd,
'Sakie, Esquawenoe and the Foundation of a
Dual-Native Tradition at Moose Factory', in
*The Subarctic Fur Trade: Native Social and
Economic Adaptations*, edited by Shepard
Krech III (Vancouver: UBC Press, 1984),
81–98; Jaenen, 'Characteristics of French-
Amerindian Contact', 88; Ray and Freeman,
'Give Us Good Measure', 136–41, 250.

22. Support for the interpretations offered in the
next three paragraphs can be found in Ray
and Freeman, *'Give Us Good Measure'*.

23. *Historical Atlas of Canada*, vol. 1, plates 37, 40,

41; Ray and Freeman, *'Give Us Good Measure'*, 26–36, 166, 180, 184, 202, 214; Eccles, 'Fur Trade', 345–8; E.S. Rogers, 'The Queen: A Cree Burial at Moose Factory, May 27, 1747', *Arctic Anthropology* 24, no. 2 (1987): 37.

24. John E. Foster, 'The Homeguard Cree and the Hudson's Bay Company: The First Hundred Years', in *Approaches to Native History in Canada*, edited by D.A. Muise (Ottawa: National Museum of Man, 1977), 49–64; Sylvia Van Kirk, *'Many Tender Ties': Women in Fur-Trade Society, 1670–1870* (Winnipeg: Watson & Dwyer, 1980).

25. Quotations: Judd, 'Sakie', 87–8. See also Charles A. Bishop, 'The First Century: Adaptive Changes among the Western James Bay Cree between the Early Seventeenth and Early Eighteenth Centuries', in *The Subarctic Fur Trade*, 26; Van Kirk, *'Many Tender Ties'*; Jennifer Brown, *Strangers in Blood: Fur Trade Company Families in Indian Country* (Vancouver: UBC Press, 1980).

26. On French dependence, see Jacqueline Peterson, 'Many Roads to Red River: Métis Genesis in the Great Lakes Region, 1680–1815', in *The New Peoples: Being and Becoming Métis in North America*, edited by Jacqueline Peterson and Jennifer S.H. Brown (Winnipeg: University of Manitoba Press, 1985), 37–71; Jacqueline Peterson, 'Ethnogenesis: The Settlement and Growth of a "New People" in the Great Lakes Region, 1702–1815', *American Indian Culture and Research Journal* 6, no. 2 (1982): 23–64. On Native women, see Dean Anderson, 'The Flow of European Trade Goods into the Western Great Lakes Region, 1715–1760', in *The Fur Trade Revisited*, edited by Jennifer S.H. Brown, W.J. Eccles, and Donald P. Heldman (East Lansing: Michigan State University Press, 1994), 93–116; Bruce White, 'The Women Who Married a Beaver: Trade Patterns and Gender Roles in the Ojibwa Fur Trade', *Ethnohistory* 46 (1999), 109–47; John Clarke, 'Sarah Ainse', *Dictionary of Canadian Biography*, vol. 6 (Toronto: University of Toronto Press, 1987), 7–9.

27. Harriet R. Gorham, 'Ethnic Identity among the Mixed-Bloods of the Great Lakes Region, 1760–1830', MA thesis (Carleton University, 1985), 65; Peterson, 'Many Roads', 48–9.

28. Quotation: Helen Tanner, 'The Career of Joseph La France, Coureur de bois in the Upper Great Lakes', in *The Fur Trade Revisited*, 179. See also Johnson, 'The Early Mississauga Treaty Process', 55; Schmalz, 'Role of the Ojibwa', 342; Lynch, 'The Iroquois', 96–7; White, *The Middle Ground*, 207–8.

29. Quotations: White, *The Middle Ground*, 209–11. See also Schmalz, *Ojibwa of Southern Ontario*, 49; Jennings, *The Ambiguous Iroquois Empire*, 156–7, 190.

30. Quotations: Jennings, *The Ambiguous Iroquois Empire*, 191, 295, 313–21; Steele, *Warpaths*, 205. See also Jane Graham, 'Wabbicommicat', *Dictionary of Canadian Biography*, vol. 3, 651–2; Percy J. Robinson, *Toronto during the French Régime: A History of the Toronto Region from Brûlé to Simcoe, 1615–1793* (1933; Toronto: University of Toronto Press, 1965), 136.

31. Quotation: David A. Armour, 'Minweweh', *Dictionary of Canadian Biography*, vol. 3, s.v. See also D. Peter MacLeod, 'Microbes and Muskets: Smallpox and the Participation of the Amerindian Allies of New France in the Seven Years' War', *Ethnohistory* 39 (1992): 42–64; Donald B. Smith, 'Who Are the Mississauga?' *Ontario History* 67 (1975): 218; Schmalz, *Ojibwa of Southern Ontario*, 59–64.

32. Quotation: John Borrows, 'Wampum at Niagara: The Royal Proclamation, Canadian Legal History, and Self-Government', in *Aboriginal and Treaty Rights in Canada: Essays on Law, Equity, and Respect for Difference*, edited by Michael Asch (Vancouver: UBC Press, 1997), 260. See also Cornelius J. Jaenen, 'The Role of Presents in French–Amerindian Trade', in *Explorations in Canadian Economic History: Essays in Honour of Irene M. Spry*, edited by Duncan Cameron (Ottawa: University of Ottawa Press, 1985), 231–50; Bruce White, 'Give Us a Little Milk: The Social and Cultural Practice of Gift Giving and the Lake Superior Fur Trade', *Minnesota History* 48 (1982): 60–71; Julian Gwyn, 'Sir William Johnson', *Dictionary of Canadian Biography*, vol. 4, 395–7; Louis Chevrette, 'Pontiac', *Dictionary of Canadian Biography*, vol. 3, 525–31.

33. Quotations: Elizabeth Fenn, 'Biological Warfare in Eighteenth-Century North America: Beyond Jeffery Amherst', *Journal of*

American History 86 (2000): 1552–80. See also Jennings, *The Ambiguous Iroquois Empire*, 447–8; Steele, *Warpath*, 239; Gregory E. Dowd, *A Spirited Resistance: The North American Indian Struggle for Unity, 1745–1815* (Baltimore: Johns Hopkins University Press, 1992), 36.

34. MacLeod, 'The Anishinabeg Point of View', 200–3; Graham, 'Wabbicommicot', 651–2; Schmalz, *Ojibwa of Southern Ontario*, 71–80.

35. Gail D. Denvers, 'Gendered Encounters: Warriors, Women, and William Johnson', *Journal of American Studies* 35 (2001): 196; White, *The Middle Ground*, 140, 482–4; Schmalz, *Ojibwa of Southern Ontario*, 53, 67–8; Borrows, 'Wampum at Niagara', 161–5.

36. Jeremy Adelman and Stephen Aron, 'From Borderlands to Borders: Empires, Nation States and Peoples In Between in North American History', *American Historical Review* 104 (1999): 814–41.

Chapter 4: The 'Men with Hats': Defining Upper Canada, 1763–91

1. Philip Ranlett, *The New York Loyalists* (Knoxville: University of Tennessee Press, 1986).

2. Richard Preston, ed., *Kingston before the War of 1812: A Collection of Documents* (Toronto: Champlain Society, 1959), xi n15.

3. For useful reviews of literature on the Loyalists, see Bruce Wilson, *As She Began: An Illustrated Introduction to Loyalist Ontario* (Toronto: Dundurn, 1981); J.M. Bumsted, *Understanding the Loyalists* (Sackville, NB: Centre for Canadian Studies, Mount Allison University, 1986); Elwood Jones, 'The Loyalists and Canadian History', *Journal of Canadian Studies* 20 (1985): 149–56; Elwood Jones, 'Loyalist Ideology: Reflections on Political Culture in Early Upper Canada', *Journal of Canadian Studies* 29 (1994): 163–8.

4. Quotations: Bruce G. Wilson, *The Enterprises of Robert Hamilton: A Study of Wealth and Influence in Early Upper Canada, 1776–1812* (Ottawa: Carleton University Press, 1983), 17 and chapter 3.

5. Quotations: Victor Lytwyn and Dean Jacobs, '"For Good Will and Affection": The Detroit Indian Deeds and British Land Policy, 1760–1827', *Ontario History* 92 (2000): 9–29.

See also John Clarke, *Land, Power, and Economics on the Frontier of Upper Canada* (Montreal: McGill-Queen's University Press, 2001), 139.

6. Quotation: Lytwyn and Jacobs, 'For Good Will and Affection'.

7. Quotation: Anthony J. Hall, 'The Red Man's Burden: Land, Law and the Lord in the Indian Affairs of Upper Canada, 1791–1851', PhD dissertation (University of Toronto, 1984), 53. See also Indian and Northern Affairs Canada, 'Backgrounder: Mississaugas of New Credit's Toronto Purchase: Specific Claim' (22 June 2003), http://www.ainc-inac.gc.ca/nr/prs/m-a2003/02332bk_e.html.

8. Quotations: Donald B. Smith, 'The Dispossession of the Mississauga Indians: A Missing Chapter in the Early History of Upper Canada', *Ontario History* 73 (1981): 67–87; David McNab, '"The Promise That He Gave to My Grand Father Was Very Sweet": The Gun Shot Treaty of 1792 at the Bay of Quinte', *Canadian Journal of Native Studies* 16 (1996): 293–314.

9. Quotations: Norman Knowles, *Inventing the Loyalists: The Ontario Loyalist Tradition and the Creation of Useable Pasts* (Toronto: University of Toronto Press, 1997), 37; Maurice E. Comfort, 'Disbanded Troops, Settled Loyalists and Emigrants in the Niagara District in 1787', *Families* 27 (1988): 231.

10. Janice Potter-MacKinnon, *While the Women Only Wept: Loyalist Refugee Women in Eastern Ontario* (Montreal: McGill-Queen's University Press, 1993).

Chapter 5: Native Peoples, Nature, and Newcomers: The Making of Rural Upper Canada, 1791–1871

1. Quotations: Douglas McCalla, 'The Ontario Economy in the Long Run', *Ontario History* 90 (1998): 97; J.K. Johnson, 'Gerald Craig's *Upper Canada: The Formative Years* and the Writing of Upper Canadian History', *Ontario History* 90 (1998): 129. See also Douglas McCalla, *Planting the Province: The Economic History of Upper Canada, 1784–1870* (Toronto: University of Toronto Press, 1993), 243.

2. Donald B. Smith, *Sacred Feathers: The*

Reverend Peter Jones (Kahkewaquonaby) and the Mississauga Indians (Toronto: University of Toronto Press, 1987), 27; Peter S. Schmalz, *The Ojibwa of Southern Ontario* (Toronto: University of Toronto Press, 1991), 106; Peggy Blair, 'Taken for "Granted"': Aboriginal Title and Public Fishing Rights in Upper Canada', *Ontario History* 92 (2000): 31–55; Brian S. Osborne, 'Organizing the Lake Fisheries: Landscapes and Waterscapes', *Historic Kingston* 38 (1990): 82–4.

3. Smith, *Sacred Feathers*, 32, 24.

4. Quotations: E. Reginald Good, 'Mississauga–Mennonite Relations in the Upper Grand River Valley', *Ontario History* 87 (1995): 165; Brendan O'Brien, *Speedy Justice: The Tragic Last Voyage of His Majesty's Vessel, Speedy* (Toronto: Osgoode Society, 1992), 34, 42, 44, 45.

5. Quotation: Smith, *Sacred Feathers*, 32. See also ibid., 30; Leo A. Johnson, 'The Mississauga–Lake Ontario Land Surrender of 1805', *Ontario History* 82 (1990): 234–5; Schmalz, *The Ojibwa of Southern Ontario*, 107–9.

6. Mary Quayle Innis, ed., *Mrs. Simcoe's Diary* (Toronto: Macmillan, 1965), 10–11 June 1796, 182–3.

7. Quotation: Christopher Vecsey, *Traditional Ojibwa Religion and Its Historical Changes* (Philadelphia: American Philisophical Society, 1983), 4; see also ibid., 10.

8. Quotation: Johnson, 'The Mississauga–Lake Ontario Land Surrender', 244. See also Grace Rajnovich, *Reading Rock Art: Interpreting the Indian Rock Paintings of the Canadian Shield* (Toronto: Natural Heritage/Natural History, 1994), 54.

9. Schmalz, *Ojibwa of Southern Ontario*, 110; Johnson, 'The Mississauga–Lake Ontario Land Surrender', 236.

10. Ibid., 249; Peter S. Schmalz, 'The European Challenge to the First Nations' Great Lake Fisheries', paper presented to the Canadian Historical Association, Calgary, 1994, 13; Brian S. Osborne and Michael Ripmeester, 'Kingston, Bedford, Grape Island, Alnwick: The Odyssey of the Kingston Mississauga', *Historic Kingston* 43 (1995): 94.

11. Quotations: Michael Ripmeester, '"It Is Scarcely to Be Believed . . .": The Mississauga Indians and the Grape Island Mission, 1826–36', *Canadian Geographer* 39 (1995):

159; Sidney L. Harring, *White Man's Law: Native People in Nineteenth-Century Canadian Jurisprudence* (Toronto: Osgoode Society, 1998), 118. See also Ripmeester, 'It Is Scarcely to Be Believed', 163–6.

12. Hope MacLean, 'A Positive Experiment in Aboriginal Education: The Methodist Ojibway Day Schools in Upper Canada, 1824–1833', *Canadian Journal of Native Studies* 22 (2002): 23–63; J.R. Miller, *Shingwauk's Vision: A History of Native Residential Schools* (Toronto: University of Toronto Press, 1996); Alan Knight, 'A Study in Failure: The Anglican Mission at Sault Ste. Marie, Upper Canada, 1830–1841', *Journal of the Canadian Church Historical Society* 45 (2003): 133–224.

13. Thorold T. Tronrud, 'Frontier Social Structure: The Canadian Lakehead, 1871 and 1881', *Ontario History* 79 (1987): 154–5.

14. Quotations: David Moorman, 'Roads and Rights: Public Roads and Indian Land in Nineteenth-Century Southern Ontario', *Ontario History* 92 (2000): 57–69.

15. For this and the next paragraph, see Victor P. Lytwyn, 'Ojibwa and Ottawa Fisheries around Manitoulin Island: Geographical Perspectives on Aboriginal and Treaty Fishing Rights', *Native Studies Review* 6 (1990): 1–29; Victor P. Lytwyn, 'The Usurpation of Aboriginal Fishing Rights: A Study of the Saugeen Nation's Fishing Island Fishery in Lake Huron', in *Co-Existence? Studies in Ontario–First Nations Relations*, edited by Bruce W. Hodgins, Shawn Heard, and John S. Milloy (Peterborough, ON: Frost Centre for Canadian Heritage and Development Studies, Trent University, 1992), 81–103; Victor P. Lytwyn, 'Waterworld: The Aquatic Territory of the Great Lakes First Nations', in *Gin Das Winan: Documenting Aboriginal History in Ontario*, edited by Dale Standen and David McNab (Toronto: Champlain Society, 1996), 14–28; Peter S. Schmalz, 'The European Challenge to the First Nations' Great Lakes Fisheries', paper presented to the Canadian Historical Association, Calgary, 1994; W.R. Wightman, *Forever on the Fringe: Six Studies in the Development of the Manitoulin Island* (Toronto: University of Toronto Press, 1982).

16. Quotation: Lytwyn, 'Ojibwa and Ottawa Fisheries', 25.

17. Quotations: Peter S. Schmalz, 'The European Challenge to the First Nations', 20, 22. See also Victor P. Lytwyn, 'Ojibwa and Ottawa Fisheries'; Lytwyn, 'The Usurpation of Aboriginal Fishing Rights'.

18. Quotation: Penny Petrone, ed., *First People, First Voices* (Toronto: University of Toronto Press, 1991), 60.

19. Ibid, 59–60.

20. Quotations: J.R. Miller, *Skyscrapers Hide the Heavens: A History of Indian–White Relations in Canada* (Toronto: University of Toronto Press, 1989), 112; Donald B. Smith, 'John A. Macdonald and Aboriginal Canada', *Historic Kingston* 50 (2002): 24, 26.

21. Quotation: Ian Radforth, 'Performance, Politics and Representation: Aboriginal People and the 1860 Royal Tour of Canada', *Canadian Historical Review* 84 (2003): 13.

22. Quotations: first and third, Susanna Moodie, in Elizabeth Hopkins, 'Susanna Moodie', in *Profiles in Canadian Literature*, vol. 3, edited by Jeffrey M. Heath (Toronto: Dundurn, 1982), 39; second, William McAlister to David Walsh, 25 May 1831, in *Selected Correspondence of the Glasgow Colonial Society*, edited by Elizabeth Ann Kerr McDougall and John S. Moir (Toronto: Champlain Society, 1994), 39; fourth, Ruth B. Phillips, *Patterns of Power: The Joseph Grant Collection and Great Lakes Indian Art of the Early Nineteenth Century* (Kleinberg, ON: McMichael Canadian Collection, 1984), 17.

23. Burwell quotation: Mary Lee MacDonald, 'The Natural World in Early Nineteenth-Century Canadian Literature', *Canadian Literature* 3 (1986): 53. See also Northrop Frye, 'Conclusion', in *Literary History of Canada*, edited by Carl F. Klinck (Toronto: University of Toronto Press, 1965), 830.

24. Quotation: Norman N. Feltes, *This Side of Heaven: Determining the Donnelly Murders, 1880* (Toronto: University of Toronto Press, 1999), 17–18. See also Good, 'Mississauga-Mennonite Relations', 163–4; John Clarke, *Land, Power, and Economics on the Frontier of Upper Canada* (Montreal: McGill-Queen's University Press, 2001), chapter 1.

25. Quotation: Linda Sabathy-Judd, trans. and ed., *Moravians in Upper Canada: The Diary of the Indian Mission of Fairfield on the Thames, 1792–1813* (Toronto: Champlain Society, 1999), xxxvi. See also Innis, ed., *Mrs Simcoe's Diary*, 24 April 1795; John Mombourquette, 'London Postponed: John Graves Simcoe and His Capital in the Wilderness', in *Simcoe's Choice: Celebrating London's Bicentennial, 1771–1993*, edited by Guy St-Denis (Toronto: Dundurn, 1992), 7.

26. Quotations: Janet Foster, *Working for Wildlife: The Beginning of Preservation in Canada* (Toronto: University of Toronto Press, 1978), 9; Clint Evans, 'The 1865 Canada Thistle Act of Upper Canada as an Expression of a Common Culture of Weeds in Canada and the Northern United States', *Canadian Papers in Rural History* 10 (1996): 138; J. David Wood, *Making Ontario: Agricultural Colonization and Landscape Re-creation before the Railways* (Montreal: McGill-Queen's University Press, 2000), 9, 13. See also Helen E. Parson, 'Reforestation of Agricultural Land in Southern Ontario before 1931', *Ontario History* 86 (1994): 238; R. Peter Gillis, 'The Ottawa Lumber Barons and the Conservation Movement', *Journal of Canadian Studies* 9 (1974): 14–30; Ian and Celina Campbell, 'Pre-European Horticultural Impact on the Forest Landscape and Forest Succession of Southern Ontario, Canada', *Archaeological Notes* (July–August 1993): 13.

27. Quotations: Elaine Theberge, 'Fothergill: Canada's Pioneer Naturalist Emerges from Oblivion', *The Beaver* (1988), 12, 18; Kenneth W. Dance, 'The Pileated Woodpecker in Ontario—Then, Now and Tomorrow', in *Ornithology in Ontario*, edited by Martin K. McNicholl and John L. Cramner-Byng (Whitby, ON: Hawk Owl, 1994), 261–6; Foster, *Working for Wildlife*, 10. See also Kirsten A. Greer, 'Recreational Bird-watching, Empire and Gender in Southern Ontario, 1791–1886', MA thesis (Wilfrid Laurier University, 2001).

28. Quotation: C.J. Houston and W.J. Smyth, 'Geographical Transiency and Social Mobility: The Illustrative Odyssey of Irish Immigrant Wilson Benson, a Well-Known Canadian Unknown', *British Journal of Canadian Studies* 7 (1992): 345–55. See also Michael Katz, *The People of Hamilton, Canada West: Family and Class in a Mid-Nineteenth-Century City* (Cambridge, MA: Harvard University Press, 1975), 94–111.

29. Terry Crowley, 'Rural Labour', in *Labouring Lives: Work and Workers in Nineteenth-Century*

Ontario, edited by Paul Craven (Toronto: University of Toronto Press, 1995), 37; Peter Russell, 'Forest into Farmland: Upper Canadian Clearing Rates, 1822–1839', *Agricultural History* 57 (1983): 326–39; Bruce S. Elliott, *Irish Migrants in the Canadas: A New Approach* (Kingston, ON: McGill-Queen's University Press, 1988), 231, 234; Gordon Darroch and Lee Soltow, *Property and Inequality in Victorian Ontario: Structural Patterns and Cultural Communities in the 1871 Census* (Toronto: University of Toronto Press, 1994).

30. Alan G. Brunger, 'The Geographical Context of English Assisted Emigration to Upper Canada in the Early Nineteenth Century', *British Journal of Canadian Studies* 16 (2002): 9.

31. Quotation: Crowley, 'Rural Labour', 37. See also John C. Walsh, 'Landscapes of Longing: Colonization and the Problem of State Formation in Canada West', PhD dissertation (University of Guelph, 2001), 61.

32. Quotations: Feltes, *This Side of Heaven*, 34–8. See also Michael Wayne, 'The Black Population of Canada West on the Eve of the American Civil War: A Reassessment Based on the Manuscript Census of 1861', *Histoire sociale/Social History* 56 (1995): 465–85. Susanna Moodie, *Roughing It in the Bush*, cited in Lorna R. MacLean, 'Common Criminals, Simple Justice: The Social Construction of Crime in 19th Century Ontario, 1840–1881', PhD dissertation (University of Ottawa, 1996), 147; Jane Rhodes, 'The Contestation over National Identity: Nineteenth-Century Black Americans in Canada', *Canadian Review of American Studies* 30 (2000): 183.

33. McCalla, *Planting the Province*.

34. Quotation: John Moodie to James Traill, 8 March 1836, in *Letters of Love and Duty: The Correspondence of Susanna and John Moodie*, edited by Carl Ballstad, Elizabeth Hopkins, and Michael Peterman (Toronto: University of Toronto, 1993), 53. See also Ian Radforth, 'The Shantymen', in *Labouring Lives*, 204–74; Wood, *Making Ontario*, 13–14.

35. *Selected Correspondence of the Glasgow Colonial Society*, 4.

36. Frank D. Lewis, 'Farm Settlement with Imperfect Capital Markets: A Life Cycle Application to Upper Canada, 1826–1851',

Canadian Journal of Economics 34 (2001): 175–6; Marvin McInnis, 'Marketable Surpluses in Ontario Farming, 1860', *Social Science History* 8 (1984): 395–424; Frank D. Lewis and M.C. Urquhart, 'Growth and the Standard of Living in a Pioneer Economy: Upper Canada, 1826–1851', *William and Mary Quarterly* 51 (1999): 151–81; Darroch and Soltow, *Property and Inequality*; Elliott, *Irish Migrants*, 238.

37. John I. Remple, 'The History and Development of Early Forms of Building Construction in Ontario', *Ontario History* 53 (1961): 10; Kim Ondaatje and Lois Mackenzie, *Old Ontario Houses* (Agincourt, ON: Gage, 1977).

38. Walsh, 'Landscapes of Longing', chapter 5; Elsbeth Heaman, *The Inglorious Arts of Peace: Exhibitions in Canadian Society during the Nineteenth Century* (Toronto: University of Toronto Press, 1999), 141–81.

39. Quotation: Karen Pearlston, '"For the More Easy Recovery of Debts in His Majesty's Plantations": Credit and Conflict in Upper Canada, 1788–1809', M.Laws thesis (University of British Columbia, 1999), 54. See also Lewis, 'Farm Settlement', 183; George Rawlyk and Janice Potter, 'Richard Cartwright', *Dictionary of Canadian Biography*, vol. 5 (Toronto: University of Toronto Press, 1983), 169.

40. Leo A. Johnson, 'Land Policy, Population Growth and Social Structure in the Home District', *Ontario History* 63 (1971): 41–60; David Gagan, 'Property and "Interest": Some Preliminary Evidence of Land Speculation by the Family Compact in Upper Canada, 1820–40', *Ontario History* 70 (1978): 63–70; J. Clarke, 'The Role of Political Position and Family and Economic Linkage on Land Speculation in the Western District of Upper Canada, 1788–95', *Canadian Geographer* 19 (1975): 18–34; J. Clarke, 'Geographical Aspects of Land Speculation in Essex County to 1825: The Strategy of Particular Individuals', in *The Western District: Papers from the Western District Conference*, edited by K.G. Pryke and L.L. Kulisek (Windsor, ON: Essex County Historical Society, 1983), 104–5; Clarke, *Land, Power, and Economics*, 295–424; Crowley, 'Rural Labour', 43.

41. Quotation: Walsh, *Landscapes of Longing*, 150. See also Lillian Gates, *Land Policies of Upper*

Canada (Toronto: University of Toronto Press, 1968), 305; John Clarke, *Land, Power, and Economics*, 157–62; Harring, *White Man's Law*, 35–61; Michelle Vosburgh, 'Bending the Rules: Inspectors and Surveyors and Upper Canada's Land Policies', *Ontario History* 94 (2002): 148–64; David Shanahan, 'Tory Bureaucrat as Victim: The Removal of Samuel Jarvis, 1842–47', *Ontario History* 95 (2003): 45–7; Walsh, *Landscapes of Longing*, 132–4, 149–51.

42. Wood, *Making Ontario*, 96–9.

43. Quotations: David Gagan, *Hopeful Travellers: Family, Land, and Social Change in Mid-Victorian Peel County, Canada West* (Toronto: University of Toronto Press, 1981). See also Crowley, 'Rural Labour', 28; R. Marvin McInnis, 'Perspectives on Ontario Agriculture, 1815–1930,' *Canadian Papers in Rural History* 8 (1992): 56; Lewis and Urquhart, 'Growth and the Standard of Living in a Pioneer Economy', 153; Wood, *Making Ontario*, 96–7.

44. McInnis, 'Perspectives on Ontario Agriculture', 56; Gagan, *Hopeful Travellers*; D.A. Norris, 'Migration, Pioneer, Settlement and the Life Course: The First Families of an Ontario Township', *Canadian Papers in Rural History* 4 (1989).

45. Quotations: *Letters of Love and Duty*, 42, 49, 50; John Carroll, *My Boy's Life* (Toronto, 1882), 212–15.

46. Quotations: John L. Ladell, *They Left Their Mark: Surveyors and Their Role in the Settlement of Ontario* (Toronto: Dundurn, 1993), 85; Shirley J. Yee, 'Gender Ideology and Black Women as Community Builders in Ontario, 1850–1870', *Canadian Historical Review* 75 (1994): 60.

47. Quotations: Janet Floyd, 'Domestication, Domesticity and the Work of Butchery: Positioning the Writing of Colonial Housework', *Women's History Review* 11 (2002): 402; Helen E.H. Smith and Lisa M. Sullivan, '"Now That I Know How to Manage": Work and Identity in the Journals of Anne Langton', *Ontario History* 87 (1995): 257; Sean W. Gouglas, 'A Currant Affair: E.D. Smith and Agricultural Change in Nineteenth-Century Saltfleet Township, Ontario', *Agricultural History* 75 (2001): 444. See also Marjorie Griffin Cohen, *Women's Work, Markets, and Economic Development in Nineteenth-Century Ontario* (Toronto: University of Toronto Press, 1988); Margaret Derry, 'Patterns of Gendered Labour and the Development of Ontario Agriculture', in *Ontario Since Confederation: A Reader*, edited by Edgar-André Montigny and Lori Chambers (Toronto: University of Toronto Press, 2000), 3–15.

48. Quotations: Robynne Rogers Healy, ed., 'Sarah Welch Diary', in *The Small Details of Life: Twenty Diaries by Women in Canada, 1830–1996*, edited by Kathryn Carter (Toronto: University of Toronto Press, 2002), 57–94; Helen M. Buss, 'Women and the Garrison Mentality: Pioneer Women Autobiographers and Their Relation to the Land', in *Re(dis)covering Our Foremothers: Nineteenth-Century Canadian Women Writers*, edited by Lorraine McMullen (Ottawa: University of Ottawa Press, 1990), 128; E. Jane Errington, *Wives and Mothers, Schoolmistresses and Scullery Maids: Working Women in Upper Canada, 1790–1840* (Montreal: McGill-Queen's University Press, 1995).

49. *Selected Correspondence of the Glasgow Colonial Society*, 40, 124; Robert Summerby-Murray, 'Statute Labour on Ontario Township Roads, 1849–1948: Responding to a Changing Space Economy', *Canadian Geographer* 43 (1999): 36–52; T.F. McIlwraith, 'The Adequacy of Rural Roads in the Era before Railways: An Illustration from Upper Canada', *Canadian Geographer* 14 (1970): 344–59; Wood, *Making Ontario*, 121.

50. Wendy Cameron, 'Defining Opportunity from Below: Assisted English Immigrants in 1830s' Upper Canada', *British Journal of Canadian Studies* 16 (2003): 50.

51. Susanna Moodie to John Moodie, 11 January 1839, in *Letters of Love and Duty*, 114.

52. MacLean, 'Common Criminals', chapters 2 and 4.

53. Quotation: Lynne Marks, 'Railing, Tattling and General Rumours: Group, Gender and Church Regulation in Upper Canada', *Canadian Historical Review* 81 (2000): 380–402.

54. Quotation: Susan Lewthwaite, 'Violence, Law and Community in Rural Upper Canada', in *Crime and Criminal Justice*, edited by Jim Phillips, Tina Loo, and Susan Lewthwaite (Toronto: Osgoode Society,

1994), 353–86.

55. Quotation: Lewthwaite, 'Violence, Law and Community'. See also Crowley, 'Rural Labour', 31.

56. Quotation: Margaret E. Turner, 'Language and Silence in Richardson and Grove', in *Future Indicative: Literary Theory and Canadian Literature*, edited by John Moss (Ottawa: University of Ottawa Press, 1987), 189. See also Dennis Duffy, *Gardens, Covenants, Exiles: Loyalism in the Literature of Upper Canada/Ontario* (Toronto: University of Toronto Press, 1982), chapter 3.

57 Charles R. Steele, 'Major John Richardson', in *Profiles in Canadian Literature*, vol. 3, 46; Ruth McKendry, *Quilts and Other Bed Coverings in the Canadian Tradition* (Toronto: Van Nostrand Reinhold, 1979); M.S. Biad, 'When Furniture Becomes Folk Art', *Canadian Collector*, s/o (1982), 46–50.

58. *Letters of Love and Duty*, 157–9.

59. Gordon Darroch, 'Class in Nineteenth-Century, Central Ontario: A Reassessment of the Crisis and Demise of Small Producers during Early Industrialization, 1861–1871', *Canadian Journal of Sociology* 13 (1988): 49–74.

60. Quotation: Lewthwaite, 'Violence, Law', 384n73; Crowley, 'Rural Labour', 100n239. See also Gordon Darroch, 'Migrants in the Nineteenth Century: Fugitives or Families in Motion?' *Journal of Family History* 6 (1981): 257–77.

Chapter 6: Place, Power, and Polity: The Emergence of Upper Canada and the Canadian Confederation, 1791–1867

1. For a useful survey of this literature up to 1990, see Colin Read, 'Conflict to Consensus: The Political Culture of Upper Canada', *Acadiensis* 19 (1990): 169–84. Wise's work is available in A.B. McKillop and Paul Romney, eds, *God's Peculiar Peoples: Essays on Political Culture in Nineteenth-Century Canada* (Ottawa: Carleton University Press, 1993). For related work that builds on, extends, and qualifies Wise's insights, see Jane Errington, *The Lion, the Eagle, and Upper Canada: A Developing Colonial Ideology* (Kingston: McGill-Queen's University Press, 1987); David Mills, *The Idea of Loyalty in Upper Canada, 1784–1850* (Kingston: McGill-Queen's University Press, 1988); Curtis Fahey, *In His Name: The Anglican Experience in Upper Canada, 1791–1854* (Ottawa: Carleton University Press, 1991).

2. Quotation: Jeffrey McNairn, *The Capacity to Judge: Public Opinion and Deliberative Democracy in Upper Canada, 1791–1854* (Toronto: University of Toronto Press, 2000), 11. See also Heather Murray, *Come, Bright Improvement! The Literary Societies of Nineteenth-Century Ontario* (Toronto: University of Toronto Press, 2002).

3. Carol Wilton, *Popular Politics and Political Culture in Upper Canada, 1800–1850* (Montreal: McGill-Queen's University Press, 2000); Paul Romney, *Mr Attorney: The Attorney General for Ontario in Court, Cabinet, and Legislature, 1791–1899* (Toronto: Osgoode Society, 1986); Bruce Curtis, *Building the Educational State: Canada West, 1836–1871* (London, ON: Althouse, 1988); Bruce Curtis, *True Government by Choice Men? Inspection, Education, and State Formation in Canada West* (Toronto: University of Toronto Press, 1992); Allan Greer and Ian Radforth, eds, *Colonial Leviathan: State Formation in Mid-Nineteenth-Century Canada* (Toronto: University of Toronto Press, 1992). On the importance of patronage, see S.J.R. Noel, *Patrons, Clients, Brokers: Ontario Society and Politics, 1791–1896* (Toronto: University of Toronto Press, 1990). On the prevalence of self-interest, see Errington, *The Lion, the Eagle*, 10.

4. Quotation: Edith Firth, ed., *The Town of York, 1793–1815* (Toronto: Champlain Society, 1962), 22. See also E.A. Cruikshank, ed., *The Correspondence of Lieutenant Governor John Graves Simcoe and Allied Documents Relating to His Administration of the Government of Upper Canada*, vol. 1 (Toronto: Champlain Society, 1923).

5. Bruce G. Wilson, *The Enterprises of Robert Hamilton: A Study of Wealth and Influence in Early Upper Canada, 1776–1812* (Ottawa: Carleton University Press, 1983); Doug McCalla, *Planting the Province: The Economic History of Upper Canada, 1784–1870* (Toronto: University of Toronto Press, 1993).

6. Errington, *The Lion, the Eagle*.

7. Quotation: Katherine McKenna, *A Life of Propriety: Anne Murray Powell and Her Family,*

1755–1849 (Montreal: McGill-Queen's University Press, 1994). See also Robin Winks, *The Blacks in Canada: A History* (Montreal: McGill-Queen's University Press, 1971), 33–4; Katherine McKenna, 'The Role of Women in the Establishment of Social Status in Early Upper Canada', *Ontario History* 83 (1990), 180.

8. Robert J. Burns, 'God's Chosen People: The Origin of Toronto Society', *Historical Papers* (1973), 213–29.

9. Wilson, *The Enterprises of Robert Hamilton*, chapter 11; McCalla, *Planting the Province*.

10. William M.T. Wylie, 'Instruments of Commerce and Authority: The Civil Courts in Upper Canada, 1789–1812', in *Essays in the History of Canadian Law*, vol. 2, edited by David Flaherty (Toronto: Osgoode Society, 1983), 3–48; Wilson, *The Enterprises of Robert Hamilton*, 106; Sid Noel, 'Early Populist Tendencies in the Ontario Political Culture', *Ontario History* 90 (1998), 173–87; S.R. Mealing, 'David W. Smith', *Dictionary of Canadian Biography*, vol. 7 (Toronto: University of Toronto Press, 1988), 811–13.

11. Quotations: J.B. Walton, 'An End to All Order: A Study of Upper Canadian Response to Opposition, 1805–10', MA thesis (Queen's University, 1977). See also G.H. Patterson, 'William Weekes', and E.H. Jones, 'Joseph Willcocks', *Dictionary of Canadian Biography*, vol. 5 (Toronto: University of Toronto Press, 1983).

12. Wilton, *Popular Politics*, 25–7; McNairn, *The Capacity to Judge*, 157; Robert L. Fraser, '"All the Privileges which Englishmen Possess": Order, Rights and Constitutionalism in Upper Canada', in *Provincial Justice: Upper Canadian Legal Portraits from the 'Dictionary of Canadian Biography'*, edited by Robert L. Fraser (Toronto: Osgoode Society, 1992), xxi–xcii; John McLaren, 'The King, the People, the Law . . . and the Constitution: Justice Robert Thorpe and the Roots of Irish Whig Ideology in Early Upper Canada', in *People and Place: Historical Influences on Legal Culture*, edited by Jonathan Swainger and Constance Backhouse (Vancouver: UBC Press, 2003), 11–24.

13. Quotation: George Rawlyk, *The Canada Fire: Radical Evangelicalism in British North America, 1775–1812* (Kingston, ON: McGill-Queen's University Press, 1994).

14. Quotations: Ibid.

15. Quotations: Ibid.; Nancy J. Christie, '"In These Times of Democratic Rage and Delusion": Popular Religion and the Challenge to the Established Order, 1760–1812', in *The Canadian Protestant Experience, 1760 to 1990*, edited by G.A. Rawlyk (Montreal: McGill-Queen's University Press, 1994).

16. Quotation: Brian Osborne and Donald Swainson, *Kingston: Building on the Past* (Westport, ON: Butternut, 1988), 49. See also George Sheppard, *Plunder, Profit, and Paroles: A Social History of the War of 1812 in Upper Canada* (Montreal: McGill-Queen's University Press, 1994).

17. Carl Benn, *The Iroquois in the War of 1812* (Toronto: University of Toronto Press, 1998).

18. Sheppard, *Plunder, Profit, and Paroles*; Osborne and Swainson, *Kingston*, 53.

19. Errington, *The Lion, the Eagles*; Mills, *The Idea of Loyalty*.

20. Quotation: Peter Oliver, 'Power, Politics and the Law: The Place of the Judiciary in the Historiography of Upper Canada', in *Essays in the History of Canadian Law: In the Honour of R.C.B. Risk*, vol. 8, edited by G. Blaine Baker and Jim Phillips (Toronto: Osgoode Society, 1999), 449. See also Barry Wright, '"Harshness and Forbearance": The Politics of Pardons and the Upper Canadian Rebellion', in *Qualities of Mercy: Justice, Punishment, and Discretion*, edited by Carolyn Strange (Vancouver: UBC Press, 1996), 77–103; R.J. Morgan and R.L. Fraser, 'Sir William Campbell', *Dictionary of Canadian Biography*, vol. 6 (Toronto: University of Toronto Press, 1987), 113–18; John C. Weaver, *Crimes, Constables, and Courts: Order and Transgression in a Canadian City, 1816–1970* (Montreal: McGill-Queen's University Press, 1995), 24–5.

21. Fahey, *In His Name*.

22. Elwood Jones, 'The Franchise in Upper Canada, 1792–1867', paper presented to the Canadian Historical Association, 1986.

23. Wilton, *Popular Politics*, 27–36; Barry Wright, 'Sedition in Upper Canada: Contested Legality', *Labour/Le travail* 29 (1992): 7–57.

24. Romney, *Mr Attorney*.

25. John Carroll, *My Boy's Life* (Toronto, 1882).

26. Paul Romney, 'From the Types Riot to the Rebellion: Elite Ideology, Anti-Legal

Sentiment, Political Violence and the Rule of Law in Upper Canada', *Ontario History* 76 (1987): 113–44.

27. Quotations: Susan E. Houston, 'The Role of the Criminal Law in Redefining "Youth" in Mid-Nineteenth-Century Upper Canada', *Historical Studies in Education/Revue d'histoire de l'education* 6 (1994): 44.

28. Quotation: S.E.D. Shortt, 'The Canadian Hospital in the Nineteenth Century: An Historiographical Lament', *Journal of Canadian Studies* 18 (1983–4): 3–14. See also C.J. Taylor, 'The Kingston, Ontario Penitentiary and Moral Architecture', *Histoire sociale/Social History* 12 (1979): 385–408; William J. Patterson, 'Surviving for 130 Years in a Male-Dominated Prison: Women in the Kingston Penitentiary, 1835–1965', *Historic Kingston* 50 (2002): 88–105; Tom Brown, 'The Origins of the Asylum in Upper Canada, 1830–39', *Canadian Bulletin of Medical History* 1 (1984): 37–58.

29. Wilton, *Popular Politics*.

30. Ibid.; McNairn, *The Capacity to Judge*.

31. Quotations: Wilton, *Popular Politics*, 124.

32. Christopher Adamson, 'God's Continent Divided: Politics and Religion in Upper Canada and the Northern and Western United States, 1775 to 1841', *Comparative Studies in Society and History* 36 (1994): 417–46.

33. R.D. Gidney, 'Egerton Ryerson', *Dictionary of Canadian Biography*, XI, 1982.

34. Michael Gauvreau, 'Covenanter Democracy: Scottish Popular Religion, Ethnicity, and the Varieties of Politico-Religious Dissent in Upper Canada, 1815–1841', *Histoire sociale/Social History* 36 (2003): 55–84; Paul Romney, 'On the Eve of the Rebellion: Nationality, Religion and Class in the Toronto Election of 1836', in *Old Ontario: Essays in Jonour of J.M.S. Careless*, edited by David Keane and Colin Read (Toronto: Dundurn, 1990), 192–216.

35. Carol Wilton, '"Lawless Law": Conservative Political Violence in Upper Canada, 1818–41', *Law and History Review* 13 (1995): 124.

36. Quotation: Colin Read and Ronald J. Stagg, eds, *The Rebellion of 1837 in Upper Canada* (Toronto: Champlain Society, 1985). See also Rhonda Telford, 'The Central Ontario Anishinabe and the Rebellion, 1830–40', in

Papers of the 28th Algonquin Conference, edited by David H. Pentland (Winnipeg: University of Manitoba, 1997), 552–70.

37. Quotation: Gauvreau, 'Covenanter Democracy'. See also Read and Stagg, *The Rebellion*.

38. Wilton, *Popular Politics*, 191; but see Wright, 'The Politics of Pardons', 96.

39. W. Thomas Matthews, 'Local Government and the Regulation of the Public Market in Upper Canada, 1800–1860: The Moral Economy of the Poor?' *Ontario History* 79 (1987): 297–326.

40. Peter Baskerville, ed., *The Bank of Upper Canada* (Toronto: Champlain Society, 1987).

41. Calculated from data in J.K. Johnson, *Becoming Prominent: Regional Leadership in Upper Canada, 1791–1841* (Kingston, ON: McGill-Queen's University Press, 1989).

42. Irving Abella, 'The Sydenham Election of 1841', *Canadian Historical Review* 47 (1966): 326–43.

43. Quotations: Mary Larrett Smith, ed., *Young Mr Smith in Upper Canada* (Toronto: University of Toronto Press, 1980), 131.

44. Quotation: Michael Gauvreau, 'Reluctant Voluntaries: Peter and George Brown; The Scottish Disruption and the Politics of Church and State in Canada', *The Journal of Religious History* 25 (2001): 152. See also Kenneth C. Dewar, *Charles Clarke, Pen and Ink Warrior* (Montreal: McGill-Queen's University Press, 2001), 101–5.

45. Paul Craven and Tom Traves, 'Canadian Railways as Manufacturers, 1850–1880', *Historical Papers* (1983): 254–81.

46. Quotations: Peter Baskerville, 'Sir Allan Napier MacNab', *Dictionary of Canadian Biography*, vol. 9; McDougall to Clarke, 17 September 1853, Charles Clarke Papers, Ontario Archives.

47. Amelia Ryerse Harris, Diary, 16 February 1859, in *The Eldon House Diaries: Five Women's Views of the 19th Century*, edited by Robin S. Harris and Terry G. Harris (Toronto: Champlain Society, 1998), 92.

48. Quotations: John Rose to Thomas Baring, Baring Brothers Papers, National Archives of Canada (NA), 4; Lydia Payne to J. Browne, September 1866, RG 19, file 9, C1, NA, 1181. See also Michael Piva, *The Borrowing Process: Public Finance in the Province of Canada, 1840–1867* (Ottawa: University of Ottawa

49. Weaver, *Crimes, Constables, and Courts*; Houston, 'The Role of the Criminal Law', 54.

50. William Westfall, *Two Worlds: The Protestant Culture of Nineteenth-Century Ontario* (Kingston, ON: McGill-Queen's University Press, 1989).

51. Quotation: Colin D. Pearce, 'Egerton Ryerson's Canadian Liberalism', *Canadian Journal of Political Science* 21 (1988): 783. See also Bernd Baldus and Meenaz Kassam, '"Make Me Truthful, Good, and Mild": Values in Nineteenth-Century Ontario Schoolbooks', *Canadian Journal of Sociology* 21 (1996): 335.

52. Quotations: Julie Mathien, 'Children, Families and Institutions in Late Nineteenth and Early Twentieth Century Ontario', MA thesis (Ontario Institute for Studies in Education, 2001), 8; Baldus and Kassam, 'Make Me Truthful', 339. See also Robert Gidney and W.P.J. Millar, 'From Voluntarism to State Schooling: The Creation of the Public School System in Ontario', *Canadian Historical Review* 66 (1985): 443–73; Bruce Curtis, '"Littery Merrit", "Useful Knowledge": The Organization of Township Libraries in Canada West, 1840–1860', *Ontario History* 78 (1986): 285–311.

53. Bruce Curtis, 'Selective Publicity and Informed Public Opinion in the Canadas, 1841–1856', *History of Education Review* 27 (1998): 1–18.

54. Quotation: J.M.S. Careless, *Brown of the Globe*, vol. 1 (Toronto: Macmillan, 1959).

55. Charles Robertson, Secretary, Toronto Board of Trade, to Galt, 3 February 1859, Galt Papers, MG 27 I D 8, vol. 1, NA.

56. E.J. Charleton to Galt, 20 February 1859, Galt Papers, MG 27 I D 8, vol. 1, NA.

57. Careless, *Brown of the Globe*, vol. 1 315.

58. Brydges to Macdonald, 22 February 1864 and 24 February 1864, Macdonald Papers, M.G. 26 A 1 B 191, NA. I wish to thank Michael Piva for sharing his insights into and sources on the significance of trade matters, especially the importance of the 'two-market' policy, and Brown's feelings on that issue, in the context of the Confederation movement. See also Piva, *The Borrowing Process*.

59. Quotation: B.W. Hodgins, 'Democracy and the Fathers of Confederation', in *Profiles of a Province: Studies in the History of Ontario*, edited by E.G. Firth (Toronto: Ontario Historical Society, 1967), 83–91.

60. Quotations: Ibid.; Norman D. Shields, 'Anishinabek Political Alliance in the Post-Confederation Period: The Grand General Indian Council of Ontario, 1870–1936', MA thesis (Queen's University, 2001).

61. Quotation: Hodgins, 'Democracy and the Fathers of Confederation'.

62. P.B. Waite, *The Charlottetown Conference*, Historical Booklet 15 (Ottawa: Canadian Historical Association, 1963), 12–13.

63. Paul Romney, 'Sir Oliver Mowat', *Dictionary of Canadian Biography*, vol. 13 (Toronto: University of Toronto Press, 1994), 728.

64. Phil Buckwer, 'The Maritimes and Confederation: A Reassessment', *Canadian Historical Review* 71 (1990): 1–45.

65. Quotation: J.M.S. Careless, *Brown of the Globe*, vol. 2 (Toronto: Macmillan, 1963).

66. P.B. Waite, *The Life and Times of Confederation, 1864–1867: Politics, Newspapers and the Union of British North America* (Toronto: University of Toronto Press, 1962), 123.

Chapter 7: Ontario in the New Dominion, 1867–1905

1. Quotations: Joseph Schull, *Edward Blake: The Man of the Other Way, 1833–1881* (Toronto: Macmillan, 1975); Douglas Owram, *The Promise of Eden: The Canadian Expansionist Movement and the Idea of the West, 1856–1900* (Toronto: University of Toronto Press, 1980).

2. Quotation: S.J.R. Noel, 'Oliver Mowat: Patronage and Party Building', in *Ontario since Confederation: A Reader*, edited by Edgar-André Montigny and Lori Chambers (Toronto: University of Toronto Press, 2000), 94.

3. S.J.R. Noel, *Patrons, Clients, Brokers: Ontario Society and Politics, 1791–1896* (Toronto: University of Toronto Press, 1990), 253–6; Peter E.P. Demski, 'Political History from the Opposition Benches: William Ralph Meredith, Ontario Federalist', *Ontario History* 89 (1997): 199–217.

4. Noel, *Patrons, Clients, Brokers*, 260.

5. Sidney L. Harring, *White Man's Law: Native People in Nineteenth-Century Jurisprudence* (Toronto: Osgoode Society, 1998), chapter 6;

A. Margaret Evans, *Sir Oliver Mowat* (Toronto: University of Toronto Press, 1992), 174–5.

6. Quotation: Kathi Avery Kinew, 'Manito Gitigaan: Governance in the Great Spirit's Garden Wild Rice in Treaty #3 from Pre-Treaty to the 1990s', in *Papers of the Twenty-Sixth Algonquian Conference*, edited by David H. Pentland (Winnipeg: University of Manitoba, 1995), 183–94. Information on the Boundary and St Catharine's cases is drawn from Evans, *Sir Oliver Mowat*; Noel, *Patrons, Clients, Brokers*; Harring, *White Man's Law*; Donald B. Smith, 'Aboriginal Rights a Century Ago', *The Beaver* 67, no. 1 (1987): 4–15.

7. Quotation: Noel, *Patrons, Clients, Brokers*, 263. See also Paul Romney, 'Sir Oliver Mowat', *Dictionary of Canadian Biography*, vol. 13 (Toronto: University of Toronto Press, 1994), 724–42.

8. Romney, 'Oliver Mowat'; Noel, *Patrons, Clients, Brokers*.

9. Quotations: Joseph Schull, *Laurier: The First Canadian* (Toronto: Macmillan, 1965), 178; *The P.P.A. in Ontario, History and Principles of the Organization* (n.d.), cited in James T. Watt, 'The Protestant Protective Association of Canada: An Example of Religious Extremism in Ontario in the 1890s', in *Canadian History since Confederation: Essays and Interpretation*, edited by Bruce Hodgins and Robert Page (Georgetown, ON: Irwin-Dorsey, 1972), 248. See also Paul-André Linteau, René Durocher, and Jean-Claude Robert, *Quebec: A History*, translated by Robert Chodos (Toronto: Lorimer, 1983), 250–1.

10. Quotation: Mark McGowan, *The Waning of the Green: Catholics, the Irish, and Identity in Toronto, 1887–1922* (Montreal: McGill-Queen's University Press, 1999), 61 (my italics). See also Peter Baskerville, 'Did Religion Matter? Religion and Wealth in Urban Canada at the Turn of the Twentieth Century', *Histoire sociale/Social History* 67 (2001), 61–96; Robert Choquette, *Language and Religion: A History of English-French Conflict in Ontario* (Ottawa: University of Ottawa Press, 1975).

11. Financing data: Livio Di Matteo, 'Fiscal Imbalance and Economic Development in Canadian History: Evidence from the Eco-nomic History of Ontario', *American Review of Canadian Studies* 29 (1999), 306.

12. 'Terms of trade' measure the export price as a percentage of import price. See *Historical Statistics of Canada*, Series G386-388.

13. Quotations: Robert L. Jones, *History of Agriculture in Ontario, 1613–1880* (Toronto: University of Toronto Press, 1946), 248, 254, 261. See also D. Lawr, 'The Development of Ontario Agriculture, 1870–1914: Patterns of Growth and Change', *Ontario History* 64 (1972): 239–51

14. Quotation: Randy Willis, *With Scarcely a Ripple: Anglo-Canadian Migration into the United States and Western Canada, 1880–1920* (Montreal: McGill-Queen's University Press, 1998), 114. See also ibid., chapters 3, 4.

15. Quotation: Noel, *Patrons, Clients, Brokers*, 263. Agricultural statistics: W. Robert Wightman and Nancy M. Wightman, *The Land Between: Northwestern Ontario Resource Development, 1800 to the 1990s* (Toronto: University of Toronto Press, 1997), table 2.1, 71.

16. Quotation: Evans, *Oliver Mowat*, 283. The classic work on this aspect of development is H.V. Nelles, *The Politics of Development: Forests, Mines and Hydro-Electric Development in Ontario, 1849–1941* (Toronto: Macmillan, 1974). See also Di Matteo, 'Fiscal Imbalance'; Noel, *Patrons, Clients, Brokers*, 268.

17. Quotation: Di Matteo, 'Fiscal Imbalance', 287. Di Matteo provides estimates for decennial census years for this period. He claims these years to be standard, that is, not exceptional in terms of income. Accordingly, for the purposes of the estimation in the text, I have assumed that the net income for the first five years in each decade was the same as that of the first census year (for the 1880s, that would be 1881), and for the last five years, the same as the second census date (for the 1880s, that would be 1891).

18. Quotation: R. Peter Gillis and T.R. Roach, *Lost Initiatives: Canada's Forest Industries, Forest Policy and Forest Conservation* (New York: Greenwood, 1986), 43. See also Di Matteo, 'Fiscal Imbalance', 310–11. On northern lumberers, see Wightman and Wightman, *The Land Between*, 124–5. For Arbor Day, see D. Diamantakos, 'Private Property Deforestation and the Clerk of the Forestry in 19th Century Ontario', *Scientia canadensis* 21

(1997): 29–48. For tourism in the north, see Patricia Jansen, *Wild Things: Nature, Culture, and Tourism in Ontario, 1870–1914* (Toronto: University of Toronto Press, 1995).

19. Quotations: Dianne Newell, *Technology on the Frontier: Mining in Old Ontario* (Vancouver: University of British Columbia Press, 1986), 77–89. See also Craig Heron, 'Factory Workers', in *Labouring Lives: Work and Workers in Nineteenth-Century Ontario*, edited by Paul Craven (Toronto: University of Toronto Press, 1995), 480; C.M. Wallace, 'The 1880s', in *Sudbury: Rail Town to Regional Capital*, edited by C.M. Wallace and Ashley Thomson (Toronto: Dundurn, 1993), 11–32; Eileen Goltz, 'A Corporate View of Housing and Community in a Company Town: Copper Cliff, 1886–1920', *Ontario History* 82 (1990): 29–51.

20. Quotation: Heather Menzies, 'Technology in the Craft of Ontario Cheese Making: Women in Oxford County circa 1860', *Ontario History* 87 (1995): 293–304. See also Terry Crowley, 'Rural Labour', in *Labouring Lives*, 55–7; Terry Crowley, 'Experience and Representation: Southern Ontario Farm Women and Agricultural Change, 1870–1914', *Agricultural History* 73 (1999): 238–51; M.J. Thompson, 'A Whey with Cheese', *This Country Canada* 6 (1994): 69–72.

21. Quotations in the last three paragraphs: Margaret Derry, 'Gender Conflicts in Dairying: Ontario's Butter Industry, 1880–1920', *Ontario History* 90 (1998): 31–47. See also Margaret Derry, 'Patterns of Gendered Labour and the Development of Ontario Agriculture', in *Ontario since Confederation*, 3–15.

22. Quotation: Christina Burr, 'The Rhetoric of Labour Reform in Toronto during the 1870s', in *Ontario since Confederation*, 61.

23. Quotations: Peter Baskerville and Eric Sager, *Unwilling Idlers: The Urban Unemployed and Their Families in Late Victorian Canada* (Toronto: University of Toronto Press, 1998).

24. Quotations: Toronto *Globe*, 26 February 1894; all other quotations in this section are from Baskerville and Sager, *Unwilling Idlers*, chapter 4.

25. The information in the last six paragraphs is drawn mainly from Baskerville and Sager, *Unwilling Idlers*, chapters 6 and 7. See also John Bullen, 'Hidden Workers: Child Labour

and the Family Economy in Late Nineteenth-Century Urban Ontario', *Labour/Le travail* 18 (1986): 163–88.

26. Gregory Kealey and Brian Palmer, *Dreaming of What Might Be: The Knights of Labor in Ontario, 1880–1900* (Cambridge: Cambridge University Press, 1982).

27. Quotations in last two paragraphs from Gerald Tulchinsky, 'Hidden among the Smokestacks: Toronto's Clothing Industry, 1871–1901', in *Old Ontario: Essays in Honour of J.M.S. Careless*, edited by David Keane and Colin Read (Toronto: Dundurn, 1990), 257–84; Robert McIntosh, 'Sweated Labour: Female Needleworkers in Industrializing Canada', *Labour/Le travail* 32 (1993), 105–38. See also Christina Burr, '"Defending the Art Preservative": Craft and Gender Relations in the Printing Trades Unions, 1850–1914', *Labour/Le travail* 27 (1991), 47–73.

28. Quotation: Thomas Conant, *Upper Canada Sketches* (Toronto, 1898), 195. Lynne Marks, *Revivals and Roller Rinks: Religion, Leisure and Identity in Late-Nineteenth-Century Small-Town Ontario* (Toronto: University of Toronto Press, 1996): 58; Andrew C. Holman, 'Manners and Morals in Victorian Ontario', in *Ontario since Confederation*, 108–9.

29. Edgar-André Montigny, *Foisted upon the Government? State Responsibilities, Family Obligations and the Care of the Dependent Aged in Late Nineteenth-Century Ontario* (Montreal: McGill-Queen's University Press, 1997), esp. chapter 5; Stormie Stewart, 'The Elderly Poor in Rural Ontario: Inmates of the Wellington County House of Industry, 1877–1907', *Journal of the Canadian Historical Association*, n.s., 3 (1992): 217–34; Richard Splane, *Social Welfare in Ontario: A Study of Public Welfare Administration* (Toronto: University of Toronto Press, 1965).

30. Quotations: Peter Oliver, '"A Terror to Evil Doers": The Central Prison and the "Criminal Class" in Late Nineteenth Century Ontario', in *Patterns of the Past: Interpreting Ontario's History*, edited by Roger Hall, William Westfall, and Laura Sefton MacDowall (Toronto: Dundurn, 1988), 206–37.

31. Peter Oliver, '"To Govern by Kindness": The First Two Decades of the Mercer Reformatory for Women', in *Essays in the History of Canadian Law: Crime and Criminal Justice*, edited by Jim Phillips, Tina Loo, and Susan

Lewthwaite (Toronto: Osgoode Society, 1994), 516–72. See also Carolyn Strange, '"The Criminal and Fallen of Their Sex": The Establishment of Canada's First Women's Prison, 1874–1901', *Canadian Journal of Women and the Law* 1 (1985), 79–92.

32. Harring, *White Man's Law*, 159–64.

33. Anna H. Lathrop, 'Contested Terrain: Gender and "Movement" in Ontario Elementary Physical Education, 1940–70', *Ontario History* 94 (2002): 165; Marks, *Revivals and Roller Rinks*; Tony Joyce, 'Canadian Sport and State Control: Toronto, 1845–1886', *International Journal of the History of Sport* 16 (1999): 22–37.

34. Quotations: Bernd Baldus and Meenaz Kassam, '"Make Me Truthful, Good, and Mild": Values in Nineteenth-Century Ontario Schoolbooks', *Canadian Journal of Sociology* 21 (1996): 340, 349. See also Colin McFarquhar, 'A Difference of Perspective: Blacks, Whites and Emancipation Day Celebrations in Ontario, 1865–1919', *Ontario History* 92 (2000): 147–60.

35. Quotation: Craig Heron, 'The High School and the Household Economy in Working-Class Hamilton, 1890–1940', *Historical Studies in Education/Revue d'histoire de l'education* 7 (1995): 221. See also Gordon Darroch, 'Families, Fostering and Flying the Coop: Normalization, Contradiction and Counterpoints in the Formation of Canadian Liberal Culture, 1871 and 1901', unpublished paper (2003).

36. Quotation: Chad Gaffield and Gerard Bouchard, 'Literacy, Schooling and Family Reproduction in Rural Ontario and Quebec', *Historical Studies in Education/Revue d'histoire de l'education* 1 (1989): 201–18. See also Michael Katz and Ian Davey, 'Youth and Early Industrialization in a Canadian City', *American Journal of Sociology* 84 (1978), 81–100; Andrew C. Holman, *A Sense of Their Duty: Middle-Class Formation in Victorian Ontario Towns* (Montreal: McGill-Queen's University Press, 2000), 152, 210, and chapter 6; Gordon Darroch, 'Scanty Fortunes and Rural Middle-Class Formation in Nineteenth-Century Central Ontario', *Canadian Historical Review* 79 (1998): 621–59; R.D. Gidney and W.P.J. Millar, *Inventing Secondary Education: The Rise of the High School in Nineteenth-Century Ontario* (Kingston, ON:

McGill-Queen's University Press, 1990).

37. Alison Prentice, 'The Feminization of Teaching', in *The Neglected Majority: Essays in Canadian Women's History*, edited by Susan Mann Trofimenkoff and Alison Prentice (Toronto: McClelland and Stewart, 1977), 49–65; Bruce Curtis, '"Illicit" Sexuality and Public Education in Ontario, 1840–1907', *Historical Studies in Education/Revue d'histoire de l'education* 1 (1989): 73–94.

38. Holman, *A Sense of Their Duty*, 98, 11, 129, 153–5.

39. The last two paragraphs are based on Peter Baskerville, 'Women and Investment in Late-Nineteenth-Century Urban Canada: Victoria and Hamilton, 1880–1901', *Canadian Historical Review* 80 (1999): 191–218; Peter Baskerville, 'Gender, Family and Self-Employment in Urban Canada, 1901 and 1996', paper presented at Canadian Business History Conference, McMaster University, 1998; Sue Ingram and Kris Inwood, 'Property Ownership by Married Women in Victorian Ontario', *Dalhousie Law Journal* 23 (2000): 404–39; Lori Chambers, *Married Women and Property Law in Victorian Ontario* (Toronto: Osgoode Society, 1997).

40. Quotation: Sharon Anne Cook, *'Through Sunshine and Shadow': The Women's Christian Temperance Union, Evangelicalism, and Reform in Ontario, 1874–1930* (Montreal: McGill-Queen's University Press, 1995); Lynne Marks, *Revivals and Roller Rinks*, 95–101. See also Carol Lee Bacchi, *Liberation Deferred? The Ideas of the English-Canadian Suffragists, 1877–1918* (Toronto: University of Toronto Press, 1983), 69, 85.

41. Quotation: M.P. Sendbuehler, 'Battling "the Bane of our Cities": Class, Territory and the Prohibition Debate in Toronto, 1877', *Urban History Review* 22 (1993): 32–3.

42. Quotation: *Globe and Mail*, 9 October 1996, cited in Anna Lee Lepp, 'Dis/Membering the Family: Marital Breakdown, Domestic Conflict, and Family Violence in Ontario, 1830–1920', PhD dissertation (Queen's University, 2001), 570–1. See also Julie Mathien, 'Children, Families and Institutions in Late Nineteenth and Early Twentieth-Century Ontario', MA thesis (Ontario Institute for Studies in Education, 2001), 19–20.

43. Annalee Golz, '"If a Man's Wife Does Not Obey Him, What Can He Do?" Marital

Breakdown and Wife Abuse in Late Nineteenth-Century and Early Twentieth Century Ontario', in *Law, Society, and the State: Essays in Modern Legal History*, edited by Louis A. Knafla and Susan W.S. Binnie (Toronto: University of Toronto Press, 1995), 323–50; Bernadine Dodge, '"Let the Record Show": Women and Law in the United Counties of Durham and Northumberland, 1845–1895', *Ontario History* 92 (2000): 127–45; Lorna McLean, '"Deserving" Wives and "Drunken" Husbands: Wife Beating, Marital Conduct and the Law in Ontario', *Histoire sociale/Social History* 35 (2002): 59–81; Lori Chambers and John Weaver, 'Alimony and Orders of Protection: Escaping Abuse in Hamilton-Wentworth, 1837–1900', *Ontario History* 95 (2003): 113–35.

44. Quotations: Ashley Thomson, 'The 1890's', in *Sudbury*, 39; Baskerville and Sager, *Unwilling Idlers*. See also Lorna Ruth McLean, 'Home, Yard and Neighbourhood: Women's Work and the Urban Working-Class Family Economy', MA thesis (University of Ottawa, 1990), 60–8, 74–6.

45. Quotation: Jamie Benidickson, 'Ontario Water Quality, Public Health, and the Law, 1880–1930', in *Essays in the History of Canadian Law in the Honour of R.C.B. Risk*, vol. 8, edited by G. Blaine Baker and Jim Phillips (Toronto: Osgoode Society, 1999), 115.

46. Quotations: Colleen MacNaughton, 'Promoting Clean Water in Nineteenth-Century Public Policy: Professors, Preachers and Polliwogs in Kingston, Ontario', *Histoire sociale/Social History* 32 (1999): 51; Heather A. MacDougall, 'The Genesis of Public Health Reform in Toronto, 1869–1890', *Urban History Review* 10 (1982), 6; Larry Sawchuk and Stacie D.A. Burke, 'Mortality in an Early Canadian Community: Belleville, 1876–85', unpublished paper (2000). See also Thomson, 'The 1890s'; Benidickson, 'Ontario Water Quality', 119–20.

47. John Hagiopan, 'The Municipalization of the City of Kingston Water Works Company', *Ontario History* 95 (2003): 67, 72; MacNaughton, 'Promoting Clean Water', 55; John Hagiopan, 'The Political Geography of Water Provision in Paris, Ontario, 1882–1924', *Urban History Review* 23 (1994):

32–51; Jeremy Stein, 'Annihilating Space and Time: The Modernization of Fire-Fighting in Late Nineteenth-Century Cornwall, Ontario', *Urban History Review* 24 (1996): 3–11.

48. Quotation: Rosemary Gagan, 'Mortality Patterns and Public Health in Hamilton, Canada, 1900–14', *Urban History Review* 17 (1989): 169. See also Sawchuk and Burke, 'Mortality in an Early Ontario Community'; Michael Mercier, 'Infant Mortality in Ottawa, 1901: An Historical-Geographic Perspective', MA thesis (Carleton University, 1997).

Chapter 8: 'A New Order of Things', 1905–23

1. Quotation: Charles W. Humphrey, *'Honest Enough to Be Bold': The Life and Times of Sir James Pliney Whitney* (Toronto: University of Toronto Press, 1985), 122. Statistics calculated from Ian A. Drummond, *Progress without Planning: The Economic History of Ontario: From Confederation to the Second World War* (Toronto: University of Toronto Press, 1987), 401, 412–13; Doug McCalla, 'The Ontario Economy in the Long Run', *Ontario History* 90 (1998): 99–100.

2. Quotations: Terry Crowley, 'J.J. Morrison and the Transition in Canadian Farm Movements during the Early Twentieth Century', *Agricultural History* 71 (1997): 335; Peter Baskerville and Eric Sager, *Unwilling Idlers: The Urban Unemployed and Their Families in Late Victorian Canada* (Toronto: University of Toronto Press, 1998), 179. Exodus statistics from W.R. Young, 'Conscription, Rural Depopulation and the Farmers of Ontario, 1917–1919', *Canadian Historical Review* 53 (1972): 319; other statistics from Drummond, *Progress without Planning*, McCalla, 'The Ontario Economy in the Long Run'; Adam Crerar, 'Ties That Bind: Farming, Agrarian Ideals and Life in Ontario, 1890–1930', PhD dissertation (University of Toronto, 1999), 13, 77. See also Terry Crowley, 'Rural Labour', in *Labouring Lives: Work and Workers in Nineteenth-Century Ontario*, edited by Paul Craven (Toronto: University of Toronto Press, 1995), 13–104.

3. Crerar, 'Ties That Bind', 15.

4. Quotation: J.M.S. Careless, 'Limited

Identities in Canada', *Canadian Historical Review* 50 (1969): 6.

5. W. Robert Wightman and Nancy M. Wightman, *The Land Between: Northwestern Ontario Resource Development, 1800 to the 1990s* (Toronto: University of Toronto Press, 1997), 107–8; Matt Bray, 'New Ontario and the Railway Revolution', in *Allegiance: The Ontario Story*, edited by Charles J. Humber (Mississauga, ON: Heirloom, 1991), 257; Livio Di Matteo, 'The Economic Development of the Lakehead during the Wheat Boom Era, 1900–1914', *Ontario History* 83 (1991): 297–316; Donald Kerr and D.W. Holdsworth, eds., *Historical Atlas of Canada*, vol. 3 (Toronto: University of Toronto Press, 1990), table 16.

6. Census of Canada, 1911, Special Report on the Foreign-Born Population, 9, cited in Julie Mathien, 'Children, Families, and Institutions in Late 19th and Early 20th Century Ontario', MA thesis (Ontario Institute for Studies in Education, 2001), 67; John H. Thompson, *The Harvests of War: The Prairie West, 1914–1918* (Toronto: McClelland & Stewart, 1989), 55.

7. Crerar, 'Ties That Bind', 17; Drummond, *Progress without Planning*, 364.

8. Quotation: E. Brian Titley, *A Narrow Vision: Duncan Campbell Scott and the Administration of Indian Affairs in Canada* (Vancouver: University of British Columbia Press, 1986), 73. See also Jean Manore, *Cross-Currents: Hydroelectricity and the Engineering of Northern Ontario* (Waterloo, ON: Wilfrid Laurier University Press, 1999).

9. Quotation: James Angus, 'How the Dokis Indians Protected Their Timber', *Ontario History* 81 (1989): 181–200. See also Janet Chute, *The Legacy of Shingwaukonse: A Century of Native Leadership* (Toronto: University of Toronto Press, 1998), 227–30.

10. Quotations: James Miller and Edmund Danziger, Jr, '"In the Care of Strangers": Walpole Island First Nation's Experiences with Residential Schools after the First World War', *Ontario History* 92 (2000): 71–88. See also J.R. Miller, *Shingwauk's Vision: A History of Native Residential Schools* (Toronto: University of Toronto Press, 1996), 357–8.

11. Quotations: Constance Backhouse, *Colour-Coded: A Legal History of Racism in Canada,* 1900–1950 (Toronto: Osgoode Society, 1999), 103–31. See also J.R. Miller, *Skyscrapers Hide the Heavens: A History of Indian-White Relations in Canada* (Toronto: University of Toronto Press, 1989), 217; Neil S. Forkey, 'Maintaining a Great Lakes Fishery: The State, Science and the Case of Ontario's Bay of Quinte, 1870–1920', *Ontario History* 86 (1995): 45–86; Stephen Bocking, 'Fishing the Inland Seas: Great Lakes Research, Fisheries Management, and Environmental Policy in Ontario', *Environmental History* 2 (1997): 52–73.

12. Quotation: Alan Brookes and Catharine Wilson, '"Working Away" from the Farm: The Young Women of North Huron, 1910–30', *Ontario History* 77 (1985): 282.

13. Carolyn Strange, *Toronto's Girl Problem: The Perils and Pleasures of the City, 1880–1930* (Toronto: University of Toronto Press, 1995), 117.

14. Quotation: Magda Farni, '"Ruffled" Mistresses and "Discontented" Maids: Respectability and the Case of Domestic Service, 1880–1914', *Labour/Le travail* 39 (1997): 77–8. See also Strange, *Toronto's Girl Problem*; Mariana Valverde, *The Age of Light, Soap, and Water: Moral Reform in English Canada, 1885–1925* (Toronto: McClelland & Stewart, 1991). Statistics from Canadian Families Project, 1901, nominal-level Public Use Sample.

15. Quotations: Dionne Brand, '"We Weren't Allowed to Go into Factory Work until Hitler Started the War": The 1920s to the 1940s', in *'We're Rooted Here and They Can't Pull Us Up': Essays in African Canadian Women's History*, edited by Peggy Bristow (Toronto: University of Toronto Press, 1994), 171–91. See also Varpu Lindstrom, '"I Won't Be a Slave": Finnish Domestics in Canada, 1911–30', in *A Nation of Immigrants: Women, Workers, and Communities in Canadian History, 1840s–1960s*, edited by Franca Iacovetta (Toronto: University of Toronto Press, 1998), 206–30.

16. Graham S. Lowe, 'Women, Work and the Office: The Feminization of Clerical Occupations in Canada, 1901–1931', in *Rethinking Canada: The Promise of Women's History*, edited by Veronica Strong-Boag and Anita Fellman (Toronto: Copp Clark Pitman, 1991), 269–85; Veronica Strong-Boag, *'Janey*

Canuck': Women in Canada, 1919–1939, Historical Booklet 53 (Ottawa: Canadian Historical Association, 1994), 5; Cynthia Comacchio, 'Mechanomorphosis: Science, Management and "Human Machinery" in Industrial Canada, 1900–1945', *Labour/Le travail* 41 (1998): 48.

17. Quotations: Joan Sangster, 'The 1907 Bell Telephone Strike: Organizing Women Workers', in *Rethinking Canada*, 249–68. See also Comacchio, 'Mechanomorphosis', 47.

18. Mercedes Steedman, *Angels of the Workplace: Women and the Construction of Gender Relations in the Canadian Clothing Industry, 1890–1940* (Toronto: Oxford University Press, 1997), 78–85. See also Douglas Cruikshank and Greg Kealey, 'Strikes in Canada, 1891–1950', *Labour/Le travail* 20 (1987): 107.

19. Ian Miller, '"Entirely from the Standpoint of Patriotic Service": Toronto Women and the First World War', paper presented to the Canadian Historical Association, Edmonton, 2000.

20. Susan Forbes, 'Gendering Corporate Welfare Practices: Female Sports and Recreation at Eaton's', *Rethinking History* 5 (2001): 59–74; Joan Sangster, 'The Softball Solution: Female Workers, Male Managers and the Operation of Paternalism at Westcox, 1923–60', *Labour/Le travail* 32 (1993): 191–3.

21. James Naylor, *The New Democracy: Challenging the Social Order in Industrial Ontario, 1914–1925* (Toronto: University of Toronto Press, 1991), 159–88, 205–7; Margaret McCallum, 'Corporate Welfarism in Canada, 1919–1939', *Canadian Historical Review* 71 (1990): 46–79.

22. Cynthia Comacchio '"By Every Means in Our Power": Maternal and Child Welfare in Ontario', in *Ontario since Confederation: A Reader*, edited by Edgar-André Montigny and Lori Chambers (Toronto: Univesrity of Toronto Press, 2000), 168–9.

23. Quotation: Jennifer Read, '"A Sort of Destiny": The Multi-Jurisdictional Response to Sewage Pollution in the Great Lakes, 1900–1930', *Scientas canadensis* 22–3 (1998–9): 123.

24. Quotations: Crerar, 'Ties That Bind', 322–3. See also Toronto, Minutes of the Council, 1912, Appendix A, 903, 1128; I am indebted to Michael Piva for this reference.

25. Quotations: Sean Purdy, 'Scaffolding Citizenship: Housing Reform and Nation Formation in Canada, 1900–1950', in *Contesting Canadian Citizenship: Historical Readings*, edited by Robert Admonski, Dorothy Chunn, and Robert Menzies (Peterborough, ON: Broadview, 2002), 135, 138; Purdy, '"It Was Tough on Everybody": Low-Income Families and Housing Hardship in Post-World War II Toronto', *Journal of Social History* 37 (2003): 459.

26. Statistics on privies are from Drummond, *Progress without Planning*, table 13.1.

27. Cynthia Commachio, *Nations Are Built of Babies: Saving Ontario's Mothers and Children, 1900–1945* (Montreal: McGill-Queen's University Press, 1993); T.R. Morrison, 'The Proper Sphere: Feminism, the Family and Child-Centred Reform in Ontario, 1875–1900', *Ontario History* 68 (1976): 45–74; Joan Sangster, 'Masking and Unmasking the Sexual Abuse of Children: Perceptions of Violence against Children in "The Badlands" of Ontario, 1916–30', *Journal of Family History* 25 (2000): 504–26.

28. Xiaobei Chen, '"Cultivating Children as You Would Valuable Plants": The Gardening Governmentality of Child Saving, Toronto, Canada, 1880s–1920s', *Journal of Historical Sociology* 16 (2003): 460–86; Paul Axelrod, *The Promise of Schooling: Education in Canada, 1800–1914* (Toronto: University of Toronto Press, 1997), 105–6; Sarah Z. Burke, *Seeking the Highest Good: Social Service and Gender at the University of Toronto* (Toronto: University of Toronto Press, 1996).

29. R.E. Spence, *Prohibition in Canada: A Memorial to Francis Stephens Spence* (Toronto: Ontario Branch of the Dominion Alliance, 1919), 206, 579–80, cited in Graeme Decarie, 'Something Old, Something New . . . : Aspects of Prohibition in Ontario in the 1890s', in *Oliver Mowat's Ontario: Papers*, edited by Donald Swainson (Toronto: Macmillan, 1972), 155.

30. Quotations: Humphries, *Whitney*, 126, 101.

31. Quotations: *Hamilton Spectator*, December 1899, in Kenneth C. Dewar, 'The Early Development of Hydroelectricity in Ontario', *Canada's Visual History*, vol. 31 (Montreal: National Film Board of Canada, 1977), illustration 6. Viv Nelles, *The Politics of Developement: Forests, Mines and Hydro-Electric*

Power in Ontario, 1849–1941, (Toronto: Macmillan, 1974), 219.

32. Humphries, *Whitney*.

33. Quotation: Nelles, *The Politics of Development*, 248–9.

34. Quotations: Ibid., 248–9; Humphries, *Whitney*, 151–68, 218–20. See also Nelles, *The Politics of Development*, 215–306.

35. Quotations: Brian McKillop, 'The Research Ideal and the University of Toronto, 1870–1906', *Royal Society of Canada, Proceedings*, 20 (1982): 273; Humphries, *Whitney*, 128. On the labour movement, see James Naylor, *The New Democracy*, 77–80.

36. Quotations: Humphries, *'Honest Enough to Be Bold'*, 19, 221.

37. Quotation: Peter Oliver, *Public and Private Persons: The Ontario Political Culture, 1914–1934* (Toronto: Clarke, Irwin, 1975), 39. See also Kerry A. Badgley, *Ringing in the Common Love of Good: The United Farmers of Ontario, 1914–1926* (Montreal: McGill-Queen's University Press, 2000), 56–7.

38. Quotation: Ian Miller, 'Our Glory and Grief: Toronto and the Great War', PhD dissertation (Wilfred Laurier University, 1999), 436. See also Barbara Wilson, ed., *Ontario and the First World War, 1914–1918: A Collection of Documents* (Toronto: Champlain Society, 1977).

39. Quotations: Mike O'Brien, 'Manhood and the Militia Myth: Masculinity, Class and Militarism in Ontario, 1902–1914', *Labour/Le travail* 42 (1998), 119, 120; Anna H. Lathrop, 'Contested Terrain: Gender and "Movement" in Ontario Elementary Physical Education', *Ontario History* 94 (2002): 166. See also Miller, 'Our Glory and Grief', 438; Wilson, *Ontario and the First World War*, xxiv; Robert Stamp, 'Empire Day in the Schools of Ontario: The Training of Young Imperialists', *Journal of Canadian Studies* 8 (1973): 32–42; Mark Moss, *Manliness and Militarism: Educating Young Boys in Ontario for War* (Don Mills, ON: Oxford University Press, 2001).

40. Paul Maroney, '"The Great Adventure": The Context and Ideology of Recruitment in Ontario, 1914–17', *Canadian Historical Review* 77 (1996): 62–98.

41. Quotation: *London Free Press*, 10 December 1915, cited in Wilson, *Ontario and the First World War*, xxxvii. See also Crerar, 'Ties That Bind', 249, 279–80, 29–37.

42. Crerar, 'Ties That Bind', 20–5; Badgley, *Ringing in the Common Love of Good*, 42–6, 66–7.

43. Quotation: Terry Crowley, 'Experience and Representation: Southern Ontario Farm Women and Agricultural Change, 1870–1914', *Agricultural History* 73 (1999): 238–51. See also Margaret Derry, 'Gender Conflicts in Dairying: Ontario's Butter Industry, 1880–1920', *Ontario History* 90 (1998): 31–47; Badgley, *Ringing in the Common Love of Good*, 127.

44. Quotation: Linda Ambrose and Margaret Kechnie, 'Social Control or Social Feminism? Two Views of the Ontario Women's Institutes', *Agricultural History* 73 (1999): 222–37. See also Monda Halpern, *And on That Farm He Had a Wife: Ontario Farm Women and Feminism, 1900–1970* (Montreal: McGill-Queen's University Press, 2001), chapter 5; Cecilia Reynolds and Harry Smaller, 'Ontario School Teachers: A Gendered View of the 1930s', *Historical Studies in Education/Revue d'histoire de l'education* 6 (1994), 155n7, 168.

45. Quotation: Crowley, 'Experience and Representation.'

46. Quotation: Terry Crowley, 'J.J. Morrison and the Transition in Canadian Farm Movements during the Twentieth Century', *Agricultural History* 71 (1997): 343. See also Charles Johnston, *E.C. Drury: Agrarian Idealist* (Toronto: University of Toronto Press, 1986); Margaret Kechnie, 'The United Farm Women of Ontario: Developing a Political Consciousness', *Ontario History* 77 (1985): 266–80; Pauline Rankin, 'The Politicization of Ontario Farm Women', in *Beyond the Vote: Canadian Women and Politics*, edited by Linda Kealey and Joan Sangster (Toronto: University of Toronto Press, 1989), 309–32; Halpern, *And on That Farm*.

47. Quotation: Craig Heron, 'The Crisis of the Craftsman: Hamilton's Metal Workers in the Early Twentieth Century', in *A History of Ontario: Selected Readings*, edited by Michael Piva (Toronto: Copp Clark Pitman, 1988), 109.

48. For an excellent overview of the interlocking effects of class, ethnicity, and gender, see Ruth A. Frager, 'Labour History and the Interlocking Hierarchies of Class, Ethnicity

and Gender: A Canadian Perspective', *International Review of Social History* 44 (1999): 217–47.

49. The last four paragraphs have benefited from the work of Naylor, *The New Democracy*. See also Cruikshank and Kealey, 'Strikes in Canada', 85–145, and Heron, 'The Crisis of the Craftsman'.

50. Quotation: Crowley, 'J.J. Morrison', 349. See also Bruce Kidd, '"Making the Pros Pay" for Amateur Sports: The Ontario Athletic Commission, 1920–1947', *Ontario History* 87 (1985), 110.

51. Quotation: Oliver, *Public and Private Persons*, 39.

52. For the last three paragraphs, see Frager, 'Labour History', 232; James Struthers, *The Limits of Affluence: Welfare in Ontario, 1920–70* (Toronto: University of Toronto Press, 1994), chapters 1 and 2; John Bullen, 'J.J. Kelso and the New Child Savers: The Genesis of the Children's Aid Movement in Ontario', *Ontario History* 82 (1990): 107–30; Margaret Little, *'No Car, No Radio, No Liquor Permit': The Moral Regulation of Single Mothers in Ontario, 1920–1997* (Toronto: Oxford University Press, 1998), 1–75; Comacchio, 'Mechanomorphosis', 51–3.

53. Quotation: Frager, 'Labour History'. For international context, see Joel Mokyr, 'Why "More Work for Mother"? Knowledge and Household Behaviour, 1870–1945', *Journal of Economic History* 60 (2000): 1–41. For a national perspective, see Veronica Strong-Boag, *The New Day Recalled: Lives of Girls and Women in English Canada, 1919–1939* (Toronto: Copp Clark Pitman, 1988), chapter 4; Kerr and Holdsworth, *Historical Atlas of Canada*, vol. 3, plate 29.

54. Naylor, *The New Democracy*, 225–9; Veronica Strong-Boag, 'The Girl of the New Day: Canadian Working Women in the 1920s', *Labour/Le travail* 4 (1979): 132; Rankin, 'The Politicization of Ontario Farm Women', 316–17; Halpern, *And on That Farm*, 204–7.

55. Badgley, *Ringing in the Common Love of Good*, 142–69.

Chapter 9: 'The Inequality of Our System': Boom, Bust, and War: 1923–40s

1. Quotations: Terry Crowley, 'The New

Canada Movement: Agrarian Youth Protest in the 1930s', *Ontario History* 80 (1988): 320.

2. Quotations: John T. Saywell, *'Just Call Me Mitch': The Life of Mitchell F. Hepburn* (Toronto: University of Toronto Press, 1991), 40.

3. Peter Oliver, *G. Howard Ferguson: Ontario Tory* (Toronto: University of Toronto Press, 1977), 78 and chapter 12; Peter Oliver, *Public and Private Persons: The Ontario Political Culture, 1914–1934* (Toronto: Clarke, Irwin, 1975), 92–125; Cecilia Reynolds and Harry Smaller, 'Ontario School Teachers: A Gendered View of the 1930s', *Historical Studies in Education* 6 (1994): 151.

4. Quotation: Oliver, *Ferguson*, 313–14. See also James Struthers, *The Limits of Affluence: Welfare in Ontario, 1920–1970* (Toronto: University of Toronto Press, 1994), 65.

5. Michael Huberman and Denise Young, 'Hope against Hope: Strike Activity in Canada, 1920–1939', *Explorations in Economic History* 39 (2002): 315–54; Robert Craig Brown, 'The Doctrine of Usefulness: Natural Resources and National Park Policy in Canada, 1887–1914', in *Canadian Parks in Perspective*, edited by J.G. Nelson (Montreal: Harvest House, 1969), 46–62.

6. Quotation: Saywell, *'Just Call Me Mitch'*, 141. See also Oliver, *Ferguson*, especially 116, 155–6; Margaret Little, *'No Car, No Radio, No Liquor Permit': The Moral Regulation of Single Mothers in Ontario, 1920–1997* (Toronto: Oxford University Press, 1998), 83.

7. Oliver, *Ferguson*, 208–14; Mark Kuelberg, '"We Have Sold Forestry to the Management of the Company": Abititi Power and Paper Company's Forestry Initiatives in Ontario, 1919–29', *Journal of Canadian Studies* 34 (1999): 187–209; Mark Kuelberg, 'Ontario's Nascent Environmentalists: Seeing the Forest for the Trees in Southern Ontario, 1919–1929', *Ontario History* 98 (1996): 138.

8. Quotations: Cynthia Comacchio, 'Dancing to Perdition: Adolescence and Leisure in Interwar English Canada', *Journal of Canadian Studies* 32 (1997): 10–11; Dorothy Choate Herriman, 'Diary', edited by Albert Braz, in *The Small Details of Life: Twenty Diaries by Women in Canada, 1830–1996*, edited by Kathryn Carter (Toronto: University of

Toronto Press, 2002), 354. See also Cynthia Commachio, 'Inventing the Extracurriculum: High School Culture in Interwar Ontario', *Ontario History* 93 (2001): 40; Lara Campbell, 'Respectable Citizens of Canada: Gender, Family and Unemployment in the Great Depression, Ontario', PhD dissertation (Queen's University, 2002), 205n29; Adam Crerar, 'Ties That Bind: Farming, Agrarian Ideals and Life in Ontario, 1890–1930', PhD dissertation (University of Toronto, 1999), 21.

9. Quotation: Pamela Sugiman, *Labour's Dilemma: The Gender Politics of Auto Workers in Canada, 1937–1979* (Toronto: University of Toronto Press, 1994), 12.

10. Quotation: Stephen Davies, '"Reckless Walking Must Be Discouraged": The Automobile Revolution and the Shaping of Modern Ontario', *Urban History Review* 18 (1989): 123–38.

11. Quotation: Cynthia Comacchio, 'Mechanomorphosis: Science, Management and "Human Machinery" in Industrial Canada, 1900–1945', *Labour/Le travail* 41 (1998): 35–67. The material in these four paragraphs is drawn from Crerar, 'Ties That Bind', 33; Drummond, *Progress without Planning*, chapter 12 and table 13.1; Davies, 'Reckless Walking Must Be Discouraged'; Gerald T. Bloomfield, 'No Parking Here to Corner: London Reshaped by the Automobile, 1911–61', *Urban History Review* 18 (1989): 139–58; Oliver, *Ferguson*.

12. Quotation: Dieter Grant Hogaboam, 'Compensation and Control: Silicosis in the Ontario Hardrock Mining Industry, 1921–1975', MA thesis (Queen's University, 1997), 44. See also Laurel Sifton MacDowell, 'Relief Camp Workers in Ontario during the Great Depression of the 1930s', *Canadian Historical Review* 76 (1995): 205; Saywell, *Just Call Me Mitch'*, 84–7; Scott Vokey, 'Inspiration for Insurrection or Harmless Humour? Class and Politics in the Editorial Cartoons of Three Toronto Newspapers during the Early 1930s', *Labour/Le travail* 45 (2000): 147; Drummond, *Progress without Planning*, 220; W. Peter Archibald, 'Distress, Dissent and Alienation: Hamilton Workers in the Great Depression', *Urban History Review* 21 (1992): 3–32; Crowley, 'The New Canada Movement': 311–25; Sally M. Weaver, 'The

Iroquois: The Grand River Reserve in the Late Nineteenth and Early Twentieth Centuries, 1875–1945', in *Aboriginal Ontario: Historical Perspectives on the First Nations*, edited by Edward S. Rogers and Donald B. Smith (Toronto: Dundurn, 1994), 250; Sean Purdy, '"It Was Tough on Everybody": Low-Income Families and Housing Hardship in Post-World War II Toronto', *Journal of Social History* 37 (2003): 460; Wayne Roberts, ed., *Miner's Life: Bob Miner and Union Organizing in Timmins, Kirkland Lake and Sudbury* (Hamilton, ON: Labour Studies Programme, McMaster University, 1979), 3–4.

13. Saywell, *Just Call Me Mitch'*, 162.

14. Quotation: Ivar Nordstram, as told to Satu Repo, 'Lakehead in the Thirties: A Labour Militant Remembers', *This Magazine* 13, no. 3 (1979): 42. See also Bryan Palmer, *Working-Class Experience: Rethinking the History of Canadian Labour, 1800–1991* (Toronto: McClelland & Stewart, 1992), 254–5.

15. Archibald, 'Distress, Dissent and Alienation', 24; Peter Archibald, 'Small Expectations and Great Adjustments: How Hamilton Workers Most Often Experienced the Great Depression', *Canadian Journal of Sociology* 21 (1996): 393.

16. Quotations: Lita-Rose Betcherman, *The Little Band: The Clashes between the Communists and the Political and Legal Establishment in Canada, 1928–1932* (Ottawa: Deneau, 1982), 166–7.

17. Quotations: *Toronto Daily Star*, 1 October 1933, cited in Irving Abella, 'Oshawa, 1937', in *On Strike: Six Key Labour Struggles in Canada, 1919–1949*, edited by Irving Abella (Toronto: Lorimer, 1974), 97; Saywell, *Just Call Me Mitch'*, 179–81. See also John Manley, '"Starve Be Damned!": Communists and Canada's Urban Unemployed, 1929–1939', *Canadian Historical Review* 79 (1998): 479.

18. Quotations: Struthers, *The Limits of Affluence*, 84–6, 91–2. See also ibid., chapter 3.

19. Carmela Patrias, 'Relief Strike: Immigrant Workers and the Great Depression in Crowland, Ontario, 1930–1935', in *A Nation of Immigrants: Women, Workers, and Communities in Canadian History, 1840s–1960s*, edited by Franca Iacovetta (Toronto: University of Toronto Press, 1998), 322–58

20. For craft workers' passivity, see Michael Bliss

and L.M. Grayson, eds, *The Wretched of Canada: Letters to R.B. Bennett, 1930–1935* (Toronto: University of Toronto Press, 1971), xxv. See also Patrias, 'Relief Strike'; Campbell, 'Respectable Citizens of Canada', 104.

21. Quotation: Nordstram, in 'Lakehead in the Thirties', 44. See also Patrias, 'Relief Strike'; Ian Radforth, *Bushworkers and Bosses: Logging in Northern Ontario, 1900–1980* (Toronto: University of Toronto Press, 1987).

22. Quotations: Campbell, 'Respectable Citizens of Canada', 83–94. See also Duart Snow, 'The Holmes Foundry Strike of March 1937: We'll Give Their Jobs to White Men!', *Ontario History* 69 (1977): 3–31; Archibald, 'Distress, Dissent and Alienation'; Gerry Tulchinsky, *Branching Out: The Transformation of the Canadian Jewish Community* (North York, ON: Stoddart, 1998).

23. Quotation: Gilbert Stelter, 'Introduction', in *Cities and Urbanization: Canadian Historical Perspectives*, edited by Gilbert A. Stelter (Toronto: Copp Clark Pitman, 1990), 10. See also Patrias, 'Relief Strike'; Drummond, *Progress without Planning*, table 10.1; Greg Kealey and Douglas Cruikshank, 'Workers' Responses', in *Historical Atlas of Canada*, vol. 3, edited by D.G.G. Kerr and Derrick W. Holdsworth (Toronto: University of Toronto Press, 1990), table 45.

24. Quotations: Patrias, 'Relief Strike', 345; Hogaboam, 'Compensation and Control', 79; Campbell, 'Respectable Citizens of Canada', chapter 4; Commachio, 'Inventing the Extracurriculum', 46.

25. Quotations: Campbell, 'Respectable Citizens of Canada', 68, 73.

26. Quotations: Ibid., 102; Margaret Hobbs, 'Equality and Difference: Femininism and the Defence of Women Workers during the Great Depression', *Labour/Le travail* 32 (1993): 201–23.

27. Quotation: Patricia Bird, 'Hamilton Working Women in the Period of the Great Depression', *Atlantis* 8, no. 2 (1982–3): 126–36.

28. Quotations: Ibid. The last three paragraphs are based on Little, 'No Car, No Radio', chapter 4; Ellen Scheinberg, 'The Tale of Tessie the Textile Worker: Female Textile Workers in Cornwall during World War II', *Labour/Le travail* 33 (1994): 161; Patricia Bird, 'Hamilton Working Women in the Period of

the Great Depression', *Atlantis* 8, no. 2 (1982–3): 126–36; Cecilia Reynolds and Harry Smaller, 'Ontario School Teachers'; Joy Parr, *The Gender of Breadwinners: Women, Men, and Change in Two Industrial Towns, 1880–1950* (Toronto: University of Toronto Press, 1990), 87–90.

29. Struthers, *The Limits of Affluence*, chapter 2.

30. Material in the last two paragraphs is from Angus McLaren, *Our Own Master Race: Eugenics in Canada, 1885–1945* (Toronto: Oxford University Press, 1990); Catherine Annau, 'Eager Eugenicists: A Reappraisal of the Birth Control Society of Hamilton', *Histoire sociale/Social History* 27 (1994): 111–33; Dianne Dodd, 'The Canadian Birth Control Movement on Trial, 1937–1937', *Histoire sociale/Social History* 26 (1983): 411–28.

31. The discussion of the Dionne quintuplets is drawn from articles by Cynthia Wright, Marianna Valverde, David Welch, Katherine Arnup, and Ian McKay in a special issue of *Revue d'études canadienne/Journal of Canadian Studies* 29, no. 4 (1994–5).

32. Quotations: Campbell, 'Respectable Citizens of Canada', 132; Nordstram, 'Lakehead in the Thirties', 40; Archibald, 'Small Expectations', 395; Crowley, 'The New Canada Movement', 320.

33. Calculated from Cruikshank and Kealey, 'Strikes in Canada', table E. On the Industrial Standards Act, see Marcus Klee, 'Fighting the Sweatshop in Industrial Ontario: Capital, Labour and the Industrial Standards Act', *Labour/Le travail* 45 (2000): 13–51.

34. Quotations: Terry Copp, 'Ontario 1939: The Decision for War', *Ontario History* 86 (1994): 269; Devlin to MacInness, 2 October 1940, file 452-20, pt 4, S, RG 10, vol. 6768, NA, in Michael Stevenson, 'The Mobilization of Native Canadians during the Second World War', *Journal of the Canadian Historical Association* 7 (1966), 209. See also Ian Miller, 'Toronto's Response to the Outbreak of War, 1939', *Canadian Military History* 11 (2002): 5–23; Sylvia Bjorkman, 'Report on Camp "W": Internment Camp "100" North of Lake Superior in World War II', *Ontario History* 89 (1997): 237–43; John Zucchi, *Italians in Toronto: Development of a National Identity, 1875–1935* (Kingston, ON: McGill-

Queen's University Press, 1988), 192; Saywell, *'Just Call Me Mitch'*, 483.

35. Quotations: Jeff Keshen, 'Revisiting Canada's Civilian Women during World War II', *Histoire sociale / Social History* 30 (1997), 250, 253, 254, 248. See also Charles M. Johnston, 'The Children's War: The Mobilization of Ontario Youth during the Second World War', in *Patterns of the Past: Interpreting Ontario's History*, edited by Roger Hall, William Westfall, and Laurel Sefton MacDowell (Toronto: Dundurn, 1988), 356–80; Scheinberg, 'The Tale of Tessie', 153–86; Ruth Roach Pierson, *'They're Still Women after All': The Second World War and Canadian Womanhood* (Toronto: McClelland and Stewart, 1986); Frager, 'Labour History', 226; Pamela Sugiman, 'Privilege and Oppression: The Configuration of Race, Gender and Class in Southern Ontario Auto Plants: 1939–1949', *Labour/Le travail* 47 (2001), 94n41.

36. Calculated from Cruikshank and Kealey, 'Canadian Strikes', table E. See also Laurel Sefton MacDowell, 'The Formation of the Canadian Industrial Relations System during World War II', *Labour/Le travail* 3 (1978): 175–96; Laurel Sefton MacDowell, *'Remember Kirkland Lake': The Gold Miners' Strike of 1941–42* (Toronto: Canadian Scholars' Press, 1983); Taylor Hollander, '"Making Reform Happen": The Passage of Canada's Collective-Bargaining Policy, 1943–44', *Journal of Policy History* 13 (2001): 299–328.

37. Donald M. Wells, 'Origins of Canada's Wagner Model of Industrial Relations: The United Auto Workers in Canada and the Suppression of "Rank and File" Unionism, 1936–1953', *Canadian Journal of Sociology* 20 (1995): 204–5; Laurel Sefton MacDowell, *Renegade Lawyer: The Life of J.L. Cohen* (Toronto: Osgoode Society, 2001).

Chapter 10: Modern Ontario: 1940s–2003

1. Mark Rupert, *Producing Hegemony: The Politics of Mass Production and American Global Power* (Cambridge: Cambridge University Press, 1995); Mark Rupert, 'Crisis of Fordism', in *Routledge Encyclopedia of International Political Economy*, edited by R.J. Berry Jones

(New York: Routledge, 2001).

2. Quotations: Keith Brownsey, 'Opposition Blues: Policy and Organization in the Ontario Conservative Party, 1934–43', *Ontario History* 88 (1996), 280; Peter Meehan, 'The East Hastings By-election of 1936 and the Ontario Separate School Tax Question', *Canadian Catholic Historical Association Historical Papers* 68 (2002): 117. See also Robert Bothwell, Ian Drummond, and John English, *Canada since 1945: Power, Politics and Provincialism* (Toronto: University of Toronto Press, 1981): 92.

3. Quotation: Terry Crowley, *Agnes Macphail and the Politics of Equality* (Toronto: Lorimer, 1990), 188. See also *Globe and Mail*, 10 July 1943; K.J. Rea, *The Prosperous Years: The Economic History of Ontario* (Toronto: University of Toronto Press, 1985), 18–19.

4. Quotation: Bothwell et al., *Canada Since 1945*, 96.

5. Steve Jobbitt, 'Re-civilizing the Land: Conservation and Postwar Reconstruction in Ontario, 1939–1961', MA thesis (Lakehead University, 2001), chapter 3.

6. Quotation: Shirley Tillotson, 'Citizen Participation in the Welfare State: The Recreation Movement in Brantford, 1945–1957', in *Ontario since Confederation: A Reader*, edited by Edgar-André Montigny and Lori Chambers (Toronto: University of Toronto Press, 2000), 310.

7. Quotations: Sid Noel, 'The Ontario Political Culture: An Interpretation', in *The Government and Politics of Ontario*, 5th ed., edited by Graham White (Toronto: University of Toronto Press, 1997), 60; Joseph Schull, *Ontario since 1867* (Toronto: McClelland and Stewart, 1978), 334. See also Roger Graham, *Old Man Ontario: Leslie M. Frost* (Toronto: University of Toronto Press, 1990); A.K. McDougall, *John P. Robarts: His Life and Government* (Toronto: University of Toronto Press, 1986); Thomas J. Courchene with Colin R. Telmer, *From Heartland to North American Regional State: The Social, Fiscal, and Federal Evolution of Ontario: An Interpretive Essay* (Toronto: Centre for Public Management, Faculty of Management, University of Toronto, 1998), 13.

8. Charles Martin, 'The Politics of Northern Ontario: An Analysis of the Political Divergencies at the Provincial Periphery',

MA thesis (McGill University, 1999), 48.

9. Quotation: A. Suzanne Hill, 'A Serpent in the Garden: Implications of Highway Development in Canada's Niagara Fruit Belt', *Journal of Historical Sociology* 15 (2002): 506. See also John C. Van Nostrand, 'The Queen Elizabeth Way: Public Utility versus Public Space', *Urban History Review* 12 (1983): 1–23; Steven High, *Industrial Sunset: The Making of North America's Rust Belt, 1969–1984* (Toronto: University of Toronto Press, 2003), 34–5.

10. Ian Allaby, 'GO Transit Moves a City', *Canadian Geographic* 108, no. 6 (1988–9): 30–6.

11. Geoffrey R. Wheeler, 'Politics and Policy in the North', in *Government and Politics of Ontario*, 288; Nancy and Robert Wightman, 'Road and Highway Development in Northwestern Ontario, 1850–1990', *Geographica* 36 (1992): 366–80.

12. John Kenneth Galbraith, *The Affluent Society* (Boston: Houghton Mifflen, 1984); Rea, *The Prosperous Years*, 84–5.

13. Ibid., 83, table 15.

14. *Globe and Mail*, 29 August 2000.

15. Quotation: Steve Jobbitt, 'Re-civilizing the Land', 135–55. See also Rand Dyck, 'The Socio-Economic Setting of Ontario Politics', in *The Government and Politics of Ontario*, 26.

16. Quotation, statistics on women, and expert opinions are from Linda Ambrose, 'Cartoons and Commissions: Advice to Junior Farmers in Postwar Ontario', *Ontario History* 93 (2001): 63, 67, 71, 72; Munro quotation from John Weaver, 'Society and Culture in Rural and Small-Town Ontario: Alice Munro's Testimony on the Last Forty Years', in *Patterns of the Past: Interpreting Ontario's History*, edited by Roger Hall, William Westfall, and Laurel Sefton MacDowell (Toronto: Dundurn, 1988), 394.

17. For rural non-farm population, see M. Toombs, 'Rising Concern in Rural Ontario re Swine Production', Ontario Ministry of Agriculture, Food and Rural Affairs (OMAFRA) website, 8 March 2000; Alison R. Locker, 'Burden of Agricultural Machinery Injuries in Ontario, 1985–1996: Descriptive and Economic Analyses', MSc thesis (Queen's University, 2001), i–ii. For primary production, see Rea, *The Prosperous Years*, 83,

table 15; farm decline calculated from Rea, *The Prosperous Years*, 136, table 31, and 'Ontario Census Farms Classified by Total Farm Area, 1991 and 1996', OMAFRA website; farm acreage from Doug McCalla, 'The Ontario Economy in the Long Run', *Ontario History* 90 (1998): 103; hog and dairy farm decline from 'Discussion Paper on Intensive Agricultural Operations in Rural Ontario', OMAFRA website; percentages of total farm revenue from 'The Protection of Ontario's Ground Water and Intensive Farming: Special Report to the Legislative Assembly of Ontario', Environmental Commissioner of Ontario, 27 July 2000, Environmental Commissioner of Ontario website; farm income calculated from 'Ontario Census Farms Classified by Total Gross farm Receipts', OMAFRA website; off-farm income from 'Rural Ontario Demographic Trends and Factors', OMAFRA website; James L. Murray, 'Agricultural Change and Environmental Consequence in Southern Ontario, 1951–1971', MA (University of Guelph, 1997).

18. Quotation: James Struthers, *The Limits of Affluence: Welfare in Ontario, 1920–1970* (Toronto: University of Toronto Press, 1994). See also Donald M. Wells, 'Origins of Canada's Wagner Model of Industrial Relations: The United Auto Workers in Canada and the Suppression of "Rank and File" Unionism, 1936–1953', *Canadian Journal of Sociology* 20 (1995): 193–225; Bryan Palmer, *Working-Class Experience: Rethinking the History of Canadian Labour, 1800–1991* (Toronto: McClelland & Stewart, 1992), 281–98.

19. Struthers, *The Limits of Affluence*, 123, 141, 213; Dan Azoulay, '"A Desperate Holding Action": The Survival of the Ontario CCF/NDP, 1948–1964', *Ontario History* 85 (1993): 17–42.

20. Quotations: Struthers, *The Limits of Affluence*, 223; Martin, 'The Politics of Northern Ontario', 49.

21. Quotations: Sean Purdy, '"It Was Tough on Everybody": Low-Income Families and Housing Hardship in Post-World War II Toronto', *Journal of Social History* 37 (2003): 465–7.

22. Quotations: Donica Belisle, 'Toward a Canadian Consumer History', *Labour/Le tra-*

vail 52 (2003): 197–8; Joy Parr, *Domestic Goods: The Material, the Moral, and the Economic in the Postwar Years* (Toronto: University of Toronto Press, 1999), 240. See also Franca Iacovetta, 'Recipes for Democracy? Gender, Family, and Making Female Citizens in Cold War Canada', *Canadian Woman Studies* 20 (2000): 12–21; Dyck, 'The Socio-Economic Setting', 40; Parr, *Domestic Goods*, 33, 107, 243–65.

23. Quotations: Struthers, *The Limits of Affluence*, 155–6, 199.

24. Quotations: Ibid., 209–10.

25. Quotations: Ibid, 146, 200, 218, 256; consumer quotation from Monda Halpern, *And On That Farm He Had a Wife: Ontario Farm Women and Feminism, 1900–1970* (Montreal: McGill-Queen's University Press, 2001), 131. See also James Struthers, 'Welfare to Workfare: Poverty and the "Dependency Debate" in Post-Second World War Ontario', in *Ontario Since Confederation*, 436–9.

26. Quotation: Rea, *The Prosperous Years*, 38. See also ibid., 29–31; Palmer, *Working-Class Experience*, 313–25; Rea, *The Prosperous Years*, 37–8; Doug Owram, *Born at the Right Time: A History of the Baby-Boom Generation* (Toronto: University of Toronto Press, 1996).

27. Rea, *The Prosperous Years*, 104; Robert Gidney, *From Hope to Harris: The Reshaping of Ontario Schools* (Toronto: University of Toronto Press, 1999).

28. A.B. McKillop, *Matters of Mind: The University in Ontario, 1791–1951* (Toronto: University of Toronto Press, 1994), 565–7; Rea, *The Prosperous Years*, 112.

29. McDougall, *John P. Robarts*, 169, 190–3; Matthew Hayday, 'Confusing and Conflicting Agendas: Federalism, Official Languages and the Development of the Bilingualism in Education Program in Ontario, 1970–1983', *Journal of Canadian Studies/Revue d'études canadiennes* 36 (2001): 50–79; Matthew Hayday, '"Pas de problème": The Development of French-Language Health Services in Ontario, 1968–86', *Ontario History* 94 (2002): 183–200.

30. Kari Carisse, 'Becoming Canadian: Federal-Provincial Indian Policy and the Integration of Natives, 1945–1969: The Case of Ontario', MA thesis (University of Ottawa, 2000), 12–13, 67, 70, 85.

31. Quotation: Ibid., 69–70. See also Joan Sangster, '"She Is Hostile to Our Ways": First Nations Girls Sentenced to the Ontario Training School for Girls, 1933–1960', *Law and History Review* 20 (2002): 59–96; Joan Sangster, 'Criminalizing the Colonized: Ontario Native Women Confront the Criminal Justice System', *Canadian Historical Review* 80 (1999): 32–60; Joe T. Darden and Sameh M. Kamel, 'Differences in Home Ownership Rates between Aboriginal Peoples and White Canadians in the Toronto Census Metropolitan Area: Does Race Matter?' *Native Studies Review* 14 (2001): 55–81.

32. Carisse, 'Becoming Canadian', chapters 3 and 4.

33. Struthers, *The Limits of Affluence*, 226–30; Jean L. Manore, *Cross-Currents: Hydro-electricity and the Engineering of Northern Ontario* (Waterloo, ON: Wilfrid Laurier University Press, 1999); Harvey McCue, 'The Modern Age, 1945–1980', in *Aboriginal Ontario: Historical Perspectives on the First Nations*, edited by Edward S. Rogers and Donald B. Smith (Toronto: Dundurn, 1994), 377–417.

34. Rea, *The Prosperous Years*, 28.

35. The last four paragraphs rely on Ross Lambertson, 'Activists in the Age of Human Rights: The Struggle for Human Rights in Canada, 1945–1960', PhD dissertation (University of Victoria, 1998), 278n14, 261–9, 407–22. See also Carmelia Patrias and Ruth Frager, '"This Is Our Country, These Are Our Rights": Minorities and the Origins of Ontario's Human Rights Campaigns', *Canadian Historical Review* 82 (2001): 1–35; James W. St G. Walker, 'The "Jewish Phase" in the Movement for Racial Equality in Canada', *Canadian Ethnic Studies/Études ethniques au Canada* 34 (2002): 1–29; Walker, 'Race', Rights and the Law in the Supreme Court of Canada: Historical Case Studies* (Toronto: Osgoode Society, 1997), esp. 172, 222–6.

36. Quotations: Nicholas Harney, 'Building Italian Regional Identity in Toronto: Using Space to Make Culture Material', *Anthropologica* 44 (2002): 46. See also Sheila L. Croucher, 'Constructing the Image of Ethnic Harmony in Toronto, Canada: The Politics of Problem Definition and Nondefinition',

Urban Affairs Review 32 (1997): 333–4.

37. Franca Iacovetta, 'Ordering in Bulk: Canada's Postwar Immigration Policy and the Recruitment of Contract Workers from Italy', *Journal of American Ethnic History* 11 (1991): 50–80; John Zucchi, *Italians in Toronto: Development of a National Identity, 1875–1935* (Kingston, ON: McGill-Queen's University Press, 1988); Nicholas De Maria Harney, *Eh Paesan! Being Italian in Toronto* (Toronto: University of Toronto Press, 1998).

38. Quotations: Franco Iacovetta, 'From Contadina to Worker: Southern Italian Immigrant Working Women in Toronto, 1947–1962', in *Rethinking Canada: The Promise of Women's History*, edited by Veronica Strong-Boag and Anita Clair Fellman (Toronto: Copp Clark Pitman, 1991), 390; Cynthia Wright, 'Rewriting the Modern: Reflections on Race, Nation, and the Death of a Department Store', *Histoire social/Social History* 33 (2000): 167. See also Franco Iacovetta, 'Defending Honour, Demanding Respect: Manly Discourses and Gendered Practices in Two Construction Strikes, Toronto, 1960–61', in *Gendered Pasts: Historical Essays in Femininity and Masculinity in Canada*, edited by Kathryn McPherson, Cecilia Morgan, and Nancy Forestall (Don Mills, ON: Oxford University Press, 1999), 210; Iacovetta, 'Recipes', 12–20.

39. Harney, *Eh Paesan*, 29, 37; Harney, 'Building Italian Regional Identity', 47–52; Franca Iacovetta, *Such Hardworking People: Italian Immigrants in Postwar Toronto* (Montreal: McGill-Queen's University Press, 1993); Michael Buzzelli, 'From Little Britain to Little Italy: An Urban Ethnic Landscape Study in Toronto', *Journal of Historical Geography* 27 (2001): 578.

40. Quotation: Moira Day, 'Canada East, Canada West: The Cultural Politics of Geography Revisited', *Prairie Forum* 21 (1996): 101. See also Alison L. Bain, 'Constructing Contemporary Artistic Identities in Toronto Neighbourhoods', *Canadian Geographer* 47 (2003): 308; Barbara C. Edwards, 'Toronto Art: A History of Connectedness, 1970–1998', MA thesis (University of Western Ontario, 1999), 41; Dyck, 'The Socio-Economic Setting of Ontario Politics', 35; Nelson Wiseman, 'Change in Ontario Politics', in *The Government and Politics of Ontario*, 424–5.

41. Quotations: Veronica Strong-Boag, 'Home Dreams: Women and the Suburban Experiment in Canada, 1945–60', *Canadian Historical Review* 72 (1991): 480, 482; Struthers, *The Limits of Affluence*, 243. See also Susan Prentice, 'Workers, Mothers, Reds: Toronto's Postwar Daycare Fight', *Studies in Political Economy* 30 (1989): 115–42.

42. Rae, *The Prosperous Years*, 32.

43. Quotations: Palmer, *Working-Class Experience*, 330–3. See also Dan Azoualay, '"The Lady from Ontario": Marjorie Wells Pinney and the Struggle for Democratic Socialism in Ontario', *Journal of Women's History* 9 (1997): 52–83; Halpern, *And on That Farm*, 121–39.

44. Quotations: Carmela Patrias and Ruth Frager, 'This Is Our Country'; Crowley, *Agnes Macphail*, 199. See also Shirley Tillotson, 'Human Rights Law as Prism: Women's Organizations, Unions, and Ontario's Female Employees Fair Remuneration Act, 1951', *Canadian Historical Review* 72 (1991): 532–57, esp. 534; Joan Sangster, *Dreams of Equality: Women on the Canadian Left, 1920–1950* (Toronto: McClelland & Stewart, 1989).

45. Quotations: Joan Sangster, 'Women Workers, Employment Policy and the State: The Establishment of the Ontario Women's Bureau, 1963–1970', *Labour/Le travail* 36 (1995): 129. See also ibid., 119–45; Dionne Brand, *No Burden to Carry: Narratives of Black Working Women in Ontario, 1920s–1950s* (Toronto: Women's Press, 1991).

46. Marcia Wharton-Zaretsky, 'Foremothers of Black Women's Community Organizing in Toronto', *Atlantis* 24 (2000): 61–71; F 2076-3-0-43, McCurdy Collection, Archives of Ontario.

47. Croucher, 'Constructing the Image of Ethnic Harmony', 320. Statistics: Ontario Ministry of Finance, Office of Economic Policy, Labour and Demographic Analysis Branch, *Census 2001 Highlights, Factsheet 6* (2001).

48. Quotation: Rae, *The Prosperous Years*, 254; see also ibid., 34.

49. Quotation: High, *Industrial Sunset*, 188; see also ibid., 103–6, 167–200.

50. Courchene, *From Heartland to North American Regional State*, chapter 5.

51. Ibid.; Lars Osberg and Kuan Xu, 'Poverty Intensity: How Well Do Canadian Provinces

Compare?' *Canadian Public Policy* 25 (1999): 186–7.

52. Martin, 'The Politics of Northern Ontario', 49–51.

53. Chuck Rachlis and David Wolfe, 'An Insider's View of the NDP Government of Ontario: The Politics of Permanent Opposition Meets the Economics of Permanent Recession', in *The Government and Politics of Ontario*, 331–7.

54. Quotation: Ibid., 336.

55. Quotation: High, *Industrial Sunset*, 200. See also Struthers, 'Welfare to Workfare', 447; Allan Moscovitch, 'Social Assistance in the New Ontario', in *Open for Business, Closed to People: Mike Harris's Ontario*, edited by Diana S. Ralph, André Régimbald, and Nérée St-Amand (Halifax: Fernwood, 1997), 82–3; Dyck, 'The Socio-Economic Setting of Ontario Politics', 32; Wiseman, 'Change in Ontario Politics', 423.

56. Quotations: Struthers, 'Workfare to Welfare', 448.

57. Quotation: Felice Martinello, 'Mr Harris, Mr Rae and Union Activity in Ontario', *Canadian Public Policy* 26 (2000): 29. See also Rachlis and Wolfe, 'An Insider's View of the NDP Government', 353–6.

58. Quotations: Mary Cornish, 'Pay Equity Gains in Peril', *Toronto Star*, 18 October 1996; Morley Gunderson and Paul Lanoie, 'Program-Evaluation Criteria Applied to Pay Equity in Ontario', *Canadian Public Policy* 28 (2002): S145n26.

59. Quotation: Ian F.G. Baxter, 'Family Law Reform: A Historical Perspective of the Ontario Experience', *Canadian Journal of Family Law* 6 (1987): 253. See also Halpern, *And on That Farm*, 134–9.

60. Quotation: Dyck, 'The Socio-economic Setting of Ontario Politics', 43.

61. Quotations: Dyck, 'The Socio-Economic Setting of Ontario Politics', 43; Ontario Human Rights Commission, *The Existence of Racial Profiling* (2002), 1, http://www.ohrc.on.ca/english/consultations/racial-profiling-report_4.shtml; Croucher, 'Constructing the Image of Ethnic Harmony', 328, 340, 332; See also Wiseman, 'Change in Ontario Politics', 435–6; Andrejs Skaburskis, 'Race and Tenure in Toronto', *Urban Studies* 33 (1996): 223–53.

62. Quotations: *Globe and Mail*, 22 January 2004.

63. Quotation: Website of the Ontario Native Affairs Secretariat, Temagami Land Claim, 21 June 2000. See also Harvey McCue, 'The Modern Age, 1945–1980', in *Aboriginal Ontario*, 377–417; David T. MacNab, 'Aboriginal Land Claims in Ontario', in *Aboriginal Land Claims in Canada: A Regional Perspective*, edited by Ken Coates (Toronto: Copp Clark Pitman, 1992), 73–99; Anthony Hall, 'Treaties, Trains, and Troubled National Dreams: Reflections on the Indian Summer in Northern Ontario, 1990', in *Law, Society, and the State: Essays in Modern Legal History*, edited by Louis A. Knafla and Susan W.S. Binnie (Toronto: University of Toronto Press, 1995), 290–320; Bruce Hodgins, Ute Lischke, and David McNab, eds, *Blockades and Resistance: Studies in Actions of Peace and the Temagami Blockades of 1988–89* (Waterloo, ON: Wilfrid Laurier University Press, 2002).

64. Peter Woolstencraft, 'Reclaiming the "Pink Palace": The Progressive Conservative Party Comes in from the Cold', in *The Government and Politics of Ontario*, 378–81.

65. Quotation: Nelson Wiseman, 'Reading Ontario Politics and Public Administration', *Canadian Public Administration* 45 (2002): 117. See also Martinello, 'Mr Harris', 29.

66. Sid Noel, 'Ontario's Tory Revolution', in *Revolution at Queen's Park: Essays on Governing Ontario*, edited by Sid Noel (Toronto: Lorimer, 1997), 1–17.

67. Osberg and Xu, 'Poverty Intensity', 190.

68. Quotations: Charles Plourde and Anthony Bruno, 'Some Economic Consequencies of Air Pollution in Selected Cities in Ontario', *Environments* 22 (1993): 54; 'Ontario Environmental Commissioner Reports Decline in Environmental Protection', website of the Environmental Commissioner of Ontario, news release, 28 April 1999. See also Robert Paehlke, 'Environmentalism in One Country: Canadian Environmental Policy in an Era of Globalization', *Policy Studies Journal* 28 (2000): 166; Anita Krajnc, 'Wither Ontario's Environment? Neo-Conservatism and the Decline of the Environment Ministry', *Canadian Public Policy* 26 (2000): esp. 114–18.

69. Krajnc, 'Wither Ontario's Environment?', 12, 126n12; 'The Protection of Ontario's Ground Water'; Environmental Commissioner of Ontario, 'State of the Industry:

Pork', OMAFRA website.

70. Quotation: Sierra Club of Canada, *Eighth Annual Environmental Report Card*, website.

71. Quotation: *Globe and Mail*, 2 October 2003. See also Roger Keil, '"Common-Sense" Neoliberalism: Progressive Conservative Urbanism in Toronto, Canada', *Antipode* 34 (2002): 579; T. Walkom, 'Labour Gearing Up for battle', *Toronto Star*, 17 June 2001.

72. Courchene, *From Heartland to North American Regional State*; John Ibbitson, *Loyal No More: Ontario's Struggle for a Separate Destiny* (Toronto: HarperCollins, 2001); for a wider context that emphasizes the east–west flow of Canada's trade, see John F. Helliwell, *How Much Do National Borders Matter?* (Washington, DC: Brookings Institution, 1998).

73. Viv Nelles, '"Red Tied": Fin de Siècle Politics in Ontario', in *Canadian Politics in the 1990s*, edited by Michael Whittington and Glen Williams (Scarborough, ON: Nelson, 1990), 94; Wiseman, 'Change in Ontario Politics', 434–5; Frank L. Graves with Tim Dugas and Patrick Beauchamp, 'Identity and National Attachments in Contemporary Canada', in *Canada: The State of the Federation, 1998/99: How Canadians Connect*, edited by Harvey Lazar and Tom McIntosh (Kingston, ON: Institute of Intergovernmental Relations, Queen's University, 1999), 316–18, 330–9.

74. Wheeler, 'Politics and Policy in the North', 284–306.

75. Christopher Armstrong, *The Politics of Federalism: Ontario's Relations with the Federal Government, 1867–1942* (Toronto: University of Toronto Press, 1981).

Index

CPSIA information can be obtained
at www.ICGtesting.com
Printed in the USA
LVOW01s1228250417
532042LV00010B/74/P